Shari'a and Politics

in Modern Indonesia

ISEAS Series on Islam

Shari'a and Politics

in Modern Indonesia

Edited by
Arskal Salim
Azyumardi Azra

LSEAS

INSTITUTE OF SOUTHEAST ASIAN STUDIES
Singapore

First published in Singapore in 2003 by
Institute of Southeast Asian Studies
30 Heng Mui Keng Terrace
Pasir Panjang
Singapore 119614

E-mail: publish@iseas.edu.sg
Website: http://bookshop.iseas.edu.sg

The responsibility for facts and opinions in this publication rests exclusively with the editors and contributors and their interpretations do not necessarily reflect the views or the policy of the Institute or its supporters.

ISEAS Library Cataloguing-in-Publication Data

Shari'a and politics in modern Indonesia / edited by Arskal Salim and Azyumardi Azra.
    1. Islamic law—Political aspects—Indonesia.
    2. Islamic law—Economic aspects—Indonesia.
    3. Islam and politics—Indonesia.
    4. Islam and state—Indonesia.
    I. Salim, Arskal.
    II. Azra, Azyumardi.
KNW479 S53   2003   sls2002026341

ISBN 981-230-187-9 (soft cover)

Typeset by International Typesetters Pte. Ltd.
Printed in Singapore by Primepak Services.

CONTENTS

ACKNOWLEDGEMENTS

Compiling various articles on the issue of *shari'a* and politics in modern Indonesia into a single volume is not a simple task. It would not have been possible without the kind contributions of Mark Cammack, Howard Federspiel, Robert W. Hefner, M. B. Hooker, Nadirsyah Hosen, Nur Ahmad Fadhil Lubis, Ratno Lukito, and Ahmad Imam Mawardi. Most of these essays originated from various sources and have been published either in refereed journals or in compiled books.

Therefore, we express deepest gratitude to the previous publishers and copyright holders for granting us permission to republish the essays: Tim Lindsey, editor of *Indonesia: Law and Society*; Chris Holt, the Federation Press publisher; Jamhari, editor of *Studia Islamika: Indonesian Journal for Islamic Studies* at the State Islamic University (UIN) Jakarta; Cik Hasan Bisri, editor of *Istiqra* at the State Institute for Islamic Studies (IAIN) Bandung; Deborah Homsher, managing editor of SEAP Publications at Cornell University; Mark Woodward, editor of *Toward A New Paradigm: Recent Developments in Indonesian Islamic Thought* and managing editor of PSEAS Publications at Arizona State University; Suryopratomo, editor-in-chief of *Kompas* daily; David S. Powers, editor of *Islamic Law and Society*; and Albert Hoffstaedt, Koninklijke Brill N. V. publisher.

We extend our acknowledgement to Kusmana, Oman Fathurrohman, Nina Nurmila, Yeti Heryati, and Fauzan Saleh for their assistance in gathering the material needed for publication. Special thanks are also due to Indriyani Permatasari, Muiz, Sudirman Hasan, Dion Hallpike, and Haya Huseini, who helped in preparing and proofreading some parts of this reader. Their assistance is deeply appreciated and gladly acknowledged.

Our thanks also go to the Institute of Southeast Asian Studies (ISEAS), Singapore for accepting this manuscript for publication. We are particularly grateful to the staff of the Publications Unit at ISEAS for their professional assistance in the preparation of this book.

Arskal Salim and Azyumardi Azra

CONTRIBUTORS

Azyumardi Azra is Professor of History and also Rector of the State Islamic University (UIN) Syarif Hidayatullah, Jakarta. In 1992, he received his Ph.D. from Columbia University. He was a Visiting Fellow at Oxford University while conducting his post-doctoral research. Since 1993 he has been the editor-in-chief of *Studia Islamika: Indonesian Journal for Islamic Studies* (Jakarta). He is also editor of *Journal of Qur'anic Studies* (SOAS, London) and *Jurnal Usuluddin* (UM, Kuala Lumpur). He has published widely on various aspects of history, religion, and politics. Among his books are *Mengenal Ajaran Kaum Sufi* (Jakarta: Pustaka Jaya, 1984), *Agama di Tengah Sekularisasi Politik* (Jakarta: Pustaka Panjimas, 1985), *Perspektif Islam di Asia Tenggara* (Jakarta: Yayasan Obor, 1989), *Jaringan Ulama Timur Tengah dan Kepulauan Nusantara Abad XVII dan XVIII* (Bandung: Mizan, 1994), *Pergolakan Politik Islam dari Fundamentalisme, Modernisme Hingga Post-Modernisme* (Jakarta: Paramadina, 1996), and *Islam Substantif: Agar Umat Tidak Jadi Buih*, (Bandung: Mizan, 2000).

Mark Cammack is Professor of Law at Southwestern University's School of Law, Los Angeles, where he specializes in comparative law with particular emphasis on Southeast Asia. He obtained his J.D. (Doctor of Jurisprudence) from the University of Wisconsin in 1983. After a clerkship for Justice Roland B. Day of the Wisconsin Supreme Court, he spent one year in Indonesia as a Fulbright scholar examining the country's legal system. His articles have been published in various international journals, including *Indonesia*, *International and Comparative Law Quarterly*, and *American Journal of Comparative Law*. He is also actively involved in the Association for Asian Studies and the Law and Society Association.

Howard M. Federspiel is Professor of Political Science at the Ohio State University, Newark. He earned his Ph.D. in Islamic Studies from McGill University in Canada in 1966. He was Visiting Professor of Islamic Studies at McGill University 1991–92 and 1995–2001 and Senior Fulbright Scholar to Indonesia in 1994. He was the general editor for *An Anthology of Islamic Studies*, vol. 2 (Montreal: Institute of Islamic Studies, 1996) and is the author of several books, including *Islam and Ideology in the Emerging Indonesian State* (Leiden: Brill Academic Press, 2001), and *Popular Islamic Literature in Indonesia* (Ithaca: Cornell Modern Indonesia Project, 1994). Recent articles include "Indonesia, Islam and U.S. Policy", *The Brown Journal of World Affairs* 9, no. 1 (Spring 2002): 107–14; "Contemporary Southeast Asian Muslim Intellectuals", in *Islam in the Era of Globalization*, edited by Johan Meuleman (London: RoutledgeCurzon, 2002), pp. 327–50, and "Islam and National Identity", in *Ethnic and Religious Conflict in Indonesia*. (Washington, D.C.: The Woodrow Wilson Center, July 1999), pp. 12–18.

Robert W. Hefner is Professor of Anthropology and Associate Director of the Institute for the Study of Economic Culture at Boston University. He obtained his Ph.D. from the University of Michigan in 1981 with the dissertation "Identity and Cultural Reproduction among Tengger Javanese". The dissertation was revised and published in 1985 as *Hindu Javanese: Tengger Tradition and Islam*. He specializes in Southeast Asian and Islamic studies, with a focus on religion, economic culture, and modern political change. He has published widely in international journals such as *Journal of Asian Studies* and *Indonesia*. Some of his publications are: *The Political Economy of Mountain Java: An Interpretative History* (Berkeley: University of California Press, 1990), *Conversion to Christianity: Historical and Anthropological Perspectives on a Great Transformation* (Berkeley and London: University of California Press, 1993), *Islam in an Era of Nation States: Politics and Religious Renewal in Muslim Southeast Asia* (Honolulu: University of Hawaii Press, 1997), *Democratic Civility: The History and Cross-Cultural Possibility of a Modern Political Ideal* (New Brunswick, NJ: Transaction Press, 1998), *Islam Pasar Keadilan: Artikulasi Lokal, Kapitalism, dan Demokrasi* (Yogjakarta: LKiS, 2000), and *Civil Islam: Muslims and Democratization in Indonesia* (Princeton: Princeton University Press, 2000).

M. B. Hooker is Professor of Law at the Australian National University. He was formerly Professor of Comparative Law at Kent University, Canterbury. He has written widely on Islamic and traditional laws in Southeast Asia. Some of his recent publications are *Adat Law in Modern Indonesia* (Kuala Lumpur and New York. Oxford University Press, 1978); *Concise Legal History of Southeast Asia* (Oxford: Clarendon Press, 1978); and *Islamic Law in Southeast Asia* (Kuala Lumpur: Oxford University Press, 1984). He is also editor of *Islam in Southeast Asia* (Leiden: Brill, 1983); *Law and the Chinese in Southeast Asia* (Singapore: Institute of Southeast Asian Studies, 2002); and (with K. Endicott et al.) *Malaysia and the "Original People"* (New York: Allyn and Bacon, 1996).

Nadirsyah Hosen is a lecturer at the State Islamic University (UIN) Syarif Hidayatullah Jakarta and also Associate Director of the Postgraduate Program at the Institute of Qur'anic Studies (IIQ), Jakarta. He was awarded a Graduate Diploma in Islamic Studies and M.A. (Honours) at the School of Classic, History and Religion of the University of New England (UNE). He obtained his Master of Laws in Comparative Law from the Northern Territory University, Australia. While studying at UNE, he served the Muslim community as the Grand Imam of UNE Mosque. His research interests are in Islamic legal theory, comparative constitutional law, and Indonesian politics.

Nur Ahmad Fadhil Lubis is Professor of Islamic Law at the State Institute for Islamic Studies (IAIN) Sumatera Utara. He is also currently Director of the Postgraduate Program of IAIN Sumatera Utara. He received his Ph.D. from the University of California Los Angeles in 1994. In the Fall of 1997, he was a Visiting Professor at the Institute of Islamic Studies of McGill University in Canada. He has presented papers on Islamic law in Indonesia at several international conferences. Some of his publications are *Pengantar Filsafat Umum* (1996), *Hukum Islam dalam Kerangka Teoritis Fiqh dan Tata Hukum Indonesia* (1997), *Introductory Readings on Islamic Studies* (1999), *Agama Sebagai Sistem Kultural* (2000) and *History of Islamic Law in Indonesia* (2001).

Ratno Lukito is a lecturer at the State Institute for Islamic Studies (IAIN) Sunan Kalijaga Yogjakarta. He is also involved in a non-government organization that focuses on research and study of culture and religion. He obtained his M.A. in Islamic Studies from McGill University in Canada. His Master thesis has been published in Bahasa Indonesia, *Pergumulan Antara Hukum Islam dan Adat di Indonesia* [Islamic Law and Adat Encounter: The Experience of Indonesia] (Jakarta: INIS, 1998), while the English version was published by Logos, Jakarta (2001). Some of his essays on Islamic law in Indonesia have appeared in *Studia Islamika: Indonesian Journal for Islamic Studies*, *McGill Journal of Middle East Studies*, and *al-Jami'ah Asy-Syir'ah*. He is currently a Ph.D. student at the Faculty of Law of McGill University.

Ahmad Imam Mawardi is a lecturer at the State Institute for Islamic Studies (IAIN) Sunan Ampel Surabaya. He obtained his M.A. in Islamic Studies from McGill University in Canada. He is also a director of the Islamic Education Center (Pondok Pesantren) and involved actively in two NGOs that undertake research and training on HRD, civic education, democracy and nationalism. He has edited *Perspektif Hukum E-Commerce* (Jakarta: PT. Mizan Grafika Sarana, 2001) and translated *E-Commerce: Revolusi Baru Dunia Bisnis* (Surabaya: Akana Press, 2001). He is the author of a forthcoming book *Perkembangan Pemikiran Hukum Islam di Indonesia* (Surabaya: Cempaka, December 2002). His articles on Islamic law and education have been published in many books, journals, and magazines, such as in *Pranata Islam di Indonesia: Pergulatan Sosial, Politik, Hukum dan Pendidikan* (Jakarta: Logos, 2002), *Perspektif Baru Pesantren dan Pengembangan Masyarakat* (Surabaya: Triguna Bhakti, 2001), *Jurnal Hukum Islam*, and *Jurnal al-Qanun*.

Arskal Salim is a lecturer in Islamic Legal Politics at the Department of Islamic Political Studies, Faculty of Shari'a of the State Islamic University (UIN) Jakarta. He is also a member of the Research Center of UIN Jakarta and has conducted a number of research projects on Islam and political development in Indonesia. He was a Ph.D. visiting student of interdisciplinary studies at McGill University in Canada (1999–2000). He is author of *Etika Intervensi Negara: Perspektif Politik Ibnu Taimiyah* (Jakarta: Logos, 1998) and *Partai Islam dan Relasi Agama Negara* (Jakarta: Puslit IAIN & JPPR, 1999). In addition, he has published in prominent Indonesian journals such as *Mimbar Agama dan Budaya, Jurnal Perempuan,* and *Studia Islamika: Indonesian Journal for Islamic Studies.* Currently, he is a Ph.D. student at the Melbourne Institute of Asian Languages and Societies (MIALS) of the University of Melbourne.

GLOSSARY

abangan	a Javanese of heterodox religious orientation; a Muslim who is greatly influenced by pre-Islamic Hindu, Buddhist, and indigenous animistic beliefs
ABRI	Angkatan Bersenjata Republik Indonesia (Armed Forces of the Republic of Indonesia)
adat	localized traditional law and custom; one of the major strands of contemporary Indonesian law
Aliran Kepercayaan	syncretic belief group
amil	lit. "worker"; in *fiqh,* it refers to a person acting as the operator to accept and distribute *zakat*
amr makruf nahi munkar	enjoining good and forbidding evil
asas tunggal	sole philosophical principle; sole basic general truth
bahts al-masail	an effort to solve religious matters
Baitul Maal	public treasury in an Islamic state
BAZIS	Badan Amil Zakat, Infak dan Shadaqah; a formal institution which accepts and distributes *zakat* and Islamic voluntary charity (*infak* and *shadaqah*) from the rich to the needy
BI	Bank Indonesia; as an independent central bank, BI is fully autonomous in formulating and implementing each of its tasks and functions as the monetary authority
BIMB	Bank Islam Malaysia Berhad
BMI	Bank Muamalat Indonesia; the first Indonesian bank with a *shari'a* system

BPR	Bank Pengkreditan Rakyat (Public Credit Bank)
bismillah	in the name of Allah
CSIS	Center for Strategic and International Studies
dakwah	call, invitation, or missionary activities seeking either to convert non-Muslims or to guide Muslims who have strayed back to the true path
DPR	Dewan Perwakilan Rakyat (House of People's Representatives)
DPR-GR	Dewan Perwakilan Rakyat Gotong Royong (House of Representatives of Functional Groups); a transitional DPR in the period of Guided Democracy in which political power shifted to the President
dwifungsi	lit. "dual function"; the dual role of the Indonesian Army as a security force and a socio-political power
faraid	(sing. *fard*) injunction, statutory portion, lawful share; action made obligatory upon Muslims by Allah
fard ayn	a duty incumbent upon the individual
fard al-kifayah	a duty incumbent upon the community, the fulfilment of which by a sufficient number of individuals excuses others from fulfilling it
fasakh	a decision of divorce based on collusion from the wife
fatawa	plural of *fatwa*
fatwa	a religious opinion issued by a competent scholar
fiqh (or *fikih*)	originally, understanding, knowledge, comprehension; technically, it refers to the science of Islamic jurisprudence
FPI	Front Pembela Islam (Front of Islamic Defenders)
GBHN	Garis Besar Haluan Negara (Guidelines of Basic State Policy); master plans and policies for Indonesia's national development
Golkar	Golongan Karya (Union of Functional groups); groupings within society, such as peasants, workers and women, that are represented by delegates to the various deliberative bodies; Golkar functions as an army-instituted and government-supported political party, winning over 60 per cent of the vote in each of the elections held during the Soeharto era.
gugat (cerai gugat)	a divorce proposed by the wife to end a marriage by law; cf. *talak*

hajj	pilgrimage to Mecca
halal	permitted by the Islamic law; legitimate
haram	prohibited by the Islamic law; forbidden
hibah	gift
hisab	a hereafter judge of all human deeds
HMI	Himpunan Mahasiswa Islam (Association of Islamic University Students)
hukum nasional	lit. "national law"; national rule made by the authority, especially those laws passed by the parliament or issued by the executive branch
HUSAMI	Himpunan Usahawan Muslimin Indonesia (Association of Indonesian Muslim Businessmen)
IAIN	Institut Agama Islam Negeri (State Institute for Islamic Studies)
ICMI	Ikatan Cendekiawan Muslim Indonesia (Indonesian Muslim Intellectuals Association)
IDB	Islamic Development Bank
Idul Fitri	the first day of the month of Syawwal; a day of celebration which marks the end of the thirty-day fasting period
ifta	issuing a *fatwa* by a recognized scholar
ijtihad	exertion, independent legal reasoning; use of logical reasoning in elaborating and interpreting the *shari'a* or in order to deduce laws from the Qur'an and the Sunnah
ijtihad jama'i	*ijtihad* on something agreed by all the *mujtahidin* (qualified persons who exercise *ijtihad*)
Inpres	*Instruksi Presiden* (Presidential Instruction)
istigfar	lit. "asking God for forgiveness"
istighotsah	a kind of prayers asking for general safety; it is usually done by a large number of people gathered in certain places such as a mosque or courtyard
Jakarta Charter	Piagam Jakarta; a name used by Muslim political activists to refer to a document produced on 22 June 1945
jihad	striving; exertion directed, individually or collectively, towards the attainment of spiritual and religious perfection; military action to defend Islam

Ka'bah	lit. "cube"; a sacred building in Mecca
KCS	Kantor Catatan Sipil (Office for Civil Records) where all births in Indonesia and marriages of non-Muslims are registered
kekeluargaan	lit. "kinship"
Keputusan Presiden	Presidential Decree
KHI	Kompilasi Hukum Islam (Compilation of Islamic Laws)
khilafiyah	lit. "disagreement"; difference in opinion among *ulama*
kitab kuning	lit. "yellow book"; old, yellowish books of Islamic sciences, especially *fiqh*, written by Muslim scholars mainly in Arabic language
Korpri	Korps Pegawai Negeri Indonesia (Corps of Indonesian State Employees)
KUA	Kantor Urusan Agama (Office of Religious Affairs); mainly to register marriages of Muslim citizens
KUHAP/KUHP	Kitab Undang-Undang Hukum Acara Pidana (Book of the Penal Law)
kyai	title given to religious scholars (*ulama*) of *pesantren*
li'an	a divorce caused by a husband's accusation of adultery to his wife
MA	Mahkamah Agung (Supreme Court)
mazhab (or *madhhab*)	school of thought; used to denote the four Sunni schools, i.e., Hanbalis, Malikis, Hanafis, and Shafi'is
Majelis Tarjih	an institution in the Muhammadiyah organization which has overall responsibility for making *ijtihad* on problems faced by Muslims from the classical era to the contemporary era
maslahat	interest or welfare consideration which may sometimes be hidden at first sight
MIAI	an Islamic organization founded on the terms of national awakening, and abolished in 1943; as a subtitute, KH Hasyim Asyari and KH Mas Mansur formed Masyumi (Majelis Syura Muslim Indonesia)
MMI	Manajemen Musyarakah Indonesia (Indonesian Co-operation Management)
MORA	Ministry of Religious Affairs

MPR	Majelis Permusyawaratan Rakyat (People's Consultative Assembly)
Muktamar	congress; a term used for major meetings of many Indonesian Muslim organizations
mubah	an action which is neither prohibited (haram) nor permitted (halal)
mudaraba	mode of business whereby two or more persons participate; one providing capital and the other (or others) providing labour and enterprise; profits are shared among the financier and the entrepreneur(s) according to mutually agreed terms; losses are borne by the financier only
MUI	Majelis Ulama Indonesia (Indonesian Council of Islamic Scholars)
murabaha	resale of goods with an additional surcharge to the stated original cost
musharaka	mode of business whereby more than one person participates with capital and labour on a basis of profit-and-loss sharing
mutasyabihat	a verse with unclear meaning
NASAKOM	an acronym coined in 1961 to promote co-operation between Nasionalis (Nationalist), Agama (Religion), and Komunis (Communist) groupings in Indonesia.
NEI	Netherland East Indies
negara hukum	a country emphasizing order based on the law system and law awareness among its members of society; the government is the authority to maintain law and order
nikah	marriage; legal union of a man and a woman as husband and wife
NU	Nahdlatul Ulama (Ulama Awakening Organization); formed by KH Hasyim Asyari and KH Abdul Wahab Hasbullah on 31 January 1926
Orde Baru	New Order; term used by the Soeharto regime for post-Sukarno policies based on realistic thinking and opposed to the personality cult and alleged lack of constitutionality of the Sukarno regime
Orde Lama	Old Order; term used by the Soeharto regime to refer to the policies of the Sukarno era

Pancasila	the five guiding principles of the Indonesian state; the basic official ideology enunciated by Sukarno and incorporated into the preamble of the 1945 Constitution; the five principles are: belief in One Supreme Being, just and civilized humanity, nationalism, democracy, and social justice.
Parmusi	Partai Muslimin Indonesia (Indonesian Muslim Party)
PBB	Perserikatan Bangsa-Bangsa (United Nations)
PDI-P	Partai Demokrasi Indonesia–Perjuangan (Indonesian Democratic Party–Struggle)
pembaharuan	lit. "reformation"; change or improvement in law system or social system
Pengadilan Agama	Islamic court; a legal institution which handles cases of family law
penghulu	an expert in religious matters, acknowledged by the society and appointed by the ruler
pesantren	Islamic boarding school
PKI	Partai Komunis Indonesia (Indonesian Communist Party)
PMA	Peraturan Menteri Agama (Policies/Regulations of the Minister of Religious Affairs)
PP	Peraturan Pemerintah (Government Regulation)
PPP	Partai Persatuan Pembangunan (United Development Party)
pribumi	indigenous Indonesian
priyayi	originally referred to the gentry (i.e. the courtiers and officials of the king) way of life but now it implies the whole set of attitudes and moral commitments adhered to by almost every white-collar Javanese, whatever his social origin
qadi	an Islamic judge who is appointed but has independent religious authority to adjudicate cases brought before him in accordance with the *shari'a*
Ramadhan	the month in which Muslims are obligated to fast from dawn to sunset
receptie	a legal theory argued by Snouck Hurgronje which states that Islamic law is acceptable if it is not contradicting the traditional law and local custom

Repelita	Rencana Pembangunan Lima Tahun (Five-Year Development Plan)
riba	lit. "increment"; refers to predetermined increase on the amount loaned which increases over time; equivalent to interest
rujuk (or ruju')	reconciliation between a man and his ex-wife after divorce; may require a re-marriage depending on the length of the divorce
RUU	Rancangan Undang-Undang (Bill)
ru'yah	sighting of the new moon to decide the start and end of the fasting month of Ramadhan
santri	a Muslim who practises Islamic doctrines devoutly, as opposed to an abangan who is less devout
shari'a (or syariah)	divine guidance as given by the Qur'an and Sunnah and includes all aspects of Islamic beliefs and practices
SKB	Surat Keputusan Bersama (Joint Letter of Decision)
surah	a chapter of the Qur'an
Syawwal	the month after Ramadhan in which Muslims celebrate Idul Fitri on the first day of month
syiqaq (or shikak)	a conflict between a husband and wife which can be solved by the family or the judge
tabligh akbar	a religious gathering in an open area, such as a field, with famous speakers (muballigh) giving orations
ta'lik talak	postponing the fall of a talak on the occurrence of an event; if the event occurred, the talak is legal
talak (or talaq)	a divorce; ending a marriage with the husband saying specific words to the wife, e.g., "I divorce you"
taqnin	making a rule or law; legislation
tarekat	an order of mystical practice
tasawwuf	Islamic mysticism which emphasizes on the purification of self and introspection in matters of religion
tauhid	the belief in the oneness of God
ukhuwah	brotherhood; fraternity
ulama	Muslim jurist, scholars, theologians; learned men who are experts in shari'a (sing.'alim)
umara	plural of amir; rulers and commanders

ummah (or *umat*)	community, group of people; esp. Muslim community as identified by the integration of its ideology, religion, law, mission, and purpose of life and group consciousness, ethics and mores, irrespective of their differences in origin, race, language, colour of the skin, and so on.
undang-undang	law; rule established by the authority
wali	guardian; manager of a thing or affair of another
waqf	a charitable trust dedicated to some socially beneficial purpose; religious endowment
wawasan Nusantara	an insight describing society, nation, mainland, ocean, and air as a union which cannot be separated; these elements are intertwined in political, socio-cultural, economic, and secure-defensive union.
zakat	the obligation on every Muslim to give away a portion of his wealth to the poor and the needy each year; there are two kinds of *zakat*, i.e., *zakat fitrah* and *zakat maal*
zakat fitrah	a form of *zakat* that is imposed on each individual Muslim regardless of his wealth and is to be given out in the month of Ramadhan, before the Idul Fitri prayers
zakat maal	a form of *zakat* imposed on Muslims who have accumulated wealth; the rate is 2.5 per cent on all financial assets and stock-in-trade of businesseses, 10 per cent on agricultural produce of rain-irrigated cultivation, and 5 per cent on the produce of artificially irrigated cultivation

1

INTRODUCTION
The State and *Shari'a* in the Perspective of Indonesian Legal Politics

Arskal Salim and Azyumardi Azra

The political atmosphere in the post-New Order era is evidently marked with the euphoria of democracy or political liberalization. One of its manifestations, as William R. Liddle ever predicted, is that in a more open political climate the expression of more formalistic Islam (the scripturalists) would appear, since "they would have many more political resources, in mass acceptance of their ideas, organization, allies, media, and access to politicians".[1]

There are at least four features of such appearance in the current scene. First is the establishment of numerous Islamic political parties that mostly adopt Islam as their basis replacing Pancasila, which the Soeharto regime forcefully implemented to be the sole basis of any organization. Two parties, the United Development Party (PPP) and the Crescent Star Party (PBB), insist that Article 29 of the 1945 Constitution be amended to reinsert the famous "seven words" (*dengan kewajiban melaksanakan syariat Islam bagi pemeluknya* [with the obligation to carry out *shari'a* for its adherents]). With these words, it will officially provide *shari'a* with the constitutional status within the Indonesian national legal system. This proposal to reintroduce the clause, which will require Indonesian Muslims to apply *shari'a*, has been unsuccessful in three consecutive annual sessions of the Majelis Permusyawaratan Rakyat (MPR) in 2000, 2001, and 2002. In the 2002 annual session, the MPR has decided not to amend Article 29 of the 1945 Constitution. However, Islamic parties continue to advocate the formal application of *shari'a*.

Second is the growing demand from certain regions of Indonesia for the formal implementation of *shari'a*. Aceh is the first province that demanded for the application of *shari'a*. In fact the application of *shari'a* in this region was sporadically undertaken when in November 1999, a young man accused of committing adultery was punished by being whipped one hundred times in public.[2] Similarly in South Sulawesi, there is an increasing aspiration to implement *shari'a* for its Muslim adherents. Abdul Aziz Qahhar Muzakkar, chief of the preparation committee for the application of *shari'a* in South Sulawesi, said that the special autonomy status granted to Aceh, including the implementation of *shari'a*, has paved the way for other provinces to secure the same status. Thus, South Sulawesi should also be granted the special autonomy status.[3] Furthermore, it has been known that at least twenty out of twenty-four heads of districts (*kotamadya/kabupaten*) in that province have expressed their willingness to apply *shari'a* in their own areas.

Third is the emergence of Muslim groups considered by many as hardliners, such the Lasykar Jihad (Jihad Troops), the Front Pembela Islam (FPI, or Front of Islamic Defenders), the Hizb al-Tahrir (Party of Liberation), and the Majelis Mujahidin Indonesia (the Council of the Jihad Fighter Groups of Indonesia), throughout the country. FPI, for example, launch radical and violent attacks on discotheques, nightclubs, and other places of entertainment in the name of *amar ma'ruf* and *nahi munkar* (enjoin good and prohibit evil), to eradicate all sorts of religiously prohibited practices such as gambling, consumption of alcohol, and prostitution. In doing so, they see themselves as the torch-bearers in the application of *shari'a* in Indonesia. In their efforts, they are frequently confronted by other groups of people, including Muslims, who cannot accept their claims and radical ways.

Last is the rising popularity of the Islamic magazine, *Sabili*, which according to surveys conducted by AC Nielsen has the second largest circulation after the women's magazine, *Gadis*.[4] This weekly magazine, which was published underground during the New Order era, currently publishes more than 100,000 copies of each edition. *Sabili* used to be a *da'wah* (call for Islam) newsletter, but it is now appearing to promote political Islam, typically from the hardliner's point of view. Some of its published opinions are clearly seen as advocating support for the formal application of *shari'a* in Indonesia. It argues elsewhere that because Indonesian national law is man-made and not divine, it can never earn the people's respect for the rule of law. *Sabili* asserts that the answer to Indonesia's legal crisis is to return to the way of God, that is, a return to the application of *shari'a*.

These four developments seem to lead to the reinforcement of Islamic law in the country, both with legal coercion and political support from the state apparatus. In other words, they aim to establish closer links between Islam and the state. Therefore, some assume that these growing aspirations towards the implementation of *shari'a* represent the latent return to the idea of an Islamic state in Indonesia.

The interaction of Islam and politics has been an integral part of the Indonesian experience since the Muslim kingdoms in the seventeenth century. Their nexus has been inexorably linked with the idea of an Islamic state. However, the actual vitality of this idea is still unclear. Given the fact that the most visible character of an Islamic state is formal implementation of *shari'a*, the interrelation between Islam and politics depends much on the extent to which *shari'a* is implemented by the state. All the essays included in this volume delineate the implementation of *shari'a* in modern Indonesia. Since the *shari'a* is believed by many Muslims as a comprehensive set of norms and values regulating all aspects of human life, these essays also deal with the various aspects of *shari'a*, such as family law, religious court, *zakat*, and Islamic banking. Taken together, all the essays will indicate the relationship between Islam and politics in which *shari'a* becomes an important factor.

This introduction seeks to articulate and identify the feature of legal politics undertaken by the Indonesian Government towards Islamic *shari'a*. There are several main questions to be investigated. Firstly, given that Indonesia is not an Islamic state, why has the implementation of *shari'a* taken place? What factors account for this? Secondly, is the implementation of *shari'a* by the rulers really reflecting the Islamic dictates or is it merely politicking, or simply the rulers' efforts to serve their interests? Thirdly, to what extent is the integration of *shari'a* into national law possible? And lastly, would this eventually lead to the founding of an Islamic state in Indonesia?

THE INTERRELATION BETWEEN STATE AND *SHARI'A*

The goal of the state, according to some Muslim political thinkers such as al-Ghazali and Ibn Taymiyyah, is to realize the *shari'a* on Earth. The existence of the state to implement the *shari'a* comprehensively at individual and societal levels, therefore, has been deemed a requirement. It has been argued that while some injunctions of Islam relating to the prayer, fasting, and *hajj* may be done individually, other rules of Islam that encompass various political, social, economic, and international relationships necessitate the existence of the state with the authority to organize society. Implicit within this logic is that all the individual's and the *ummah*'s (community) actions and initiations are subject to Allah's commands and prohibitions (that is, *shari'a*). Accordingly, the sovereignty neither belongs to the state nor to the *ummah*, but to the *shari'a*.[5] It is a widely accepted notion that where Muslim kingdoms or Islamic states exist, the *shari'a* should be implemented. Therefore, the relationship between Islam and the state has been signified by the implementation of *shari'a*, whatever it covers, within the governmental legal system.

In the modern world, several states declare themselves Islamic and attempt to develop Islamic alternatives to, or adaptations of, legal institutions and legislation. While some other Muslim countries have integrated more *shari'a* injunctions into their secular legislation, others are interfering with the teaching and development of *fiqh* (Islamic jurisprudence), the practice of *ifta'* (issuing Islamic legal opinions on questions relating to Muslim law), or the codification of *shari'a*. In Indonesia, the application of *shari'a* has a deep-rooted history, since the time of the Muslim kingdoms. Anthony Reid points out that as early as the seventeenth century, thieves in Banten and Aceh were punished with amputations. This kind of punishment was enforced by amputating the right hand. If the crimes were repetitively committed, the subsequent punishments would be to amputate the left leg, the left hand, and then the right leg. And finally, the thief would have to be isolated in Sabang Island off the coast of Aceh.[6] These severe punishments were undoubtedly taken from Islamic penal law (*hudud*). The existence of this practice obviously rejects the predominant view among many observers who argue that no Islamic laws were practised by the early Islam in Indonesia.

It must be admitted, however, that the implementation of *shari'a* ultimately depends much on the attachment of the Muslim rulers to *shari'a*. The history of *shari'a* implementation in Indonesia does not necessarily show any permanency or sustainability. As an example, when Susuhunan Amangkurat replaced Sultan Agung of Mataram as the holder of power, he soon liquidated the Surambi court, the court that was established in accordance with Islamic traditions during the reign of Sultan Agung. Amangkurat instead revived the Pradata court, a Hindu Majapahit court that had existed in Java prior to the coming of Islam.[7] Another example worth mentioning is the refusal of Sultan Iskandar Thani of Aceh to continue with the evidence procedures that had been established by his predecessor, Sultan Iskandar Muda. The procedure required disputing parties to put their hands into boiling water in order to investigate and to prove which party's claim was true.[8]

The implementation of *shari'a* through the state power involves a long and bitter debate in modern Indonesia. The history of *shari'a* in modern Indonesia has been the struggle of Muslims to attain a proper place for *shari'a* within non-Islamic, or even anti-Islamic, regimes. At the earliest stage of Indonesian independence, Muslim leaders struggled to introduce in the preamble of the 1945 Constitution a phrase to the effect that Muslim citizens would be obliged to carry out their religious duties. The preamble, later known as the Jakarta Charter, which includes the "seven words" (that is, *dengan kewajiban melaksanakan syariat Islam bagi pemeluknya*), is believed to give a constitutional basis for the application of *shari'a* in Indonesia. The effort nonetheless was unsuccessful because of strong resistance from the circles of non-Muslims and also secular nationalists, most of whom were Muslim as well.[9]

The debates on the Jakarta Charter or the *shari'a* implementation continued within the Constituent Assembly in 1959. They seemed to end with the issue of the Decree of President Sukarno on 5 July 1959, which stated that the Jakarta Charter had inspired the 1945 Constitution and formed a unity with that Constitution. Therefore, there is no need to put it in an explicit way. However, the issue was far from resolved. In the post-Sukarno era, or precisely in the early years of the New Order, the debates continued when Islamic parties once again demanded the government to revive the Jakarta Charter as an integral part of the preamble to the 1945 Constitution. This effort again ended in failure because the army did not allow such an agenda to be discussed in the MPR session of 1966–67.[10]

It is noteworthy that although the Jakarta Charter was not accepted by the Soeharto government to be in the 1945 Constitution, which would have given *shari'a* a constitutional status, a number of aspects relating to *shari'a* have been legislated in the national laws. At least five laws that contain strong *shari'a* influences were legislated in the era of Soeharto. These are the marriage law, *waqf* (charitable foundation) regulation, religious court law, the law that allow the operation of the Islamic Bank, and the codification of Islamic family law that includes the rules of inheritance. President Habibie during his stay in power (1998–99) added two laws which covered the administration of *hajj* and *zakat*. All these laws that accommodate the elements of Islamic law have been enacted without any reference to the Jakarta Charter.

Given that some Islamic injunctions have been legislated while Indonesia is not an Islamic state, same question might be raised. Why has this happened? What factors account for this? In order to understand the implementation of *shari'a* in modern Indonesia, one should not only look at its Constitution or at its broad outlines of national policy; more importantly, the law in the final analysis is a political product.[11] Thus, all elements of Islamic law that have been integrated into national law are mainly the result of political interaction between the Indonesian Government and the Islamic communities, particularly Muslim élites. The study of legal politics in Indonesia, therefore, is insufficient by researching only what is written in the statute texts; what had happened prior to and during the debate of its drafting process and enactment by the legislature must be analysed, too.

Legal politics, as has been defined by Mahfud, is a legal policy that will be or has been nationally applied by the government, which also includes the explanation on how politics controls law-making by looking at the political configuration behind its enactment process.[12] Thus, laws are ultimately the crystallization of political aspirations that have interacted and have been contested. The laws then should not be merely perceived as the imperative articles or requirements that have *das sollen* features, but it should be seen as a subsystem that in reality is much influenced by politics, either in formulating its contents or in its implementation. It is not amazing, therefore, that the law has been frequently associated with power; in order to maintain the status quo certain regimes have exploited the law. The politics, in short, is an independent variable, while the law is a dependent variable. In fact, politics is often more powerful than the law.

In the light of the above definition of legal politics, it can be concluded that the survival, or even revival, of the religious court that implements *shari'a* in modern Indonesia is certainly a political product. Its survival had resulted from the contested position between *adat* court and religious court in the national legal system immediately after the independence of Indonesia. A detailed discussion on this issue can be found in Ratno Lukito's contribution to this volume. His article portrays the political interaction between the supporting camps of both courts, in which he discusses debates between two contending camps — the "pluralist" versus "uniformist" groups on the one hand, and the "secular nationalist" versus "Muslim" groups on the other. The former centred their arguments on the notion of the unification of law and of pluralism within the law, while the latter put the focus of discussion in the general or civil court as opposed to religious court.

Lukito's essay suggests that the religious court's survival or revival was implicated by the initial legal policy taken by the New Order government of Indonesia, which proposed the unification of law in order to eventually abolish all elements of colonial law. It is believed that the unification of the country after prolonged colonialization could also be achieved through a unification of law. Conversely, legal diversity would inevitably lead to conflict. Differences are perceived as equivalent to conflict, and hence should not be permitted. To prevent conflicts, there should be a unified law for all citizens. The unification of law then is viewed as the only method to serve Indonesian pluralistic society. Since the *adat* courts would imply legal pluralism, and hence are not parallel to the unification of law, their existence in national legal system should be terminated. This situation had indirectly given advantages to the position of the religious courts in Indonesia, which surprisingly have not been affected by the process of unification of law in the country. In contrast, as will be depicted below, the principle of the unification of law and the existence of Islamic court/law has not been mutually exclusive.

THE STATE'S INTERESTS ON THE APPLICATION OF *SHARI'A*

It might be observed that the final decision to allow any part of Islamic law to be integrated into national positive law during the New Order period comes from the President's hand. But a question remains as to why the government has a very strong control over the legislation of law in Indonesia, particularly in the New Order era. The most determining legal political aspect that could explain this matter is that the President has been provided by the 1945 Constitution with an overwhelming quantity and quality of executive power. As Hooker notes in his article in this volume, the crucial role of the President in law-making has a long history in Indonesia, since independence. Almost all the implemented *shari'a* in Indonesia could get a status as national positive law after the President's intervention into the legislature. In addition, the role of the President in law-making is also often exercised by way of "Presidential Instruction" (*Instruksi Presiden*), which is not a statute (*undang-undang*) but has the force of law. One such instruction relating to *shari'a* is the Presidential Instruction Number 1 of 1991 to the Minister for Religious Affairs to disseminate the Compilation of Islamic Laws to various government agencies, mostly Islamic judges, and to apply the Compilation in conjunction with other laws. This unlimited power, of course, may provide the chances for the government to attach its interests in the application of Islamic law.

The political configuration, particularly during the New Order era, has surely, shaped the state's interests in the application of *shari'a* in Indonesia. There were, at least, three features of the state's interests. First, as has been briefly explained above, is the unification of law. The unification of law has become a blueprint in the development of Indonesian national legal system. This policy regarding law implementation is founded on two perspectives. First is nationalism, which emphasizes that the Republic of Indonesia is a national state, not a state founded upon a racial, cultural, or religious base. Therefore, there must not be any regulation that discriminates between people based on ethnic group, class, race, religion, or the like. Second is the *nusantara* perspective, which upholds the idea that the whole *nusantara* — Indonesian archipelago — is an integrated, compact unity of *tanah air* ("land and water" mother country). This perspective requires the same laws to be valid for the whole country, all the regions to have the same rights and responsibilities, and no region will be discriminated against or privileged over another, under the unitary state of Indonesia.

Nur Ahmad Fadhil Lubis emphasizes in his article in this volume that even though the prime motive of the regime was to create a single united legal system, it could not be entirely applied since the population of the country consists of citizens who have other differences, for example, gender, age, occupation, and religion. Thus, they should be treated in different ways in terms of the application of law, because enforcing a unified rigid law for this plural society may only inflict injustice and, thus, could incite resentment. Therefore, a certain extent of variety in laws is permitted as long as it does not endanger the integrity and unity of the nation. This notion of legal diversity has been eventually accepted as the complementary perspective to the principle of the unification of law in the development of national legal system. Therefore, looking at the Broad Outlines of National Policy (GBHN) of 1973, 1978, 1983, and 1988, the development of national law was oriented to the codification and unification of law. The Marriage Law of 1974, among other things, is one such unified law. Nevertheless, the GBHN of 1993 provides a new direction in Indonesian legal development; all process of law-making should pay attention to the plurality of legal awareness of the citizens.[13] This change means that certain Islamic rules could also be exclusively applied to Muslim citizens. This change came into being coincidentally with the resurgence of Islam in the political arena of the New Order regime in the 1990s.

It is interesting to note that both the principles of the unification of law and legal diversity have already been used or abused depending on the government interests. It is fair to say that both principles are more politically formulated rather than lawfully laid down. The cases of the Marriage Law of 1974 and the Religious Judicature Act of 1989 will clearly elucidate this tendency. In the case of the Marriage Law, since the 1950s the government had attempted to propose a unified national marriage law regardless of religion; and only resulted otherwise eventually in 1974. This attempt was motivated in part by a desire to forge an Indonesian national consciousness and civic identity to overcome the seeds of national disintegration originating from ethnic, religious, and cultural attachments.

In the case of the Religious Judicature Act, the government has ignored the basic principle of the unification of law and tended to diversify the courts due to the state's responses to the special needs of Muslims. Responding to the objections raised by non-Muslims regarding the Bill of the Religious Judicature Act — in which they contended that the Bill was a discrimination against citizens based on religion — Minister for Religious Affairs, Munawir Sjadzali, said: "Not every legal distinction should be perceived as inequality before the law. It cannot be said either that the principle of equality before the law is valid only if all factual conditions are similar. Therefore, there should have been certain specific laws for particular group of citizens."[14] Although the government seemed to recognize the principle of equality before the law, they cannot apply this principle given the plurality of Indonesian citizens. Some political observers noted that this state's response, instead of fulfilling what Muslims truly expected, was put forward as a means to gain Muslim political support for President Soeharto. It is because of such state's interests that the government could introduce one regulation for all citizens at one time, and introduce a specific law for particular citizens at another time.

The enactment of the Religious Judicature Act, however, can also be analysed within the perspective of the unification of law. In his article in this volume, Cammack explains that one reason for the promulgation of the law is that there were three different labels and varied jurisdictions under which the religious courts had operated prior to 1989. So, the enactment of the law eliminated these differences and unified all procedures and authorities of the religious court. With the same token, it is true that this law includes the unification of law, but it is only applicable to Muslim citizens, not to the entire Indonesian citizens.

A similar case can also be found in the enactment of the Compilation of Islamic Laws or Kompilasi Hukum Islam (KHI). The KHI is perhaps the best example of how the government has tried to unify and codify the diverse material on *fiqh* (Islamic law). Ahmad Imam Mawardi, in his contribution to this volume, emphasizes that the KHI is "one of many vehicles used by the Indonesian government to unify and codify Islamic law". Despite allowing Muslim citizens to apply Islamic law in accordance with their respective faiths and schools of thought (that is, *mazhab*), the government has sought to unify the application of Islamic law for Muslims.

The unification of law has been one of the KHI's purposes. Although it is not a statute (*undang-undang*) with a binding effect, because it was passed through Presidential Instruction No. 1/1991, the KHI has become a guide to applicable law for judges within the jurisdiction of the institutions of the religious court in solving submitted cases. Thus, this function of the KHI has inevitably unified all Muslims' performance on applying *shari'a* though limited only in three areas of law: marriage, inheritance, and *waqf*. In short, the idea behind the KHI's issuance is based on the need to unify all references of Islamic law, which are under the religious court's authority, so that the problem of differences in the application of *shari'a* can be resolved. As noted by Mawardi, the KHI is an instrument to "eliminate disparity in legal decisions in the interest of social justice and of legal certainty". Viewed in this light, the government deliberately created a harmonious and practicable law for its Muslim citizens to avoid disorder and, accordingly, to maintain political stability as one of the prerequisites of national development. However, in the name of legal certainty, this attempt has abandoned the principle of legal pluralism; Islam has acknowledged various schools of thought (*mazhab*) and allowed different legal opinions to exist, and that every Muslim is free to apply whichever suits him/her.

The second state's interest is social engineering. It is clear that Indonesian legal politics, particularly that of the New Order, was carried out to implement and justify the government's agenda of economic growth, social development, and modernization. This kind of legal politics had been taken basically in order to maintain political stability and sustainability of national development. To this end, the law was practically manipulated by the New Order as a tool of social engineering. It seems that for the New Order regime, the law can be an instrument for evolutionary or revolutionary changes, or as a tool of social engineering. Thus, almost all legislation projects were devoted to national development. The efforts of the government to enact the marriage law, as part of a chain of Islamic legal developments in Indonesia, should be analysed in this light. In this regard, it seems unnecessary for the government to deal with the question: how does the marriage law meet the legal needs and practices of Indonesian Muslims? Instead the government has to show the reforms or innovations that the marraige law offers and its significance in preparing the Indonesian society to face the challenges of modernization.

Among the government's purposes in proposing the marriage legislation were to limit arbitrary divorce and polygamy and to eliminate or reduce child marriages. Azyumardi Azra's essay in this volume, which focuses on the marriage law, emphasizes that the marriage law has succeeded in accelerating social changes in Indonesia. Azra shows some impacts of the marriage law, which among others are the creation of healthy families and control of population growth, divorces, and polygamy. The stricter regulations and more difficult procedures provided by the marriage law have contributed towards a dramatic decrease in divorce rate. In West Java for instance, the divorce rate in 1955 was 58 per cent of registered marriages, but in 1985 and 1986 the rate went down to 16.53 per cent and 14.05 per cent respectively. With regard to the difficult procedures for polygamy, the marriage law has successfully painted an unfavourable image of polygamy among Indonesians; and as a result, the practice of polygamy has been less common nowadays.

The third state's interest is to express a symbolical gesture that the relationship between the government and Islam has been partly changed from coerced marginalization to controlled inclusion. Wertheim notes that although Indonesian Muslims constitute the majority of the population, they tended to behave like a minority, particularly under the Sukarno and early Soeharto regimes. By 1968, tension between the government and Islam was openly acknowledged; from then on, Islamic political parties and Muslim activists were treated as subjects of state repression and political marginalization. The relationship between Islam and the state, accordingly, became more tense, if not hostile.[15]

Since the late 1980s, however, there have been some changes in the New Order's policy towards Islam. The New Order regime shows a more accommodative attitude towards Islamic socio-cultural and political interests. According to some observers, this was due to the rise of "cultural Islam". The rise of cultural Islam is a result of a new approach to develop Islam after Pancasila has been accepted as the sole ideological basis. In the light of cultural Islam, Islam or the Muslim community was no longer seen as a threat to the existence of the nation-state of Pancasila. Indeed, the New Order regime began to treat it sympathetically by implementing a number of policies which were apparently to meet the aspiration of the Indonesian Muslims — for example, the passing of the Religious Judicature Act (1989), the founding of ICMI (Ikatan Cendekiawan Muslim Indonesia, or Indonesian Muslim Intellectuals Association) (1990), the issuance of the Presidential Instruction to disseminate the Compilation of Islamic Laws (1990), the issuance of the Joint Ministerial Decree on the guidance of *zakat* administrator or BAZIS (1991), the holding of an Islamic Cultural Festival (1991), the establishment of the Islamic Bank (1992), and the annulment of the national lottery (1993) (cf. Effendy 1998). All these new trends have been seen as signs of reconciliation between the state and Islam after two decades of antagonism.

Robert Hefner seems to share the above opinion. In his article in this volume, he states that the founding of the Indonesian Islamic Bank (Bank Muamalat Indonesia or BMI) was one of the positive result from Indonesia's Islamic renewal that began in the early 1970s under the guiding influence of such figures as Nurcholish Madjid, Dawam Rahardjo, and Abdurrahman Wahid. He adds that the changing government attitude towards Islam, as the outcome of the exchanged strategy from political Islam to cultural Islam, could not be put aside in generating such fruits of renewal. In Hefner's opinion, the government's support for the founding of Bank Muamalat — despite objections from secular technocrats and certain segments of the military — was an indication of the government's acknowledgement to and welcoming Muslim community to contribute more to the national economic development.

A fourth item can be added to the aforementioned state's interests: that all those concessions in the field of the application of Islamic law might have been seen as a way to increase the regime's own legitimacy. The New Order regime had sought to subordinate Muslim community under its control and to derive political advantage from the emergence of Islam in Indonesian politics during the 1990s.[16] From this point of view, it may be assumed that the government's efforts — to codify or transform various Islamic legal doctrines into national law or government regulations — were not sincere responses to the needs of Muslim citizens. The regime considered it more important to maintain its political status quo.

It is interesting to highlight that although the state's interest could have strongly influenced the process of *shari'a* implementation in Indonesia, mainly on the legislation projects, it cannot completely dictate the *fatwa* (Islamic legal opinion) issued either by individual *ulama* or a body of the legal commission within Muslim organizations such as the MUI (Council of Indonesian Ulama), NU (Nahdlatul

Ulama), or Muhammadiyah. This is perhaps due to the character of the *fatwa*, which has no legal enforcement, but echoes the political or ethical vibes, and due to the nature of the *mufti* (person or a body that issues the *fatwa*) who are generally independent from the political co-optation.

A number of *fatwas* have been issued in Indonesia for the purpose of supporting the government policies as well as opposing the government. Nadirsyah Hosen's article "*Fatwa and Politics in Indonesia*" in this volume portrays how *fatwas* were issued as a response to the temporal emerging issues of social life or a response to the government policies on religious life. It is worth noting that the *fatwas*, which supported the government policies, were particularly related to the government's effort in social engineering. The *fatwa* on family planning is a good example of how the Indonesian Government has been able to gain the support from almost all large and important Muslim organizations such as the MUI, NU, and Muhammadiyah.

The *fatwas* opposing the government are mainly in response to the government's attempt to establish itself as the highest authoritative body in the public sphere, by offering judgements upon and endorsing legality of the religious affairs in the daily life of citizens. The *fatwa* of the MUI on prohibiting Muslim attendance at Christmas celebrations and the *fatwa* of the NU on determining the first of day of Syawwal or Idul Fitri in a manner different from the government's decision are the examples of this kind of *fatwa*. In the former case, the government's initiative to promote harmonious relationship between Muslims and Christians could be assumed as a way to relinquish the faith in Islam. In the latter case, the government's attempt seeks to unify the celebration of Idul Fitri was seen as an unacceptable effort to intervene in religious matters.

THE CHARACTERISTICS OF THE IMPLEMENTED *SHARI'A*

Given the state's motives on the implementation of *shari'a* are mostly socio-political, it is important to point out two distinctive characteristics of the implemented *shari'a*: private and optional. Before elaborating on this, it is necessary to present the five levels of Islamic legal spheres, which are adapted from Daniel E. Price. Muslims believe that *shari'a* is a comprehensive set of norms and values regulating human life down to the smallest detail. The comprehensiveness of *shari'a* can be broken down into the following five legal spheres:

1. Issues of personal status such as marriage, divorce, *waqf*, and inheritance.
2. The regulation of economic matters such as banking and business practices.
3. Prescribed religious practices such as restriction on women's clothing, consumption of alcohol, gambling, and other practices that are considered un-Islamic.
4. The use of Islamic criminal law, including its punishment.
5. The use of Islam as a guide for governance.[17]

The first characteristic of the implemented *shari'a* in Indonesia is that its application is merely limited to those elements that are viewed as private Islamic law. Under this comes the marriage law, inheritance rule, *waqf* regulation, Religious Court law, and Islamic banking system. The *hajj* arrangement law and *zakat* administration law can also be added to this list since both laws could be regarded as prescribing religious practices, but none of the articles of either law obliges Muslim citizens to perform the *hajj* or to pay *zakat*. Both laws are simply guidelines to manage or facilitate the performance of *hajj* and *zakat*. Looking at the five levels of Islamic legal spheres, the first and second levels could be categorized as private Islamic law, while the third to the fifth levels should be regarded as public law.

The application of *shari'a* being limited only up to the second level, or only to contain private Islamic law, was a result of political contestation between the Islamic group on the one hand and the nationalist group on the other. The Islamic group seeks to apply the whole elements of *shari'a* through the state power, while the nationalist group, particularly non-Muslim citizens, are wary of the attempts to implement *shari'a*, because they regard the legislation of Islamic law as a gradual effort to revive the Jakarta Charter. Since the New Order politics was directed at promoting harmony among citizens, both sides had been positioned by the regime in a *fait accompli* situation to accept unnegotiable settlement in which none was able to completely have its way. This kind of settlement, which limits the application of *shari'a* only to the private Islamic law, however, has been still undeclared, and therefore it could potentially lead to new dispute or even a clash in the future, especially if efforts are made to go further than the second level. This has been obvious among some Muslim groups in Jakarta, such as the Front Pembela Islam (FPI) and Front Hizbullah, who had attempted to restrict the operational time or even to close down amusement places during the fasting month of Ramadhan in 2000. These radical activities, however, have provoked strong resistances, and even physical confrontations, especially with those who have certain objections to the *shari'a* implementation agenda.[18]

The second characteristic of the implemented *shari'a* is optionality. This means that no state apparatus should be involved in imposing on Muslim citizens to perform their religious duties. Given such a characteristic, no punishment may be meted out by the state to those who completely neglect the performance of Islamic duties. Article 49 of the Religious Judicature Act states that the religious court can examine the inheritance, testaments, and gifts only if they are performed according to Islamic law. Cammack (in this volume) explains that this has provided a "choice of law" in which, before submitting the case to the court, the parties involved in the division of an estate can select the law to be followed: either civil law or Islamic law. Likewise, the *zakat* administration law does not state the punishment for those who are unwilling to give a small percentage of their wealth to the eight *asnaf* (categories of *zakat* recipients). In short, the performance of Islamic duties depends much on the devotion of each individual Muslim citizen, while the state merely acts as the facilitating institution for that purpose.

Given the two characteristics of the implemented *shari'a*, it is safe to say that the Indonesian state has not significantly changed its policy towards Islamic law despite the fact that some of its precepts have been legislated into national law. The policy of the regime to keep Islam under its control is still evident. Taking *zakat* administration as a case study, Arskal Salim in his article in this book points out that all government policies towards *zakat* administration in Indonesia have not contributed significantly towards either considerable political accommodation or developments of Islamic teachings. Although there is some form of state involvement, the state confines its role to simply supervising the *zakat* administration to prevent abuse. Similarly, Cammack in his conclusion regarding the promulgation of the Religious Judicature Act points out that although the government's regulatory efforts are now articulated with a vocabulary supplied by Islam, the regime's basic objective of controlling Indonesian family law remains unchanged.

In addition, we may say that by controlling Islamic law, the Indonesian state has successfully instituted a new "reception theory" — that the implementation of *shari'a* is officially legitimate only if it has been ratified as national positive law. This is true for some of the contents of *shari'a* that have been put into bureaucratic formulae; and its emergence into legal force is possible only with the government's political will.

RESPONSES TO THE IMPLEMENTED *SHARI'A*

The formal implementation of *shari'a* by the state has elicited a at least three kinds of responses from Indonesian citizens. First is from within the government circle that allow the integration of *shari'a* into national legal system, but only in limited areas. The second stems from non-Muslim and nominal Muslims who oppose *shari'a* manifestation in any legal matters because its ratification would certainly infringe the principle of equality. The last originates from certain groups of Muslims who seek to have more elements of Islamic law to be legalized. The account of these issues can be found in Howard Federspiel's contribution in this volume. His essay portrays the wide variety of views manifested by Indonesians regarding Islamic values and law. Federspiel also identifies a greater change in perception among Indonesian citizens, especially Muslim intellectuals and activists, about the manner in which Islamic values and law are to manifest themselves in society and the nation. They have come to regard the values and mores of Indonesian culture as important and necessary considerations in the establishment of Islamic law in the country.

Federspiel is correct. Despite growing demands among certain groups of Muslims to apply more of *shari'a* at the state level, all these efforts are unsuccessful in obtaining greater support among the general Muslim population and the majority votes in the Parliament as well. Indeed, the leaders of the Muslim largest social-religious organizations, such as KH Hasyim Muzadi (general chairman of the NU) and Ahmad Syafi'i Ma'arif (chief national leader of Muhammadiyah), openly declare that they reject any attempt to revive the Jakarta Charter. In addition, Azyumardi Azra noted that the emerging aspiration to implement more formalistic *shari'a* that appeared in regions of Indonesia, such as South Sulawesi, or manifested in certain groups of Muslims who attacked nightclubs, discotheques, and houses allegedly used for prostitutions, has more to do with the failure of the Indonesian Government in enforcing law and eliminating crimes, thus providing a *raison d'être* to take Islamic law as the solution.[19]

What notions can be drawn regarding the development of formal implementation of *shari'a* in Indonesia so far? What would the implementation of *shari'a* in Indonesia imply? Would it lead to the establishment of an Islamic state? Looking at the formal implementation of *shari'a* in Indonesia within the light of the five levels of Islamic legal spheres, which have been described earlier, it can be concluded that it could not lead to the founding of an Islamic state. Since the current Indonesian legal system reached no further than the second level, this proves that Indonesia is not an Islamic state, although the majority of its population adheres to Islam. Moreover, if we take into consideration the two characteristics of the implemented *shari'a* — private and optional — it is clear that the Indonesian Government would never allow the application of *shari'a* to lead to the founding of an Islamic state.

One may still wonder if Indonesia would be more inclined to subscribe to the idea of an Islamic state. This is not impossible, since it would certainly be a contesting process in Indonesian political system. But, given the current trends that almost all aspirations to the formal application of *shari'a* gain no positive feedback, the transformation of Indonesia into an Islamic state is likely to be a remote possibility only.

CLOSING REMARKS

It will be clear to the readers of this book, however, that the relationship problem between religion and the state in Indonesia is far from being resolved. It is not the intention of this book to offer a solution for such a problematic topic. In fact, the essays collected in this volume are offered as a contribution to the subject by assessing the role of the Indonesian Government in implementing *shari'a*. In so doing, this book seeks to contribute to a better explanation on how the Indonesian state, which is neither secular nor religious, has played a role in implementing *shari'a* for its Muslim citizens in a pluralistic society.

There are of course those who would enthusiastically argue that the existence of *shari'a* in certain areas are simply representation of the rulers' interests rather than the true aspiration to apply *shari'a*. The implemented *shari'a* provides the rulers with a symbol to acquire the legitimacies from their Muslim citizens and influences among other Muslim kingdoms.[20] This view has answered the question of the motive behind the actions taken by the Indonesian Government in allowing the formal implementation of *shari'a* in its limited parts.

The collection of essays in this volume originated from various sources. Most of them have been earlier published either in refereed journals or in compiled books, while the rest are derived from unpublished papers or Master theses. They are brought together in this book for they have revealed strong connections with the implementation of *shari'a* that has been taking place in Indonesia. This book deals with special themes, issues, and perspectives that no other works have put forward. It must be admitted, however, that several chapters within this book need updating because they were produced several years ago and, therefore, have not covered the recent political issues in Indonesia. Considering this, we include an epilogue whose main focus is to reveal the developments of Islamic law during recent Indonesian political transitions. The application of *shari'a* in Aceh and the similar growing demands in some other regions, in line with the beginning of the decentralization era, are discussed in the epilogue. For further understanding and analysis, complete texts of several Indonesian laws pertaining to Islamic rules are provided in the Appendixes. These English texts are official translations that are taken from the publications of the Ministry of Religious Affairs.

Notes

1. William R. Liddle, "*Media Dakwah* Scripturalism: One Form of Islamic Political Thought and Action in New Order Indonesia", in *Toward a New Paradigm: Recent Development in Indonesian Islamic Thought*, edited by Mark R. Woodward (Arizona: Arizona State University, 1996), pp. 323–56.

2. "Seorang Pezina Dicambuk 100 kali di Aceh" [An adultery committer whipped 100 times in Aceh], *Media Indonesia*, 30 November 1999.

3. Abdul Aziz Qahar Muzakkar, "Otonomi Khusus Aceh dan Sulsel" [Special autonomy for Aceh and South Sulawesi], *Fajar*, 2 June 2000.

4. Ali Said Damanik, *Fenomena Partai Keadilan: Transformasi 20 Tahun Gerakan Tarbiyah di Indonesia* (Jakarta: Teraju, 2002), p. 160.

5. See Arskal Salim, *Etika Intervensi Negara: Perspektif Politik Ibnu Taimiyah* [The ethics of state intervention: Ibn Taymiyah political perspectives] (Jakarta: Logos, 1988), p. 54.

6. Anthony Reid, *Southeast Asia in the Age of Commerce 1450–1680*. Volume One: *The Lands Below the Winds* (New Haven: Yale University Press, 1988), p. 143.

7. John Ball, *Indonesian Legal History 1602–1848* (Sydney: Oughtershaw Press, 1982), p. 68.

8. Reid, *Southeast Asia*, pp. 143–44.

9. B. J. Boland, *The Struggle of Islam in Modern Indonesia* (The Hague: Martinus Nijhoff, 1982), pp. 15–39.

10. Ibid., pp. 100–101, 159.

11. Mohd Mahfud, *Politik Hukum di Indonesia* [Legal politics in Indonesia] (Jakarta: LP3ES, 1998), p. 7.

12. Ibid., p. 9.

13. Cik Hasan Bisri, "Aspek aspek Sosiologis Hukum Islam di Indonesia [Sociological aspects of Islamic law in Indonesia]", in *Hukum Islam dalam Tatanan Masyarakat Indonesia* [Islamic law in Indonesian social order] (Jakarta: Logos, 1998), edited by Cik Hasan Bisri, pp. 109–44.

14. Munawir Sjadzali, "Landasan Pemikiran Politik Hukum Islam dalam Rangka Menentukan Peradilan Agama di Indonesia", in *Hukum Islam di Indonesia: Pemikiran dan Praktek*, edited by Eddi Rudiana Arief et al. (Bandung: Rosda Karya, 1991), p. 52.

15. W. F. Wertheim, "Indonesian Moslems under Sukarno and Suharto: Majority with Minority Mentality", Studies on Indonesian Islam, *Occasional Paper* No. 19, Center for Southeast Asian Studies, University of North Queensland Australia, 1986.

16. William R. Liddle, "The Islamic Turn in Indonesia: A Political Explanation", *Journal of Asian Studies* 55, no. 3 (1996): 613–34.

17. Daniel E. Price, *Islamic Political Culture, Democracy and Human Rights: A Comparative Study* (Westport, Connecticut: Praeger, 1999), p. 145.

18. *Adil*, 14 December 2000.

19. Azyumardi Azra, "Islamic Perspective on the Nation-State: Political Islam In Post-Soeharto Indonesia", Paper presented at International Conference on "Islamic Perspectives on the New Millennium", The Australian National University (ANU), Canberra, 20–21 November 2000.

20. Olaf Schumann, "Dilema Islam Kontemporer: Antara Masyarakat Madani dan Negara Islam" [Dilemma of contemporary Islam: Between civil society and the Islamic state], *Jurnal Pemikiran Islam Paramadina* 1, no. 2 (1999): 48–75.

2

LAW AND POLITICS IN POST-INDEPENDENCE INDONESIA
A Case Study of Religious and *Adat* Courts

Ratno Lukito

INTRODUCTION

The shift from colonial to sovereign status did not bring any direct or pervasive changes to bear on the stature of law in the young Republic of Indonesia. By the time the proclamation of independence was issued on August 17, 1945, law in Indonesia had essentially changed little since the Japanese occupation of Java.[1] As most of the nation's elite was, in the early days of independence, people who had dominated Indonesian politics during the colonial era, the revolutionary ideas of grass-roots movements had not yet penetrated common legal parlance. This elite did not constitute a radical, social element interested in the reformulation of the former colonial state apparatus. On the contrary, they were quite content to fall back on the familiar. Strategies for social revolution, or even social change were hardly mentioned formally within the legal sector at this time.[2] Symptomatic of this situation was the Transitional Provision in Article 2 of the 1945 Constitution which stipulates that "All existing institutions and regulations of the state shall continue to function so long as new ones have not been set up in conformity with this Constitution."[3] Hence, to avoid creating a legal vacuum, the new government

Previously published as "Law and Politics in Post-Independence Indonesia: A Case Study of Religious and *Adat* Courts", *Studia Islamika: Indonesian Journal for Islamic Studies* 6, no. 3 (1999): 65–86. Reproduced with permission of the author and the publisher, State Institute for Islamic Studies (IAIN).

was forced to reintroduce many laws inherited from the colonial era. An example of this is the *Wetboek van Strafrecht* measures, enacted in 1915, which continued to regulate criminal law in Indonesia, except in those regions outside of Java where native courts remained operative. In the latter, only a few articles of laws inherited from the Dutch were applied through the provisions of Law No. 80 of 1932.[4]

This paper will address the development of Indonesian law in the post-independence era. In the following pages, I aim to demonstrate that changes in the country's political climate affected both the Islamic and *adat* (customary) courts, in spite of the inflexibility with which both legal traditions had weathered the political upheavals of the first half of the century. To this end, the place of both *adat* and religious courts in post-independence Indonesia will be analyzed in light of this political change. Two major avenues of investigation will be discussed. The first explains the debate between "pluralist" and "uniformist" groups regarding legal development in the young Republic of Indonesia, while the second discusses contentions between the so-called "secular nationalists" and "Muslims". The discussion provided in these sections is intended to provide a basis for understanding the legal controversies, which unavoidably arose as a result of the shift from a colonial to a national legal philosophy.

LEGAL ISSUES IN INDEPENDENT INDONESIA

Consisting of thousands islands, the Indonesian archipelago is inhabited by various ethnic, social, religious and cultural groups, each of which retains unique customs and ways of life.[5] Embracing this pluralism, the Republic of Indonesia has coined the official motto: *"Bhinneka Tunggal Ika"*, or "Unity in diversity." That diversity is evident in the legal dualism that exists within the unified state. In the immediate post-colonial era, several groups of laws survived the transition from the Dutch colonial government: (1) laws governing all inhabitants, e.g. the Law on Industrial Property and Patents; (2) customary laws which applied to indigenous Indonesians; (3) Islamic law applicable to all Indonesian Muslims; (4) laws tailored to specific communities in Indonesia, such as the Marriage Law for Christian Indonesians; and (5) the *Burgelijk Wetboek* and the *Wetboek van Koophandel* measures, originally applied to Europeans only, but later extended to cover the Chinese. Certain provisions in the latter, however, had also been declared to apply to native Indonesians.[6]

In the wake of the demise of colonial power and the assertion of national sovereignty, the new Indonesian leaders were inclined to view law as an essentially "rational-legal" organ of the state. Limited reforms to the system of law were, naturally, aimed at diminishing the vagaries of colonial law as much as possible. A new legal policy was to be constructed to replace colonial legal policy.[7] However, the legal pluralism of the country rendered the zeal for legal reformation somewhat premature. Legal controversies unavoidably arose between contending camps: the "pluralist" versus "uniformist" groups on the one hand; and the "secular nationalist" versus "Muslim" groups on the other. In the former, debate centered on the notion of the unification of law and of pluralism within the law in relation to *adat* law, while in the latter the focus of discussion was Islamic law. These groupings will be analyzed in detail in the following pages.

PLURALISM VERSUS UNIFORMISM

The concept of statehood is usually associated with the promulgation of uniform regulations for the governance of all citizens, irrespective of their ethnicity, religion or social status. While Indonesia's early leaders may not have been inclined towards radical political or social innovation, they were, nonetheless, committed to the unification of the country. For many leaders, this could only be achieved through a unification of law. In this manner, Indonesia would, it was reasoned, hasten to modernize. In fact, intertwined with the express need to modernize Indonesia, was the added desire on the part of national leaders, to exercise the spirit of colonial law. With "equality before the law" as its motto, the new state refrained from overturning the decision by the Japanese colonial authority to abolish the dualist composition of the legal courts. The dualism of the judicial structure, which had differentiated the European from the native, had been replaced by a single three-instance hierarchy of courts using a procedural code for all Indonesians.[8] The bureaucracy, the courts, and the offices of prosecution all came to be staffed with Indonesian officials. Thus, in theory, the colonial yoke of authority had been broken.

In spite of this advance, the total abolition of colonial law and its substitution with a uniform legal code was to prove a formidable task in a heterogeneous country like Indonesia. Extant laws were so intermingled with religious beliefs and culturally specific in nature as to render these attempts futile. In addition, the instability of the immediate post-colonial political climate led the republic's leaders to focus their attention on national unity rather than on institutional innovation.[9] As a consequence, the unification of law in the early years of independence proved to be unworkable. Different categories of law continued to be applied to different classes of residents, a fact that betokened the tenacity of legal pluralism as inherited from the Dutch colonial administration.

The unification of the law was, in fact, the first issue raised by the new republican leaders who were preoccupied with the notion of erasing colonial law. Instead, they proposed the promotion and development of indigenous law as the substance of future national law. What in fact occurred was that all theoretical strategies to unify the law in Indonesia were frustrated in practical application. The ensuing difficulties were a consequence, not only of the plurality of ingrained religious and cultural values, but also of the fact that the modern judicial system as defined by the colonial apparatus, had taken root in Indonesian society.[10] That aside, indigenous legal culture as propounded by Indonesian jurists at that time, was at odds with the notion of constructing "the same law for all." This is hardly surprising given the fact that these jurists studied under Dutch teachers, and were sufficiently impressed by the Dutch understanding of law to preserve its tenets.[11] Thus, while they may have presented themselves as exponents of Islamic or *adat* law, their vision of national law rarely transcended the bounds of colonial philosophy.

Retaining the skeleton of the former legal system was in fact also an imperative if the young republic were to avoid creating a legal vacuum in which conflicting social groups might advance competing political and legal doctrines. This explains why the Transitional Provision of the 1945 Constitution, which put faith in the pluralism of law, was a matter of necessity. As Lev points out, this "was not merely a matter of convenience ... nor was it simply because no one had any ideas"; rather ". . . the colonial law provided an available and appropriate framework", and this law ". . . was a . . . secular neutrality between conflicting religious and social groups, . . . that also kept the existing dominant elite in control of national institutions."[12]

However, as the revolution provided national impetus to the dismantling of colonial power in all its forms, the idea of a unified national law was endorsed in earnest. In some regions, this was marked by a grassroots mobilization to undermine local elites through the adoption of national institutions. The momentum from this movement facilitated the first real steps towards the unification of the law.

As one might expect, the decolonialization and nationalization of law in Indonesia had direct consequences for the institution of *adat* law. Outside Java especially, the demolition of customary courts proceeded gradually but persistently, as social mobilization fostered the expansion of national institutions.[13] Every effort was made to replace judicial institutions that rested on local power with a unified state judicial system. The reorganization of the judicial institution can be characterized as a political strategy aimed at unifying the young, pluralist country under the umbrella of a centralized power. In the judicial sphere, this gave rise to the central government's unfortunate compulsion to simplify the judicial system and, moreover, to eradicate all courts backed by village power. This was in contrast to Java where the administrative apparatus was relatively accustomed to the notion of unification. Beyond Java, the political climate was such that the notion of unification proved problematic.[14] In Sumatra, for example, the nationalization of the courts and the displacement of the sultanates' authority, from which the authoritative basis of customary law was derived, led to violent uprisings.

The intentions of the government regarding the unification of law, as a means to national unification, were made clear with the promulgation of Law No. 7 on February 27, 1947. This article stipulated that the organization and powers of the Supreme Court (*Mahkamah Agung*) and Chief Public Prosecutor (*Kejaksaan Agung*) were declared retrograde as of August 17, 1945. The clarification of this law amply reflected the government's conviction that a unified court system was a prelude to a unified state. At a later date, on August 29, 1947, Law No. 23 was promulgated expressly abolishing the customary courts of the former self-governing areas of Java and Sumatra.[15] Lev notes that the clarification of this law served as strong validation for the policy of unification, and quotes the law to this effect:

> The Government of the Republic of Indonesia is not all merely the successor of the Netherlands-Indies Administration . . . The Republic of Indonesia is a State which we, the whole Indonesian people, have established together as a united and sovereign State. Its Government consists of our own people. . . The justice established

throughout our State for all citizens (including those living in special regions [i.e., the former self-governing areas]) is justice "in the name of the Republic of Indonesia." Nor is that justice limited by the existence of various regions, and it would not be appropriate to divide it up into so many "sferen van rechtspraak" [areas of independent administration of justice, as in the colony]. From the beginning it has been the responsibility of the central Government to administer justice, as intended by Article 24 of the Constitution.[16]

Further modifications to judicial unification were marked by the enactment of a new law in June 1948. Due to the Dutch army's reassumption of power in the country, this law never came into effect, but the idea of a unified court system had taken root.[17] Most significantly, Law No. 19 of 1948 recognized only three spheres of government justice, i.e., general, administrative, and military. With general justice, there were only three judicial levels: the *Pengadilan Negeri* (court of first instance), *Pengadilan Tinggi* (appeals court), and *Mahkamah Agung* (supreme court).[18] Surprisingly, one finds no mention of either *adat* or religious courts in these provisions. Such an omission betrays the ineptitude of the new Indonesian legal architects in grasping the complexity of the inherited conflict between the exponents of *adat* and Islamic law.

With regard to *adat* courts, Article 10 of the 1948 law stipulates that the resident legal authority in a region be allowed to continue mediating certain conflicts and crimes covered under the "living law of society." In Lev's view, the vague language which denotes the institution of customary law as a "living law of society" and not as "*adat* laws" implies "a number of worries beginning to burden justice officials and also some emerging political conflicts."[19] On the one hand, this legitimized the abolition of *adat* laws, and yet on the other it also created more problems than the simple recognition of these laws would have done. Gradually, but persistently, every venue of opportunity to marginalize the *adat* courts was taken by justice officials. In fact, the so-called "living law of society" also camouflaged "an increasingly tense issue between those who controlled the new national government and the forces of Islam."[20] The on-going conflict between one group of people who favored the Dutch concept of *receptie*, in which Islamic law could be recognized only to the extent that it was absorbed by *adat* law, and another group who acknowledged Islamic law as a living law in society, was, at least for the moment, muted. In view of the fact that the term "living law of society" could be taken to mean either Islamic or *adat* law, the government took the initiative by conceding this status to both Islamic and *adat* law, in the hope that this would remove a source of conflict.

This situation remained in effect until the emergence of the United Republic of Indonesia (*Republik Indonesia Serikat*) in 1949.[21] On August 17, 1950, the United Republic of Indonesia came to an end. This marked the return of the country to its earlier form as the Republic of Indonesia, as first proclaimed in August 1945. With sovereignty, the effort to extend the jurisdiction of national institutions was intensified across Indonesia.[22] The dilemma of whether it would be the idea of unification, embodying the spirit of the national struggle, or that of realism-pluralism, was decided by ideological and political considerations which paved the way for the victory of the unificationists. Unification of law was in fact understood not only as a social or juridical argument, but also as the other side of the same coin of centralized political power, while *adat* law, which was pluralistic in nature,[23] symbolized the preservation of local autonomy; indeed, it was this symbolism that unavoidably rendered *adat* law somewhat suspect.[24] As may be imagined, the issue of unification during this period had wide ramifications. The dispute now erupted beyond the issue of unification of law *vis-à-vis* pluralism of law *per se*, to include contending arguments in favor of the centralization of state power *vis-à-vis* its decentralization.[25] Thus, law was now interwoven with politics.

Since the 1950s, Indonesian leaders have faced the challenge of building a coherent legal system in a pluralistic country without extinguishing the diverse ethnic, cultural and social practices of its society. The emergence of the uniformists on the one hand and the pluralists on the other was, therefore, a natural outcome of efforts at unifying the law. The former group, represented by those who strove for the modernization of Indonesia, argued that the country should adapt itself to models of "modern" nationhood if development and growth were to be encouraged. This could only be done if ". . . a clearly articulated legal system which as far as possible reflected the unity of Indonesia"[26] were put into place. Hence, *adat* law, a symbol of local autonomy for them, was perceived as "backward" and anti-modern.[27] The pluralists, on the other hand, maintained that the only practical law for a society like Indonesia was a pluralistic one. Proponents of *adat* law could not countenance the alteration of social conditions by the mere process of creating laws because, on a functional level, law had to accommodate itself to social conditions. More importantly, they argued, one cannot begin to unify the law when social conditions foster its fragmentation.[28] For this group, *adat* law continued to be regarded as a symbol of national pride which underscored the identity of indigenous Indonesian society and which deserved to be preserved. These two arguments monopolized the discussion on law in Indonesia until the end of the 1950s; indeed, as Ball states "the nature of legal developments in independent Indonesia has been largely determined by opinions (of the Indonesian lawyers) on the role of 'adat' law."[29]

Later developments did indeed facilitate what seemed to be the imminent recognition of *adat* law. Amid new outbursts of conflict between Indonesians and the Dutch concerning the liberation of West Irian, the zeal for demolishing all colonial vestiges from Indonesia gained momentum. In the legal arena, the notion of preserving *adat* law as a symbol of the spirit of indigenous values became suddenly credible. This shift was marked by a change in the official symbol of the Indonesian legal system. Lady Justice (*dewi yustisia*), a European symbol of justice, was replaced in 1960 by the Banyan Tree (*pohon beringin*), which in Javanese culture represents guardianship.[30] In the same year, a decree of the Provisional People's Assembly (*Ketetapan Majelis Permusyawaratan Rakyat Sementara*), No. II/MPRS/1960, explicitly identified *adat* law as a source for the development and elaboration of law in Indonesia.[31] This provision seemed to weaken the mandate of the movement for legal unification. Nonetheless, for the exponents of *adat* law, the battle was far from won.

The decree recognizing *adat* law is not, upon careful reading, unequivocal; it is stated therein that *adat* law should "not hamper the development of a just and prosperous society."[32] An ambiguous phrase, indeed, unavoidably invites competing interpretations and proclamations from leading scholars. Mohammad Koesnoe,[33] for instance, refuses to acknowledge any such fetters upon *adat* law.[34] As its leading exponent, he argues that the conditions imposed upon *adat* law are irrelevant as the conditions are themselves an expression of the imperative character of the law. *Adat* law, he continues, is a dynamic law that develops in conjunction with the development of society.[35] The logical underpinnings of that condition are therefore invalidated. In his conception, *adat* law would serve as the basis of national law not in its substantive sense, but in its principles, postulates, and basic values. The counter argument, characterizing *adat* law as backward and uncertain, could therefore only result from a misreading of the law.[36] Other scholars, who did not challenge the decree openly, advanced arguments against the pro-*adat* group. Simorangkir, for example, argued that *adat* laws hampered the modernization of society since, as an unwritten law, *adat* law engendered legal uncertainty.[37]

Whatever the pros and cons of the arguments for or against the inclusion of *adat* law in Indonesian public life, the ambivalence of national leaders on the question of plurality *vis-à-vis* uniformity of law could not be disguised. On a basic level, they accepted notions of legal unification in keeping with the spirit of Indonesian nationalism, but remained skeptical as to whether *adat* laws could simply be brushed aside. In actuality, the dilemma facing the new national leaders was essentially the same as that faced by colonial policy makers a half centuries earlier,[38] when arguments between liberals and conservatives or universalists and particularists were the order of the day.[39] The status of law remained unchanged in spite of the vigor with which a national law as derived from indigenous Indonesian values was pursued. Indeed, changing the symbols of national law, as in the shift from *dewi yustisia* to the *pohon beringin*, proved easier than changing the substance of the law itself.[40]

The enthusiasm with which national leaders greeted the reconstruction of the law as promoted in the Decree No. II/MPRS/1960 could be seen in the enactment of the Basic Law on Agrarian Affairs in 1960. This law amply reflects the difficulties encountered by leading legal scholars attempting to construct a truly "nationally oriented law" as stipulated by the Decree. Theoretically, this law substituted the colonial law pertaining to agrarian matters contained in the *Burgelijk Wetboek* (book II) with *adat* law; this appeared to be a step towards diminishing the role of colonial law, in that the law clearly stated that it would take Indonesian *adat* law as its source. Yet, the law, in practice, preserved many colonial rules since rights found in the *Burgelijk Wetboek* could also be found in the new law. One also finds no mention of land rights based on *adat* law, i.e., *hak ulayat*, as all land was now subject to the imperatives of national security and unity.[41] As a consequence, Gautama stated at the time, "the western principles are adopted 'silently'... by the legislators," adapting to modern principles and operating within a modern western model of agrarian reform such as that "the new statute means that the reception of western law will continue in Indonesia. . ."[42]

Further developments were marked by a shift in government from Soekarno to the "New Order" administration of 1966. With this shift in the political landscape, legal patterns also changed. If the law had previously been "the law of revolution", law in the new era assumed a fresh role as "the law of development";[43] law as a vehicle to rapid development. Furthermore, as the word "development" in the New Order era had the connotation of economic progress, national law was increasingly perceived as a means to that end. At this juncture, the articulation of laws functioned as a tool of social engineering, an idea that quickly gained popularity. This idea was, in fact, first set forth by Mochtar Kusumaatmadja,[44] who argued for the need to combine sociological considerations with the study of law in developing countries in an effort to alleviate their socio-economic problems.[45]

Kusumaatmadja assumed a neutral posture with respect to whether the law should be uniform or pluralist in nature, for in spite of perceiving the role of *adat* law as incompatible with the requirements of economic development, he also questioned the benefits of imported Western law, which he felt at the time had had "little effect on the modernization process as a whole."[46] He concluded that hasty decisions concerning the development of law in Indonesia should be avoided, i.e., that the government of the day should continue the colonial legal tradition or simply make use of *adat* law in national law. The distinction should be made between the areas of law in which innovations could be made and those areas in which they could not. He was of the opinion that the areas most intimately connected with the cultural and spiritual life of the people should be left undisturbed, while in other neutral areas regulated by the social intercourse of modern imperatives the government could benefit from imported legal concepts.[47] He proposed what might be termed a selective unification of the law.

It was Kusumaatmadja's legal model which most contributed to the law's new role as a vehicle of modernization in the New Order era.[48] His concept of a selective unification of the law was adopted as government policy on law in modern Indonesia. Backed by the executive power, Kusumaatmadja's ideas carried enough weight to dampen the debate between pluralists and uniformists. As the main concern of the New Order was improving the economy,[49] legal institutions were accordingly geared towards the accommodation of economic development. As a consequence, the government was forced to become more vigilant in those areas where native values played a persistent role in law making. Otherwise the wrong decision could undeniably impede the national program itself.

What is important to note about this new policy is that the law had now actually become a governmental tool of social control. With law fully in the hands of the government, the appeals of pro-*adat* groups, who argued that law should not come from above (state power), but should, rather, spring forth from society,[50] went unheard. The pluralist group therefore lost its philosophical arguments. To make matters worse, the unfortunate position of *adat* law had been exacerbated by a shortage of qualified scholars who could have provided fresh ideas on the role of *adat* in the modern era of Indonesia.[51] So when the government reopened the debate on national law making, exponents of *adat* law could no longer compete with their counterparts, the exponents of national law. At this stage, as law emerged as an organ of the government apparatus of the New Order, *adat* law began to fade.

SECULAR NATIONALIST *VS.* MUSLIM

In contrast with *adat* law, which had been weakened by the process of unification of the law, the position of Islamic law in the country did not seem to have been affected in any way. While *adat* was, by its nature, powerful only locally,[52] Islam was powerful nationally.[53] As a result, the centralization of power had little influence on the status of Islamic law.

In his analysis of the nexus between politics and religion in Islam, Allan Christelow argues that the point of maximum stress between the two is located in the office of the *qadi*, "a state-appointed religious judge."[54] This is true of the accommodations reached between the state and Islam since the emergence of the nation-state in Islamic countries, the latter phenomenon a result of their encounter with Western values through the colonization process. In Indonesia, these accommodations can be discerned in the case of the religious courts. Since independence, the evolution of the court systems has reflected the encounter between nationalist groups, who represent state power, and Muslim groups.

In the early days of independence, the courts continued to function in their juridical capacities, as the colonial courts had done, while all efforts to extend their jurisdiction were frustrated.[55] This may have been the result of a failure to reorganize the system. The courts, which had been administered by the Ministry of Justice during the Japanese occupation, came under the jurisdiction of the Ministry of Religion in 1946.[56] Surprisingly, only two years later, the government promulgated Law No. 19,[57] which decreed that religious courts would be amalgamated under regular courts. Cases involving Muslim litigants which required resolution under Islamic law, would be decided by a Muslim judge. However, since this law was never actually put into effect by the Indonesian government, based on the Transitional Provision of the 1945 Constitution, the existence of the religious courts continued to exist in the form stipulated in *Staatsblad* 1882 No. 152, especially in Java and Madura.[58] What is important to note is that this policy represents an early official attitude toward the inherited political conflict between secular nationalists and Muslims. Although the 1948 law was never implemented, the spirit and letter of this law had the effect of subordinating Muslims to the former. This situation was exacerbated with the abolition of the Sultanate Courts outside Java and Madura in 1951, which created confusion over the settlement of religious disputes.

Yet, six years later, through the issuance of government regulation (*Peraturan Pemerintah*) No. 45/1957, the confusion over religious disputes outside Java and

Madura was resolved by the government's reestablishment of religious courts for those areas. In effect, this regulation provided religious courts with more extensive jurisdiction than the courts in Java, Madura or South Kalimantan. Until this time the pluralism of religious law continued to define the religious courts in terms of their structure, procedure and even their designation which varied between the three regions: (1) in Java and Madura, the courts were called *Pengadilan Agama* and the appeals court *Mahkamah Islam Tinggi*; (2) in Banjarmasin (South Kalimantan), the *Kerapatan Qadi* or *Pengadilan Qadi* had *Kerapatan Qadi Besar* or *Pengadilan Qadi Tinggi* for its appellate; and (3) for the rest of Indonesia, the courts were called *Mahkamah Syar'iyah*, while appeals courts were called *Mahkamah Syar'iyah Propinsi*. The courts in the first two regions continued to apply laws inherited from the Dutch, while the government, through the regulation of 1957, acquired jurisdiction over courts in the rest of Indonesia.[59]

Later developments in the religious court system were not without difficulties. The notion of a "reception theory", inherited from the Dutch, influenced many Indonesian legal experts and led to their antagonism towards the existence of religious courts. The most prominent among these experts was Dr. Raden Soepomo, a nationalist adviser to the Justice Department, who seemed very antagonistic to Islam and who exercised great influence in the preparations for the introduction of the 1945 Constitution.[60] The fact that most officials in the Department of Justice and civil courts were graduates of Dutch law schools, which de-emphasized Islamic law in their curriculum, compounded the problem. Most of them were acquainted with Islamic law only from their study of the Shafi'ite school as applied by Indonesian Muslim traditionalists. They neglected, however, to familiarize themselves with the basic tenets of Islam.[61] Consequently, they felt estranged both from Islam and from Muslims who expressed a desire to practice Islamic law.

The problem was also worsened by the fact that the Muslim judges who ran the religious courts were traditionalists whose knowledge of Islamic law was confined to the classical Shafi'ite school, and officers whose judicial knowledge was very limited. This unavoidably created a huge gap between judges or legal experts educated under the Dutch, who possessed a very westernized understanding of law, and Muslim judges trained along traditional lines in Islamic educational institutions.[62] These circumstances only widened the gulf between the nationalist and Muslim groups.

This polarization came to a head in 1970 with the promulgation of Law No. 14. As a substitute for Law No. 19 of 1964, it affirmed and bolstered the standing of religious courts in Indonesia's New Order. Article 10 of the 1970 Law states that judicial power was to be exercised by courts of justice in the spheres of religious, military and administrative law. This law therefore ensured that the religious courts would operate within the judicial system and, indirectly, granted religious courts a status equal to that of the other two courts operating in the country.

At the practical level, however, the principle of equality among the three judicial bodies remained unrealized. Colonial regulations, stipulating that all decisions of the religious courts were to be ratified by regular courts before being officially implemented, even if decided by the High Court of Appeal, still survived. The "fiat of execution" (*executoire verklaring*) was only required if the disputants did not voluntarily abide by the court's decision. This trend was then reinforced by the Marriage Law (Law No. 1 of 1974), viewed mainly as a concession to Islamic law, stipulating that all religious court decisions were to be approved by its counterpart, the regular court. This change from specific approval to a general imperative obviously denotes the subordination of religious courts to regular courts.[63] Thus, while Islamic law had received formal recognition, nationalist lawyers continued to regard the judicial institution of religious law with disdain. Many Muslim writers opposed this "fiat of execution" by arguing that it was contradictory to the general norms of the Basic Judiciary Law.[64] The subordinate status of the religious courts, however, continued to underline the uneasy tension between nationalists and Muslims in the early years of the New Order.

The debate among Indonesian politicians and legal experts over the existence of the religious courts continued unabated into the 1980s. This situation was indicative of the bias that existed against the position of Islam in the state. The religious courts themselves, wracked by poor administrative and work procedures, did little to improve their own image. Even Hazairin, recognized as the most outspoken critic of reception theory,[65] had at one time expressed his disagreement with the courts.[66]

Hazairin's attitude was typical of many Muslims who, while counting Islamic law as an important source of the Indonesian law-making process, were of the opinion that the practice of Islamic law was not dependent upon the existence of religious courts. Islamic law, they argued, could simply be applied in the regular courts. Other Muslims, however, argued that the religious courts were indispensable for the application of Islamic law, and warned against the danger of allowing the regular courts and their secular-trained lawyers to meddle in sacred law.[67]

In spite of these impediments, however, the religious courts were partially successful in fulfilling their role as problem-solvers in marriage disputes. For villagers in particular, the religious courts performed a vital role in this area, offering as they did consultation services. Given judicial norms in the secular decision-making process, people could not expect to find such services in an ordinary civil court. Islamic judges on the other hand have traditionally played an advisory role in cases of marriage and divorce, particularly in areas where there was no advisory committee on marriages and settlement of divorces (*Badan Penasehat Perkawinan dan Penyelesaian Perceraian= BP4*).[68]

Against the background depicted above, the Indonesian government, to the surprise of many observers, issued on December 29, 1989, Law No. 7 on Religious Courts, initiating the most recent changes to religious courts as an institution. The modernist Muslim ideal of promoting religious courts in conjunction with a modern judicial system was realized with the passage of this law. In contrast to the court system devised by the Dutch, this new law gives all religious courts throughout Indonesia a uniform name, i.e., *Pengadilan Agama* (Religious Court), and *Pengadilan Tinggi Agama* (Higher Religious Court) for the courts of appeal. More importantly, the jurisdiction of the courts was expanded to include all cases of Muslim family law, namely marriage, divorce, repudiation, inheritance, bequest, gift (*hibah*) and endowment. Additionally, the religious courts now share an equal status with that of the regular courts, so that the *executoire verklaring* is no longer warranted.

Much has been written about the most recent Islamic developments in Indonesia. Most of the literature suggest that there has been a rapprochement between the state and Islam in Indonesia since the second half of the 1980s. New legal statutes, such as the Basic Law on Education, the Presidential Instruction No. 1 of 1991 on the Compilation of Islamic Law, and broad government support for Muslim intellectual organizations such as ICMI (Ikatan Cendekiawan Muslim Indonesia) have made clear the intention of the New Order regime under Soeharto to address the needs of Muslim society. This development would seem to mark a turning point in the relationship between nationalists and Muslims, wherein they no longer see each other as enemies, but as full partners in the New Order's efforts at nation building.[69]

The regime's softened attitude towards Islam surprised many observers, given the fact that the voice of the non-Muslim factions in Indonesian political discourse was still heard well into the late of 1980s; this was illustrated during the debate over the law on religious courts in the House of Representatives (Dewan Perwakilan Rakyat). Non-Muslim and nationalist groups expressed a great opposition to the draft of the Religious Courts Act of 1989.[70] Interestingly, they suspected this step of being a prelude to Muslim efforts to revive the Jakarta Charter. In their view, the enactment of Law No. 1 of 1989 was a signal that Indonesian Muslim elements were intent on building an Islamic state.

Their suspicions seem unfounded in light of the fact that Muslim idealists promoting the notion of a state based on Islamic ideology have consistently been defeated by accommodationist Muslims over the past decade. For other Muslims the notion of an Islamic state, whatever that may mean, has been discarded. This fact, coupled with the adoption by all political parties and mass organizations of the principles of Pancasila as their sole ideological basis, has led more Muslim leaders to question the relevance of the debate for the Republic of Indonesia. The discussion no longer revolves around the pros and cons of building an Islamic state, but rather focuses on the ways in which Islamic values are to be integrated into national ideology. As one Islamic leader put it after 1965, ". . . we do not talk any more about an Islamic State but at best about an Islamic society."[71] In other words, Islam may have declined as a political force, but its cultural strength continues to exert potent influence on contemporary Indonesian politics. This condition appears to have stimulated the enactment of the latest series of laws on religious courts. These now retain an independent status in the Indonesian judicial system. As long as they continue to fulfill the requirements of any modern court, their status, in relation to other judicial bodies in Indonesia, cannot be undermined.

CONCLUSION

The emergence of a new pattern of legal policy-making in the country has unavoidably invited heated debate and sometimes resentment among certain Indonesian groups, over the question of instituting both *adat* and religious courts. Critics of this policy argue that such courts might eventually come to be affiliated with local powers beyond the formal political powers of the central government. It is in this way that the climate that featured the banishment of the *adat* courts as its final result can be understood. Religious courts, on the other hand, did not seem to have been affected by the process of unification of the law in the country. Although political upheaval in the early days of independence tended to weaken the role of the courts in the Indonesian judiciary system, the practical benefit of the courts at the grassroots level of Muslim society helped to maintain its stature. This might also be due to the fact that the institution's political power is more national in its extent and more powerful in its endurance as it is backed by religious values. As a result, the centralization of power had little influence on the status of the religious courts. The resilience of the religious courts in Indonesia's changing political climate, especially since the second half of the 1980s, is also the result of the accommodations reached between the state and Islam in the heyday of the encounter between nationalist groups, who represent state power, and Muslim groups.

Therefore, although the nation's changing political constellations have had an unavoidable influence on the position of the two court systems, with the banishment of the *adat* courts being one of the results of these changes, the political role played by the religious court system seems unable to be impeded. While the *adat* courts were *willy-nilly* dampened from their natural growth, religious courts have maintained their position, and have even strengthened in conjunction with the rise of the domination of central power and its accommodation of Islam.

Notes

1. R. Subekti, *Law in Indonesia* (Jakarta: Yayasan Proklamasi, Center for Strategic and International Studies, 1982), p. 6.
2. Daniel S. Lev, "Judicial Unification in Post Colonial Indonesia," *Indonesia* 16 (October 1973): 13.
3. This English version is taken from Subekti, *Law in Indonesia*, p. 6.
4. Subekti, *Law in Indonesia*, p. 7.
5. Gouwgioksiong, "The Marriage Laws of Indonesia with Special Reference to Mixed Marriages," *Rabels Zeitschrift* 28 (1964): 711–31.
6. Subekti, *Law in Indonesia*, pp. 6–7.
7. On using the word "new" vs. "old" in the debate over legal politic of Indonesia see Sajuti Thalib, *Politik Hukum Baru* (Bandung: Binacipta, 1987), pp. 52–53.
8. Daniel S. Lev, "Judicial Institutions and Legal Culture," in *Culture and Politics in Indonesia*, edited by Claire Holt (Ithaca, N.Y.: Cornell University Press, 1972), p. 257.
9. See Lev, "Judicial Unification," p. 13.
10. Wignjosoebroto, *Dari Hukum Kolonial ke Hukum Nasional* (Jakarta: Raja Grafindo Persada, 1994), pp. 176–87.

11. See Lev, "Judicial Institutions," pp. 261–63.

12. Lev, "Judicial Unification," p. 14.

13. Wignjosoebroto, *Dari Hukum*, pp. 192–93; see also a brief explanation of this in Lev, "Judicial Unification," pp. 15–37.

14. See Lev, "Judicial Unification," pp. 14–18.

15. Koesnodiprodjo, *Himpunan Undang2, Peraturan2, Penetapan2 Pemerintah Republik Indonesia*, as cited in Lev, "Judicial Unification," pp. 19–20.

16. As taken from Lev, "Judicial Unification," p. 20 (the interpolation in square brackets are Lev's).

17. Lev, "Judicial Unification," p. 20.

18. See Articles 6 and 7 of the law. This judicial hierarchy is still in place today.

19. Lev, "Judicial Unification," p. 21.

20. Lev, "Judicial Unification," p. 22.

21. This was the result of the Round Table conference (*Konferensi Meja Bundar*) between Indonesia and the Netherlands, held on December 27, 1949.

22. Lev, "Judicial Unification," pp. 22–23.

23. On the pluralistic nature of *adat* law see M. M. Djojodigeono, *Adat Law in Indonesia* (Jakarta: Djambatan, 1952).

24. Lev, "Judicial Unification," pp. 23–24.

25. See Wignjosoebroto, *Dari Hukum*, pp. 202–23.

26. S. Takdir Alisjahbana, *Indonesia: Social and Cultural Revolution* (Kuala Lumpur: Oxford University Press, 1966), p. 67.

27. Lev, "Judicial Unification," p. 23; see also his "Judicial Institutions," p. 255; see in addition his "Colonial Law and the Genesis of the Indonesian State," *Indonesia* 40 (October 1985): 69–74.

28. See this argument in Djojodigoeno, *Adat Law in Indonesia*, pp. 5 ff.

29. John Ball, *Indonesian Law Commentary and Teaching Materials* (Sydney: Faculty of Law, University of Sydney, 1985), p. 202. See also his *The Struggle for National Law in Indonesia* (Sydney: Faculty of Law, University of Sydney, 1986) in some related issues.

30. See Wignjoseobroto, *Dari Hukum*, pp. 210–11.

31. The Provisional People's Assembly Decree No. II/MPRS/1960, Enclosure A, paragraph 402 explains the national politics of law as follows:

    a) The principle of the construction of national law shall be in accordance with the state direction and based on *adat* law which does not hamper the development of a just and prosperous society.

    b) In an effort to homogenize law, extant legal practice in Indonesian society must be considered.

    c) In the process of perfecting marriage and inheritance laws, religious and *adat* factors should be considered.

    See R. Soerojo Wignjodipoero, *Kedudukan Serta Perkembangan Hukum Adat Setelah Kemerdekaan* (Jakarta: Gunung Agung, 1982), pp. 24–30; also Soerjono Soekanto, *Kedudukan dan Peranan Hukum Adat di Indonesia* (Jakarta: Kurnia Esa, 1987), pp. 73–74.

32. See the Decree No. II/MPRS/1960 paragraph 402 point (a) in note 31 above.

33. He is one of leading scholars on *adat*, and is a graduate of Leiden University.

34. See Mohammad Koesnoe, "Hukum *Adat* dan Pembangunan Hukum Nasional," *Hukum dan Keadilan* year 2, no. 3 (March/April 1970): 32–43. Also his "Menetapkan Hukum Dari *Adat*," *Hukum Nasional* year 2, no. 3 (January–March 1969): 3–11.

35. Koesnoe, "Hukum *Adat*," pp. 40–41.

36. Koesnoe, "Hukum *Adat*," pp. 36–37.

37. B. Simorangkir, "*Adat* Versus Emansipasi," *Sinar Harapan*, August 10, 1968.

38. Wignjosoebroto, *Dari Hukum*, pp. 209–10.

39. See A. D. A. de Kat Angelino, *Colonial Policy*, tr. G. J. Renier (The Hague: M. Nijhoff, 1955) vol. 2, pp. 171–93.

40. See Daniel S. Lev, "The Lady and the Banyan Tree: Civil Law Change in Indonesia," *American Journal of Comparative Law* 14 (1965): 282–307.

41. See Wignjosoebroto, *Dari Hukum*, pp. 212–13.

42. Soedarto Gautama, "Law Reform in Indonesia," *Rabels Zeitschrift* 26 (1961): 535–53.

43. See Wignjosoebroto, *Dari Hukum*, pp. 224–27.

44. He was a professor of international law at the University of Padjadjaran, Bandung, serving from 1974–1978 as Minister of Justice and after that as Minister of Foreign Affairs.

45. Mochtar Kusumaatmadja, "The Role of Law in Development: The Need for Reform of Legal Education in Developing Countries," in *Role of Law in Asian Society*, vol. II, *Papers for Special Congress Session in 28th International Congress of Orientalists (1973)* as cited from Wignjosoebroto, *Dari Hukum*, p. 231.

46. Kusumaatmadja, "The Role of Law," p. 4.

47. Kusumaatmadja, "The Role of Law," p. 8.

48. See for example Sajuti Thalib, *Politik Hukum Baru*, pp. 65–67; C. F. G. Sunaryati Hartono, *Politik Hukum Menuju Satu Sistem Hukum Nasional* (Bandung: Penerbit Alumni, 1991), pp. 1–2.

49. Wignjosoebroto, *Dari Hukum*, pp. 233–35.

50. See for example the argument asserted by the exponent of *adat* law that law should not appear to contravene with the feeling of justice of the society in Halimah A., *Kebhinnekaan dan Sifat-Sifat Khas Masyarakat Hukum Adat Indonesia* (Padang: Laboratorium PMP/IKN FPIPS Institute Keguruan Ilmu Pendidikan Padang, 1987), p. 4.

51. Wignjosoebroto, *Dari Hukum*, pp. 240–41.

52. Theoretically, *adat* was weakened on a national level because it was divided by van Vollenhoven into 19 distinct areas based on shared custom or culture.

53. Lev, "Judicial Unification," p. 22.

54. See Allan Christelow, *Muslim Law Courts and the French Colonial State in Algeria* (New Jersey: Princeton University Press, 1985), p. 262.

55. See Lev, *Islamic Courts in Indonesia* (Berkeley: University of California Press, 1972), pp. 62 ff.

56. This was based on Government Decree No. 5/S.D. promulgated on March 25, 1946. Furthermore, based on the Second Announcement of the Ministry of Religious Affairs (Maklumat Menteri Agama II) all judges of the religious courts came under the organization of the Department of Religious Affairs. See *Kitab Himpunan Perundang-undangan R.I.*, vol. I: *Siaran Pemerintah tanggal 15 Juli 1960*, p. 1697 as cited in B. Bastian Tafal, "Pengadilan Agama," *Hukum Nasional* year 2, no. 7 (1976): 96.

57. See a case of the same law concerning the institution of *adat* law on page 80.

58. Zain Ahmad Noeh and Abdul Basit Adnan, *Sejarah Singkat Pengadilan Agama* (Surabaya: PT. Bina Ilmu, 1983), p. 54.

59. Eddy Damian and Robert N. Hornick, "Indonesia's Formal Legal System: An Introduction," *The American Journal of Comparative Law* 20 (1972): 517–18.

60. Deliar Noer, *The Administration of Islam in Indonesia* (Ithaca, NY: Cornell Modern Indonesia Project, Southeast Asia Program, Cornell University, 1978), p. 45.

61. Noer, *The Administration of Islam*, pp. 45–46.

62. Lev, "Judicial Institutions," p. 297; Noer, *The Administration*, pp. 46–47.

63. Nur Ahmad Fadhil Lubis, "Institutionalization and the Unification of Islamic Courts Under the New Order," *Studia Islamika* 2/1 (1995): 22–26.

64. See for example T. Jafizham, "Peranan Pengadilan Agama dalam Pelaksanaan Undang-Undang Perkawinan," in *Kenang-Kenangan Seabad Peradilan Agama* (Jakarta: Departemen Agama, 1985), pp. 170–72; and H. Dahlan Ranuwihardjo," Peranan Badan Peradilan Agama dalam Mewujudkan Cita-Cita Negara Hukum," in *Kenang-Kenangan*, pp. 201–12.

65. See Hazairin, *Hukum Kekeluargaan Nasional* (Jakarta: Tintamas Indonesia, 1982), pp. 7–10, wherein he calls the reception theory a "teori iblis" ("theory of the devil").

66. See Lev, *Islamic Courts*, p. 88.

67. Noer, *Administration of Islam*, pp. 48–49.

68. Noer, *Administration of Islam*, p. 50.

69. Lubis, "Institutionalization," pp. 34–35.

70. See Ismail Saleh, "Wawasan Pembangunan Hukum Nasional," *Kompas*, June 1 and 2, 1989, as quoted in Lubis, "Institutionalization," p. 47. This article appeared during the heated debate in the Parliament as well as in public over the bill proposing reform of the Religious Courts. See also Zuffran Sabrie, ed., *Peradilan Agama Dalam Wadah Negara Pancasila: Dialog Tentang RUUPA* (Jakarta: Pustaka Antara, 1990), pp. 124–31.

71. See B. J. Boland, *The Struggle of Islam in Modern Indonesia* (The Hague: Nijhoff, 1982), p. 159.

3

THE STATE AND *SHARI'A* IN INDONESIA

M. B. Hooker

For Muslims, the authority of Islam is an alternative to the authority of the state, regardless of that state's particular ideological persuasion. This is as true now as it was for the Abbasids, the Ottomans, the former Soviet Union and the Imperial European powers of the 19th and 20th centuries. The issue has not subsided with the demise of imperialism. The successor states must still face and accommodate it. In the past 50 years, the relationship between the Indonesian state and Islam has changed constantly depending on the political circumstances of the time, ranging from oppression, conflict and control to an uneasy accommodation. It is a relationship that is difficult to characterise with any precision. It would be over-facile, for example, to describe any period of the relationship only in terms of conflict. Equally, accommodation, or attempts at accommodation, have not been overwhelmingly successful. Recently, however, the Indonesian state appears to have struck a more positive balance with Islam. The government has provided for the integration of *syariah*[1] into the rapidly developing state.

Essentially, the issue is authority. Islamic purists claim authority from Revelation; secular nationalists claim authority from the Constitution of the state. The ideal for some Muslim activists is the 'Islamic state'. However, this in itself is a contradiction. Authority can have only one locus. The issue is always who has the power to exercise authority, and how this power is to be divided, controlled and transferred. As Pakistan shows, Islamic jurisprudence provides no sufficient answer for the contemporary nation state. Indeed the arguments about the nature

Previously published as "The State and *Syariah* in Indonesia 1945–1995", in *Indonesia: Law and Society*, edited by Tim Lindsey (Sydney: Federation Press, 1999), pp. 97–110. Reproduced with permission of the author, the editor, and the publisher.

of the Islamic state in the contemporary Muslim world usually reduce themselves to little more than vague generalities supposedly founded in seventh century Muslim practice. On the other hand, proponents of an Islamic basis for the state can and do point to parts of Islamic law (for example, family law) where rather more specific provisions are available.

The forms and expressions of the nation-state, such as constitutions, legal codes, and the distribution and separation of powers have developed from European political history over the past two centuries. Although the nation-state and its components can encompass an Islamic element, overlay or colouring, the impact of Islam can never be fundamental. An element of tension will always exist simply because the sources of authority are irreconcilable.

This is as true for Indonesia as any other state populated by Muslims. Islam has been an ideology of resistance, in both the former Netherlands East Indies (NEI) and the independent Republic. The history of *syariah* in Indonesia has been the struggle to attain a "proper" place within a non- or even anti-Islamic polity. It was not until 1882 that *syariah* received minimal recognition in the NEI and even this was substantially reduced in 1937 (Hooker, 1984). The period from the 1880s to World War II was characterised by an intense debate within the official circles governing the NEI as to the place of Islam and its relation to law, in particular to *adat* law. The proponents of *adat* argued that the Indonesian Muslims were "nominal" if not even "heretical" Muslims. They came to this conclusion by emphasising the non-scriptural nature of Indonesia Islam, particularly in social custom including, especially, inheritance. The proponents of Islam, on the other hand, including especially Snouck Hurgronje, emphasised the local nature of Islamic forms and practices throughout the Muslim world. A non-scriptural expression of religion, they argued, did not make a Muslim into a "nominal" Muslim.

On the other hand, the Japanese interregnum gave Islam a place in the wartime state for the first time (Benda, 1958) and since 1945, Islam (and hence *syariah*) has been a fundamental element of Indonesian political life. It is not as though the Japanese really promoted Islam, except possibly in the last few months of the war. What they did, however, was to give the religion a recognised space in national life. The nature and extent of this space has greatly varied in the past half century but its existence has never been called into question since.

THE COLONIAL RELIGIOUS COURT SYSTEM (1882–1989)

The colonial Religious Court System was the main legacy of the Dutch. In 1882, they promulgated the first regulation concerning the Colonial Religious Court system.[2] The law, revised in 1937, established Religious Courts in Java, Madura, Banjarmasin and associated areas of southern Borneo.

In 1957, the Indonesia Government promulgated regulations extending the system to the whole archipelago.[3] These regulations constituted the Religious Court system until the reforms of 1989 discussed below. Essentially, the function and content of this legislation was procedural. The majority of the provisions regulated the appointment of court officers and defined their functions. The substantive principles of *syariah* were not stated.[4] The structure of the Religious Courts was based directly on the secular model. They were collegiate; they had appeal systems; and they followed secular rules of describing, validating and filing judgments. It is not difficult to understand how this restricted the application of *syariah*. For example, the secular procedures left no room, or very little, for the application of the principles of classical (that is, Arabic) *fikh* (rules of law) and classical rules of evidence were totally excluded.

Syariah was formally limited in other ways. From 1937, the jurisdiction of the Religious Courts was quite severely restricted, mainly to matters of dowry, marriage and divorce.[5] Other claims for money or goods generally fell under the jurisdiction of the civil courts. The secular courts also had jurisdiction over property matters, as the Dutch considered them to be *adat* issues. The post-independent Indonesian government has maintained the position that *syariah* should not be used to settle property disputes. This issue has and continues to cause substantial difficulties simply because family matters (as regulated in *syariah*) cannot be separated from land, the most important form of property in peasant communities.

The colonial principle that civil power had ultimate authority affected the jurisdiction of the Religious Courts. The dominance of the secular courts has been re-stated and reinforced in independent Indonesia. The Law on Judicial Authority of 1970 gives the *Mahkamah Agung* or Supreme Court overriding cassation[6] powers over all branches of the judicature, including the Religious Courts. Even at district court level, the Religious Courts were never granted exclusive jurisdiction. A dissatisfied party could apply to the district court for another adjudication on the case, based on either civil (that is, Dutch-derived) law or the *adat* of the area or district.

Although pre-war jurisprudence is scarce, Daniel Lev (1972*a*) has illuminated two things about the post-independence workings of the Religious Courts important to the present discussion. First, the quite artificial limits on Religious Court jurisdiction are widely ignored. Religious Court judges use *fatwa* (a ruling on a point of law) as a way around the circumscribed jurisdiction. In the classical *fikh* the *fatwa* is rather formal. Indeed, its formal character has been a feature of Islamic legal history from the earliest times. Governments in Muslim history (for example, the Ottoman Empire) have used *fatawa* (plural version of *fatwa*) to validate purely secular or state interests. However, the Indonesian interpretation of *fatwa* has been quite different. *Fatawa* have provided judicial recognition to the reality of urban and peasant life, despite the restrictive (pre-1989) colonial-derived laws.

Similarly, the courts have innovatively interpreted *sjiqaq* (*shikak*), or "serious disagreement" in divorce proceedings in the absence of any legislative provision. In the classical *fikh*, *shikak* is primarily a process of mediation with the *hakam* (arbitrator) and not a cause *for* divorce. According to the *fikh*, only the husband can initiate divorce. However, according to Lev's data, pre-1989 Religious Court practice was generally to hold that *shikak* gave women the option to initiate divorce proceedings in the Religious Court. *Shikak*, then, appears to have been used, with court sanction, to allow wives to escape marriages when they have had no grounds for any classical *fikh* remedy. Again, this is a response to the limited jurisdiction given to the Religious Courts. The practice is not classically correct but is an attempt to overcome the restrictive colonial legacy.

Although the issue of jurisdiction has not been entirely resolved, the use of these methods eased the problem. However, the reforms of 1991 have rendered the rather sophistic use of *fatwa* and *shikak* unnecessary. These reforms will be discussed below. On a more general note it is worth recalling Hazairin's call in the early 1960s (1964) for the development of a distinctly Indonesian *Mazhab* (school of law).[7] In one sense, this is impossible but in terms of the reality of law — legal realism, itself a respectable position in jurisprudence — that position is by no means untenable. *Fatawa* and *shikak* certainly provide evidence of innovation and, I suggest, a careful analysis of *yurisprudensi* ("jurisprudence", in Indonesia, the decisions of the court) from the Religious Courts from 1945 to 1990 would probably go a long way toward showing the appropriateness of Hazairin's position. To my knowledge, this has not been done.

THE FIRST INITIATIVE ON ISLAM:[8] THE MINISTRY OF RELIGION

In January 1946, the Republic of Indonesia established a Ministry of Religion with a range of functions. For the purposes of this chapter,[9] the most important were: the regulation of marriage and divorce, the organisation and staffing of the Religious Courts (*Pengadilan Agama*), and the supervision of religious foundations (*wakaf*). These functions were an advance on the pre-war position. Most importantly, they introduced a unitary scheme of *syariah* administration. This, for the first time, gave Islam a significant bureaucratic presence. However, the formal administrative jurisdiction of the Ministry and its various components remained rather restricted.

A good example is Law No 22 of 1946, which repealed the colonial Marriage Law of 1929 and replaced it with a new system of organisation. The law did not affect the substantive law of marriage. Indeed, the text does not mention Muslim marriage rules. The Law's structure and content owed much to the repealed legislation. Thus, the Law established Registrars (*pencatat*) for marriage, divorce, and reconciliation to register all such agreements, receive fees and issue copies of the registration to the parties. Persons entering into these contracts without registration could be fined and Registrars who failed to perform their functions properly could be fined or imprisoned. Although purely formal and procedural, the Law attempted to impose an Indonesia-wide and uniform administration for Muslim marriage for the first time. The Law applied only in Java and Madura until it was extended to the remaining territories of Indonesia in 1954 (Katz & Katz, 1975: 656–81).

According to the Law, Registrars are paid public servants under the control of the Ministry and the scope of their territorial competence is defined by the Ministry in terms of its own area arrangements. These revolve around the *Kantor Urusan Agama* (KUA), the office of Religious Affairs, which is organised in a hierarchy descending from the Ministry in Jakarta down through provinces, sub-provinces and districts to village religious officials. Its function is to register marriages, divorces, and reconciliations, although in the early 1950s it did not claim competence to annul marriages. In the same period, it also undertook judicial functions on a wide range of subjects in the those areas in which Religious Courts had not been established.

The KUA procedure for the registration of marriage, divorce or reconciliation is quite simple. The parties need only produce proof of identity and any previous unions. However, if the application is for a marriage certificate (*surat nikah*), a statement of prenuptial conditions must be provided. If the husband breaches these conditions, his wife may divorce him. The standard conditions are absence for six months, failure to maintain for three months, assault and neglect.

The Ministry's effect on the substantive private law of Muslims has been minimal. Its main functions are political — to promote religion generally and Islam in national politics particularly. Its lesser administrative function is to regulate marriage and divorce by insisting upon bureaucratic procedures. The Religious Courts have been left to effect necessary reforms.

Before 1965, the Directorate of Religious Justice within the Ministry heard appeals from decisions of the Religious Courts. The staff of the Directorate includes Muslim legal experts who provide advice to the Ministry and other government departments when requested. The Directorate also examines Religious Court decisions. This activity, combined with the importance of the Ministry as a centre of Muslim policy-making, directly brings substantive questions of Islamic principle into the arena of national politics.

The Directorate was formally given power to review decisions of the Religious Courts in respect of "conditions and rules laid down by statute" by a Ministerial Decision in 1963 (Bambang Pranowo, 1990). In an elucidation of this power the following passage occurs:

> Whether the implementation of the Ministerial Decision will be limited only to statutory [procedural] requirements or will involve the subject matter of the Religious Courts' decisions, largely based on *syariah* rules, will also be left to the discretion of the Head of the [Directorate of] Religious Justice. ... For in essence the application of religious justice cannot be separated from consideration of *syariah* rules and [the effort] to strengthen the application of *syariah* rules as an element in the positive law of the Republic of Indonesia based on the rule of law (Bambang Pranowo, 1990: 493).

This statement comes close to suggesting that the Directorate had become a Court of Cassation in its own right. However, in 1965, the Supreme Court was specifically authorised to grant cassation in Muslim matters (see below). At the time of writing, the Directorate's review power seems to have been exercised infrequently, and with care. Data are sparse but, in the available cases, the Directorate has shown itself aware of the policy aspects of Islam and Muslim law.

One Supreme Court case involved the issue of jurisdiction (reported in Lev, 1972: 99–101). The suit involved the West Java Religious Court, the *Mahkamah Islam Tinggi* (Islamic Appellate Court) and the *Pengadilan Negeri* (District Court, the lowest court in the secular judicial system). There had apparently been procedural errors at all levels and in all jurisdictions. The Directorate intervened and quashed the Religious Court judgments. A later Religious Court came into issue with the secular court over the issue of the Directorate's powers. It was on the question of spheres of jurisdiction that an appeal was lodged with the Supreme Court.

The court declared that there was no legal basis for the Directorate's assumption of judicial or quasi-judicial powers. However, the court implicitly contradicted itself by finding that exercising judicial discretion (*kebijaksanaan*) might itself involve judicial elements. The court refused to interfere with any of the Islamic judicial issues in the suit.

The contradictions within this judgment merely reflect the contradictions within the Indonesian legal system. The status of "Ministerial Decisions", the form of the law which established the Directorate's appellate function, has never been clear. The late President Soekarno introduced this form of executive law-making on 5 July 1959. On 5 July 1966, the MPRs,[10] or provisional People's Consultative Assembly, prohibited the further issuance of such Decrees and ordered a review of all such laws which contradicted the Constitution (Hooker, 1984: 260). Some were repealed, and others were upgraded to, or replaced by, statutes (*undang-undang*). Nothing has been done about this particular decision.

THE POLITICAL IDEOLOGY SURROUNDING *SYARIAH*

The issue of Islam *vis-à-vis* the state is best approached through an investigation of past and current ideology. An obvious starting point is the Jakarta Charter (*Piagam Jakarta*) of June 1945. Although later deleted from the 1945 Constitution of which it briefly formed a part, it has been influential in the debate on the status of Islam in Indonesia. Regarding Islam, the Charter stated:

> [The state is based upon, among others] Belief in the One Supreme God with the obligation to carry out *syariah* for adherents of Islam.

The Jakarta Charter set an agenda, the simplicity or apparent simplicity of which can be misleading to positivist lawyers. It does not amount to the creation of a *Negara Islam* or Islamic state. While the Charter specifically refers to *syariah*, it is vague as to its exact scope and competence, leaving much room for debate over its jurisdiction. As discussed above, the rather restricted colonial view that *syariah* was to be restricted to certain elements of family law and *wakaf* has continued to the present day. Furthermore, the functions of the Ministry of Religion are conducted within a secular state that draws its legitimacy from a Constitution. Nevertheless, Islam as an ideology for state legitimacy can be advanced as an alternative or corrective to state practice. There are plenty of examples of past and present Muslim politicians achieving some successes in this way (Lubis, 1995).

The political dimensions of *syariah* are concerned less with its prescriptions and more with the varying ideologies which surround "an" Islam, or a view or views of Islam. The *Qur'an* and *Sunna* (practice of the Prophet as reported in *Hadith* — tradition) are primary starting points for all Muslims. However, from thereon in, there is a wide divergence in opinion in many areas such as literature, history and philosophy. This fluidity and variation is as true for Islam in Indonesia as it is elsewhere. It has been customary to speak in terms of reformist, traditionalist and modernist Islam. These terms are of little direct importance to Indonesian law. It is more significant that the laws which reference *syariah* contain ideological references to *Pancasila*.

Pancasila is the well-known and often-asserted five fundamentals on which the Indonesian state is, or claims to be, based. The principles of *Pancasila* most important to *syariah* are its first, a Belief in One Supreme God, and fourth, which embodies a commitment to democracy. For Muslims, the reference to God embodies the *Qur'an* and *Sunna*; however, the mention of democracy refers to a political system for which these sources provide no direct authority. There is of course an Indonesian dimension to these comments. Democracy can be "guided", and the words of God, which is how we know Him, can be interpreted variously and through the ages.

In short, there are no certainties for *syariah* in *Pancasila* — a constant theme in Indonesian Islam since independence. There are excellent current examples on the debate. For example, Bambang Pranowo (1990) poses a pertinent question: "Which Islam and which *Pancasila*"? He notes that the New Order government seems to be moving toward an interpretation of *Pancasila*, which, while viewing it as an incorporated whole, also seems to be playing down its secularity. In his view, some degree of Islamic infusion into at least the first *sila* is now becoming government policy. He instances the use of the specifically Islamic term *taqwa* (obedience) in a wide variety of contexts, including the oath which government officials must take and the P4 (*Pancasila* education program) Guidelines. Pranowo gives other examples, and concludes that the New Order interpretation of *Pancasila* is "more religious" and hence more acceptable to "modernist" Islam. Evidence of this new trend may be the new regulation of *syariah*, which is the subject of the rest of this chapter. Before turning to this issue, the Indonesian Constitution of 1945 must be briefly discussed.

THE 1945 CONSTITUTION

The Indonesian Constitution is short and many of its provisions are vague and imprecise. There are brief references to the One Supreme God (in the Preamble and Art 29). The Constitution also provides the President with an overwhelming quantity and quality of executive power. This is most often exercised by way of "Presidential Instruction"' (*Instruksi Presiden*), which is not a statue (*undang-undang*) but has the force of law. Presidential law-making has had a long history in Indonesia since independence.

The President is also the final arbiter of *Pancasila*'s meaning and content. Taken together with his law-making powers, the implications for Islam are striking. The function and jurisdiction of *syariah* are almost exclusively under his control. Muslim views on the laws of the Indonesian Republic can and have been put successfully in the past (for example, the amendments to the Marriage Bill of 1974 before its enactment). The initiative, however, remains with the President. This is a long way from a *Negara Islam*.

LAW NO 7 OF 1989 ON RELIGIOUS JUSTICE[11]

This part highlights the significant features of Law No 7 of 1989. It is a formal law, as opposed to a Presidential Instruction, and was passed by the Peoples' Representative Council (DPR),[12] with the assent of the President in December 1989. It consists of a Preamble and seven chapters. There are three noteworthy features of the Preamble. First, religious justice is described as pertaining to the certainty of law, itself a basic function of Law No 14 of 1970 on Judicial Power. This reference to the general court structure of the Republic of Indonesia clearly indicates the full integration of religious justice within the national court system. Secondly, the pre-existing regulations on the Religious Courts (that is, the colonial and immediate post-colonial regulations) are described as "disjointed" and thus not suited to a national system of judicial administration. Thirdly, the Preamble proposes a "unified law ... in a national legal system ... based upon *Pancasila* and the Constitution of 1945".

General Provisions (Articles 1–5)

These provisions formally establish Religious Courts and a Religious Appeal Court. For our purposes, the most important is Art 5(1) which states that, "the technical development of justice in the Religious Court shall be undertaken by the *Mahkamah Agung*". However, responsibility is not totally within the ambit of the Law No 14 of 1970 on Judicial Power. Article 5(2) of the Law on Religious Justice states that the Minister for Religion is to be responsible for the organisation, administration and finance of the Religious Courts. According to the Law on Judicial Power and Law No 14 of 1985 on the *Mahkamah Agung*, the Supreme Court has a general supervisory jurisdiction exercised through cassation (*kasasi*). This provision was intended to establish the Supreme Court as the final arbiter over matters arising from all branches of the Indonesian judicature. Up to the time of writing, it appears that the Director of Islamic Justice within the Ministry of Religion resolved appeals from the lower level Religious Courts.

The Composition of the Court (Articles 6–48)

These Articles establish the qualifications the religious judiciary must hold, and provide for the appointment and dismissal of judges and administrative staff. A judge must be a public servant and a "graduate in *syariah* law or a graduate with a mastery of Islam". Neither qualification is further defined. All officers of the court must take an oath in the name of Allah and swear to "be faithful to and defend and apply the *Pancasila* as the basis and ideology of the state, [and] the Constitution of 1945".

This part of the Law also regulates the perennial subject of jurisdiction. The Minister for Justice, the Minister for Religion, the Chief Justice, the Attorney General and, of course, the President generally share authority over the appointment, dismissal, suspension and arrest of judges. The President appoints and dismisses Religious Court judges on the advice of the Minister for Religion with the assent of the Chief Justice of the Supreme Court (Art 15(1)). If a judge acts criminally, negligently or culpably, the Chief Justice and the Minister for Religion must formulate appropriate investigation procedures (Art 19(3)) to ascertain whether he should be removed. The President can suspend a judge from office on the advice of the Minister for Religion with the assent of the Chief Justice (Art 21(1)). A judge can be arrested by the Attorney General (*Jaksa Agung*) with the assent of the Minister for Religion and the Chief Justice. The Minister for Religion has jurisdiction over these matters with regard to lower level administrative staff and generally supervises Religious Court judges (Act 12(1)). The new legislation has been in operation now for almost 10 years but we are little wiser as to how it actually works. The reported *yurisprudensi* is sparse and, when available, minimalist. The only constant feature is the use of *Pancasila* as a sort of basic reference point but this tells us nothing about legal reasoning.

The Powers of the Court (Articles 49–53)

Two points of particular interest emerge from this short chapter of the Law. First, Art 49 establishes the courts' jurisdiction over marriage, inheritance and *wakaf*. However, it goes on to provide (Art 49(2)) that marriages are to be "based on or regulated by the operative marriage laws". This is a reference to the Law No 1 of 1974 on Marriage, which, as will be discussed below, is also cited in the Compilation. The significance of this Article lies in its reference to *syariah* as defined in a state law — it is not a reference to *syariah* alone.

Secondly, Art 50 provides that where property or "other civil matters" arise in cases of marriage, inheritance or *wakaf*, the general courts, that is, the civil courts, must first decide the issue. This provision retains the colonial practice of separating property matters from personal relationships. As mentioned above, it is practically almost impossible to split jurisdiction in family law this way (with the possible exception of *wakaf*). Therefore, this provision is often avoided using various devices (especially *fatwa*), or at worst, is inoperable.

Law on Procedure (Articles 54–91)

This chapter is divided into three parts: a general Article; investigation of marriage disputes; and fees. There are two interesting features in the general provisions.

First, the Religious Courts must follow the laws of civil procedure operating in the civil courts (Art 54). The particular legislation is not actually specified. Secondly, Art 62 states that all decisions must "contain the provisions of relevant regulations on the unwritten source of law which forms the basis of the decision". This may be a reference to *adat* or local Muslim practice. Indonesian *yurisprudensi* must be examined to answer this question.

Regarding marriage disputes, the court's function is solely to regulate divorce. The Articles relevant to divorce in this chapter are clearly aimed at controlling the process of divorce by removing it from individual initiative and subjecting it to administrative procedure and, hence, delay. The same steps were taken in Singapore in the late 1950s (see Djamour, 1966) and slightly later in Malaysia.[13]

The first method of divorce regulated under the Law is *talak* (divorce by unilateral repudiation by the husband). Muslim countries throughout the world have been concerned to restrict the use of *talak*, and thus the negative societal consequences (single parent families) which follow from it. However, to destroy the right itself would be unacceptable because it is prescribed in the *Qur'an*. The Law therefore requires the husband to apply to the Religious Court to witness his declaration of *talak* (Art 66(1)). He must accompany his request with reasons for the divorce (Art 67(6)). The court is to investigate the matter within 30 days (Art 68(2)).

Article 70 sets out the restrictions on *talak* in more detail. The court may allow the husband's request if no reconciliation is possible, *and* there are reasons to justify the *talak*. Thus, the court has a measure of discretion when hearing *talak* cases. Furthermore, a wife may appeal the court's decision to allow the *talak* (Art 70(2)), an act entirely unknown in the classical *fikh*. The Religious Court is thus able to make *talak* virtually impossible to obtain.

The Law also empowers the wife to apply for divorce if her husband is imprisoned, has a physical impediment or they suffer an irreconcilable difference (*syiqaq*) (Art 73 ff). This is essentially a summary of *syariah fasakh* divorce with the additional requirement that the husband pay alimony and maintenance (Art 78). Article 81(2) states that a divorce has formally occurred when, "the decision of the court receives legal binding force". Where does this leave *syariah*? An examination of recent *yurisprudensi* would indicate current practice.

Adultery is the final ground for divorce. Classical Islamic law requires that divorce by accusation of infidelity (*lian*) must always be supported by oath. According to the Law,[14] the husband's oath is in *fikh* form, but the wife's must be in accordance with the "existing procedural law" which is rather more difficult to obtain.

Concerning fees, there is a familiar division of responsibility. They are regulated by the Minister for Religion with the *assent* of the Supreme Court. Finally, the law repeals existing legislation on religious justice (Art 107(1)).

The Law can be interpreted in a number of ways and on a number of levels. The legislator clearly intended to unify administration within the Republic of Indonesia. Individual judges must subscribe to the unifying ideology of *Pancasila* and the 1945 Constitution. The Law also creates administrative diversity. Various Ministries have an interest in the administration of *syariah*. This may be bureaucratic diversity, or a representation of different bureaucratic interest groups. In the Indonesian context such formalism as the separation of powers can be quite misleading. Nevertheless, there does seem to be recognition that some functions are better kept or treated separately. For individual claimants, the real test of the Law will come in seeing whether the Religious Courts will consistently exercise the considerable administrative control they have over individual (*syariah*-based) initiatives in divorce.

THE *KOMPILASI* — COMPILATION OF ISLAMIC LAW, 1991

This *Kompilasi* is certainly the most important document on *syariah* promulgated in modern Indonesia. The idea of enacting a "Muslim Code" or "Islamic Code" is not new. It has been discussed, to the writer's knowledge, for the past quarter century, and almost certainly in earlier years. The realities of post-independence Islamic politics are clearly the explanation for the considerable delay (Zifirdaus Adnan, 1990: 441–78).

The *Pancasila* surrounds the Compilation. Article 1 of the Elucidation states:

> For the people and nation of Indonesia which is founded upon the *Pancasila* and the Constitution of 1945 there is a right to the existence of a single national law which will guarantee the continuation of religious life based upon the principle of Belief in One Almighty God, while simultaneously representing the embodiment of the legal awareness of the Indonesian community and people.

The Compilation is not a Law (*undang-undang*), but "a guide to applicable law for Judges within the jurisdiction of the Institutions of Religious Justice in solving the cases submitted to them" (Elucidation, Art 5). Article 3 and 4 of the Compilation's explanatory memorandum or Elucidation — which like all the Elucidations that accompany laws in Indonesia should be read as part of the text of the law itself — appear to state what the "applicable law" is, by setting out the following sources for *syariah*: (a) standard texts of the *Shafi'i mazhab*, (b) additional texts from other *mazhab*, (c) existing *yurisprudensi*, (d) the *fatwa* of *ulama*, and (e) "the situation in other countries". This is a formal acknowledgment of eclecticism for sources of *syariah*. The Compilation claims to be a summary of these sources for use by Religious Court judges, but seems to overlook the *Kitab Kuning* or "yellow books" which are the bases for instruction in the *Pesantren* (local Islamic schools) (Van Bruinessen, 1995).

The *Kompilasi* came into force by way of Presidential Instruction which, as mentioned, it is not an *Undang-undang*. The authority for Presidential Instructions is found in Art 4(1) of the 1945 Constitution, which merely states that the President "holds the power of government in accordance with the Constitution". The Presidential Instruction directed the Minister for Religion, "to implement the Instruction". The Minister then issued a "Ministerial Decision" to implement the

Instruction. The Decision declares its own legal basis to be Art 17 of the 1945
Constitution, which states that "Ministers shall lead Government Departments"
(Art 17(3)) and "assist the President" (Art 17(1)).

The decision provides detailed instructions to various government agencies[15]
to "apply the Compilation in conjunction with other laws". Neither the Ministry
of Justice, nor the Supreme Court are mentioned. The Ministerial Decision refers
to the Religious Ministry's own decisions on Organisational Structure.[16]

The Compilation itself consists of three books. The first concerns Marriage
Law (Arts 1–170); Book II relates to Inheritance (Arts 171–214); and *Wakaf* is the
subject of Book III. As will be recalled, the colonial legislation regulated these
same three subjects. The provisions of the Compilation, however, are far more
detailed. What follows is a discussion of some of the issues arising out of the
Compilation.

The contents of Book I on Marriage[17] (which includes divorce) fall into three
categories: (a) straight-out reproduction of *fikh*, though in a much simplified form;
(b) *fikh* rules, the operation of which are contingent on the completion of bureaucratic
procedure; and (c) rules of *fikh* as amended or controlled by the judicial process in
the Religious Courts. These categories will be discussed in turn.

Several points flow from the straight-out reproduction of *fikh*.[18] First, the
Compilation's rules are very simple statements — they are obviously drafted to be
understood by judges with only a limited knowledge of *fikh*. The implication of
this appears to be that these simple versions are themselves sufficient for
adjudication on *fikh*. However, this view is subject to confirmation by post-1991
yurisprudensi. That there is no mention of any classical text tends to support this
conclusion. Additionally, although it may be assumed that the rules are taken from
the *mazhab Shafi'i* this is by no means conclusive. Again, post-1991 Religious Court
yurisprudensi must be examined to answer these questions.

The rules of *fikh* which have been put into bureaucratic formulae are also
interesting. Chapter XVI of the Compilation deals with termination of marriage.
Articles 129–142 and 146–148 require a daunting quantity of paperwork to be
completed before a marriage is validly terminated. Although these "rules" do not
affect the substance of *fikh*, they subject it to a secular process which actually
determines its application. Without procedural compliance, the *fikh* will not be
applied. Thus, a husband who wishes to declare *talak* must submit an oral and a
written request to the Religious Court. If the judge permits the *talak*, then copies
of the declaration are made and registered "as evidence of the divorce". The Law
also contains provisions regulating the summons to attend court hearings. Various
methods of delivery are specified, including the requirement that it be displayed
on public notice boards and in newspapers. There are further examples of *fikh*
being restricted by bureaucratic procedures in the compilation.

The purpose of these restrictions is to control personal status. The state has a
vested interest in this because divorced wives and fatherless children throw a
burden onto state agencies. Singapore realised this in the late 1950s and Malaysia
some years later. Indonesia now grasps the point. The *ulama* still equivocate. On

the one hand the much abused *talak* is divinely permitted; on the other, the social consequences are plain for all to see. To retain the divine permission but to formulate a bureaucratic obfuscation is a sensible response.

As to instances where the rules are amended and controlled by judicial processes, the policy of the Compilation is clearly stated early on in the text. According to Art 4, the validity of a marriage is determined by (a) *syariah*; and (b) the Law on Marriage. *Syariah* alone is insufficient. For example, the Law on Marriage regulates the age at which people may marry. A Muslim man's right to take more than one wife is likewise severely restricted. To enter into a polygamous marriage, the man must obtain permission from a Religious Court. Without judicial approval, the marriage "shall have no legal force" (Art 56(3)). Referring to Art 5 of the Law on Marriage, the Compilation states that he must also obtain the permission of his existing wife or wives (Art 58(1)). However, a wife's refusal to grant permission is not absolute; the Religious Court may override it if the wife is barren, unable to fulfil her marital obligations, or has an incurable illness (Art 59 referring to Art 57). The husband must still show he is capable of behaving justly towards all his wives and children and ultimately this will be a matter of fact for the court.

Other provisions of the Compilation have a similar effect. For example, Chapter X of the Compilation aims to prevent any marriage forbidden by "legislation or Islamic law". The Religious Court has jurisdiction over the matter, but the Marriage Registration Office (Clerk), who must also be informed of the marriage, is forbidden "to implement or aid in the implementation" of a marriage which contravenes the Law on Marriage (Arts 8, 68–69). Similarly, the Compilation sets out two methods for the termination of marriage (Chapter XVI): *talak, or,* a "claim for divorce" (Art 114). The grounds for divorce are set out in Art 116. This part of the Compilation appears to aim to control *talak* and also to give the wife an avenue to initiate divorce. As discussed above, this option was a feature of the pre-Compilation administration of *syariah* through the use of *shikak*. *Talak* is controlled by way of judicial supervision. The Religious Court may refuse a request by a husband for *talak*, but the refusal is open to appeal and cassation (Art 130). A wife may submit a claim for divorce on specific grounds which include desertion for two years, lack of a harmonious domestic life, and imprisonment of the husband for five years. In addition, the court may order alimony payments and the protection of the wives' assets during the period of the divorce claim. The important conclusions is that *talak* is controlled, and, the wife has an initiative outside of and separate from *syariah*.

The remainder of Book I merely repeats *syariah* rules in simple form. The same is true for Book II (Inheritance) and Book III (*wakaf*). In these two areas, the Compilation is concerned with administrative procedures, and there are no substantive variations on the *fikh* rules.

From the above discussion, it is clear that "pure" *syariah* is restricted to inheritance and *wakaf* and that in marriage and divorce it is accommodated to secular legislation and strictly controlled by the Religious Courts. Theoretically, the husband's rights in *talak* are preserved. However, a wife now has a right to divorce, though a limited grounds outside the *fikh*. The important change is that the husband's consent does not seem to be necessary: the wife's claim is by way of judicial process (*fasakh*). In this respect, the Compilation has not gone so far towards secularisation as some of the Malaysian legislation where "irretrievable breakdown" actually appears as a cause for divorce. This is, or appears to be, subsumed under *fasakh* in Indonesia.

CONCLUSION

Several conclusions can be drawn. The first is that the recent legislation is a considerable advance over the colonial and post-colonial position. The Religious Courts are now fully a part of the national legal system with a defined and (comparatively) extensive jurisdiction. The Law on Religious Justice has certainly repaired pre-1989 internal inconsistencies. However, responsibility for various aspects of Religious Justice administration remains divided between a number of Ministries. The Supreme Court has a rather restricted function in cassation. The Ministry of Religion is the prime source of authority, and given that political power resides in the Indonesian bureaucracy — underpinned by the executive nature of the 1945 Constitution — this is not likely to change in the future. The *Negara Hukum* (state based on law) particularly where *syariah* is involved, remains problematic.

Secondly, and following from the recognition of executive control — which is ultimately located in the office of the President — one has always to consider the ideology of the executive government. For Indonesian Islam it is the *Pancasila*, in particular the first principle, "Belief in One God". While this is somewhat acceptable to Muslims it also carries the strong implication of secularism. The authority for *Pancasila* and its definition is in government hands. By contrast to *syariah*, its derivation is not direct from Revelation.

The practical expression of accommodation is best illustrated by the Compilation. It has been approved by the *ulama*, but ultimate approval for its implementation comes from the authority of the President in the name of *Pancasila*. Thus, we have the authority of those learned in *syariah*; the authority of the President, that is, the secular state; and the ideological authority of *Pancasila*. It is tempting to rank these authorities but I think that would be a mistake. It is probably more sensible to take them as interdependent. *Syariah* is part of the state process and, with the ebb and flow of the political process, the balance of authority will also vary.

Thirdly, we do not know how these laws are being applied. This is most likely to be found in the *yurisprudensi* of the Religious Courts. There are pre-1989 collections published; however, it appears that no detailed analysis has been done. Post-1991 *yurisprudensi* is likely to be even more interesting.

Finally, the system of religious justice in Indonesia is now, formally speaking, on a level comparable to Singapore, Malaysia and (on paper at least) the Philippines.

This is worth remembering because with the increased movement of people within South-East Asia, the issue of foreign judgment recognition is likely to arise sooner rather than later. This will be a further test for the reformed religious justice system of Indonesia.

Notes

1. The whole corpus of Islamic jurisprudence.
2. For details see Hooker (1984).
3. For details see Hooker (1984).
4. Until 1991.
5. See the revised *Priesteraad* Regulation, 1937, Art 10(3).
6. Review by the Supreme Court on the facts, law and reasoning of a law or court. The result might be a confirmation of the law or court decision or a direction to re-hear.
7. For the Sunni Muslim the schools of law are Hanafi, Hanbali, Maliki and Shafii. The latter is the school of adherence in Indonesia and Malaysia.
8. I deal with the 1945 Constitution and the *Pancasila* in the next section. For the moment, I take administrative/public law only.
9. The following summary is taken directly from Hooker (1984: 256ff).
10. *Majelis Permusyawaratan Rakyat* (*Sementara*), Indonesia's supreme sovereign body.
11. The translations of Law No 7 of 1989 and the Compilation were done by Bernard Quinn. I would like to acknowledge the excellence of his work and his generosity in allowing me to use it.
12. *Dewan Perwakilan Rakyat*, Indonesia's parliament.
13. See the recent (post 1980s) legislation. A good summary is in Horowitz (1994), 233–94, 543–80.
14. See the Elucidation to the Law No 1 of 1974 on Marriage for another and perhaps more complex example.
15. "This Decision shall be delivered to the honourable:
    1. The Minister for the Coordination of Public Prosperity
    2. The Ministers of the Fifth Development Cabinet in the Public Prosperity sector
    3. The Minister for Justice
    4. The Secretary of State
    5. The Secretary of the Fifth Development Cabinet
    6. The Finance Supervisory Board in Jakarta
    7. Secretary General, Inspector General, Directors General, the Head of the Religious Research and Development Bureau and the technical staff of the Minister for Religion
    8. Heads of Bureaus, Directors, Inspectors, Head of the Religious Research and Development Centre and the Head of the Administrative Staff Education and Training Centre in the Department of Religion
    9. The Heads of the Provincial Regional Offices of the Department of Religion throughout Indonesia."
16. Presidential Decisions No 44 of 1974 and No 15 of 1984, Ministerial Decisions No 18 of 1975 and No 75 of 1984.
17. Chapters 1, 5–8, 12 and 18.
18. If we except the restriction on fragmentation in Art 189.

4

THE STATE'S LEGAL POLICY AND THE DEVELOPMENT OF ISLAMIC LAW IN INDONESIA'S NEW ORDER

Nur Ahmad Fadhil Lubis

The growing discontent under guided democracy and the pressure of deteriorating economic conditions under Sukarno brought about political violence and social conflict on an unparalleled scale in Indonesia's history. This was the opposite of Sukarno's ideal of uniting different ideological stream — nationalism, communism and Islam — under his guided democracy. The abortive coup of September 1965 which was followed by the destruction of the communist party and its anti-religious ideals marked a turning point in the history of the Indonesian nation. While the full story behind the September 30th movement, as it was named thereafter, remains subject to conflicting interpretations, there can be no doubt about the result of the coup.[1] The most important result was the end of the Sukarno era and the emergence of the New Order government.[2]

This article will look at the legal and judicial changes brought about by the New Order government and will seek to analyze the impact of "Pancasila" ideology and "developmentalism" (*pembangunan*) — the two key words of the New Order regime's basic policy — on Islamic law and institutions, especially the *agama* (religious) courts. The weakening, and later disappearance, of formal Islamic

---

Previously published as "Institutionalization and the Unification of Islamic Courts under the New Order", *Studia Islamika: Indonesian Journal for Islamic Studies* 2, no. 1. (1995): 1–51. Reproduced with permission of the author and the publisher, State Islamic University (UIN), Jakarta.

political parties from the national political stage and the enforcement of singular adherence to "Pancasila" have usually been understood as having suppressed and curbed the progress of Islamic law and institution in the search for national legal system. However, this article will seek to show that those policies and programs, in addition to posing a tremendous challenge to the proponent of Islamic law and institution, at the same time created a valuable opportunity and a favorable climate for Islamic law and its institutions to develop, adapt and participate in the formation of the national legal and judicial system.

THE RISE OF THE NEW ORDER

The political power of Sukarno, who had been nominated as president for life and had dominated the Indonesian political scene since before independence waned considerably soon after the abortive coup. His remaining influence was effectively broken when he kept trying to play down the demands of fast growing counter-movements led by the anti-communist army generals, Muslim organization and student leaders. The decisive transfer of political power occurred on March 11, 1966, when President Sukarno reluctantly signed an order empowering General Suharto, "to take all steps deemed necessary to guarantee the security, tranquility and stability of the government machinery and the process of the Revolution. . . [and] the personal safety and authority of the President. . ."[3] It was later obvious that the steps "deemed necessary" by Suharto included the abolition of the Indonesian Communist Party and its affiliates and the arrest of many of Sukarno's ministers, something that Sukarno refuses to do.

The New Order came into existence as a reactive response to the deteriorating conditions under the pretext of the "guided democracy" of President Sukarno, who sought to integrate existing conflicting political ideologies. The divide and rule policy of Sukarno enhanced tension in particular between the communist and left wing parties, and the Islamic and other anti-Communist exponents. The army's rank and file, which had bitter experience of communist rebellions and uprisings, generally disapproved of the favorable position given to the Communist Party and its leaders by Sukarno. The army's suspicion grew stronger when the PKI wanted to arm its members as a voluntary militia. All these developments culminated with the abortive coup of September 1965. The counter movement temporarily united all fronts against the establishment.

However, when everything cooled down, the prime beneficiary of this crisis was the Indonesian army, whose surviving leaders moved to establish a "quasi-military" regime under Suharto.[4] During the period of violent transition (1966–1968) the radical parties were destroyed and other parties were weakened. The military assumed control of government. Instead of cooperating with the available politicians, the regime sought the assistance of academicians, especially economic professors most of whom had graduated from Western universities and who had no political followers, and also those who came from minority groups, especially

Christians. The coalition of these two groups formed a new cabinet with two urgent programs: political stability and economic development.

Recovery was greatly assisted by a considerable expansion of crude oil production and the developments of natural gas resources which were encouraged by two unanticipated increases in the price of oil and gas in 1973 and 1979. The favorable treatment by industrialized donor countries to help the country also played a remarkable role in helping the government to realize its prime objectives.

Learning from the failure of Sukarno government, the New Order regime, as opposed to the "Old Order" of Sukarno, insisted on its legality by claiming to uphold the constitution integrally and by maintaining that its basic objective was a constitutional mission to create stability and prosperity for the whole nation. The new provisional People's Consultative Assembly, now cleansed of all communist influence and Sukarno's backers, acknowledged the validity of the presidential command letter (MPRS Decree no. IX/1966), discharge Sukarno of his executive power in the following year (MPRS Decree no. XXXIII/1967), and in 1968 appointed Suharto outright as the second president of the Republic (MPRS Decree XVIV/1968).[5]

THE IDEOLOGY OF THE NEW ORDER

The New Order aims to create a system in which political, economic and cultural life is inspired by Pancasila, and by means of which a stable and institutionalized structure and prosperous and just nation are to be built.[6] This idea was encouraged by a conviction that much of the national interest and development had previously been neglected due to the struggle over ideological differences. Stability and economic progress were two principal goals which the Old Order was accused of failing to achieve and these two became the prime goals and the channel of legitimacy of the New Order government. The goals were embodied in Pancasila which became the ideological foundation of the state and nation. The present government claimed that the true principles of Pancasila had been pushed aside by Sukarno and the PKI (Indonesian Communist Party) under the pretext of Guided Democracy. Therefore, the New Order wanted to put an end to the ideological debates that had dominated the early years of independence and so emphasized the compromising ideas of Pancasila. The new political systems based on Pancasila values are being built specifically to fulfill the basic need of the whole Indonesia population.

Many studies dismiss the New Order regime's determination to adopt and apply the Pancasila ideology as an essentially self-serving strategy promoted by the existing regime to preserve the status quo and to continue its ravaging of state resources. Most of the students overlook the significance of promoting an indigenous compromising ideology in this critical new nation. It was also obvious that the prevailing mood among national leaders was to stop the disintegrating factors that had ravaged the nation since its independence. A few writers seek to go beyond this and try to understand how the actors perceived their actions. In other words, this latter type of study sees how the New Order regime was determined to design its own policy and tries to conceptualize this polity, in terms that are consistent with the ideological concepts that they use in their self-understanding and analysis.[7]

The New Order government, however, does not merely retain Pancasila, but has also campaigned to elucidate and disseminate its existence. A short course was designed to educate the Indonesian people, starting with civil servant and then community leaders and students, about the directives for the realization and implementation of Pancasila and some other civic subjects. The manifest intention has been to establish a strong national solidarity and to prevent conflict arising from ideological differences, and this objective, being compounded by other conditions, seems to have reduced political tension and ideological debates. However, this nation-wide compulsory systematic dissemination of a strictly formulated "philosophy" may have a negative impact and destructive effect upon social integration and political dynamism.[8]

The rejection of the "Islamic" state and the failure of the liberal system and guided democracy during the Sukarno era, had forced the New Order regime to find a common ideology which would prevent the disintegration of Indonesia's plural and heterogeneous societies. Besides, they also have to prove that the claim of exponents of an "Islamic" state, that never had a chance for this to be tried in a national Indonesian context, is beyond any probable option. The existing political parties were affected and weakened by the suffering of the whole country. This trauma and a distrust of the political leaders made the policy of the New Order, to exclude them from the cabinet and any important key positions, look normal and acceptable. The only existing alternative, which may challenge the ruling government, comes from the Islamic circle. Too much pressure on Islam or too drastic a distance from it may backfire by facilitating the Islamic groups' claim that the existing government is detrimental to Muslim interest and rights.

The goals of stability, national integration and development filled the regime's political discourse during the first decades of the New Order. Because of the continuing silence of concepts like consensus (*mufakat*), deliberation (*musyawarah*) and mutual cooperation (*gotong-royong*), among the general population, the policy makers of the New Order regime sought to inscribe Pancasila, which contains those values, into the national consciousness, in spite of the fact that the same terms had been used (or abused) by Sukarno. Thus, the very first act of the People's Assembly (MPR) was to reaffirm its commitment to and the centrality of the reinstated 1945 Constitution, and to declare that Pancasila "cannot be changed by anybody, including the elected MPR, because changing the content of the preamble means the dissolution of the state", thus signaling its ideological significance in shaping the government's policies. In order to prevent the possibility of any deviant interpretation of Pancasila, the People's Assembly promulgated a decree elaborating basic interpretation of it. The government established a nation-wide institution to devise, supervise and organize "upgrading courses" on Pancasila for government officials and society leaders.

In this respect, the New Order was more consistent and fortunate than its predecessor. With the disappearance of the communist party and the weakening of most of the politicians, the newly established government was not plagued by conflict over ideological issues and the priority of national interests. There was a general tendency then to eschew ideological slogans and to play down political niceties in favor of pragmatic economic action.[9]

Another basic claim of New Order government is its insistence on upholding the 1945 Constitution. This constitution was designed by a Javanese-sponsored preparatory committee under the pressure of an on-going struggle. Consequently, it was intended more as a provisional constitution and gave great power to its executive leader to lead and guide the nation in a time of struggle and revolution. Sukarno himself on many occasions in the early days of independence stressed that the Constitution was only a "temporary", "lightning" and "revolutionary" constitution, which in due time could and must be perfected by the elected representatives of people.[10] However, it was Sukarno who decreed the return to this temporary constitution and used it to support his guided democracy.

No wonder some observers call this document an "authoritarian constitution"[11] which justifies the authoritarian action of any ruling regime as "constitutional". This may partly be the reason why Sukarno, as well as Suharto, took every step necessary to prevent this constitution from being repealed or amended.

THE IDEAL STATE: *NEGARA HUKUM*

The break-up of guided democracy revived a strong hope among many people for the rule of law and the authority of the judicial system. Constitutionally, the conduct of the government is to be based on the rule of law, since Indonesia is a *rechtstaat* (*Negara Hukum* or a state based on law), not a *machtstaat* (a state based on power). The constitution also stated that Indonesia is a democracy in which sovereignty resides with the people and is vested in the People's Consultative Assembly as the institutional embodiment of the entire Indonesian people. However, the drafters of the constitution did not endorse the *Trias Politica* theory of Montesquieu which advocated a separation of powers among executive, legislative and judicial branches of government. Instead, it adopted a distribution of powers among different but cooperative organs of government which individually or collectively serve the national interest. The formulation and decision concerning national interests at the practical level are more often than not in the hands of the president who acts beyond his capacity as the head of the executive branch of the government.

Soon after the "Old Order" was toppled, in response to the many forms of influential executive law-making introduced by Sukarno, and in an effort to clarify the types and order of law permitted and regulated by the 1945 Constitution, the reshuffled People's Assembly stipulated that Pancasila must be the source of all laws, and on this basis, it adopted the following order of laws proposed by the House of Representatives:

a. at the top is the Constitution (*Undang-undang Dasar*) which can be implemented in three ways: by a decree of the People's Assembly, by statute and by Presidential Decision;

b. Decrees of the People's Assembly (*Ketetapan MPR*). These fix the broad outlines of national policy for legislative and executive spheres of government. Those directed at the legislature must be implemented by statute, those at the executive by Presidential Decision;

c. Statutes (*Undang-undang*). These are enacted by the House of Representatives and ratified by the President. They are passed for the purpose of implementing either the Constitution or a Decree of People's Assembly. The President also has emergency power to promulgate a "regulation in lieu of statute" (*Peraturan Penganti Undang-undang*), which is of the same rank as statutes but must be withdrawn unless approved by the House of Representatives at its next session;

d. Government Regulations (*Peraturan Pemerintah*). These are promulgated by the President for the purpose of implementing a statute;

e. Presidential Decisions (*Keputusan Presiden*). These are also promulgated by the President, for one of three purposes: to implement the Constitution, to implement a decision of the People's Assembly in the executive sphere, or to implement a Government Regulation;

f. Other implementing regulations. For the purpose of applying a higher order of regulation, other regulations of a lower priority are authorized. Normally, these are promulgated by a Minister.[12]

The promulgation of new laws had been very slow which led to greater reliance on executive regulations. The few laws that have been promulgated so far have mostly been initiated, designed and heavily influenced by the executive branch of the government. This situation has been more obvious under the New Order government. The complex plural colonial legacy, complicated by "revolutionary" policies and neglect of the legal progress and facilities of the Sukarno and early Suharto regimes, has contributed to the existence and persistence of the "vast and extensive jungle of law". Another effect of this situation has been to give extraordinary discretion to government authorities. The very complexity and vagueness of the Indonesian legal system in itself constitutes an obstacle to achieving a high degree of justice and legal certainty besides leaving wide latitude for discretion to government authorities.

The term *rechtstaat* is mentioned in the Elucidation of the 1945 Constitution. It is interesting to see that foreign word is cited directly without further explanation which means that either the term is well-known and understood by everybody or that this foreign concept did not have any acceptable equivalent among the drafters. The latter seems to be case. The Indonesian phrase *Negara Hukum* (state based on law, state based on the Rule of law, state law) became popular in later discussion. The New Order has formally proclaimed itself committed to the idea of *Negara*

Hukum as stipulated by the Constitution and under the guiding principles of Pancasila. Discussions on the implementation of this grand policy have been more political than legal. The prevailing modes of governance which inclined more towards the *beamtenstaat* (bureaucratic state), patrimonialism and the so-called *integralistich staatsidee* (ideal integralistic state), let alone military guided democracy, have colored the discussion and formulation of legal development during the New Order government.

THE LEGAL POLICY AND THE LEGAL DEVELOPMENT

The idea of a state based on law within the framework of integralistic state seemed to be the guiding principle of the government in the second decade of its establishment.[13] During the first decade despite some formal statements in favor of legal reform, this was superseded by the urgency of economic development. The concept of an integralistic state was proposed by Supomo, a legal scholar with specialization in Indonesian customary (*adat*) law who held an important post at the Ministry of Justice under the Japanese occupation government. He was later Minister of Justice in early independent Indonesia while holding a professorship at a leading law school in Jakarta. His ideas seemed to represent an embodiment of the whole nation, in which the leader acted as the benevolent father of the people. It also represented a strong state with an emphasis on unity, with no dualism between state and individuals since all individuals are an organic part of the state. It has been claimed to represent the character of communal and family life in Indonesian society. In Supomo's perception, a new state must emerge as a strong state because only a strong state with a strong leader can bring unity and prosperity to the people. The new state must be based on a totalitarian ideology which integrated the whole nation. Consequently, the whole nation rejects the idea of separating, let alone dichotomizing, different powers of the state. Many scholars hold the opinion that constitutionally, the *integralistich staatsidee* had been defeated when the 1945 Constitution subscribed to the *rechtstaat* principle, to the norm of republic, and to limited human rights guarantees.[14] But others, especially those who hold power and influence in the government, maintained the basic ideas that had never been rejected and they have been immersed in the stipulation of Pancasila and *kekeluargaan* basis in the Constitution.[15]

The elements of these two different, often conflicting, concept of *rechtstaat* and *integralistisch staatesidee* may be traced to the statutes promulgated by the New Order government which seek to integrate them into the Indonesian legal system. A new law on the Judiciary (Law no. 14/1970) restored some principles of judicial authority by revoking the presidential right to interfere in judicial matters, but at the same time, it opened the way for executive interference through the control of appointment, promotion, transfer, dismissal and salary of the judges. The government keeps on emphasizing that there should be harmony between the branches of power. The opening of this possible interference strengthened an argument that the judiciary has become an extension of the larger bureaucracy. As such, the notion of the bureaucratic state or *beamtenstaat* practiced during the colonial times remains. In this respect, Lev's observation may have continued up to present:

> ...With political parties steadily weakening and the *pamongpradja* (bureaucrats) securely in palace, both *Guided Democracy* and the New Order were generally linked to the structure of the colonial state. In this respect, at least, the independent state was not merely similar to the colonial state. It was the same state.[16]

Another important principle which seems to have guided the legal policy of the New Order government is the notion of law as a "tool of social engineering", which practically means that the law are directed to facilitate and regulate the developmental programs of the movement. Suharto, 1974, implicitly emphasized this principle in his formal speech:

> Even though development definitely brings about a chain of substantive and urgent changes, it is absolutely necessary to maintain stability and order. This must not be understood to mean statistic that is just maintaining a status quo. Law, as an important means to keep order, must be developed and nurtured in such a way as to give an appropriate moving space for those changes. Absolutely not the other way around, this hampers developmental efforts just for the sake of the desire to conserve old values. Indeed, law must come forward, leading the way and smoothing the road for progress.[17]

At the formal constitutional level, the 1993 Guidelines of State Policy (GBHN) which have been decreed by the People's Consultative Assembly promulgate that all the planning, implementation, supervision and improvement of developmental efforts and state policy must be guided by nine basic principles as follows: (1) belief and piety toward the One Almighty God which is the spiritual, moral, and ethical foundation of national development, (2) utility, (3) democracy, (4) justice and equality, (5) balance, harmonious and appropriate, (6) rule of law, the essence of which is justice and truth, (7) self-confidence and reliance, (8) heroism, and (9) belief in science and technology.[18]

In connection with the nation's legal condition and its development, the Guidelines state the following:

> Developments in the field of law and legal statutes have created a legal system and legal product which gives legal protection and a legal foundation for society and developmental activities. Gradually improved legal conscience and more rapid development demand the formation of a national legal system and legal products which support and come from Pancasila and the 1945 Constitution. Legal development, furthermore, still needs to pay attention to the improvement of the socialization of law, the improvement of consistent and consequent law enforcement, the improvement of qualified and responsible law enforcing officials, and the creation of their adequate supporting means and facilities.[19]

Based on the perceived actual legal conditions of the country, and guided by the general basic principles of national development, the legal development for the next twenty-five years of the New Order government are directed towards "the formation and function of a strong national legal system, based on Pancasila and the 1945 Constitution, by paying attention to the plurality of the existing legal order, which is able to guarantee legal certainty, stability, enforcement and protection; the essence of which is justice and truth, besides being able to safeguard and support national development which is backed up by law enforcement agencies, adequate legal services and facilities as well as by a law-aware and abiding society.[20]

These ideas have been formulated further in the Guidelines of State Policy which reiterate that a legal development is directed to create a united national legal system by gradually developing three important fields of legal systems; (1) Substantive Material Laws (*Perangkat Hukum*), (2) Systematic Legal Order and Structure (*Tatanan Hukum Nasional*), and (3) Legal Culture (*Budaya Hukum Nasional*).[21]

The legal development in the field of substantive material laws consist of the following: (a) Extension of the Principles of National Law, (b) Development of Legal Statutes in accordance with the aspirations and needs of modernizing and improving the Indonesian population, (c) Development of Jurisprudence as a real legal source of national law, and (d) Establishment of customary law (*hukum kebiasaan*) which is based on Pancasila philosophy and the 1945 Constitution.

The order and structure of the national legal system are directed to solidly build the following aspects: (a) establishment of national laws as a compact system, which comprises the organization, institutions, structure and legal mechanisms, (b) improvement of qualified and respected law enforcing officials and institutions, (c) improvement of legal service professionals, (d) improvement of expertise, skills of law professionals, as well as the clear division of rights and responsibilities among various law professions, (e) ordering and intensification of the existing legal institutions, (f) creation of necessary new legal institutions, (g) improvement of legal information, e.g., the establishment of law libraries and a Law Documentation and Information Network System, (h) improvement of legal planning, research and development facilities, (i) improvement and modernization of physical facilities and supporting materials for legal development.

The Guidelines of State Policy also emphasized the development of the abstract ideas upon which a national legal system is to be built. This is called the development of national legal culture (*pembangunan budaya hukum nasional*). To achieve this, the Guidelines reiterate the following programs: (a) to establish and to socialize the national legal philosophy and national legal theory, (b) to maintain and intensify legal conscience and law abiding behavior, (c) to improve legal education and professional ethics.

The development of national legal system under the New Order government, at least as formally expressed by the Ministry of Justice and other high-ranking officers, has been based on three fundamental perspectives.[22] First is nationalism in the sense of emphasizing the idea that the republic of Indonesia is a nation-state, not a state founded upon a racial, cultural or religious basis. Therefore, under the national legal system, as far as possible, there must not be any regulation, written or otherwise, that discriminates between people based on ethnic group, class, race, religion or the like. Second is the *nusantara* perspective which is the view of the Indonesian upholding the idea that the whole *nusantara* Indonesian archipelago is an integrated, compact unity of *tanah air* (land and water mother-country). This perspective requires that the same laws be valid for the whole country, all the regions have same rights and responsibilities, and no region will be discriminated against or privileged over another, under the unitary state of republic. Last but not least is the theme of *Bhinneka Tunggal Ika* (Unity in diversity). This phrase is also on the coat of arms of the nation.

Even though the prime principle and objective of the development of a national legal system is to create a single united legal system which is directed to realize national interests (*kepentingan nasional*), the law must not overlook the reality that the population of the country consists of those who have different religions, race, ethnicity, culture and interests. Enforcing the same rigid law for this plural society may inflict injustice and incite resentment which are against the objectives of maintaining and improving a just and harmonious society of the whole population. Thus, a certain extent of variety is permitted as long as it does not endanger the integrity and unity of the nation. The existence of this variety is viewed as a subsystem which integrates itself harmoniously in the national legal system and serves the national interest.

These principles and points of view have been expressed time and again not only by the bureaucracy but also by the legal community at large. It may be safe to suggest that the legal debates and discussions on legal reform during the New Order era government had used, or possibly abused, these principles.

There are three general dimensions in applying all the above ideals and objectives. The first dimension is that of safeguarding against the appearance of a legal vacuum in which a legal uncertainty, or even a chaotic situation, may erupt. The second is a dimension of improvement in the sense of modifying the inherited colonial legacy to be more in line with the spirit of independence and national aspirations. Only in the third dimension is an outright enactment of new laws in order. As suggested above, one of the main priorities of the New Order government is to replace those colonial laws and regulations that continued to function as transitory regulations until the new ones promulgated in accordance with the Constitutional principles that exist. It has been estimated that there are at least 400 colonial laws and regulations waiting to be reformed.[23] The first two dimensions mentioned above contributed to a persistence of colonial legacy, and eventually may have contributed to the existence of the bureaucratic state as suggested before by some scholars. Likewise, the reluctance of some bureaucrats to reform those outdated regulations may have been encouraged by the fear of losing their privileges. Legal reforms through executive regulations may have been more profound and easier to implement because, among other factors, they do not have to go through complicated and time-consuming parliamentary debates and public opinion. However, further studies need to be undertaken to substantiate this contention.

This condition may be explained by the historical legacy of the Indonesia legal system as well as its legal bureaucrats and professionals who have been heavily influenced by the Dutch legal system which can be traced back to the Roman-Germanic civil law traditions. One of the characteristics of the civil law system has been an emphasis on the development of law in a codified manner, rather than in the resolution of individual disputes. Max Weber characterizes civil law as having a logically formal rationality. It is logical, as explained by Trubek,[24] to the extent that the decisions in specific cases are reached by the process of specialized deductive logic proceeding from previously established rules or principles. It is formal to the extent that the criteria of decisions are intrinsic to the legal system. It is rational in the sense that it relies on some justifications that transcend a particular case and is based on existing, unambiguous rules. So, compared to common law system, a civil law system is particularly more open to philosophical and doctrinal influence. In this system, these influences come largely from academics and rulers, whereas in a common law system they lie mostly in the hands of judges.[25]

Even though executive influence has been very strong in shaping the country's legal process and products, be it formal or informal, written or otherwise, it does not mitigate the contribution of judge-made laws and judicial jurisprudence, especially that of the Supreme Court.

JUDICIAL AUTHORITY AND INDEPENDENCE

Having said all this, no one can deny that the New Order government has been successfully producing new kinds of legal statutes (*Undang-undang*), and more executive regulations. The most important legal statutes are those that regulate the judicial institutions and their procedural regulations. Some substantive laws have also been enacted in the field of criminal law and some commercial and financial laws. This latter category of laws has been urgently needed due to rapidly growing economic activities during the last two decades of the New Order era. In the following section, some of these laws pertaining to the judiciary will be discussed.

The relatively separated and independent judicature stipulated by the Constitution, which was neglected by the Sukarno regime, was supposed to be restored by the New Order government. However, the founding fathers of the nation who drafted the 1945 Constitution did not entertain the idea of a separate independent judicial branch of the government. An independent judiciary is not explicitly stated in the 1945 Constitution. Article 24 simply says that judicial powers shall be exercised by a Supreme Court and other courts in accordance with the promulgated statute. Meanwhile Article 25 of the Constitution prescribes that the structure and jurisdiction of the courts, and the conditions for appointment and dismissal of judges be regulated by the statute.

These two short Articles mentioned above have become the prime reference and basis for enacting "fundamental rules" (*ketentuan-ketentuan pokok*) statutes. As observed by some scholars, it is customary for the so-called "fundamental rules" law of Indonesia to function more as policy declarations than as statutory schemes. Implementation usually depends on the enactment of subsequent legislation and the promulgation of special implementing regulation usually in form of government regulations or ministerial decisions. On a practical level, these lower implementing regulations also function as authoritative interpretations of the basic laws. Until such organic laws and implementing rules are established, the basic laws operated more as a statement of national intent. Many court decisions denied a defense's argument based on an enacted statute because it had not had any implementation guidance yet.[26]

The principle of a limited "independent judiciary" is contained in the Elucidation to the judicial articles of the 1945 Constitution, which states that the judiciary should be free from government/executive influence and that the position of judges should be protected from such influences by statute. The elucidation does not spell out what is meant by "independent judiciary". It is left to be elaborated and promulgated in subsequent laws aimed at implementing the Constitution. By reading the laws promulgated after independence, this principle has been understood and applied differently depending on the political whims of those who are in power. As a result, during the guided democracy period of Sukarno, the president was authorized to interfere at any time when revolution or the national interest was at stake.[27] The judiciary was subordinate to the executive, personified by the President, who was perceived as a benign father of the nation and the leader of the revolution. Historically speaking, this was a continuation of what a king was supposed to be in pre-colonial times. Furthermore, centuries of colonization by the Dutch who ran the country more as a bureaucratic state gave strong influence to the country's elites. This influence dies hard even after independence and the proponents of the rule of law and an independent judiciary must encounter it.

The ideas of the rule of law and independent judiciary have fluctuated in Indonesian legal discussions. During the parliamentary years (1950–1957) it served as the legitimating ideology of the constitutional republic, but many of its symbols were attached conservatively to Dutch colonial institutions, procedures and codes that were carried over into independence. This conservative stance and colonial legacy were repugnant to many revolutionary fighters and nationalist leaders. These smoothed the way for Sukarno to introduce his integralistic patrimonial guided democracy (1959–1965) which submerged the principle of the rule of the law and the independent judiciary and emphasized substantive, rather that procedural, justice. When the Old Order was toppled, those dormant ideas were rapidly revived. During the early days of the New Order period, many of its leaders blamed the previous regime for trampling the principle of the rule of the law and supporting the ideas of *Negara hukum* (state based on law).

The discussion and debates later came to a climax with the promulgation of Law No. 14/1970 which was more of a compromise and middle-way between the ideas of the rule of law and an independent judiciary and that of an integralistic state.[28] The New Order government took the initiative to introduce a law which could bring about substantial changes in Indonesia's judicial system, particularly in emphasizing the independence of the judicial bodies from executive interference. Thus Law No. 19 of 1964, notably Article 19, which allowed the president to intervene in judicial matters was revoked and replaced by Law No. 14 of 1970, the Basic Law of the Judiciary. Article 4, paragraph 3 of the Law eliminated Article 19 of Law No. 19/1964 and stipulated against any intervention in judicial matters by non-judicial forces, thereby reconfirming formal judicial independence.

In addition to confirming the principle of judicial independence the new law also authorizes increased authority for the judiciary and several new provisions. These include the presumption of innocence until proven guilty (Article 8), the right to legal aid (Article 36), the right to be tried in an open court (Article 16), and the right to compensation for illegal detention (Article 9); all speak to the recognition of some basic human rights. The renewed interest in rights of the individual in law enforcement, made possible by the mental climate and political environment of this period, had its manifestation in the field of criminal law in the creation of a completely new code of criminal procedures (*KUHAP-Kitab Undang-undang Hukum Acara Pidana*) in 1981. The KUHAP can be viewed as the logical continuation of the recognition of the citizen's basic rights in the 1970 Basic Law on Judiciary Power. However, in the field of substantive criminal law, the old colonial code of criminal law (*Wetboek van Strafrecht*) promulgated in 1918 is still in force. At the time of this writing, a bill on national criminal law has been introduced and discussed in parliament, and the upsurge of public comments and debates on the bill show the enthusiasm for and importance of this law for the people at large. (Even until early 2002, it is still a legal draft.)

Returning to the provisions of the Law No. 14/1970, perhaps the most interesting move in strengthening judicial power is the application of the judicial review of the Supreme Court. According to Article 26, the Supreme Court (*Mahkamah Agung*) has the authority to declare invalid all regulations below the level of statute (*Undang-undang*) on the grounds that they are contrary to higher-level regulations statutes. Thus for the first time a judicial remedy is authorized for eliminating, *inter alia*, various executive decrees which contradict the legislation they are supposed to implement. However, this formal stipulation still needs to be tested in actual cases, especially because the Supreme Court can use this power only if an appeal is raised to it.

However, the same law contains a stipulation that might not always be in line with the ideal of judicial independence. Article 31 of the Law No. 14/1970 stipulates that judges are appointed and dismissed by the president. Furthermore, in day-to-day practice, all the judges are government officers under the supervision of the Ministry of Justice whose minister is an assistant of and is responsible to the president. Besides, the judges are also members of official KORPRI (*Korps Pegawai Republik Indonesia*/Corps of Government Employee of the Republic of Indonesia) which is part of the ruling party, Golkar.

The Law retains the existing structure of four court system with a Supreme Court at the apex. Those courts are *Peradilan Umum* (General Court), *Peradilan Agama* (Religious Court), *Peradilan Militer* (Military Court), and *Peradilan Tata Usaha Negara* (State Administrative Court). The General Courts are courts of general jurisdiction in both civil and criminal matters. They have three levels: District Courts (*Pengadilan Negeri*), Provincial High Court (*Pengadilan Tinggi*) and National Supreme Court. These levels, with slight variations, also exist in the other courts with the Supreme Court as the highest judicial body of the nation.

The other three courts sub-system is considered special courts of justice. Agama Courts have special jurisdiction over disputes between husbands and wives of Islamic faith, and over disputes involving Islamic Law in enumerated to the extent that such areas have not been superseded by statutory law applicable to the Muslim population. Military courts try and determine cases involving armed forces personnel in accordance with the military codes. The State Administrative Courts, which were the last to be established in the country, hear and decide upon complaints and disputes concerning the policy and decision of government offices and officials.

At this point, it is appropriate to say more about the Supreme Court, because this court supervises all the existing courts, including the Religious Courts. As the highest judicial body in the country, as regulated by the Law No. 14/1985, the Supreme Court is authorized to hear cases from all types of court that are brought before it. Unlike the High Court at the provincial level, the Supreme Court does not concern itself with either the facts or the evidence of the case, but limits its examination to the legal aspects or points of law of the case. What this means is that the Court investigates whether the lower courts (i) have infringed the law, or (ii) have applied the law erroneously. Thus, the Supreme Court's principal role is to ensure the uniformity of the law, or whether the lower court interprets and applies law correctly. Appeals to the Supreme Court in Indonesia are known as *kasasi*. This term is derived from French "cassation", indicating that this system originated from France and was brought to Indonesia by the Dutch.[29]

In addition to the above judicial duty, the Supreme Court has some other important functions: (i) to supervise legal processes across the country, (ii) to exert control over judges' activities, (iii) to give legal opinions and advice to high state institutions, including the President, for example in granting/refusing presidential legal clemency. The Supreme Court is headed by a chair person (*ketua*), assisted by one Vice Chair (*wakil ketua*) and six Junior Chairpersons (*ketua muda*). The Chair and Vice Chair are nominated by the House of Representatives and appointed by the president. The President also appoints the Junior Chairpersons from those supreme justices proposed by the Chair. The current law limits the appointment of supreme justices only from those who have adequate and satisfactory judicial positions or other legal professions. Ordinarily, there are panel of three justices to hear each case. However, the Chair and Vice Chair are not limited to the judicial and legal professions only. Articles 11 to 13 of the Law No. 14/1985 regulates that the retirement and dismissal of the Chair, Vice Chair and Justices of the Supreme

Courts are in the hands of the President in accordance with statute without any obligation to seek approval from the House of Representatives.

As mentioned above, the 1970 Basic Law of the Judiciary maintains and strengthens position of the *Agama* Court in Indonesia's New Order. Article 10 states that the judicial power is exercised by courts of justice in the spheres of general, religious (*agama*), military and state administrative courts. It further stipulates that the Supreme Court is the highest court in the nation having responsibility for, among others, the supervision and hearing of final appeal (cassation) cases from A*gama* Courts. Traditionally, it was assumed that a case was finalized after being heard and decided by the High *Agama* Court. This is why there was some resentment against the submission of the religious court's decisions to the scrutiny of the "secular nationalist" Supreme Court. This transfer seems to ensure that the *Agama* Courts operated within the judicial system and, indirectly, to indicate that the status of the *Agama* Courts is equal to that of the other three courts operating in the country.

At the theoretical level this was indeed encouraging to the proponents of Islamic courts. At the practical level, the principle of equality among the four judicial bodies remained a subject of debate. For one thing, the surviving colonial rule determined that all decisions of the *Agama* Court were to be sanctioned by the local civil court in order to be officially enforceable, even if they had been decided by the High Court of Appeal. The fiat of execution (*executior verklaring*) was needed only if the disputants did not carry out the decision voluntarily. But, a new marriage law (Law No. 1/1974) which was mainly viewed as a concession to Islamic law, stipulated that all Religious Court decisions must mandatorily be approved (*pengukuhan*) by its counterpart general civil court. This change from specific approval to a general imperative obviously indicates that the Islamic courts were subordinated under the civil courts.[30] The main reason cited was the lack of an executing agent (*juru sita*), someone like court bailiff in the U.S., in the *Agama* Courts.

However, it was through the enactment of the new Marriage Act in 1974 as Law No. 1 of 1974, that the existence of *Agama* Courts was more solidified and their functions were extended. Article 63 of this Law stipulates that for Muslim Indonesians their marital and divorce disputes will be tried and decided by the *Agama* Court in accordance with their religious norms. The extension and re-affirmation of *Agama* Court jurisdiction as stipulated in the Marriage Law of 1974 includes the following:

What are intended as the matters of marriage which are regulated in the Act No. 1 year 1974 concerning Marriage are among others:

1. permission to have more than one wife;
2. permission to conclude a marriage for those who are not yet 21 (twenty-one) years of age, when the parents or guardian or relatives of the straight lineage have different opinions;
3. marriage dispensation;

4. marriage prevention;
5. refusal of Marriage Registrar to register a marriage;
6. marriage cancellation;
7. negligence suit of the spouse's responsibility;
8. repudiation divorce;
9. divorce suit;
10. settlement of common property;
11. child custody and alimony;
12. child custody and alimony whose father fails to perform his responsibility;
13. maintenance support of the ex-wife and determination of the responsibility of the ex-wife;
14. child's legal status;
15. termination of parental custody;
16. termination of guardianship;
17. appointment of non-relatives as legal guardians in cases in which relative guardians fails to fulfill the responsibility:
18. appointment of a guardian in cases of child of minor age who is abandoned by parents;
19. financial compensation punishment of guardian who has caused a loss to the property of the child under guardianship;
20. determination of the origin of a child;
21. determination of the refusal to conclude mixed marriages;
22. determination on the validity of marriages concluded before the promulgation of Act No. 1 year 1974 concerning Marriage and which were concluded in accordance with other regulations.[31]

Before concluding the discussion of judicial development during the New Order government, there is one remaining issue. Although customary courts, which were abolished and then reinstated under Dutch colonial rule, were formally abolished in 1951 by the government, peaceful settlement and village justice is still practised in many rural areas. My observation in seven provinces, some of them in the hinterland, although preliminary, indicates that this grass-roots method of setting disputes still survives. Even though they look to the state legal system for guidance, more and more village authorities that are asked to mediate still adapt their procedures and formulations to local conditions. The influence of the local *ulama'* and *kiyai* have been great not only in setting disputes but also in socializing the religiously-valued legal rules. This type of settlement is recognized and recommended by formal courts of justice. The importance of grass-roots informal leadership of the Islamic *ulama'* has come to the attention of the government which seeks to co-opt them into disseminating its programs.

THE DEVELOPMENT OF ISLAMIC LAW IN NATIONAL LEGAL SYSTEM

In discussing Islamic Law (both in the sense of *shari'âh and fiqh*) in Indonesia, the focus here is on the position and contribution of Islamic law in the national legal system. The Indonesian legal system characterizes pluralism in many senses of the term, even though various laws that comprise its sub-systems are coming closer to forming a united national legal system. This pluralism is not only in the field of substantive law, but also in procedural law and the judicial institutions that enforce it. The best way to describe the legal condition of the country is its national motto: *Bhinneka Tunggal Ika* (Unity in Diversity). The diverse laws that have been applied in Indonesia are indigenous Customary Law (*Adat*), Islamic Law and Western Law, or more specifically Dutch, and to a lesser extent also British law. The oldest among these three is the Indigenous Customary law, and then the Islamic law, which came together with the spread of the Islamic religion in the region, and lastly Dutch law, which was enforced by the colonial government starting from the sixteenth century.

In the light of this background, we will start by looking at the relationship between Islamic and *Adat* law. When Islam entered into the archipelago, the populations of this vast area were subject to their respective customary rules which were different from one tribe to another and from one region to the next. Islamic legal theory (*Usûl al-Fiqh*) recognizes the significance of '*âdat* (Customs) and '*urf* (usages) as supplementary sources of Islamic law. This means that the population who convert to the Islamic religion may continue to practise their customs and usages, as long as they do not contradict the injunctions of the primary sources, i.e. al-Qur'ân and al-Sunnah. Considering the broad legal injunctions of the Qur'ân, plus the tolerant attitudes of the Sufi and mercantile Muslims who introduced the religion to this region, it may be assumed that most existing customs and usages were revived after the conversion. The Islamization of local customs must have been a long and peaceful process, a process which some writers observe is still continuing to date.[32] In some areas, such as Aceh and later also in Minangkabau, *adat* has been integrally immersed into Islamic Law.[33]

The Islamic legal theory of *adat* and the on-going process of interaction between *shari'âh* and *adat* took a different turn and a dichotomous dimension when the Dutch colonial government interfered. Initially the Dutch adopted a non-interference policy but later, when colonial interest lay more in the preservation of locally oriented and conservative *adat* than universal and egalitarian Islamic law, the Dutch took the side of local *adat* leaders in their struggle against Islamic proponents. The best case in point was the "*paderi* war" in Central Sumatra in the early twentieth century. Islam, as a universal and egalitarian religion, was conceived as a threat to Dutch colonial domination. This was obvious when van Vollenhoven defended *Adat* law because, among others, if *adat* was not revived and defended, surely Islamic law would become prevalent.[34] More and more legal scholars and Muslim leaders in Indonesia over the last few decades have maintained that the conflict between Islamic law and *adat* was created, or at least exaggerated, by the colonial officers.

The interest in *adat* law became stronger when a debate flared up over which law was best for the Indonesian population. Many colonial officers favored the imposition of modern Western laws after being adapted to Indonesian conditions.

However, the idea that *adat* law, into which some Islamic legal elements had been integrated, was the actual positive law of the people, as put forward by Snouck Hurgronje and van Vallenhoven, gained momentum and supporters during the last phase of the Dutch colonial government. The prominence of *adat* over Islamic law was adopted as a formal legal policy as it was promulgated in Basic Law of the colony in 1927.

Basically, *adat* law is unwritten rules which grow, develop and disappear along with the growth and development of the concerned community. On one occasion, there have been efforts to collate the existing community conventions into written forms. Many ethnographic monographs have been produced to record this *adat* law. One good example of the integration of some principal elements of *adat* law into legal statute is the Basic Agrarian Law of 1960. Many scholars argue that after being transformed into statute, the characteristics of *adat* law are lost.

This latter characteristic is also shared by Islamic law. The source of Islamic law are in written forms, as are the formulations by legal scholars in *fiqh* texts, but they are not codified. These materials must go through *taqnîn* (enactment) by the caliphs or Muslim rulers, or by *qadâ* (adjudication) of a *qâdî*, or by *fatwâ* (legal opinion) of a *muftî* (jurist consult) to transform them into "positive law". Most Islamic law has never been enacted as positive law by the ruler; it is followed and respected as a part of religious conviction and due to moral consciousness and social sanctions.

After the enactment of Law No. 14/1970 in which the authority of the Supreme Court also covers the Islamic Courts, there were increasing contacts and cooperation between the Supreme Court and the Ministry of Religion in supervising and developing Islamic Courts in the country. Even though the Act implicitly stipulates that the cases of the *Agama* courts may be appealed to the Supreme Court, its application was hampered by the absence of appropriate procedural laws. In the meantime, the policy in the Islamic courts and the Ministry of Religion, considering that no new law was enacted to regulate it, continued to follow the colonial regulation which stated that the decisions of appeal from the High Religious Court were final.[35]

The enactment of the Marriage Law in 1974 extended the jurisdiction of the Religious Courts, and case dockets increased considerably. At the same time, more and more disputants wanted to present their cases at the level of the Supreme Court. In light of this situation, the Supreme Courts issued its own regulation in 1977 to regulate procedures in the examination and decision of appeal cases originating from religious courts. However, the Ministry of Religion maintained the existing law and tradition. This dualism created a debate among legal scholars and bureaucrats and only ended when the Chairman of the Supreme Court and the Minister of Religion met and issued a common statement in 1979. This agreement has been followed by mutual cooperation between the two institutions. This cooperation was also enhanced by the establishment of a special chamber dealing with cases from religious courts, and six Supreme Court justices were appointed to it with a chair appointed among them.[36]

In the early eighties, the Supreme Court presented its opinion that one of the basic reasons for judicial uncertainty and legal confusion in the Islamic courts was the absence of judicial procedures and codified Islamic laws. Moreover, the selection, promotion and supervision of the judges were also cited as needing urgent improvement to elevate and integrate Islamic courts into a national judicial system. In March 1985 a joint program was launched by the Supreme Court and the Ministry of Religion with a specific objective to gradually overcome these problems.[37]

This cooperation has borne fruit in the form of the compilation of Islamic law. One of them is the use of Presidential Instruction (*Inpres*), instead of statute (*Undang-undang*), Government Regulation (*Peraturan Pemerintah*) or even Presidential Decision (*Keputusan Presiden*) which have a higher level in the national legal order. Even those who approved the formulation of this compilation through a Presidential Instruction, acknowledged that ideally it should be enacted as a legal statute through Parliament and President as regulated by articles 5 and 20 of the Constitution. However, they realized that this ideal is not realistic considering the sensitivity of the issue among some nationalist and non-Muslim leaders. Furthermore, in a country with a strong executive system and a patrimonial political culture, an executive order may be practically as effective as formally enacted statute. In some cases, it has been more effective because there have been several *undang-undang* enacted by the parliament, such as the Law on the Environment, which remained idle for quite some time because its implementing regulations had not been issued by the executive branch of government. In the light of these conditions, it might have been a wise and effective choice, and a "by-pass road",[38] to apply the compilation with the Presidential Instruction No. 1 on June 10, 1991, and based on it, the Minister of Religion issued the Decision No. 154 in July 1991, to formally implement the compilation as a guidance and reference for all government agencies, especially the *Agama* Courts, as well as society at large, in settling disputes in the fields of marriage, inheritance and *waqf*.[39]

This is a prime example of the significance of the executive function in the formation of a national legal system, not only in enforcing the promulgated laws but also more so in legal-finding and law-making. The national legal system is an open system in the sense of considering any existing laws in the world as its raw materials as long as they are not contradictory to Pancasila values, 1945 Constitution norms and national interests as well as being in line with the legal needs of the Indonesian state and nation.[40]

Given all these requirements, one may ask: what is the position of Islamic law in the national law? Does the Muslim community which comprises the great majority of the country's population adhere to Islamic law regardless of whether it has been transformed into national law or not? Has the requirement of testing the elements of Islamic law through Pancasila values, the 1945 Constitution norms and official law-making procedures created another kind of reception theories? What is implied by this is that the Islamic law is not valid by itself, but only if it has been ratified as "national" law, and as such it is followed not as Islamic law but more as national law.

To answer these challenging questions, government officials maintain that since there has been a national consensus in the form of Pancasila and 1945 Constitution, national development should be built in accordance with the agreed consensus. However, as the first principle of Pancasila is Belief in God and given the demographic factor that the majority of the population is Muslim, Islamic law has a special position and function in the formation of a "unified modern national legal system".[41]

Given all these facts, the possibility of Islamic legal values influencing national law or the elements of Islamic law, so that it is received as positive law, is extensive if not imperative. Alternatively, the existence of legal products which are contradictory to basic Islamic values is unlikely, and if enacted, they are likely to be ineffective, or even counter-productive. However, the positive contribution of Islamic law to national law will be hampered if Islamic law does not reform and actualize itself in responding to the pressing demands of modern life.

There have been many legal statutes enacted during the New Order government that may be cited as having adopted Islamic law as national positive law. Some of these have been repeatedly mentioned in the previous discussion: Law No. 1/1974 on Marriage and Law No. 7/1989 on the *Agama* court. Besides these, various regulations have been issued to implement Islamic law in the country, for example, Government Regulation No. 9/1975 on the Implementation of the 1974 Marriage Law, Government Regulation No. 28/1977 on Islamic religious foundations (*Perwakafan Tanah Milik*), Presidential Instruction No. 1/1991 on the Compilation of Islamic Law, and Minister of Religion Regulation No. 2/1990 on the guardian of Islamic marriages.[42]

The application of Islamic law is not only confined to those fields of law that are traditionally at the heart of the religion, i.e. family and inheritance law, but also occur in more mundane fields. In this sense, one may cite the new Education Law, tabled after exhaustive drafting in early 1989 and after heated debates, which enshrined with more certainty the role of religious instruction at every level and in every kind of formal education, and appeared to grant more security to private religious school. Let us conclude the examples of transformation of the elements of Islamic law into national law by looking at the newly promulgated Law on Banking (Law No. 7/1992). It is interesting to note that this Law recognizes the institution of *mudârabah* (profit-loss sharing agreements) as one of the functions of general banks in Indonesia. In order to regulate this new banking activity, a government Regulation No. 72/1992 was issued, in which reference is formally made to Islamic *shari'âh*. Article 2 of this Regulation states: "The profit-loss sharing principle as intended by the above-mentioned article 1 is a profit-loss sharing principle based on *shari'âh*." Article 5 further stipulates:

1. A bank based on the principle of profit-loss sharing must possess a *Shari'âh* Supervisory Council (*Dewan Pengawas Syari'at*) which has a duty to ensure that all banking activities in collecting funds from the community and in distributing them to the community are in accordance with *shari'âh* principle;

2. The formation, of this Shari'âh Supervisory Council is to be carried out by the concerned bank based on consultations with the institutions in which the Indonesian *ulamâ* associate themselves.

The elucidation of this article further explains that the function of this Shari'âh Council is to determine the legality of any banking activity/product/service from the point of view of Islamic *shari'âh*; consequently, the members of this council must consist of those who have wide and deep knowledge of *shari'âh*.[43] This law did not remain on the books very long, because soon afterwards a new Islamic Bank, *Bank Muamalat Indonesia*, was established in which Suharto, his family and several Muslim ministers and high ranking officers own portions of the shares.

These are good examples of how Islamic law is transformed into national law. Even though no one denies the emergence of a favorable social climate and a better political environment during this most recent phase of the New Order government in terms of the transformation of Islamic law into positive national law, accepting the conclusion that Islamic law has enjoyed an upper hand the formation of a national legal system is fraught with risk an exaggeration. Those legal products and developments mentioned above seem to be *ad hoc* and unsystematic. However, they give a beneficial precedent and a clearer picture for Islamic law proponents on the condition and possibilities of defining and applying Islamic law elements into national positive law. The strict and complete imposition of Islamic law in the nation-state of Indonesia, even if only for the adherents of Islam, may not only be impossible, but also detrimental to Muslim interests at large.

Islamic law as expounded in *fiqh* literature and practices by the Muslim community has been accepted and succeeded as raw material for the formation of national law through a legal channel of national law-making. Ismail Suny, a famous scholar of constitutional law and Muslim leaders, is of the opinion that the position of Islamic law in the Indonesian legal structure is stronger than just "raw material". Borrowing a theory in constitutional law, he put forward the terms "persuasive source" and "authoritative source". Persuasive source is that people have to be convinced to accept and implement it, while as an authoritative source it is valid by itself. He maintained that Article 29 of the 1945 Constitution which states that: "The State guarantees the freedom of each and every citizen to profess a religion and to worship in accordance with one's religion and belief", has established Islamic law as an authoritative source at least for those Islamic law adherents and canceled completely the *receptie* theory which denied the validity of Islamic law until it was received by a community as part of its *adat* law. The Presidential decree of July 5, 1959 to return to the 1945 Constitution mentioned in its consideration the factor that the Jakarta Charter[44] was an inherent part of the Constitution, which strengthened the authoritativeness of Islamic law as a source of the national legal system.[45]

Suny also argued that the validity of Islamic law only for Muslim does not contradict the principles of equality before law which is stipulated in Article 27 of the 1945 Constitution. Systematic interpretation of Articles 27 and 29, he argues, is a relationship between general rule (*lex generalis*) and specific rule (*lex specialis*). Equality before law in which each and every citizen is treated equally without any discrimination based on race, color, class, religion etc. applies as a general principle. Meanwhile the right to profess a religion and to worship accordingly is also guaranteed by the Constitution and is applied as a specific rule which exempts it from a general rule. This kind of argument has also been cited by a former Minister of Religion, Munawir Sjadzali, in defending the constitutionality of the Law on *Agama* Courts.[46] In his writing, he quoted a former Minister of Justice, Omar Senoadji, who maintained that not all legal distinctions are to be seen as a breach of the principle of equality before law, even treating unequal people equally may not be in the line with justice and the constitution.

CLOSING REMARKS

To pursue and upgrade this phenomenon, the Islamic law proponents must exercise a new *ijtihad* in the sense of carrying out systematic and endless effort to derive legal principles and rules from its sources by considering wisely the legacy of Islamic legal traditions and literature. Those studies are directed to answer the actualities and problems of the present-day Indonesian population, the great majority of which are Muslims, and to guide them in advancing their welfare and capabilities in the modern world.

On this point, Ismail Saleh, a previous Minister of Justice, forwarded an interesting and viable theory. When the bill of *Agama* Courts was heatedly debated in parliament and public, an article by him appeared in one of the catholic-owned leading newspapers in Jakarta with a nation-wide circulation, which maintained that a national legal system is to be a more unified system of law. However, it is an open system in the sense that any system or doctrine that is in line with Pancasila and the 1945 Constitution may become a source in its formations. In this context, Islamic law is in a better position. But, Islamic law has also to go through the mechanism of national law-making. What is important is to find out the norms of Islamic law so that they be accepted by every segment of the population and as such they will be accepted more easily and transformed into a national legal order. If there is a difference between Islamic Law and other sources, efforts should be directed to find a common core (*inti*) and common denominators among these different sources, so that the gap can be filled or at least minimized. Only if all this proves ineffective, it may be wise and just to adopt the concept of *Bhinneka Tunggal Ika* (Unity in Diversity) in the sense that each distinct group is subject to its distinctive law without making the others subject to it.[47]

As reiterated above, the success of implementing some sections of Islamic law and the adoption of certain elements of Islamic values into national positive law are made possible by a favorable political situation and by cooperation with other segments of the population. This conditioning may be imperative if this trend is to continue. The contribution of those Muslim legal bureaucrats and professionals who are generally not conversant, or even some those are unsatisfied with traditionally formulated Islamic law, has been critical in this process. Mutual cooperation and constructive dialogue between these two proponents of Islamic law, irrespective of their differences in what constitutes this, are required to make Islamic law not only enforceable as a national law but also in reinvigorating it as an actual legal system that fits the demand of a modern society.

Notes

1. The literature on the Indonesian *coup d'état* is extensive. Some of the representative material with conflicting opinion are the following: Arthur J. Dommen, "The Attempted Coup in Indonesia", *The Chine Quarterly*, 25 (January–March 1966); Jon Hughes, *Indonesian Upheaval*, (New York: McKay, 1967); Donald Mindley, "Political Power and the October 1965 Coup in Indonesia", *Journal of Asian Studies*, XXVI/2 (February 1965), pp. 103–10; John O. Sutter, "Interpretations of Gestapu, the 1965 Indonesian Coup", *World Affairs*, XXXII/4 (March 1970), pp. 305–17, and W. F. Wertheim, Indonesia before and after the Untung Coup", *Pacific Affairs*, 39 (Spring-Summer 1966). These interpretations and many others are summarized in Arnold C. Backman's book, *The Communist Collapse in Indonesia*, (New York: W. W. Norton and Co., 1969). Some scholars at Cornell University also conducted research and put forward their interpretation, see Benedict R. Anderson and Ruth T. McVey, *A Preliminary Analysis of the October 1, 1965 Coup in Indonesia*, (Ithaca, NY: Cornell Modern Indonesia Project, Intern Report Series, Cornell University Press, 1971). For an official Explanation of the coup, see Nugroho Notosusanto and Ismail Saleh, *The Coup Attempt of the September 30th Movement*, (Djakarta: Pembimbing Masa, 1968).
2. For a good introduction to the emergence of the New Order, see J. M. van den Kroef, *Indonesia since Sukarno*, (Singapore: Asia Pacific Press, 1971), and another book with the same title by Peter Polomka (Melbourne: Penguin Books, 1971).
3. Donald Hindley, "The September 30 Movement and the fall of Sukarno", *The World Today*, XXIV (August 1968), pp. 345–46. For an interesting discussion of the backgrounds of the March 11th Order, see Peter Polomka, *Indonesia since Sukarno*, p. 89. The text of this order itself is reprinted in *Far Eastern Economic Review*, (24 March 1966), p. 550.
4. There has an endless debate over which category of state the Indonesia policy belongs to. Most Western analysis continue to purvey New Order Indonesia as an authoritarian military state, some prefer to call it a quasi-military state and others a bureaucratic state. However, the new Order exponents call it a "Pancasila Democratic state". See Chua Beng Huat, "Looking for Democratization in Post-Suharto Indonesia", *Contemporary Southeast Asia* 15, no. 2 (September 1993); and Richard Langil, *Military Rule and Development Policy in Indonesia under the New Order*, 1966–1974 (Ph.D. dissertation, American University, Washington, D.C.), p. 61.
5. All the decrees and decisions of the Provisional People's Consultative Assembly are compiled by Kansil and Erwin, *Kitab Himpunan Karya MPRS*, (Djakarta 1970). See also Eddy Daiman and Robert N. Homick, "Indonesia's Formal Legal System: An Introduction", *America Journal of Comparative Law*, 20/3 (Summer 1972).
6. On the development of Pancasila democracy in the New Order, see, among others, Abdul Haris Nasution, *Pancasila Democracy Today and Tomorrow* (Djakarta, nd) and

Orba: a Guide to the Order Government Policy (Djakarta: Department of Information, Republic of Indonesia, November 1967). Also useful is Donald, "Indonesia 1970; The Workings of Pancasila Democracy", *Asian Survey*, XI (February 1971), and "Indonesia, 1971: Pancasila Democracy and the Second Parliamentary Election", *Asian Survey*, XII (January 1972.)

7. One example of study using the liberal democratic category is Andrew MacIntyre, *Business and Politics in Indonesia*, (Sydney: Allen and Unwin, 1990), while a cultural essentialist tendency is represented by Richard Robison, *Power and Economy in Suharto's Indonesia*, (Clayton: Center for Southeast Asian Studies, Monash University, 1990). For a good example of a new approach, see Chua Beng Huat, "Looking for Democratization", pp. 131–60.

8. For extensive study on this subject, see Christine Drake, *National Integration in Indonesia: Pattern and Policies* (Honolulu: University of Hawaii Press, 1989).

9. The pragmatic and realistic if not simplistic, approach of the early New Order government is noted by many observers of Indonesia. See, among others, Guy Pauker, "Indonesia: The Year of Transition", *Asian Survey*, VII (February 1967); Guy Pauker, "Indonesia Age of Reason?", *Asian Survey*, VIII (February 1968); John Allison, "Indonesia: Year of the Pragmatists", *Asian Survey*, IX (February 1969); and Mochtar Lubis, "Indonesia's Goals and New Realities", *Pacific Community*, II (April 1971).

10. As quoted by B. J. Boland, *The Struggle of Islam in Modern Indonesia* (The Hague: Martinus Nijhoff, 1982), p. 37.

11. See for example, Guy J. Pauker, "Policy Implication of Political Institutionalization and Leadership Change in Southeast Asia", *Asian Affairs An American Review*, 13/3 (Fall 1986).

12. MPRS Decree No. XX/MPRS/1966 of July 5, 1966 concerning the DPR-GR (House of Representative) memorandum about sources of the legal order and forms of regulation. See Kansil and Erwin, op. cit., p. 150. See also Eddy Damain and Robert N. Hornick. "Indonesia's Legal System an Introduction", *American Journal of Comparative Law*, 20/3 (Summer 1972), pp. 524–26.

13. See, for instance, the remark made by the ruling party Golkar on the draft bill of the Supreme Court and the General Court respectively, September 17. 1985, See also the reply of Minister of Justice to remarks made by members of the House of Representatives on the draft bill, October 4, 1985. The Minister, among others, said "The government actually is applying integralistic principles in accordance with the spirit of Pancasila and the 1945 Constitution in supervising the judges by emphasizing a priority on togetherness and consultation between the government and judiciary". For further discussion see Todung Mulya Lubis, *In Search of Human Right: Legal Political Dilemmas of Indonesia's New Order, 1966–1990* (Jakarta: Gramedia, 1993), pp. 86–96.

14. See Ismail Suny, *Mekanisme Demokrasi Pancasila*, (Jakarta: Aksara Bari, 1978); Marsilam Simanjutak, *Unsur Hegelian dalam Pandangan Negara Integralistik*, (a thesis submitted to the Law School, University of Indonesia, 1992) and Lubis, op. cit., p. 87.

15. Among those who subscribe to the integralistic state are Padmo Wahyono and Oemar Senoadji, both of whom have had influential positions either in the Supreme Court or the Ministry of Justice. See Wahyono, "Hak dan Kewajiban Asasi berdasarkan Cara Pandang Integralistik Indonesia", *Forum Keadilan*, 9 (1989), Senoaji, "Kekuasaan Kehakiman di Indonesia sejak kembali ke Undang-undang Dasar 1945", a paper presented at the Seminar on "Thirty Years of the Return to the 1945 Constitution" held in Law School, Pajajaran University, Bandung, July 5–6, 1989, as quoted by Lubis, op. cit., p. 87.

16. See Daniel S. Lev, "Colonial Law and the Genesis of the Indonesian State", *Indonesia*, 40 (1985), p. 72.

17. As quoted by Sunaryati Hartono, a current directrice of the Nation Law Department Center, in her article, "Pembinaan Hukum Nasional Pada Pembangunan Jangka Panjang Tahap II Dalam Konteks Hukum Islam", *Mimbar Hukum*, IV/8 (1993), p. 1.

18. The Decree No. II Year 1993 of the People's Consultative Assembly on Guidelines of State Policy (Garis-garis Besar Haluan Negara) in which a master plan for the second twenty-five year national development paln is formulated. See *Ketetapan-ketetapan Majelis Permusyawaratan Rakyat Indonesia Tahun 1993*, (Jakarta: BP7 Pusat, 1993), pp. 19–20. This publication is in Bahasa Indonesia and the translation here is mine.

19. Ibid., p. 30.

20. Ibid., p 33.

21. Information and quotation on the Guidelines of State Policy in the sphere of legal development, besides being taken from the official publication cited in footnote 18, are also taken from Sunaryati Hartono, op. cit., pp. 1–18.

22. See Ismail Saleh, Minister of Justice, "Wawasan Pembangunan Hukum Nasional", *Kompas* (June 1 and 2, 1989). This article appeared in one of the largest daily newspapers in Indonesia during the heated debate in the Parliament and public on the bill of Religious Court. This article is later also included in Zuffran Sabrie (ed.) *Peradilan Agama dalam Wadah Negara Pancasila: Dialog tentang RUUPA* (Jakarta: Pustaka Antara, 1990), pp. 124–131. See also Sunaryati Hartono, op. cit., pp. 3–4.

23. This estimate was given by Mrs. Hartono. See op. cit., p. 12.

24. See David M. Trubek, "Max Weber on Law and the Rise of Capitalism, *Wisconsin Law Review*, 3 (1972), pp. 720–53.

25. For further discussion on the civil law system, see J. T. Merryemen, *The Civil Law Tradition*, (Stanford University Press, 1969), and Alan Watson, *The Making of Civil Laws*, (Cambridge: Harvard University Press, 1981).

26. This condition had been observed by Eddy Damain and Robert N. Hornick in the early seventies. In general this condition, to a lesser extent, is still true. See their article "Indonesia's Formal Legal System: An Introduction", *American Journal of Comparative Law*, 20/3 (Summer 1972), p. 510.

27. Article 19 of Law No. 19/1964 says: "In the interests of revolution, the honor of the state and nation, or the urgent interest of society at large, the President can engage or interfere in court proceedings". While Article 23 of the Law No. 13/1965 states "In cases where the President interferes, the court proceedings have to be stopped and the decision of the President should be announced". For further discussion on the perspective of human right debates in Indonesia, see Lubis, op. cit., pp 96–102.

28. For a detailed discussion of the background and debates about this law, see Daniel S. Lev, "Judicial Authority and the Struggle of an Indonesian *Rechtstaat*", *Law and Society Review*, 13/1 (Fall 1978), pp. 37–71.

29. See R. Subekti, *Law in Indonesian*, (Bandung: Karya Nusantara, 1976), and Bambang Waluyo, *Implementasi Kekuasaan Kehakiman Republik Indonesia*, (Jakarta: Sinar Grafika, 1992), especially chapter 6 on the Supreme Court, pp. 95–116.

30. Many Muslim writers criticize this institution of "execution permit" and argue that it is contradictory to the general norms of the Basic Law of Judiciary. See, among others, T. Jafizham, "Peranan Pengadilan Agama dalam Pelaksanaan Undang-undang Perkawinan", in *Kenang-kenangan Seabad Peradilan Agama* (Jakarta: Departemen Agama,

1985), pp. 170–72; and H. Dahlan Ranuwiharjo, "Peranan Badan Peradilan Agama dalam Mewujudkan Cita-cita negara Hukum," ibid., 201–12.

31. The jurisdictions which are established by the 1974 Act of Marriage are enumerated in the Elucidation of Article 49 paragraph (2) of the Act No. 7 Year 1989 concerning the Religious Court, State Gazette No. 49 Year 1989. See Abdul Gani Abdullah (ed.) *Himpunan Perundang-undangan dan Peraturan Peradilan Agama* (Jakarta: Intermasa, 1991), pp. 302–303.

32. See Mitsuo Nakamura, *The Crescent Arises over the Banyan Tree,* (Yogyakarta: Gadjah Mada University Press, 1983).

33. The integration of adat into Islamic law may be discerned from the proverbs of each community. In Aceh, for example, there is a famous saying: *Hukum ngon adat hantom cre, ladee zat ngon sipeut* ([Islamic] law and *adat* cannot be separated; as between a thing with its attribute). The proverb from Minangkabau reveals the connection between Islamic law and adat in a clearer position: *Syara' mengato, adat memakai* (*Shari'ah* decides, *adat* applies). For further discussion see Muhammad Daud Ali, *Asas-asas Hukum Islam,* (Jakarta: Rajawali Press, 1990), p. 201. In the case of Minangkabau, see Hamka, "Hubungan Timbal Balik antara Adat dan Syara' di dalam Kebudayaan Minangkabau", *Panji Masyarakat,* 61/IV (1970), and Amir Syarifuddin, *Pelaksanaan Hukum Kewarisan Islam dalam Lingkungan Adat Minangkabau,* (Jakarta: Gunung Agung, 1984).

34. This remark has been used time and again by the proponents of Islamic law to point out the implicit colonial background that backs up *"adat"* law. Even Bustanul Arifin, a Supreme Court Judge, and later the Junior Chair for Agama Courts appeals in the Supreme Court, quoted it. See article in Muchtar Na'im *Menggali Hukum Tanah dan Hukum Waris Minangkabau* (Padang: Center for Minangkabau Studies, 1986).

35. This was regulated in Article 7 State Gazette No. 601 of 1937 in conjunction with Article 15 State Gazette no 638 of 1937 and continued to be valid based the stipulation of chapter Article 11, Government Regulation No. 45 of 1957. See *Kenang-kenangan Seabad Peradilan Agama di Indonesia,* (Indonesia: Departemen Agama, 1985), p. 46.

36. These Supreme Court justices who were appointed to the chamber by the chief of the Supreme Court in 1979 were Sri Widoyati Wiranto Soekito, Z. Asikin Kusuma Atmaja, B. R. M. Hanindyo Poetro Sosropranoto, Poerwata S. Gandasubrata, Kaboel Arifin and Bustanul Arifin. The last mentioned justice was later in 1982 officially appointed to be the chief of chamber with the title Junior Chief (Ketua Muda) of Supreme Court by the President. All six justices were Muslim and had formal education in "secular" national law schools and none, excepting the chief, can be considered 'ulama in the traditional background in Islamic religion. This was a matter of contention among Agama court judges, Ministry of Religion officials and Muslim leaders at large. Therefore, many had good reason to feel relieved when in late 1982, more Supreme Court Justices with some religious education but not at level of *'ulama* were appointed. See H. A. Muhaimin Nur, et al. (eds.), *Kenang-kenangan Seabad Peradilan Agama di Indonesia,* (Jakarta: Departemen Agama, 1985), pp. 52–53. Special research on the sociological background and judicial behavior of these judges, or in the matter of all the Supreme Court justice, is needed and essential in order to comprehend the judicial system.

37. See Bustanul Arifin, "Kompilasi: Fiqh dalam Bahasa Undang-Undang", *Pesantren* 2, no. 2 (1985): 26–27. For extensive discussion of the Islamic Law Compilation, see H. Abdurrahman, *Kompilasi Hukum Islam di Indonesia,* (Jakarta: Akademika Pressindo, 1992).

38. The term "by-pass road" (*jalan pintas*) was used by Supreme Justice Harahap to refer to the Compilation of Islamic law and the way it is enacted and implemented.

39. For further discussion on the background and efforts to implement the compilation, see Abdul Gani Abdullah, "Pemasyarakatan Inpres No. 1/1991 tentang Kompilasi Hukum Islam", *Mimbar Hukum: Aktualisasi Hukum Islam*, III/5 (1992), pp. 1–6, K. H. Sjechul Hadi Permono, "Sosialisasi Inpres No. 1/1991 tentang Kompilasi Hukum Islam", ibid., pp. 7–16, and Ahmad Azhar Basyir, "Pemasyarakatan Kompilasi Hukum Islam melalui Jalur Pendidikan Non Formal", ibid., pp. 17–20.

40. See Ismail Saleh, "Eksistensi Hukum Islam dan Sumbangannya terhadap Hukum Nasional", *Kompas* (June 3, 1989).

41. The attributes of a "modern unified national legal system" have been expressed by the Minister of Justice and high ranking officer. See, for example, Ismail Saleh, Ibid. This article was later complied by Zuffran Sabrie (ed.) op. cit., pp. 132–36.

42. All laws, government regulations and legal documents pertaining to the jurisdictions of Agama Court have been compiled by Abdul Gani Abdullah, *Himpunan Perundang-undangan dan Peraturan Peradilan Agama*, (Jakarta: Intermasa, 1991).

43. For further discussion of the new Law on Banking in Indonesia, see Widjanarto, *Hukum dan ketentuan Perbankan di Indonesia*, (Jakarta: Grafiti, 1993)

44. Those who argued against the validity of Islamic law and the existence of separate courts for Muslim citizens in a national legal judicial system have criticized some Muslim leaders for wanting to establish an Islamic state and to reassert the Jakarta Charter which had been defeated and refused once and for all. Based on this, they opined that the existence of separate Islamic court which enforces Islamic Law is unconstitutional, against the national consensus and detrimental to national integration, and most of all, contradictory to Pancasila. See, for example, Franz Magnis-Suseno, "Seputar Rencana UU Peradilan Agama", *Kompas* (June 16, 1989); S. Widjoyo, "Antara Negara Agama dan Negara Pancasila", *Majalah Hidup*, 7 (February 12, 1989); S. Widjojo, "Kesaktian Pancasila dan Tantangan", *Majalah Hidup*, 10 (March 1989); P. J. Suwarno, "Peradilan Agama di Negara Pancasila", *Suara Pembaruan* (April 6, 1989); T. B. Simatupang, "Menyempurnakan RUUPA demi Makin Mantapnya Persatuan & Kesatuan Bangsa", *Suara Pembaruan* (June 29, 1989).

45. Ismail Suny is a professor of constitutional law and legal theory at the school of Law, Universitas Indonesia, Jakarta, from which he graduated in 1957. He also obtained his Masters in Civil Law at McGill University, Montreal, Canada (1960) and a jurist Doctorate from Universitas Indonesia (1963). He comes from Aceh, a predominantly Islamic area in the northern tip of Sumatra and has been active in the Muhammadiyah organization as one of the chairman of its national board and Rector of Muhammadiyah University in Jakarta (1973–1980). He was also the Vice Director of the National Law Development Center, Ministry of Justice (1964–1974), for a short period a member of the House of Representatives (1973–1980) and a consultant to the prestigious National Defense and Security Board (1980–1987). Despite all these positions in official institutions, he was a consistent scholar whose writings sometimes criticizes unconstitutional practices of the New Order government. Because of this, he had been detained by the security officers. When Suharto's policy leaned to cooperate more with Muslims, he joined the ICMI (*Ikatan Cendekiawan Muslim Indonesia*) and was appointed as one of its national chairmen. He was later appointed as Ambassador to Saudi Arabia. Some of his writings which are relevant to the topic of this study are: "Kedudukan Hukum Islam dalam Sistem Ketatanegaraan Indonesia", in Juhaya S. Praja (ed), *Hukum Islam di Indonesia: Perkembangan dan Pembentukan* (Bandung: Remaja Rosda Karya, 1991), pp. 73–81,

"Hukum Islam dalam Hukum Nasional", *Hukum dan Pembangunan*, XVII/4 (August 1987), pp. 351–57; "Tradisi dan Inovasi Keislaman di Indonesia dalam bidang Hukum", *Mimbar Hukum*, IV/8 (1993), pp. 19–28.

46. See Munawir Sjadzali, "Landasan Pemikiran Politik Hukum Islam dalam Rangka menentukan Peradilan Agama di Indonesia", in Juhaya S. Praja (ed.), op. cit., pp. 41–67.

47. See Ismail Saleh, "Eksistensi Hukum Islam dan Sumbangannya terhadap Hukum Nasional", *Kompas* (June 3, 1989). This article was later included in Zuffran Sabrie (ed.), op. cit., pp. 132–36.

5

THE INDONESIAN MARRIAGE LAW OF 1974
An Institutionalization of the
Shari'a for Social Changes

Azyumardi Azra

INTRODUCTION

Indonesia is the largest Muslim nation in the world. According to estimation, Muslims make up more than 87 per cent out of the total Indonesian population.[1] The rest of the populations are Christians, Hindus, Buddhists, and smaller groups of adherents of local mystical cults and primal religions. Despite its large Muslim population, Indonesian Islam is still a neglected area of scholarly studies. Furthermore, when Indonesian Islam is studied, much attention have been paid by scholars mainly to the political and cultural aspects; while Islamic law has not yet received an equal treatment.

It has been recognized that the rapid spread of Islam in this archipelago, beginning in the twelfth century, takes a form of "penetration pacifique". Thus by and large, as Arnold points out, no gun was fired, nor was any sword drawn for the propagation of Islam in Indonesian soil. Arnold concludes that, "the history of Malay Archipelago during the last six hundred years furnishes us with one of the most interesting chapters in the story of the spread of Islam by missionary efforts. . . . In every instance, in the beginning, their works had to be carried on without any patronage or assistance

Previously published as "The Indonesian Marriage Law: An Institutionalization of the *Shari'a* for Social Change", *Istiqra* 6 (July–December 1992): 20–38. Reproduced with permission of the author and the publisher, State Institute for Islamic Studies (IAIN) Bandung.

from the rulers of the country, but solely by the force of persuasion, and in many cases in the face of severe opposition, especially on the part of the Spaniards".[2]

It is important to note that Islam arrived in Indonesia when the centers of Islamic political power in the Middle East were in the decline. In the middle of the thirteenth century when Islam gained a foothold in Sumatra, the Muslim all over Islamdom had fallen on evil days. The Abbasid were already torn apart; the Fatimids who ruled over the Arab countries, and North Africa were in the process of disintegration; Persia was the vantage ground for self-interested upstarts; while Spain, once the pride of Muslim culture and philosophy, had forgotten its traditions and was in the throes of death, surrounded as it was by the Christian hordes who were bent upon giving it short shrift.

While Islam lost its political supremacy, on the contrary, the sufistic brand of Islam gained momentum. The reign of the philosophical and legal aspects of Islam was replaced by the *tasawwuf*, which, to some extent, was a sort of Muslim escapism in facing political and economic disintegration. Apart from the supposedly negative side of the *tasawwuf*, it must be kept in mind, however, that it had in fact become the last strong bastion in keeping the dynamic impulses of Islam. In this respect, it was Islam which had been heavily infused by the *tasawwuf* arrived in Indonesia. Thus, as Gibb points out; the spread of Islam in the new territories to the East in Southeast Asia and Africa was largely the work of the Sufi brotherhoods which were in many cases tolerant of traditional usage and thought which ran contrary to the strict practice of Islamic orthodoxy.[3]

Considering that above-mentioned socio-historical discourse, it can be concluded that the conversion of Indonesia to Islam was very largely the work of the Sufi *tariqàs*, since at all events their interpretation of Islam certainly fit into the background of the Indonesians which was heavily influenced by Hindu-Buddhist syncretism and indigenous custom (*adat*). As early as the seventeenth century a number of great *ulama* played a crucial role in implanting the seeds of Islamic orthodoxy. This is in turn provided *raison d'etre* for the rise of reform movements. This was followed by the Padri movement in West Sumatra in the first half of the nineteenth century, which also had objectives to purify Islamic doctrines and practices from un-Islamic influences and ultimately to establish a more *shari'a*-oriented *umma*. This movement, which developed into a sort of civil war among Minangkabau Muslims, was later suppressed by Dutch colonial power, though its influence remained viable for a long time in various parts of the archipelago. And since beginning of the twentieth century, various Islamic modernist movements flourished in the Indonesian world. Therefore, one of the unifying themes of the history of Islam in Indonesia is the spread and improvement of Islamic religious life toward a more genuine Islam as prescribed by the Qur'an and the Hadith.

As far as marriage law is concerned, from the coming of Islam up to 1974, there was no unified marriage law implemented in Indonesia. Marriage was carried out among people according either to religious law or to indigenous tradition and custom (*adat*), or even to Western marriage laws. This variety of marriage laws was recognized and implemented, and later was maintained in force by the government of the newly independent Republic of Indonesia after the Second World War up to 1974. In the meantime, it has long been felt by many Indonesian Muslims that they needed a new marriage law. After a series of efforts, in 1974 a new marriage law was promulgated. Since Indonesia is not an Islamic state, the new law is not formally declared as an exclusive Muslim marriage law. Rather, it is intended to apply to all Indonesians regardless of their religion. It is must be admitted however, that after it was passed by the Parliament, the new marriage law in one way or another is sort of codification of Islamic marriage law, for all of its articles have been amended in order to be in line with the *shari'a*. Therefore, the promulgation and implementation of the new marriage law to a great degree is an institutionalization of the *shari'a* in Indonesia.

Since its implementation in 1975, the new marriage law has brought about social changes, especially among the vast Muslim population. Considering a great deal of statistics, it has succeeded in term of decreasing divorce rate, polygamy, marriage of minors, and other related matters. This paper will briefly uncover the development of Muslim marriage law *vis-a-vis* non-Muslim marriage laws before the promulgation of the Indonesian marriage law of 1974. It also tries to describe and analyse the Indonesian marriage law of 1974 according to the *shari'a* viewpoints, and social changes it brought in Indonesian society.

MARRIAGE LAW BEFORE THE LAW NO. 1 OF 1974

Before the coming of Islam into Indonesia, there were a variety of traditions and custom (*adat*) of the indigenous people in the life of the society. The *adat* itself varies according to ethnic origins and cultural backgrounds of the natives, given the diversity of ethnic groups and cultural bounds of the population of Indonesia. As far as marriage is concerned, it is in *adat* laws, in varying degrees, a matter of kinship group, family, community and personal concern. As Ter Haar maintains, marriage is also the means by which the organized relationship groups which form autonomous communities preserve their existence, be they sub-clans, sub-tribes or extended families. Within the community, marriage is also the means by which the individual family extends its line into the future, and this makes it a family matter.[4] Therefore, marriage and marriage laws have very important position in *adat* law.[5]

The introduction of Islam into Indonesia brought about a great degree and transformation of the indigenous *adat*. As Nasution and Khatib argue, the *adat* of the Islamized communities has more or less incorporated elements of Islamic teachings, especially the rules for marriage and other areas of family law.[6] Because of this amalgamation of *adat* laws with Islamic tenets, it is not surprising that later on the British and Dutch authorities at first assumed that *adat* laws were basically the same as those of Islam. The person who was mainly responsible for this opinion was Christian van den Berg, a prominent Dutch advisor; he called this opinion as the theory of *receptio in complexu*. Later, Snouck Hurgronje through the so-called *receptie* theory proposed that *adat* law was not the same as Islamic law with some deviations in it, but it was based upon the indigenous Indonesian way of life and culture.[7] In other words, *adat* law was not just Islamic law mixed with local custom, but also contained many additional elements which were greatly varied as one moved from one Indonesian locality to another.[8] On the other hand, Hazairin, a leading Indonesian legal scholar, maintained that *adat* law was to some extent the same as that of Islam because of its adoption of Islamic tenets.[9] I would suggest that besides its adoption of certain Islamic tenets, *adat* law apparently keeps its own distinctive character which differs from those of genuine Islam.

The Dutch East Indies Company, which began to exercise its control on parts to the whole region of the Indonesian Archipelago from 1619 up to the eruption of the Second World War, initially did not to pay much attention to the rule of law among the natives. It was only in and around their main settlements that the Dutch laws was later introduced; the implementation was adapted to local conditions and supplemented by special laws and regulations applicable to the Dutch East Indies. When the British temporarily controlled the East Indies between 1811 to 1816, they also implemented a legal system which treated Islamic law as identical with the native customary law, particularly by attaching a Muslim adviser (*penghulu* or *qadi*) to the general court. After the Dutch returned to the Archipelago, by their regulation of 1819 regarding civil and criminal procedure for the native population, they maintained the legal conditions as they found them.[10] Thus, until the later part of the nineteenth century the predominant Dutch view of Indonesian law was that it was basically Islamic. In the subsequent development, however, the Dutch recognized the distinction between *shari'a* and *adat* law. And in the struggle between Islam and *adat* everywhere in Indonesia, the Dutch naturally took the side of *adat* and tended to promote the development of *adat* law in order to curb the progress of Islam. Therefore, they began to change the *status quo* of the law.

This change was reflected in the law policy of the Dutch colonial administration which began to take a clear shape in 1848 by starting to make a codification of law in Indonesia. The Dutch also enacted a Civil Code (*Burgerlijk Wetboek*) and a Commercial Code (*Wetboek van Koophandel*) for Europeans in Indonesia which later on were developed as a different group of laws in order to be applicable to all different groups of the population.[11] Therefore as far as the marriage laws are concerned, there were four kinds of marriage laws in force in Indonesia during the Dutch colonial rule, as follows:

1. The Islamic marriage law regulating the marriage among all Muslim Indonesians.[12]
2. The Civil Code (*Burgerlijk Wetboek*) regulating the marriage among persons who are subjects to western law, i.e. the Europeans and the Chinese.[13]
3. The ordinance of 1933 for marriage of Christian Indonesians.[14]
4. The *adat* law (customary law) for marriage of persons who are neither Muslims nor non-Christians (differing from one area to another).[15]

We are not going to discuss the content of each marriage law above, but what is important to note is that actually there was no definitive legal codification of the Islamic marriage law enacted by the Dutch. In other words, the regulations of the so-called "Islamic marriage law" were preserved merely in various *shari'a* and *fiqh* books. Since the vast majority of Indonesian Muslims follow the Shafi'i school of law, it is mostly the principles and practices of this school that are implemented.[16]

It is relevant to mention here that after the British interregnum in Indonesia, the Dutch also followed the British[17] model in administering Islam. Later, the Dutch established Islamic courts which were called *priesterraden* ("priest-court") on the mistaken assumption that the Muslim *penghulu* (*qadi*) and their subordinates functioned as priests in Christianity. These *priesterraden* exercised judiciary functions concerning Muslim family matters such as marriage, divorce, reconciliation (*ruju'*) and to a certain extent, inheritance (*fara'id*). These Islamic courts initially were established for Java and Madura in 1882 and later also for other islands. They functioned alongside the *landraaden* (civil court).[18] The decisions of Islamic court, however, could only be executed after the civil court had given its affirmation (*executoir verklaard*). Therefore, the Islamic court was in quite a weak position *vis-à-vis* the civil court, since it was very possible for the latter to nullify decisions of the former if it considered that Islamic court had overreached civil court jurisdiction.[19]

For practical purposes, I would say that there was no substantial change both in Muslim marriage law and in Islamic court in the period of Japanese Occupation (March 1942–August 1945). After the independent Republic of Indonesia was proclaimed on August 17, 1945, a substantial change was carried out. The administration of Islamic courts and matters concerning Muslim marriages which previously had been administered by the Ministry of Justice now came under the jurisdiction of the newly established Ministry of Religion. This change was announced in 1946. While the Ministry of Religion maintained the structure and composition of the Islamic courts, in a very short time after its establishment the Ministry introduced the law No. 22 of 1946,[20] which was intended to unify the administration of Muslim marriage and divorce throughout the country under the control of the Ministry itself.[21] This law provided that henceforth all Muslim marriages, divorce and reconciliation (*nikah, talaq, ruju'* or NTR) would be brought under the solitary formal supervision of the registrars (the *pegawai pencatat NTR*) appointed by the Minister of Religion or his delegate. The seat of the registrars of the NTR would be determined by local religious office (the *Jawatan Agama Daerah*, later became the *Kantor Urusan Agama* or the District Religious Office) directly controlled by the Minister of Religion.[22]

The promulgation of the law No. 22 of 1946 did not go uncontested. The law was hotly debated in the revolutionary parliament (KNIP), where nationalists and secularists of various kinds stood opposed. Their opposition was mainly because of the fear that the law in one way or another would strengthen the position of either the *qadi* (the *penghulu*) and other Islamic functionaries of Islamic law in the new state. However, the law was finally passed in parliament after strong pressures by Muslim leaders. Although the implementation of this law could not be carried out effectively due to the Indonesian revolution, it was, however, considered as a victory for the Muslims. This law made the distinction between Muslims and non-

Muslims become clear — as far as the procedure of marriage is concerned. The crucial differences between the law No. 22 of 1946 and other laws concerning the procedures of marriage, which were enacted before, were that for Muslims registration was not necessary for the validity of their marriages, divorces and reconciliations. It was sufficient for Muslims to register these acts at the local, Muslim-run District Religious Office (*Kantor Urusan Agama*) rather than at the Civil Registrar's Office (*Kantor Catatan Sipil*) which then merely served non-Muslims and was under the jurisdiction of the Ministry of Justice.[23]

In order to implement the law No. 22 of 1946, the Ministry of Religion issued Instructions No. 4 of 1946, Law No. 32 of 1954, Instructions No. 1 of 1955, and Decree No. 15 of 1955. These regulations gave the registrars advisory powers with respect to forced marriages, divorces, and polygamy.[24] Beside regulated marriage procedures, the last two regulations also contained provisions of the *taklik talak* (Arabic: *ta'liq al-talaq*) which had long been customary in Indonesia.[25] The *taklik talak* is the condition in the marriage contract, breach of which enabled the wife to apply for divorce. The formulae and conditions of the *taklik talak* have been standardized by the Ministry of Religion, and they are printed in the last page of the official marriage certificate. Immediately after contracting his marriage, the husband has to declare to his wife's *wali* (guardian) and the witnesses that there are four reasons upon which his wife may initiate divorce proceeding against him: if he deserts her for six consecutive months, if he does not give her proper maintenance for three consecutive months, if he physically mistreats her, or if he neglects her for six consecutive months.[26]

THE STRUGGLE FOR THE MARRIAGE LAW OF 1974

It is must be admitted that for various reasons those above mentioned regulations did not have much effect, particularly on the betterment of Muslim marriage practices. The divorce rate among Indonesian Muslims was very high; indeed one of the highest in the world. According to Lev, from 1947 to 1972 the number of repudiation (*talaq*) registered each year in Indonesia run from about 50 per cent to 58 per cent of the number of registered marriages. On the contrary, the total number of reconciliation (*ruju'*) cases was approximately from 5 per cent to 10 per cent of repudiations.[27] This drew the attention of those who wanted to reform the marriage laws on the grounds that a very high rate of divorce had created social instability, work hardship on mothers and children, and was fundamentally unfair to women. These reasons were generally brought to the forefront of the society by the activists for the emancipation of women.[28]

The impetus for the reform of marriage laws came from the nationalists who struggled for a unification of Indonesian marriage laws. They argued that in sphere of national unity based upon the idea of a national unitary Republic, that the diversity of laws of the Dutch's heritage, especially concerning marriage and divorce, should be abandoned. It would be in accordance with the national aspirations if a uniform law could be regulated applicable to all citizens irrespective of their ethnic origins, religions, and social conditions. As Lev points out, after 1950 the legal system came under attack because it was considered not only as colonial, but also divisive and discriminatory in its nature.[29]

The attempt to formulate a unified national marriage law irrespective of religion, began in 1950 when the Minister of Religion formed a Governmental Committee to draft a Marriage Bill. In 1952, in response to demands from religious groups, the Committee had abandoned its original aim and, instead, to formulate drafts based on diversity of laws according to the different religious groups. In March 1954, the Committee completed its works on a draft for Muslim marriage. The draft was not discussed in the parliament until 1958, together with a counter draft submitted by the religiously neutral nationalist groups. The result was a deadlock in the parliamentary debates, and both were tabled. New attempts were made when the government submitted two Marriage Bills to parliament; in 1967 a Marriage Bill for Muslim Indonesians, and in 1968 a Marriage Bill on basic principles of marriage applicable to all religious groups. Parliamentary debates on these bills during the years of 1967–1970, however, did not produce any result.[30]

The main reason for the failure is, of course, closely related to irreconcilable interests of the conflicting groups. Muslims groups wished to preserve the *status quo* or to confine small changes to a special statute applicable just for Muslims.[31] They feared that the general statute might introduce an opening wedge of uncontrollable reform and, that it finally would weaken Islamic law over Muslim family life.[32] On the other hand, Christian group favored a more general statute which would better accord with their own marriage rules and which would minimize Islamic influence. They feared that statutory autonomy in marriage law — which they might otherwise favor — could lead to similar demands for Islamic autonomy in other areas of social, political, and economic life, which ultimately would threaten the minority interests of Christians.[33] Even the Chinese resistance to a unified marriage law was even stronger. Unification, as Lev points out, would place them on an equal footing with Indonesians, possibly even subjecting them to a certain principles of Islamic law.[34] Thus unification of marriage law posed the gravest challenge to Chinese minority social status and group cohesion.

Apart from the failure before and conflicting interests of different religious groups, the government once again submitted a new Marriage Bill to the Parliament on July 31, 1973. The new Bill however, caused one of the most controversial and most hotly debated issues and the 1970s both among the Muslims outside Parliament's building and among the members of Parliament itself. The Muslims were outraged because neither Minister of Religion nor any Muslims leader had been consulted when it was drafted. Furthermore, they felt that most of the Bill's articles in many respects were contradictory to the doctrines of *shari'a*, thus it was seemingly intended to uproot Islamic influence in the country. It is not surprising, therefore, that the atmosphere at the time was full of rumors of plots of Christianization.[35]

There were several main articles of the proposed Bill which aroused controversy. Firstly was article 2(1), which stipulated that civil registration was necessary for the validity of a Muslim marriage; secondly were Articles 3 and 40, which stipulated that Muslim seeking a divorce, and a Muslim wishing to conclude a polygamous marriage was required to apply for the necessary permission to a civil court instead of an Islamic court; thirdly was Article 11(2), which stipulated that religious differences were not an obstacle to marriage; fourthly were Articles 8(c) and 62 concerning the status of adopted children who would have the same status as natural children; and fifthly were Articles 13 and 49, which gave legal status to engagement and stipulated that if pregnancy resulted from an engagement, then the man have to marry the woman (if she wanted) — an act which by this law would give the child the same legal status as a child born in wedlock.[36]

Johns has pointed out that each of these Articles, in effect, set civil law above the revealed law of Islam in a manner perceived as blasphemous.[37] Since, according to the *shari'a* all that was necessary for a valid Muslim marriage was an *ijab qabul* — marriage contract made in accordance with the *shari'a,* between the groom and the bride's father or *wali* (guardian). It is clear that civil registration is not stipulated by the *shari'a* as a condition of valid marriage. Although for approximately the past twenty years Muslims prior to the proposed Bill have been required by the Indonesian government to register their marriages with Islamic registrars, it has never been suggested that this registration was necessary for a valid marriage. Furthermore, the Muslims feared that making civil registration for a condition for a valid marriage would be to make marriage less of a religious affair and more a matter of state administration.[38]

The requirement the applications to divorce or to conclude a polygamous marriage be made to a civil court was likewise an affront. The Muslims objected to both the substance and procedure of these provisions, especially the latter. For Muslims, to go to civil courts instead of Islamic courts in marriage matters is to make Islamic courts subservient to civil courts, and this is an offense against God. Furthermore, since the Islamic court is a symbol of Islamic authority and a guarantor of the application of the *shari'a,* then the proposed articles clearly were deemed a grave threat to Islamic power in Indonesia.[39] The Muslims felt that those proposed articles were intended to eliminate the power and function of Islamic courts, which according to the Law No. 14 of 1970 of equal rank with the civil courts.

There is no doubt that the Bill's article which proposed that religious differences were not an obstacle to marriage, had practical implications that were anathema to Islamic law and Muslims. It simply provided a means by which a Muslim woman could opt out of the constraints of Islamic law and marry a non-Muslim man. Muslims' objection to this proposed article has a long history; for decades they had objected to a similar article in the regulation on Mixed Marriages, which was promulgated by the Dutch in 1898, and which was still valid at the time of the proposed marriage law.[40] To a Muslim, allowing intermarriage simply means a rejection of the belief that Islam is a way of life, and a legal permission to Christianize or to convert Muslim woman to other religions. Furthermore, children of such a mixed marriage most likely would be non-Muslims.[41] For this reason, some Muslim leaders criticized the proposed Bill in general as "Veiled Christianization".

Two other proposed articles concerning the status of adopted children gave rise to controversy. The articles proposed a prohibition of marriage between an adopted child and his or her adoptive parents or their children, and stipulated that an adopted child has the same status as natural child, and that an adoption severed the relationship between an adopted child and his or her natural parents. Muslims' objection to these articles was that according to the *shari'a*, adoption is not a legal matter and does not sever the relationship between a child and his natural parents.[42] Furthermore, the *shari'a* provides that the blood relationship is the basis of the laws in regulating inheritance and guardianship and supervision of a child; adoption may not alter these laws.[43] The Muslims also strongly objected to Articles 13 and 49 which gave legal status to engagement and a child born in wedlock as a result of that engagement. The Muslims opposed these proposed articles since Islam does not recognize the status of engagement. They also believed that to legitimize a child resulting from an engagement would be to legitimize sexual relations outside of marriage.[44]

It is not appropriate to describe in detailed manner the debates in the parliament and the demonstrations by the Muslims outside the Parliament Building. What is important was that after the seizure of the floor of the parliament by the angry Muslim demonstrators, the government finally agreed to accept radical change in the Bill. President Soeharto lastly conceded to the Muslim United Development Faction (FPP) in the parliament that all Articles contrary to Islamic law would be deleted.[45] Finally, the revised Bill was passed by the parliament on December 22, 1973, and was signed by President Soeharto on January 2, 1974, and become Indonesian Marriage Law No. 1 of 1974. Following the promulgation of this new marriage law, its Implementing Regulation was enacted on April 1, 1975 by Government Regulation No. 9 of 1975, and was enforced on October 1, 1975. This Implementing Regulation is mainly concerned with the procedures of marriage, divorce, and the like, and other technical matters.

By and large, the new Marriage Law incorporated almost all demands of the Islamic groups. Anything that had been deemed contrary to Islamic law in the original Bill was changed, taken out, or left subject to Implementing Regulation. For instance, in the new Law civil registration is no longer necessary for the validity of a Muslim marriage.[46] The prohibition against marriage between adoptees and their adoptive parents or sibling is not mentioned at all,[47] or is taken out from the original Bill. Former Articles such as 11(2) and 62 concerning the propriety of inter-religious marriage and the legal status of adopted children were also deleted from the new Law. Likewise, the former Article 13 on the legal status of engagement was taken out and the former Article 49 on the status of a child born outside the wedlock was left subject to future government regulation.[48] The former Articles 3 and 40, which required a Muslim to get permission from a civil court before he may marry more than one wife and before Muslim man or woman may divorce his or her spouse also were changed. Instead of getting permission from a civil court, in the new Law those who want to do the above acts must get permission only from Islamic courts.[49] To sum up, there is no longer any question in the new Law of Islamic law requiring ratification of civil law. The regulation of marriage, polygamy, forced marriage,[50] and divorce now is fully in the hands of Islamic courts. The possibility of Muslim woman marrying a non-Muslim man has also been removed.

With regard to all the above-mentioned amendments to the original Bill, it is not surprising that Muslims in general are satisfied with the new Law. Johns is of the opinion that from several standpoints the new Law represents a milestone in the history of Islam in Indonesian public life.[51] For the first time in Indonesia a substantive marriage law for Muslims has been codified by the state,[52] while the Westerners, Chinese, and Christian groups have had their own codified substantive marriage laws.[53] The codification of Muslim marriage law to an appreciable extent in the new Indonesian marriage law, according to Johns, is law better able to ensure consistency in Islamic courts' decisions than simply "the teaching of the Prophet and the learned scholars of early Islam". Not only this, but to the degree that Islamic law is embodied in this marriage law, it is now part of the positive law of Indonesia.[54] Therefore, it undoubtedly enhances and formalizes the public position of Islamic law in Indonesia. Consequently, the position of Islamic court also becomes more powerful by requiring that its decisions be given confirmation — ministerial rather than discretionary act — by the state (civil) court.

A lengthy discussion would be needed to analyse all body of the new Indonesian Marriage Law with regard to the view of the *shari'a*. Aside from the major issues that have been amended in order to be in line with the *shari'a*, we would describe briefly the general content of the new law which hopefully would give us a clearer picture of it. Therefore we can gain a more complete and more comprehensive idea of the so called-"codification of Muslim marriage law" Indonesian style.[55]

1. Concept of Marriage

Marriage is relationship of body and soul between a man and woman as husband and wife with the purpose of establishing a happy and lasting family (household) founded on the belief in God Almighty.[56] Marriage is legitimate, if it is has been performed according to the respective religions and beliefs of the parties concerned.[57] Marriage in principle is monogamy. However, at the request of the husband and his wife consents, a court under certain circumstances may authorize polygamy.[58] Polygamy is only allowed when wife has a physical disability disease, or is unfertile or unable to fulfill her sexual duties to such extent that the marriage is threatened. In polygamous situations, the husband must guarantee the necessities of live for his wives and their children and promised fair treatment of them.[59]

2. Procedures

Matters with regard to registration and suit of marriages, divorces and reconciliations are carried out and decided by Islamic courts (*Pengadilan Agama*) for Muslims and civil courts for all others.[60]

3. Legal Capacity

Both the husband and the wife have the capacity to take legal action.[61]

4. Prerequisites for Marriage

In order to enter matrimony, a person who has not attained the age of 21 years should obtain the consent of both the aspirant bride and the aspirant bridegroom unless their religious law does not state otherwise.[62] The minimum marital age is 19 years for a male aspirant and 16 years for a female aspirant.[63]

5. Impediment to Marriage

No marriage is allowed between two persons who have either an ascending or descending line of blood relationship; relationship by marriage; foster relationship; and sibling relationship.[64]

6. Prevention of Marriage

A marriage may be prevented in the case of any party who is not satisfied with the prerequisites for the performance of the marriage. Those who may prevent a marriage is the family members in a straight line of either ascendancy or descendancy, siblings, marriage guardian supporter of either the aspirant bride or aspirant bridegroom and any interested parties.[65]

7. Marriage Contract and Ceremony

The marriage contract will not be legalized if it is in violation of legal, religious and moral limits.[66] The marriage ceremony is performed according to the respective religion before the registrars and the presence the witnesses.[67]

8. Rights During Marriage

The rights and obligations of the wife are equivalent to those of the husband with regard to both the marital relationship and the couple's relationship to society.[68] The husband, however, is obligated to support his wife to the best of his abilities, while the wife is obligated to maintain the household. Thus, the husband is the head of the household and the wife is the homemaker.[69]

9. Property

Goods acquired during marriage become joint property. Unless otherwise agreed by the spouses, property brought into the marriage by either husband or wife, or acquired by gift or inheritance, remain under ownership of the respective party.[70] In the case of divorce, the joint property will be dealt according to the laws of their respective religion, customary law and other law.[71]

10. Parental Rights and Duties

Both parents are responsible for the care and education of their children but the father has the primary responsibility for meeting these expenses. A father's financial obligation to his child (children) continues even after divorce.[72] Children are required to respect their parents and to obey their just wishes. When the children reach their maturity, the responsibility of care is reversed and children are obligated to care for their parents.[73]

11. Guardianship

A child who has less than 18 years of age and has never married is under parental authority, except where the parents are discharged from such an authority. The parents are not allowed to transfer a right or to mortgage property possessed by a child under the authority.[74] In case there are no parents, the child is placed under guardianship. Such guardianship applies both to the person and property of the child.[75]

12. Divorce, Separation and Alimony

Divorce is obtainable from the court upon sufficient proof. The grounds for divorce are the same for either party.[76] Adultery or other vices; abandonment, imprisonment for a substantial period; abuse and cruelty; disease or disabilities which prevent the fulfillment of marital duties; and general incompatibility.[77] Divorce will only be granted after the court has attended to achieve a reconciliation to no avail.[78] In the event of such a reconciliation, a second suit for divorce may not be based on the same grounds as the first.[79]

The law provides for separation pending the outcome of the divorce suit. The court has the power in the divorce proceedings to determine alimony, to decide property rights, and to take measures to safeguard and maintain the children's education and the property in dispute.[80]

13. Waiting Period

There is waiting period for a woman whose marriage has been dissolved.[81] The waiting period for the marriage terminated due to death is 130 days; due to divorce is three times of menses with minimum 90 days — and for those who have stopped menstruating is also 90 days. If the marriage has been dissolved while the woman is pregnant, the waiting period is until childbirth.[82]

14. "Common Law" Mixed Marriage

There is no common law regulated by this law. A valid marriage must satisfy the religious law of the spouses.[83] Mixed marriage is understood as a marriage between two persons in Indonesia subject to different laws because of difference in citizenship, and one of the parties is a foreign citizen while the other is an Indonesian citizen.[84]

THE SOCIAL IMPACT OF THE NEW MARRIAGE LAW

When the Law No. 1 of 1974 was promulgated on January 2, 1974, and implemented on October 1, 1975 many Indonesian legal experts were sceptical about its impact on accelerating social changes in Indonesia. They considered the new Law as lacking in clarity which they viewed as a crucial obstacle in implementing it successfully. Even some of them predicted that such a law would fail in changing marriage practices among the population.[85] Their scepticism mainly have to do with the controversy prior to the promulgation of the law. And when the revised Bill was passed by the parliament, it was the turn of the Christians to feel uneasy about it. As Katz and Katz point out, particularly disturbing to them was what they discerned to be a tendency in the new Law for the state not only to allow but to require the application of religious laws, at least in marriage. This they felt was antithetical to true religious freedom; instead they would have liked the law to offer the possibility of a marriage according to secular law.[86]

The scepticism and gloomy prediction above, however, are far from the real development after the new Law has been enforced for some time. Katz and Katz, who revisited Indonesia almost two years after the implementation of the new Law, conclude that it has succeeded in dramatically affecting Indonesian society.[87]

The success of the new Law, of course, means achievement of most of the goals which are stated in the promulgation and implementation of the Law. These goals include the creation of stable families, the control of population growth, the control of divorce and polygamy, the equalization of the rights and status of women; and last but not least, the unification of the nation through unification of the Law. Following we would describe briefly several impacts of the new Law:

1. Divorce

The more strict regulations and more difficult procedures provided by the new Law have caused striking decrease of divorce rate. According to figures kept by Ministry of Religion, there is an overall decrease of approximately 70 per cent in the Muslim divorce rate.[88] The most recent figures of divorce rate in several provinces also show the same tendency. In West Java province, for instance, in 1955 the divorce rate was 58 per cent of the registered marriages, but in 1985 the figure was 16.53 per cent and 1986 was 14.05 per cent.[89] In the special territory of the Capital Jakarta, the divorce rate between 1954–1975 was approximately 26 per cent, but in 1985 rate became 11 per cent. The decrease of divorce rate is also found in the Special Territory of Aceh in the northwestern tip of Sumatra. The divorce rates in Aceh were 22.37 per cent (1974), 17.53 per cent (1975), 6.68 per cent (1976), 7.64 per cent (1985) 7.15 per cent (1986).[90] It is also interesting to note that divorces initiated by Muslim women increased steadily. For example, take the figures kept by Islamic court of South Jakarta. There was no divorce suit initiated by Muslim women in the period between 1968–1976. But there were 58 cases in 1977, 79 (1978), 118 (1979), 103 (1980), 103 (1981), 90 (1982), 126 (1983), 108 (1984), 120 (1985) and 169 cases in 1986.[91] These very facts reflect the rise of new awareness among Muslim women to take legal actions if their husbands do not meet their duties in their marriages.

2. Polygamy

It clearly becomes much more difficult for a Muslim man to practise polygamous marriage after the implementation of the law No. 1 of 1974. Especially for Muslims who are the government employees, the chance to have more than one wife is even far more difficult. This is because the implementation of the Government Regulation No. 10 of 1983, which provides that if a government employee wants to have another wife, he has to get permission from his superior,[92] in addition to permission from the court of laws as provided by the new Marriage Law.

Actually, before the implementation of the new Law, the practice of polygamy was not very widespread, accounting only 5 per cent of all marriages.[93] Though there is no recent figure of polygamous marriage, with regard to the strictness of the law concerning polygamy, it is safe to assume that the practice becomes very rare nowadays. The rarity of polygamous marriage has certain share in establishing familial and economic stability and in slowing down population growth.

3. Minimum Age of Marriage

The new Marriage Law provides that the minimum marital age is 19 and 16 for a man and a woman respectively. There must be a special permission from a court if the person who wants to get married have not yet attained that minimum marital age. Based on their survey, Katz and Katz report that the Law has raised the marriage among the population.[94] In addition to the minimum age of marriage as stipulated by the new Law has influenced the attitudes toward minor marriages, it is important to note the other factors also contribute to the tendency of young people to get married a bit later. The factors such as the rising standard of education, the widespread campaign of family planning, the tightening economic burden, and other reasons also give rise to the delay of marriages among young people in particular.

In addition to the impacts mentioned above, the new Law has contributed to the rise of new awareness of the society as a whole toward the rule of law. Since the new Law regulates very important aspect of the life of the people, it is true that it has attracted their very concern with the law. For the government's part, the new Law is also a big step toward the improvement of the system of law as a whole. By promulgating and implementing this new Law, the government has to improve, for instance, the infrastructure needed to carry it out. The Islamic courts, which are responsible for serving the bulk of the population have to be strengthened, after long being the objects of much criticism. For that purpose, the government has allocated much more money to improve the facility and the number of the Islamic courts as well as the quality of Islamic judges and other court employees. These all increase the stature of Islamic courts in particular, and the rule of law in general in the eyes of the population.

CONCLUSION

Islam in Indonesia has its own characteristics which are relatively different than those of the Middle East, given the diversity of ethnic groups cultures and social systems in the archipelago. Islam to certain degrees has to soften and adapt itself to local situations. For centuries, indigenous beliefs and practices (*adat*) blended into Islamic tenets. The history of Islam in Indonesia, therefore, is a history of continual struggle for the Islamization of Indonesian society, which gave rise to tensions and conflicts both among the Muslims and the Indonesian population. The conflict during the submission of the marriage Bill described above should be understood in that framework.

Despite its huge Muslim population, Indonesia is not an Islamic state since Islam is not formally declared as the state religion.[95] However, in legislating law in implementing its policies, the government has to take Islamic teachings and Muslims' opinion into crucial consideration; acting otherwise the government will face a strong opposition from the vast majority of its population, which in turn will bring its legislations and policies into a total failure. The success story of the new Marriage Law is closely related to the fact that the Bill had been amended almost completely in order to be in line with the doctrines of the *shari'a*. After the insistence of all parties concerned particularly the *ulama* and other Muslim prominent leaders that no substantive change has occurred in Muslim marriage law, the Muslim population in general does not hesitate to follow the provisions of the new Law. Therefore, the new Law, finally receive strong support from all levels of the society, which in turn, brings far-reaching social changes in the country.

Notes

1. *The World Almanac and Book of Facts 1986* (New York: Newspaper Enterprise Association Inc., 1985), p. 596. See also the Table of the people of Islam 1986, which is published by the American Institute for Islamic Affairs, Washington, 1986. In the current time, Indonesian population is estimated more than 210 million people, while Muslims are still the largest part; no less than 80 per cent.
2. Thomas W. Arnold, *The Preaching of Islam*, Reprinted ed. (Lahore: Ashraf, 1961), p. 363. For more discussion concerning the coming and the spread of Islam in the Archipelago, see, for example; Sayyid Muhammad Naguib Al-Attas, *Preliminary Statement on A General Theory of the Islamization of the Malay-Indonesian Archipelago* (Kuala Lumpur: Dewan Bahasa & Pustaka, 1970); N. A. Baloch, *Advent of Islam in Indonesia* (Islamabad: National Institute of Historical and Cultural Research, 1980); H. J. De Graaf, "Southeast Asian

Islam to the Eighteenth Century", in P. M. Holt et. al. (eds.), *The Cambridge History of Islam* (London: Cambridge University Press, 1987), pp. 123–54, etc.

3. H. A. R. Gibb, *Modern Trends in Islam* (Chicago: University of Chicago Press, 1945), p. 25. Further accounts on the role of Sufism and *sufis/ulama* in the spread and development of Islam in Southeast Asia as a whole, see my "The Transmission of Islamic Reformism to Indonesia; Networks of Malay-Indonesian Ulama in the 17th and 18th centuries," PhD dissertation, Columbia University, 1992.

4. B. Ter Haar, *Adat Law in Indonesia*, translated from the Dutch and edited with an Introduction by E. Adamson Hoebel and A. Arthur Schiller (New York: Institute of Pacific Relation, 1948), p. 163. This is an excellent treatment of *adat* laws with their many aspects during the Dutch colonial period. On the conflicts and accommodation of the *shari'a* and *adat*, see, M. B. Hooker, *Islamic Law in South-East Asia* (Oxford: Oxford University Press, 1984).

5. On marriage according to *adat* laws with its aspects such as the preliminary steps to marriage, marital forms, child (minor) marriage, polygamy, divorce, marital property, etc., see, Ter Haar, ibid., p. 164–94.

6. Harun Nasution and Ahmad Khatib, "The Positions of *Adat* Law, Shari'a and Secular Law in Indonesia", *Studies in Islam*, 11 No. 1–2, New Delhi, 1974, pp. 62–67. See also, M. B. Hooker, "The State and *Syariah* in Indonesia 1945–1995" in Timothy Lindsey (ed.), *Indonesia: Law and Society* (Sydney: The Federation Press, 1999), pp. 97–110.

7. Ibid., p. 63.

8. On the examples of the degrees of *adat* adoption of Islamic Law, see Ter Haar, pp. 177–79 and pp. 182–83; Hooker, "The State and *Syariah*", pp. 98–99.

9. See, Hazairin, *Hukum Kekeluargaan Nasional* [National Family Laws] (Jakarta: Tintamas, 1962), and *Pergolakan Penyesuaian Adat kepada Islam* [the Struggle of *Adat* Adoption of Islam] (Jakarta: Bulan Bintang, 1952).

10. See, H. Waster, *Custom and Muslim Law in the Nederlands East Indies* (London: Transaction of the Grotius Society, 25, 1940), p. 51 ff.

11. On the development of the Dutch law policy, see Supomo, *Sistem Hukum di Indonesia Sebelum Perang II* [Law Systems in Indonesia before World War II] (Jakarta: Noodhoff — Kolff, 1953); Subekti, *Law in Indonesia* (Jakarta: Gunung Agung, 1973), pp. 9–15.

12. Subekti, ibid., p. 15.

13. Ibid., pp. 12–13. On the complete Civil Code concerning marriage, see Ali Affandi, *Hukum Keluarga Menurut Kitab Undang-undang Hukum Perdata* [Family Law According to Burgerlijk Wetboek] (Yogyakarta: Jajasan Badan Penerbit Gadjah Mada, 1964).

14. Subekti, p. 11.

15. Ibid., p. 16.

16. For a brief but excellent treatment of the regulations and practices of Islamic marriage law before the promulgation of the marriage law of 1974, see, Ahmad bin Mohd. Ibrahim, "The Administration of Muslim Law in Indonesia", *Islamic Culture*, Vol. XLIII No. 2, Hyderabad, The Islamic Culture Board, April 1969, pp. 113–24.

17. Sir Stamford Raffles, the British Governor General in Indonesia (1811–1816), referred to these Islamic court as *"the court of penghulus"*. See Mohd Ibrahim, "The Administration", p. 110.

18. On this issue, for example, see, Notosutanto, *Organisasi dan Jurisrudensi Peradilan Agama di Indonesia* [Organization and Jurisprudence of Religious Courts in Indonesia] (Yogjakarta: Jajasan Badan Penerbit Gadjah Mada, 1963); Daniel S. Lev, *Islamic Courts*

in Indonesia (Berkeley: University of California Press, 1972). Both books, of course, do not include the accounts about the growing position of the Islamic courts after the implementation of the marriage law of 1974.

19. For more information on the weakness of Islamic courts in particular and the Dutch colonial policies on administering Islam in general, see; H. Aqib Suminto, *Politik Islam Hindia Belanda* [Dutch Indies Islamic Politics] (Jakarta: LP3ES, 1985); W. J. A. Kernkamp, "Government and Islam in the Netherland Indies", translated by N. A. C. Slotemaker de Bruine, *The Muslim World*, Vol. 35, Hartford, 1945, pp. 6–26, esp. pp. 19–22 on the condition of Islamic courts and the Dutch's efforts to interfere Muslim marriage affairs.

20. The complete provisions of this law is given in Koesnodiprodjo, *Himpunan Undang-undang, Peraturan-peraturan, Penetapan-penatapan Pemerintah Republik Indonesia 1946* [Compilation of Laws, Regulations and Decrees of the Government of the Republic of Indonesia, 1946) (Jakarta: Seno, 1947), pp. 73–78.

21. The Dutch colonial administration had also to push through similar requirement in 1937, as a part of a broader effort to reform Islamic marriage rules, but on the whole plan was rejected by Islamic leadership as unwarranted intrusion into Islamic affairs. See, Lev, *Islamic Court*, p. 57.

22. Lev, *Islamic Courts*, p. 55.

23. June S. Katz & Ronald S. Katz, "The New Indonesian Marriage Law; A Mirror of Indonesia's Political, Cultural and Legal System", *The American Journal of Comparative Law*, 23, 1975, p. 658; Ali Afandi, *Hukum Keluarga,* p. 10.

24. Wirjono Prodjodikoro, *Hukum Perkawinan di Indonesia* [Marriage Law in Indonesia] (Bandung: Penerbit Sumur Bandung, 1971).

25. Many Muslims especially in Java regarded that the *taklik talak* (*ta'liq al-talaq*) originated from a regulation of a King of Mataram of Central Java in the seventeenth century. Whether this notion is right or not, it is clear that similar provision can be found in the Hanbali School of law regarding conditions in marriage. The doctrinal basis of nearly all *taklik talak* decisions in Indonesia is a maxim from the sixteenth century commentary *al-Tahrir* by Zakaria al-Ansary, edited by al-Sharqawi (d. 1812). Whoever makes his *talaq* dependent upon an action, then the *talaq* occurs with the existence of that action according to the original pronouncement". On this issue, see for example, Mohd. Ibrahim, p. 115; Notosusanto, pp. 90–92; Lev, *Islamic Courts*. p. 163; and Joseph Schacht, "Talaq" in *The Encyclopedia of Islam*, Vol. I Part 2, E. J. Brill, Leiden, p. 639.

26. The official form of the *taklik talak* formulated by the Ministry of religion is as follows:

Having signed the marriage contract (*akad nikah*), I ＿＿＿ bin ＿＿＿ promises sincerely that I will fulfill my obligations as a husband and will live amicably with my wife, name ＿＿＿＿ binti ＿＿＿＿ according to the teachings of the law of Islam.

Furthermore I hereby pronounce the *taklik* formula (*sighat taklik*) with regard to my life as follows:
If ever I;

1. Leave my wife for six months consecutively, unless I am performing a state responsibility,
2. Or I do not give her obligatory support (*nafkah*) for three months,

3. Or I maltreats my wife physically,

4. Or I neglect my wife for six month consecutively,

Then, should I violate anyone of these promises, and my wife refuses to acquiesce and so charges before the *Pengadilan Agama* (Islamic courts) or similar court or other agency competent to deal with this accusation, and the accusation is upheld and accepted by the court to other instance, and my wife pays 1,000 *rupiah* as an *iwad* (compensation), my first *talak* falls upon my wife. To the court and or instance mentioned above which examines and decides upon the accusation of my wife, I give authority to accept the *iwad* money and to contribute it for charitable purposes.

This English translation is provided by Lev, *Islamic Courts*, pp. 163–64 from the Indonesian original form in Sidik Sudarsono, *Masalah Administratif dalam Perkawinan Ummat Islam Indonesia* [Administrative Matters in Indonesian Islamic Marriage] (Jakarta: Fa.Dara, 1965), p. 236. A slightly different English translation is in Mohd. Ibrahim, "Administration", p. 115.

27. Lev, *Islamic Courts*, pp. 140–41; Cora Vrede-de Stuers in *The Indonesian Woman; Struggles and Achievements* (The Hague: Mouton, 1960), p. 131 notes that 1956 divorces in Egypt numbered 26 per cent of marriages, in Algeria 15 per cent, in Iraq 10 per cent, in Iran 18 per cent, in Syria 8 per cent, and Indonesia 52 per cent. These divorce rates among Muslim countries are quoted by Elizabeth H. White, "Legal Reform as an Indicator of Women's Status in Muslim Nations", in Lois Beck and Nikki Keddie (eds.), *Women in the Muslim World* (Cambridge, Mass.: Harvard University Press, 1980), p. 58; Nani Soewondo suggests in *Seminar on Law and Population* (Jakarta: National Training and Research Center Indonesian Planned Parenthood Association, 1974), p. 74, that the divorce rate in Indonesia was 50 per cent from 1960 to 1968 and 30 per cent from 1969 to 1970.

28. For accounts on the woman movements concerning the efforts to reform of marriage laws, see Vrede-de Stuers, *The Indonesian Woman,* esp. pp. 120–140; Nani Soewondo, *Kedudukan Wanita dalam Hukum dan Masyarakat* [The Position of Women in Law and Society], 2nd Edition (Jakarta: Timun Mas, 1968), esp. pp. 175–88.

29. Daniel S. Lev, "The Lady and the Banyan Tree", *The American Journal of Comparative Law*, Vol. 14, 1965–66, p. 285.

30. The information of these attempts are based on Deliar Noer, *Administration of Islam in Indonesia,* (Ithaca, NY: Cornell Modern Indonesia Project, 1978), pp. 51–52; and *The Indonesian Marriage Law,* 2nd print (Department of Information of the Republic of Indonesia, 1976), pp. 5–7.

31. Katz & Katz, "Indonesian Marriage Law", p. 657.

32. Lev, *Islamic Courts*, p. 140.

33. Ibid., pp. 139–40.

34. Lev, "The Lady", pp. 287–89 and see note 13 and text accompanying it on p. 6.

35. Katz & Katz, "Indonesian Marriage Law", p. 660; Anthony H. Johns, "Indonesia; Islam and Cultural Pluralism", in John L. Esposito (ed.), *Islam in Asia; Religion, Politics and Society* (New York: Oxford University Press, 1987), pp. 217–18.

36. Proposed Marriage Law of 1973, articles 2(1); 3; 40; 11(2); 8(c), 62; 13; 49 respectively for the five central issues; see, Katz & Katz, "Indonesian Marriage Law", pp. 661–62.

37. Johns, "Indonesia", p. 218.

38. Katz & Katz, "Indonesia Marriage Law", p. 661.

39. Ibid.

40. Regeling op de Gemengde Huwelijken (the Ordinance on Mixed Marriages) published in *Staatsblad* (State Gazette) 1898, No. 158, Art. 7(2). The same provision can also be found in Huwelijks-Ordonantie voor Christen-Indonesiers (the Marriage Ordinance for Christian Indonesians) published in *Staatsblad* 1933 No. 74. The last articles of this Ordinance deal with the questions of differences of religious and conversions in marriages. See, Notosusanto, *Organisasi*, pp. 31–32; Subekti, *Law in Indonesia*, p. 13.

41. HM. Rasjidi, *Kasus RUU Perkawinan dalam Hubungan Islam-Kristen* [The Case of the Proposed Marriage Bill in Islamic and Christian Relations] (Jakarta: Bulan Bintang, 1974), p. 12, quoted in Katz & Katz, "Indonesian Marriage Law", p. 662. Rasjidi, a prominent Muslim professor and former Minister of Religion, strongly criticizes the proposed Bill in general as "veiled Christianization".

42. Katz & Katz, "Indonesian Marriage Law", p. 662; Soewondo, *Kedudukan Wanita*, p. 60.

43. Katz & Katz, "Indonesian Marriage Law", p. 662, see also debates among the Dutch and Indonesian legal experts on this issue in Lev, *Islamic Courts*, pp. 20–21.

44. Katz & Katz, "Indonesian Marriage Law", p. 662.

45. A detail account regarding the Muslim pressures and the reversal of the government stand, see Katz & Katz, ibid., pp. 663–66.

46. Law, No. 1, 1974, Art. 2.

47. Ibid., Art. 8; and see also the clarification of law No. 1, 1974, Art. 8.

48. Law, No. 1, 1974, Art. 43(2).

49. Ibid., Art. 4 and 63.

50. Ibid., Art. 14, 45, 46, 47, and 50.

51. Johns, *Indonesia*, p. 219.

52. Ibid., Katz & Katz, "Indonesian Marriage Law", p. 669.

53. See notes 12, 13, 14, 15, 16 and the text accompanying them.

54. Johns, *Indonesia*, p. 219; this very fact is also confirmed by the Indonesian legal scholars, see for example a reader on aspects of Law No. 1 of 1974 entitled *Perkawinan dan Hukum Perkawinan* [Marriage and Marriage Law] (Surabaya: Fakultas Hukum Universitas Airlangga, 1976), esp. parts III (pp. 47–50), IV (57–70), V (71–86), and VI (87–102).

55. The following description is based on The *Indonesian Marriage Law* (see, note 30). This publication contains; 1. Introduction, 2. Law of the Republic of Indonesia No. 1 of Year 1974 on Marriage. 3. Clarification on the Law on Marriage of the Republic of Indonesia No. 9 of 1974. 4. Government Regulation of the Republic of Indonesia No. 9 of 1975 concerning Implementation of Law No. 1 of 1974 on Marriage. 5. Clarification on the Government Regulation of the Republic of Indonesia No. 9 of 1975 concerning the Implementation of Law No. 1 of 1974 on Marriage.

56. Law No. 1, 1974 Art. 1

57. Ibid., Art. 2.

58. Ibid., Art. 2.

59. Ibid., Art. 3–5; Implementing Regulation No. 9, 1975, Art. 40–44.

60. Law No. 1, 1974, Art. 63.

61. Ibid., Art. 31

62. Ibid., Art. 6

63. Ibid., Art. 7

64. Ibid., Art. 8
65. Ibid., Art. 13, 14.
66. Ibid., Art. 29(2).
67. Implementation Regulation No. 9, 1975, Art. 10.
68. Law No. 1, 1974, Art. 31.
69. Ibid., Art. 34, 31.
70. Ibid., Art. 35–36.
71. Ibid., Art. 37, and Clarification of the Law No. 1, 1974, Art. 37.
72. Law No. 1. 1974, Art. 45, 41.
73. Ibid., Art. 46.
74. Ibid., Art. 47, 48.
75. Ibid., Art. 50.
76. Ibid., Art. 38, 39, 40 and Implementing Regulation No. 9, 1975, Art. 14, 15, 16, and 17.
77. Implementing Regulation No. 9, 1975, Art. 19.
78. Law No. 1, 1974, Art. 39; Implementing Regulation No. 9, 1975, Art. 31.
79. Implementing Regulation No. 9, 1975, Art. 32.
80. Ibid., Art. 24.
81. Law No. 1, 1974, Art. 11.
82. Implementing Regulation No. 9, 1975, Art. 39.
83. Law No. 1, 1974, Art. 2.
84. Ibid., Art. 57.
85. Katz & Katz, "Indonesian Marriage Law", p. 680.
86. Ibid., p. 665.
87. June S. Katz & Ronald S. Katz, "Legislating Social Change in a Development Country; The New Indonesian Marriage Law Revisited", *The American Journal of Comparative Law*, Vol. 26, 1978, p. 309.
88. Ibid., p. 310.
89. "Perceraian Paska UU Perkawinan" [Divorce after the New Marriage Law]", *Panji Masyarakat* [The Banner of Islam; an Islamic Magazine], No. 532, March 1, 1987, p. 17.
90. Ibid.
91. Ibid., p. 23
92. Ibid., p. 20.
93. Nani Soewondo, "Seminar on Law", p. 34.
94. Katz & Katz, "Legislating Social Change", p. 313.
95. Constitutionally, Indonesia is a national unitary Republic with sovereignty vested in the people. The political system of the Indonesian government is democracy based on the 1945 Constitution and the *Pancasila* (the Five Principles), the philosophical basis of the state, with consists of five inseparable and mutually qualifying principles: (1) Belief in the One Supreme God, (2) A just and civilized humanity, (3) Unity of Indonesia, (4) Democracy led by the wisdom of unanimity arising from deliberations among the representatives of the people, and (5) Social justice for the whole of the people of Indonesia. These five basic principles are embodied in the Preamble to the 1945 Constitution. For a short information, see for example; *Indonesia 1978; An Official Handbook* (Jakarta: Department of Information of the Republic of Indonesia, 1979), pp. 59–67.

6

INDONESIA'S 1989 RELIGIOUS JUDICATURE ACT
Islamization of Indonesia or Indonesianization of Islam?

Mark Cammack[1]

I. INTRODUCTION

In 1989 the Indonesian legislature passed and President Suharto signed a new law governing the country's Islamic courts. The statute, known as the Religious Judicature Act[2] (the Act), significantly enhanced the legal and institutional standing of the Islamic courts by providing formal legal guarantees of their security and increasing the level of state support. The Act also expanded and equalized the courts' powers. Prior to the passage of the Act the substantive competence of Islamic courts on the populous islands of Java and Madura extended only to matters of marriage and divorce. The 1989 Act expanded the Islamic courts' jurisdiction to include inheritance throughout the country. The Act also strengthened the standing of the Islamic courts in relation to the civil courts by eliminating a rule dating from the nineteenth century which had required that decisions of Islamic courts must be ratified by a civil court to be enforceable.

Previously published as "Indonesia's 1989 Religious Judicature Act: Islamization of Indonesia or Indonesianization of Islam?", *Indonesia* 63 (April 1997): 143–68. Reproduced with permission of the author and the publisher, SEAP Publications, Cornell University.

The enactment of the Religious Judicature Act seemed to signal a reversal in New Order policy on the role of religion in public life and the enforcement of Islamic Law. Although Islamic interests provided critical support in President Suharto's rise to power in the mid-1960s, the regime's actions over the ensuing two decades did not support Islamic involvement in the exercise of state power. Once in control, the New Order set about systematically to neutralize Islam as a basis for political and legal mobilization. Most observers in the 1970s would have found it unthinkable that in the 1990s the Suharto government would be actively promoting state enforcement of Islamic doctrine.

This article seeks to place these recent developments in Islamic law in a broader context, and qualifies the initial assessment of their importance. Though significant, the Religious Judicature Act does not mark the dramatic shift in policy that at first blush it seems to indicate. Rather, it is to a large extent the culmination of events set in motion twenty years earlier. Moreover, while the Suharto government is clearly presenting a more Islamic demeanor, it has not abandoned its historic policy of controlling Islamic law and politics.

The next section of the article provides a brief historical introduction to the Islamic courts in Indonesia as background to more recent developments. In Part III I survey the key provisions of the 1989 Act and point out changes it makes to prior law. Part IV looks more closely at one specific issue treated in the Act — divorces initiated by men — to illustrate my thesis that recent events are largely continuous with policies established a quarter century earlier.

II. HISTORICAL BACKGROUND TO THE 1989 ACT

Islamic judicial institutions have operated in island Southeast Asia for centuries,[3] but the lineage of the present Indonesian Islamic courts is commonly traced to a Dutch Royal Decree of 1882. That Decree formally chartered a system of Islamic tribunals called "Priests' Councils" (*priesterraden*) to operate alongside the existing ordinary courts in Java and Madura.[4] The courts were to consist of the *penghulu* — the chief religious official of the district — and from three to eight members, with a minimum of three required to constitute a quorum.[5] The collegial character of the courts was a Dutch innovation, apparently based on a misunderstanding of contemporary practice in which the *penghulu*, not well versed in the law, took advice from others who were more learned.[6] Although the *penghulu* received a small civil service salary in his capacity as religious advisor to the civil court, the member judges were not civil servants and received no government compensation. Instead, they served on a per session basis and were compensated out of fees paid directly by litigants and a share of the estate in inheritance cases, which was also a principal source of emolument for the chairmen.[7] Under an earlier regulation issued in the 1830s, Islamic court decisions had to be ratified by a civil court to be enforceable.[8]

The next significant intervention in the administration of Islamic law occurred in the 1930s. A series of regulations in 1937 called for a number of changes to the courts in Java and Madura, which were renamed "Penghulu Courts" (*penghulu-gerecht*), and established new tribunals, called "Kerapatan Qadi," in South Kalimantan.[9] The regulations provided for the payment of salaries to the court chairmen and the addition of a salaried clerk. These reforms, which were not actually implemented for nearly a decade,[10] were intended to promote the independence of the courts by reducing or eliminating their dependence on exactions from litigants, and to make them more modern and efficient. The regulations also provided for the formation of Islamic appeals courts, a change that had been recommended by C. Snouck Hurgronje, the renown Islamicist and colonial advisor on native affairs, as a means of promoting more informed and uniform decision making.[11] This aspect of the law was implemented with the formation of the Kerapatan Qadi Besar in Banjarmasin to serve the new courts in Kalimantan and the Mahkamah Islam Tinggi for Java and Madura.[12]

The most significant change made in 1937 related to the jurisdiction of the courts. The law transferred authority over inheritance from Islamic to civil tribunals.[13] This left the Islamic courts with jurisdiction over marriage and divorce only. The same limitation was also applied to the new courts in South Kalimantan. The elimination of Islamic inheritance jurisdiction reflected the views of the so-called *adat* law school, a group of Dutch scholars and their Indonesian students who favored neither Islamic nor Dutch legal institutions but the customary rules (*adat*) of the archipelago's numerous ethnic groups.[14] The priority given to *adat* over Islam found legal expression in the so-called reception theory, which holds that Islamic rules have the force of law only insofar as they have been received into the local *adat*.[15] Apart from the doctrine's practical significance in restricting the applicability of Islamic law, *shariah* oriented Indonesians have, since its inception, considered the reception theory especially pernicious because of its denial of any independent standing for Islamic law.[16]

In preferring *adat* over Islam, the Dutch scholars of Indonesian custom and their Indonesian students were, in an important respect, simply aligning themselves on one side of a conflict that was both deeper and more enduring than the narrow legal question of whether Islamic or customary rules would govern inheritance questions.[17] Conceived most broadly, *adat* and Islam represent more than simply alternative sets of legal rules: they represent competing bases of social authority. From this broader and symbolically weightier perspective, the loss of jurisdiction over inheritance, which is everywhere regarded as a core religious concern for Muslims, represented a victory for anti-Islamic forces and a serious setback in the historic advance of Islam in the archipelago.[18]

An effort was also launched in 1937 to reform the substantive law of marriage, although the initiative failed.[19] For several decades, Indonesian women's groups had been agitating for legislation limiting or prohibiting polygamy and curbing the Muslim husband's power of unilateral repudiation.[20] The colonial government's proposal would have established a registration procedure whereby a woman whose marriage had been registered gained legal protection against unilateral divorce and polygamy. The proposal was opposed both by Islamic groups, who saw it as an improper interference with the infalliable and everlasting religious law, and by the major nationalist parties, who regarded it as an illegitimate intrusion by the Dutch into native affairs, and was withdrawn.[21]

With independence there occurred a number of changes of importance to Islamic courts, but the departure of the Dutch did not dramatically alter the terms of the debate over the courts or the balance of power between supporters and detractors.[22] One development that proved critical was the creation of the Ministry (later Department) of Religion.[23] The establishment of the Ministry, then unique in the Muslim world, made possible the consolidation of the entire Islamic administration under a single authority and ensured that Islamic institutions would be under the control of Islamic groups, rather than that of more secular minded nationalists who dominated the Ministry of Justice and the rest of the state bureaucracy.[24] Also critical to the courts' survival was the emergence of Islamic political parties, which were able to check to some degree the secularizing and modernizing impulses of the executive bureaucracy. Although Islamic leaders often disagreed over issues relating to Islamic courts and many favored the eventual absorption of the Islamic courts into the civil judiciary, there was enough support for the continued existence of a separate Islamic court system to prevent the abolition of the courts or further encroachment on their powers.[25] Thus, by the time the nation's first law on judicial organization and procedure was enacted following the transfer of sovereignty,[26] Islamic interests could marshal enough clout to secure the recognition of the existence of Islamic courts, even though the drafters of the statute in the Justice Ministry clearly favored their abolition.[27] The 1951 statute did not expressly authorize Islamic courts, but stated that provision for the administration of Islamic justice would be made through a separate government regulation[28] — language that provided the foundation for the eventual establishment of a nation-wide system of Islamic courts.

Following the passage of the 1951 law, the Ministry of Religion, which had taken over administration of the Islamic courts on Java and Madura in 1946, set about to unify, centralize, and, to the extent possible, expand the Islamic court system into those parts of the country where courts were not then formally established.[29] Over the next several years the Ministry worked with local leaders to acquire control over existing Islamic tribunals and established a limited number of new courts by means of ministerial regulations. The Ministry was also able to use local religious affairs offices, which existed throughout the country, to assert some control over the administration of marriage and inheritance in areas without Islamic courts. Finally, in 1957 the cabinet approved a regulation authorizing the formation of Islamic courts everywhere in the outer islands where they did not already exist.[30] Patterned after the Royal Decree of 1882, the 1957 regulation authorized the establishment of Islamic courts, labeled Pengadilan Agama/ Mahkamah Syariah, wherever there were civil courts exercising a territorial jurisdiction co-extensive with the civil court.[31] The new Islamic tribunals were to have the same collegial organization as the courts set up under the Dutch era regulations.[32] Unlike the existing courts, however, the substantive competence of the new courts would include inheritance as well as marriage and divorce cases,[33] producing a disparity between the courts in Java, Madura, and South Kalimantan compared with the rest of the country.

The promulgation of the 1957 regulation, as a result of which there existed a legal basis for Islamic courts throughout the country, represented a significant victory for advocates of Islamic law. The issuance of the regulation was more a result of the persistent lobbying of the Ministry of Religion and a confluence of political developments that made the granting of concessions to Islam and the outer islands momentarily expedient than of any change in policy toward Islamic law.[34] Shortage of funds delayed the implementation of the regulation. By the early 1970s, however, first instance Islamic courts existed in most districts throughout the country, and additional appeals courts — four in Sumatra and one in Sulawesi — were added to existing appellate tribunals in Java and Kalimantan.[35]

Thus, the Islamic court system was able to survive and even expand in independent Indonesia despite opposition to the courts from some segments of the bureaucracy, especially the Ministry of Justice, whose lawyers — trained in the civil law tradition — considered the existence of sectarian tribunals to be incompatible with a modern national state.[36] But while defenders of Islamic courts had enough leverage to protect them against threats of abolition or absorption into the civil judiciary, the Islamic courts suffered from inadequate budgets and a general neglect that left them ill-housed and with staffs that were both too small and inadequately trained.[37] Many courts, especially in the outer islands, did not have their own physical facilities; court sessions were held in the back rooms of other government offices or the residence of the court chairman.[38] All Islamic courts suffered from insufficient support staff. Some courts did not have a full-time court chairman, but relied exclusively on part-time member judges.[39] By comparison to civil court judges, Islamic court judges were badly paid and poorly educated.[40]

The post-independence era also witnessed a number of efforts to enact legislative reforms of Islamic marriage law, none of which, however, resulted in changes to the substance of Islamic rules. A statute passed in 1946 required that all marriages, repudiations, and reconciliations be registered in the local religious affairs office.[41] Failure to register could subject the party to a small fine, but did not affect the validity of the action. More ambitious proposals that would have affected substantive rights were considered by the legislature in both the late 1950s and again in the late 1960s, but none of the proposals was enacted.[42]

Although there were no similar legislative initiatives concerning Islamic inheritance law, the matter of inheritance provoked a scholarly debate in the 1950s and 60s that laid the groundwork for developments in the late 1980s. The figure at the center of the debate, Professor Hazairin of the University of Indonesia, was Indonesia's most prominent and daring exponent of Islamic modernism, the jurisprudential theory that the original sources of Islamic law should be reinterpreted in light of contemporary social realities.[43] Hazairin argued that the classical Islamic legal doctrines that developed in the Arabian Peninsula were incompatible with Indonesian circumstances, and advocated the development of a distinctively Indonesian school of Islamic law or "*mazhab*" alongside the four existing schools.

He paid particular attention to inheritance law, arguing that the patrilineal bias of classical inheritance doctrine was incompatible with both Indonesian social realities and the spirit of the Koran.[44]

Hazairin's views won some adherents in academic circles, but had little influence on judges or policy makers. During this period, both the Islamic bureaucracy and the religious courts were dominated by "traditionalists" committed to following the legal doctrines (*fiqh*) of the early jurists as contained in the classical legal texts.[45] A quarter century later, however, the principle of an Indonesian *mazhab* would provide part of the justification for state intervention in the development of Islamic legal doctrine.

The change in administration following the events of 1965 raised expectations among many Muslims that organized Islam would play a larger role in the country's public life in the new regime than it had under Sukarno. It soon became apparent, however, that Muslim support for Suharto in his bid for power — support that was probably critical to his success — would not translate into Muslim participation in the exercise of power once Suharto's authority was established.[46] Upon assuming control, the new regime systematically set about to consolidate the primacy of the executive bureaucracy and to emasculate political parties and other non-state sources of political power.[47] Although all groups challenging the dominance of the bureaucracy came under suspicion, during its first two decades, the Suharto government was especially repressive of Islamic groups, which were regarded as the chief threat to stability following the elimination of the communist party.[48] Nor did strongly identified Muslims acquire influence within the bureaucracy, the upper echelons of which were dominated by military officers not oriented toward Islam. Indeed, beginning in 1971 organized Islam lost control of the Ministry of Religion, its traditional stronghold within the government, when Professor Mukti Ali, a Western trained educator with strong ties to neither of the major Islamic groups, was appointed Minister of Religion.[49] An even more significant appointment was made seven years later when the Religion portfolio was given to General Alamsjah Ratu Perwiranegara, a military man and member of Suharto's inner circle of advisors.[50]

Muslim expectations that the New Order would be friendlier toward Islamic law than the Old also proved mistaken.[51] By 1973, two years after the government scored a decisive victory over Muslim parties at the polls, Islamic courts were fighting for their survival. In July of that year the administration put forward a marriage law proposal which, on its face, would have thoroughly secularized Indonesian marriage law and effectively abolished much of the country's Islamic court system.[52] Both the Department of Religion and organized Islam were largely excluded from the preparation of the draft.[53] Although this was ostensibly a Department of Justice initiative, the impetus for the proposal apparently came from the influential clique of informal Presidential advisors lead by Ali Murtopo and the group's Catholic dominated research arm, the Center for Strategic and International Studies.[54] This group was not especially concerned about Islamic courts per se, but found the marriage law issue provided them with an opportunity to strike a blow at political Islam.[55]

The proposal provided for a single set of marriage and divorce rules applicable to all Indonesians regardless of religion. It required civil registration for marriage and court approval for divorce and polygamy.[56] Both divorce and plural marriage, moreover, would become subject to tight restrictions.[57] Enforcement of the law was to be entrusted to the civil courts,[58] which would have reduced the jurisdiction of the outer island courts to matters of inheritance only and left the Islamic courts in Java, Madura, and South Kalimantan with literally nothing to do.

The proposal met with angry and determined Muslim opposition both inside and outside the legislature.[59] At one point several hundred Muslim youth occupied the floor of the legislature, and the army had to be called in to restore order.[60] A solution to the conflict was reached only after high-ranking military officers initiated discussions with Muslim leaders outside the formal legislative process.[61] The parties to this negotiation agreed to a framework for revising the bill, in which Muslim interests acceded to demands for legal restrictions on arbitrary divorce and polygamy in exchange for promises that the substantive law of marriage would not be altered and the role of the Islamic courts not diminished.[62] A statute implementing this agreement was approved by the legislature in late 1973 and signed into law by the President as the 1974 Marriage Act.[63]

The effect of the 1974 Marriage Act on Indonesian Islamic law is a matter of dispute. Many Muslims have hailed Article 2(1) of the law, which states that a marriage is valid when it is performed according to the religious law of the parties, as marking the first formal recognition of Islamic rules as Indonesian law and the end of the hated reception theory. A more extreme version of this view interprets that provision as importing the entire corpus of Islamic marriage doctrine into state law. The Supreme Court and the Department of Religion, on the other hand, have been promoting a dramatically different interpretation of the Marriage Act, which attaches more importance to the positive content of the statute than to Islamic doctrine.[64] According to this interpretation, the Act effects significant changes in the marriage law of Indonesian Muslims, including registration as a requirement for marriage and court approval for divorce and polygamy. It is my contention that the 1989 Religious Judicature Act is, at least in part, an effort to influence the outcome of the debate over the meaning of the Marriage Act.

III. THE 1989 RELIGIOUS JUDICATURE ACT

The Minister of Religion presented the government's proposal for a new law governing Islamic courts to the Indonesian legislature in December of 1988. Consideration of the bill continued throughout the following year, during which time it was widely debated in the public press. The public discussion focused primarily on the broad question whether a separate system of sectarian courts was appropriate for an officially pluralist nation.[65] That issue, however, was not really open to debate in 1989. By the time the Bill was introduced the survival of the Islamic courts was virtually assured as a result of changes made following the implementation of the 1974 Marriage Act. In December of 1989 the legislature approved the Bill with only minor changes from the original draft, and it was signed into law by the President shortly thereafter.

The Act is contained in 108 sections divided into seven chapters [see Appendix II]. As with all legislative enactments in Indonesia, it is accompanied by an official elucidation that provides a section by section commentary on the text.

Chapter I is labeled "General Provisions" and contains sections on the definitions, status, location, and organization of the Islamic courts. It defines the "Religious Judiciary" (*Peradilan Agama*)[66] as the "judiciary for adherents of Islam."[67] This judiciary consists of "Religious Courts" (*Pengadilan Agama*), identified in the following chapter[68] as courts of first instance, and "Religious High Courts" (*Pengadilan Tinggi Agama*), which exercise appellate jurisdiction.[69] Together they "exercise judicial power" for Muslim litigants limited to civil matters specified in the Act.[70] The first instance courts are to be located in municipalities (*Kotamadya*) or districts (*Kabupaten*) with territorial jurisdiction throughout the municipality or district. Appeals courts are to be located in the provincial capitals with province-wide jurisdiction.[71]

The specification of a uniform designation for Islamic courts throughout the country replaces the three different labels under which the courts had operated in the past. Like so much else in the Act, this change had already been effected by means of a Ministerial Decision several years earlier.[72] In 1989, there were more than three-hundred first instance Islamic courts operating in most districts and municipalities throughout the country, and appeals tribunals had been established in eighteen of the country's twenty-seven provinces.[73]

The Act assigns responsibility for what is labeled "technical juridical" matters to the Supreme Court while the organization, administration, and finances of the courts are under the auspices of the Minister of Religion.[74] This division of responsibility for Islamic courts between the Supreme Court and the Department of Religion represents a change from the practice that had prevailed until the late 1970s. As noted, the Ministry of Religion had assumed administrative control of the Islamic courts in 1946. As an adjunct to that administrative function, the Directorate of Religious Justice, the division of the Ministry responsible for the courts, had also exercised some control over the law the courts applied, and eventually acquired powers of appellate review in 1964.[75] Around this same time Justice Ministry officials were urging the creation of an Islamic chamber in the Supreme Court to serve as a court of cassation for the Islamic system.[76] For a time the Directorate of Religious Justice lent guarded support to this limited integration of the Islamic courts into the civil system as a means of improving the profile of the courts without entirely losing their identity.[77] Other segments of the Islamic community — Islamic political leaders and probably most Islamic judges — opposed the idea on the ground that the courts should remain tied to the Islamic community rather than attaching themselves more firmly to a non-Islamic state. When a new Basic Law on Judicial Authority was passed in 1970, supporters of the idea of an Islamic chamber had enough influence to gain inclusion of a provision granting the Supreme Court review powers over all Indonesian courts, including the Islamic court system.[78]

Nothing was done to enforce the Supreme Court's powers with respect to Islamic courts until after the implementation of the Marriage Act. Then in 1977 the Supreme Court issued a regulation establishing procedures for Supreme Court review of Islamic court decisions.[79] The Directorate of Religious Justice initially resisted the move, instructing Islamic courts not to cooperate with litigants seeking cassation in the Supreme Court. The conflict was finally resolved following a meeting between the Minister of Religion and the chairman of the Supreme Court that resulted in the appointment of six Supreme Court justices to an Islamic panel.[80] This ushered in a new era in relations between the Department of Religion and the Supreme Court. By the time the Religious Judicature Bill was proposed, the Supreme Court had assumed a major role in the administration of the Islamic courts in addition to the exercise of its review powers over those courts.

Chapter II of the Act governs the structure and composition of the courts.[81] Among its more significant provisions are the rules treating the appointment and qualification of judges. The power to appoint and terminate judges is vested in the President as Head of State upon the recommendation of the Minister of Religion and the agreement of the Supreme Court.[82] The provision granting the Supreme Court a voice in the selection of judges, which had been the practice for several years before the Act was proposed, formalized Supreme Court involvement in the management of the Islamic judiciary contrary to the earlier tradition of exclusive Religion Department control.

Articles 14 and 15 of Chapter II specify the qualifications for judges. Appointment as an Islamic judge requires, among other things, that the candidate be a civil servant, hold a law degree or a *shariah* degree, and be a Muslim.[83] The requirements that all Islamic judges have academic credentials and civil service status represent a change from prior law. As noted, under the 1882 statute only the court chairman was a civil servant, and prior law did not specify any educational qualifications for judges, the vast majority of whom did not have university degrees.[84] Both the educational qualification and civil service status for judges had been enforced as a matter of executive policy for several years before the statute was proposed,[85] and by the time the Act was passed significant progress had already been made toward their full implementation.[86] With the passage of the Act, all judges not meeting its requirements were retired. Since most of those who served as Islamic judges before the mid-1970s did not meet the qualifications required under the Act, the effect of the imposition of the new qualifications was dramatically to transform the Islamic judiciary over the space of less than two decades.

Chapter III specifies the powers of the Islamic courts. Article 49 states that "Religious Courts have the responsibility and authority to examine, decide, and resolve cases at the first instance between Muslims in the areas of: a) marriage; b) inheritance, testaments, and gifts, that are performed according to Islamic law; c) charitable foundations."[87] The high courts are granted appellate jurisdiction coextensive with the competence of the lower courts.[88]

The courts' jurisdiction over marriage is further specified as relating to "matters regulated in or based on applicable marriage legislation."[89] This vague reference is clarified in the elucidation as referring to the 1974 National Marriage Act.[90] The elucidation then lists twenty-two specific subject areas relating to marriage that are treated in the National Marriage Act. The effect of granting the Religious Courts plenary authority to apply the Marriage Act for Muslims is significantly to expand the courts' powers. Prior to the passage of the Religious Judicature Bill, the competence of the Islamic courts extended only to those matters that had been treated in executive implementing regulations issued in 1975.[91] All other matters had to be referred to the civil courts. The regulations that had been issued under the 1974 Marriage Act covered matters relating to the validity of marriage, including the granting of permission to enter a polygamous marriage or dispensation from statutory age requirements, and the procedures for dissolving marriages. They did not address child custody following divorce or any matters relating to financial obligations or property rights after termination of the marriage. The Supreme Court had held that in the absence of government regulations implementing the Act's provisions on these matters, they were to remain under the jurisdiction of the civil courts. The enumeration of powers in the elucidation to the Religious Judicature Act makes it clear that these matters are now within the authority of the Islamic courts.

The provision granting all Islamic courts power to decide issues of property distribution following death is likewise a change from prior law, since the Islamic courts for Java, Madura, and South Kalimantan had lost their inheritance jurisdiction in the 1930s. The Act clarifies the courts' inheritance powers as including "designation of heirs, designation of the estate, designation of individual shares, and distribution of the estate."[92] Resolution of disputes regarding ownership of property remains under the jurisdiction of the civil courts.[93]

As a practical matter the restoration of the courts' inheritance jurisdiction may not be as significant as it appears. First, although the courts for Java, Madura, and South Kalimantan lacked formal jurisdiction over inheritance matters prior to the passage of the Act, many people had been taking non-contentious inheritance questions to Islamic courts for "advisory opinions" (*fatwa*).[94] These opinions were made enforceable by means of a private agreement to abide by the court's decision that was negotiated by the parties under the supervision of the court. Moreover, the Act includes an important limitation on the courts' inheritance jurisdiction buried in the introduction to the elucidation. It is there provided that before the initiation of proceedings the parties can decide to select the law that will be used in the division of the estate. This "choice of law" provision was hotly debated during the consideration of the Bill.[95] The principle that the claimants to an estate be allowed to choose the legal regime governing distribution of property has its source in the historic debate over the extent to which Islamic rules had supplanted *adat* in matters of inheritance. The argument advanced by opponents of state enforcement of Islamic rules — that the state should not be a party to the Islamization of the country — prevailed, resulting in the provision for an election determining whether Islam or *adat* should govern distribution of property on death.

Chapter IV treats procedure in Islamic courts. The first part of the Chapter contains general provisions, beginning with the general rule that the procedural law to be followed in Islamic courts is that contained in the Code of Civil Procedure and applicable in the civil courts, except as specifically provided in the Act.[96] This first part also contains provisions relating to the means of exercise of judicial power generally as well as provisions unique to Islamic courts. For instance, one section requires that justice be carried out "with simplicity, expedition, and minimal expense," and also provides that decisions and decrees be opened with the recital of the *Bismillah*,[97] the ritual invocation of God's name that occurs at the beginning of each *surah* of the Koran. Other provisions require that in order to be valid, decisions and decrees must be announced in open court,[98] and that decisions and decrees must recite the reasons and basis for the result, including specific statutory provisions or unwritten law.[99]

Part two of the Chapter lays out special procedural rules for divorce actions. It begins, however, with the general injunction that "Divorce can only be carried out (*dilakukan*) in open court after the court has attempted unsuccessfully to reconcile the parties."[100] This provision is potentially very significant if construed as denying the validity of a Muslim husband's unilateral repudiation of his wife or *talak*. However, the language of the provision, which is identical to that contained in a provision of the National Marriage Act,[101] is ambiguous. As will be discussed below, the comparable provision in the Marriage Act was widely interpreted as rendering judicial divorce mandatory, giving rise to penalties for those who do not comply, but not affecting the legal validity of a non-conforming *talak*. As will become clear, moreover, the whole question of the legal effect of extra-judicial *talak* was a principal theme of the debate during the legislative consideration of the bill.

The Act next specifies three different procedural schemes for three different types of divorce: *talak* divorces; "complaint" (*gugat*) divorces; and divorces on grounds of adultery. The procedures for *talak* divorces, which generally track corresponding portions of the executive regulations issued in 1975 to implement the Marriage Act,[102] provide for a husband to recite the repudiation formula or *talak* — "I divorce you" — in court under judicial supervision. According to classical Islamic doctrine, a husband has an absolute power to repudiate his wife at any time for any reason. Under the Act, following the 1975 regulation, a husband wishing to repudiate his wife must file a petition requesting the court "to convene to witness his pronouncement of the *talak*."[103] In a modest change designed to provide greater protection to wives, the husband must file his petition with the court in the district where his wife resides, rather than in his own district, as permitted by the 1975 regulation.[104]

The husband's petition must recite the name, age, and residence of both parties, as well as "the reasons that form the basis for the *talak* divorce."[105] The Act does not specify what reasons qualify as sufficient reasons.[106] The court must examine the petition in closed session within thirty days after the file is enrolled by the clerk.[107] In keeping with the policy of attempting to reduce the frequency of divorce, the court is charged with attempting to reconcile the couple at the first hearing[108] and then throughout the pendency of the case.[109] If the couple cannot be reconciled and if there are "sufficient reasons for divorce the court decrees that the petition is granted."[110]

The Act provides that the wife may appeal the court's decree declaring that there exist grounds for a *talak*.[111] Only after the decree has become final through the exhaustion of all appeals or the expiry of the period for filing an appeal does the court schedule a hearing for the purpose of witnessing the husband's *talak*.[112] This procedure was established by means of a Supreme Court Circular issued in 1985.[113] Before the issuance of the circular, the wife could appeal the sufficiency of the husband's reasons for divorcing her only after the divorce became effective through the husband's pronouncing the *talak*. This procedure was unacceptable from the Muslim perspective because the *talak* was an accomplished fact that could in nowise be invalidated through a judicial decision on appeal. Reformers, on the other hand, were anxious that there be some means for an appeal of the first instance court finding of sufficient grounds in order to preserve the contentious nature of the action and impose meaningful limits on the husband's power to divorce his wife. The device used by the statute of simply deferring the pronouncement of the *talak* until any appeals have been completed provides an adequate solution for the narrow problem it addresses. However, the problem of appealing a *talak* exemplifies a broader difference in interests and outlooks that the Act must negotiate. Stated most broadly, the difference is between a view which sees law as emanating from the law-making organs of the state and a view which sees the source of law in the revealed word of God.

A woman wishing to be divorced from her husband proceeds under the "complaint" procedure outlined in the following part.[114] Like the rule setting forth the *talak* procedure, the complaint procedure largely follows the pattern set out in the implementing regulations to the 1974 Marriage Act.[115] Furthermore, though not explicitly stated in the text, the drafters undoubtedly contemplated the continuation of the courts' practice under the 1975 regulations. The Islamic courts had interpreted the complaint procedure in the regulations as simply vindicating the courts' powers to grant divorces initiated by women in accordance with Indonesian Islamic doctrine. The Shafi'i school of Islamic law as applied in Indonesia recognized a number of means by which a dissatisfied wife could terminate her marriage.[116] Unlike her husband, all the divorce options for wives required cooperation of the court. In applying the Marriage Act and its implementing regulation, the courts had essentially assimilated traditional Islamic doctrine to the list of grounds for divorce stated in the positive law.[117] That is, the specific grounds stated in the statute were identified with one of the avenues for divorce recognized in Islamic law. For instance, the statutory grounds of irreconcilable differences was interpreted as a codification of the Islamic *syiqaq* procedure. *Syiqaq* is ostensibly a mechanism for resolving differences between spouses through appointment of arbiters for each. However, it had evolved into a divorce procedure once it became recognized that the husband's arbiter, typically one of the judges, had the power to terminate the marriage if reconciliation efforts failed. Following the effective date of the Marriage Act and its implementing regulations, the Islamic courts "applied" the rule regarding divorce based on irreconcilable differences by appointing arbiters as required by the *syiqaq* procedure. The Act contains no list of grounds for complaint divorces. It was clearly anticipated that the courts would continue to apply the substantive law in effect before the Religious Judicature Act was passed, which was understood to be essentially Islamic doctrine. Indeed, the Act expressly provides for the appointment of arbiters when the complaint is "based on the grounds of *syiqaq*."[118]

The complaint initiating the proceeding is to be filed in the court in the district where the complainant resides unless the wife has left the marital residence without permission,[119] a change designed to redress the unequal legal standing of women. The complaint procedure contains the same charge to the judge to try to reconcile the couple[120] and the same rules and timetable for examining the complaint as are contained in the *talak* procedure.[121]

On the issue of proof, the Act states that a copy of a judgment of conviction is sufficient proof when the asserted ground for the complaint is that the husband has been convicted of a crime and sentenced to prison,[122] and that the court can order the husband to submit to a physical examination when the basis of the complaint is that he suffers from a handicap or illness which prevents him from performing his conjugal obligations.[123] As observed, the statute also sets out the *syiqaq* procedure. Apart from these references, however, there is no specification of the kinds or quantities of evidence required to prove either a *talak* or a complaint claim. The Act states that the court's "decision" on the complaint is to be announced in open court and that the divorce and its consequences are deemed to have occurred from the time the court's decision acquires the force of law.[124]

The third type of divorce action regulated by yet another set of procedural rules is divorce based on adultery. The explanation for the separate treatment of adultery cases lies, once again, in Islamic doctrine, specifically the procedure known as *li'an*. The *li'an* divorce procedure derives from the criminal law.[125] A Muslim husband who suspects his wife of adultery takes four solemn oaths that his wife has committed unchastity or that the child born to her is not his. The wife is then offered the chance to deny the accusation with four oaths of her own. The requirement that the parties swear four times to the same thing has its source in the requirement of testimony from four witnesses to prove the crime of adultery, and if the wife refuses to make her denial she stands convicted of that crime. If she does deny, then the only effect of the procedure is permanently to dissolve the marriage.

The proposal codified the traditional *li'an* procedure, but broke from tradition by making it available to either spouse. Not surprisingly, the inclusion of the *li'an* rule was controversial.[126] Publicly expressed opposition to the provision insisted that the rule had no place in an essentially procedural statute because of its substantive character, and that the extension of the *li'an* option to wives was inconsistent with Islamic doctrine.[127] It seems likely that a more important but unstated basis for opposing the proposal is the highly irrational character of the rule. In the enacted version the rubric for the procedure is changed from *"li'an"* to "divorce on account of adultery." Another amendment provides for a different procedure depending on whether the charge is brought by husband or wife. If the husband makes the oath of accusation the case proceeds and is resolved according to the *li'an* procedure. When a wife accuses her husband then the case is resolved under the "applicable rules of procedure."[128]

The inclusion of the *li'an* procedure reflects the basically modernist jurisprudential outlook of the Act.[129] Although, as discussed above, Islamic modernism authorizes the reinterpretation of the original sources to meet changing needs, the limits of legal change are highly restrictive. The standard modernist position authorizes a reinterpretation of rules based on authorities deemed uncertain, but insists on strict adherence to those legal doctrines that are based on divine texts that are certain.[130] Because the *li'an* procedure is regulated in some detail in the Koran,[131] the premises of modernist jurisprudence require its recognition.

The influence of Islamic modernism in the preparation of the Act is indicative of a more general shift in the position of modernist Islam *vis-à-vis* the Indonesian state. In contrast to the situation before 1970s, the upper echelons of the Department of Religion are now dominated by modernists, the most notable example being H. Munawir Sjadzali, the two-term Religion Minister who shepherded the Act through the legislature and whose legal reform proposals in the 1980s sparked a firestorm of controversy.[132] The overhaul of the Islamic judiciary that resulted from the imposition of new educational qualifications in the early 1980s has also changed the profile of the Islamic bench. Once the preserve of traditionalist judges trained exclusively in *pesantren*, the courts are now overwhelmingly staffed by graduates of the State Islamic Institutes, which are decidedly reformist in orientation.[133]

The remainder of Chapter IV and the last three chapters of the Act address a variety of technical matters including costs,[134] the responsibilities of court personnel,[135] and a set of concluding provisions repealing conflicting statutes and providing that the Act shall take effect on the date that it is enacted.[136]

IV. AN INDONESIAN *MAZHAB*: THE CASE OF *TALAK* DIVORCES

Like many legislative enactments, the 1989 Religious Judicature Act is not an expression of any one purpose or coherent ideology or set of policies. It reflects, rather the outcome of a negotiation in which no single interest or outlook was able completely to have its way.

To illustrate the various conflicting tendencies embodied in the Act, I propose to take a closer look at one narrow aspect of the statute — its treatment of divorces initated by men. The provision governing *talak* divorces was one of the more contentious features of the proposal. The reason the *talak* provision engendered controversy is that the question of the husband's power unilaterally to repudiate his wife focuses the disagreement between two conflicting points of view. It engages both the jurisprudential conservatism of the advocates of state enforcement of Islamic law and the statist orientation of the New Order's leaders. An examination of the Act's treatment of the issue in the context of the broader history of New Order policy toward Islamic law shows that the Act failed to resolve the tension between the two tendencies. Instead it effects an unsteady compromise, the precise terms of which are the subject of continuing negotiation.

In order to appreciate the tensions that lie behind the divorce provisions of the Religious Judicature Act, it is useful to recount the course of divorce reform legislation beginning in the early 1970s. The government's 1973 draft national marriage law would have abolished the *talak* by converting divorce into a contentious judicial proceeding. The draft stated that anyone wishing to divorce must prove statutory grounds in court, included an exhaustive list of legal grounds, and required that the court's "decision" terminating the marriage had to be announced in open court.[137]

The divorce provisions in the enacted version differed in important respects from the initial draft. The treatment of divorce in the statute itself is very brief, by its own terms incomplete, and on its face extremely obscure. The statute states only that marriage can be terminated by death, divorce, or court decision; that divorce must be "performed" in court; that before a divorce can be carried out there must be sufficient reasons; and that procedures for divorce would be set forth in separate implementing regulations.[138] The statute itself does not specify what reasons qualify as "sufficient reasons" for divorce, but a list of grounds for divorce is contained in the official elucidation accompanying the Act.[139]

The intent of these obscure provisions became clear only in the government's implementing regulations[140] and the practice of the courts. Under the regulations as interpreted by the courts, a Muslim man wishing to divorce his wife must file a petition with the Islamic court for permission to repudiate his wife. The regulation directs the courts to examine the petition to determine if it is based on statutory grounds, and to convene for the purpose of witnessing the husband's repudiation only if the court finds the couple can no longer live together in harmony. After witnessing the husband's *talak*, the court verifies the divorce by issuing a "Certificate Respecting the Occurrence of a *Talak*."[141]

The appeal of this scheme from the Islamic perspective is its recognition of the *talak* as the mechanism for dissolving the marriage. In the Muslim understanding the statute does not alter the substance of the divine law but simply institutes procedures for its enforcement. Instead of prescribing legal grounds or conditions for divorce, the statute seeks to control the incidence of divorce by imposing legal requirements for the use of the husband's *talak*. From the Muslim perspective at least, the law regulates the occurrence of legally significant events, rather than declaring new legal meanings. And since the law addresses itself exclusively to when a man may repudiate his wife and not to the issue of when the repudiation is effective, a *talak* pronounced in violation of the Act may be illegal but is nonetheless efficacious.[142]

The Religious Judicature Act abjures the coy approach of the Marriage Act and explicitly provides that the procedure for divorces initiated by men involves a court-sanctioned *talak*. Like the Marriage Act, however, the language of the Bill equivocates on the question whether compliance with its procedures, though unquestionably obligatory, is necessary for the divorce to be valid.

The debate over the proposal clearly indicated the existence of conflicting views on that question. At one point during the consideration of the Bill, the Unity Development Party — the government contrived coalition that functions as the only authorized voice for Muslim interests in the legislature — proposed an amendment to Article 66 that would have recognized the validity of extra-judicial *talak*.[143] Under the proposed amendment, which went nowhere, a husband who either wished to or "had already repudiated his wife" could petition the court to certify his action.[144] Despite the failure of the amendment, the Unity Development faction maintained in its comment on the final draft of the Bill that the language of the statute did not preclude a finding that extra-judicial *talak* are valid. Citing the Basic Law on Judicial Authority for the proposition that judges may take account of "the legal values that exist in society," the comment argued that, "in calculating the wife's waiting period [following an extra-judicial *talak*], due consideration must be given to religious precepts."[145] What this means, expressed ever so indirectly, is that judges can find that extra-judicial *talak* are legally effective. The Armed Forces faction countered with its own interpretation of the relevant provisions in its final written comments to the Bill. Its comment states flatly that the statutory language means that "as a matter of law *talak* divorces are valid only if performed in court."[146]

There was no attempt to resolve this difference before passage of the law. An unequivocal declaration that extra-judicial *talak* either do or do not have the force of law would undoubtedly have created a serious obstacle to the Bill's approval. This absence of clarity on such an important point was not viewed as problematic. Like many legislative enactments, this statute was not regarded as providing a definitive resolution of what the law is, but as providing a basis for a continuing negotiation over what the law should be. Moreover, the ambiguous and inconclusive character of the provision provided the opening for the Supreme Court and the Department of Religion gradually and quietly to promote their interpretation of what the law means.

A 1990 circular containing instructions for the implementation of the Act indicates the direction the Supreme Court wishes to take the law and the means by which this is being accomplished. It states that "A *talak* divorce is in principle a contentious marriage action between the two parties to the case, and as a consequence the judicial product from the judges must have the form and title of *decision* with an order in the form of *decree*."[147] The import of labeling the judges' output as a "decision" is to give or attempt to give the proceeding a judicial cast. This is in line with the general purpose of the directive which is to discourage the treatment of *talak* proceedings as simply ministerial ceremonies that result in an official recognition of the occurrence of a *talak*. By characterizing the proceeding as a contentious action, the circular emphasizes the judges' role as adjudicators having the power to grant or withhold approval of the divorce subject to the husband's proving legislatively prescribed grounds. The change represents at best a partial step toward the eventual aim of acquiring state control over Islamic divorces. But it is precisely by means of such obscure and incremental actions that the government is attempting to move its agenda forward.

Another much more significant vehicle by which the Supreme Court and Department of Religion are pressing an alternative interpretation of Islamic divorce rules is the Compilation of Islamic Laws. The Compilation is an Indonesian language manual of rules covering marriage, divorce, inheritance, and charitable foundations. It was drafted under the direction of the Department of Religion and the Supreme Court over a period of several years,[148] and given the force of law in 1991 through a presidential decree.[149] In addition to the classical texts of Islamic legal doctrine, other sources that were surveyed in the preparation of the Compilation included works on Islamic law by Indonesian scholars, the rulings of Indonesian Islamic organizations, the decisions of Indonesian Islamic courts, and legislation from other countries. The ostensible purpose of the project was to provide certainty and uniformity in the application of Islamic law. It has also been the means by which the government has attempted to promote an understanding of Islamic law consistent with its aims.

The Compilation provides a more comprehensive treatment of the law of divorce than the Religious Judicature Act, including some thirty-six articles on the subject. The general approach tracks the Marriage Act and the Religious Judicature Act in setting up two procedures, one available only to men, in which the husband repudiates his wife in court, and the other for women. Like the Religious Judicature Act, the Compilation does not explicitly declare extra-judicial *talak* invalid. But the suggestion in the Compilation that a *talak* without judicial approval does not have the force of law is stronger than in the Act. The Compilation, like the Act, states that a divorce can only be performed in court[150] and that a husband who wishes to repudiate his wife must file a petition with the court to convene for that purpose.[151] But the Compilation also says that "A *talak* is a declaration of the husband *in the presence of the members of the court* that consititutes one cause of the dissolution of marriage."[152] Read literally, this language would seem to indicate that an extra-judicial repudiation is not a "*talak*" and therefore is of no effect. Another provision states that "Divorce takes effect from the moment it is expressed in the presence of the members of the court."[153] This provision likewise suggests that a husband's attempt to repudiate his wife outside of statutory procedures is ineffective, though the use of the generic word for divorce rather than the word *talak* creates some ambiguity.

That which is obliquely intimated in the Compilation of Islamic Law is stated with unmistakable clarity in a comment on the text written by a Justice of the Supreme Court.[154] The article, entitled "Codifying the Abstractions of Islamic Law," is contained in a periodical published by the Department of Religion and designated as required reading for all Islamic judges. Sounding a popular modernist refrain, the article begins by distinguishing *fiqh* — temporal rules — from *shariah* — the eternally correct path of life.[155] The author goes on to explain that the *fiqh* that were derived by the medieval jurists and contained in the classical texts are not "Islamic law," since they represent only the opinions of their authors. Nor do the Koran and the Traditions comprise Islamic law since they hardly present a comprehensive treatment of legal problems. Thus, the author concludes, in the *fiqh* and the Koran Indonesian society has only "abstractions" of Islamic law.[156] Hence the necessity for a codification of these abstractions in the Compilation of Islamic Laws.

The author then proceeds to elaborate his jurisprudential theory for the derivation of legal rules from the divine sources, and summarizes the aims and content of the Compilation. Among the avowed purposes of the Compilation is to "banish the understanding [of law] as a private affair." The traditional understanding of Islamic law, the author writes, has been that the principles of the law are regarded as a private matter between the individual and God. As a result, it is a matter in which the state may not interfere. But with the implementation of the Compilation, the application of the law is no longer left in the hands of individuals. "The emergence of the Compilation inaugurates a new era in Indonesian history, in which Islamic law has been elevated to the status of valid civil law that has a public character and can be enforced by the instrumentalities of the state."[157]

The author also offers an analysis of the substance of the Compilation, including the divorce provisions. As interpreted by the Supreme Court Justice, the *talak* procedure is "elevated to the status of a contentious proceeding," and he states unequivocally that extra-judicial *talak* "are not valid and not binding."[158] With this the government has successfully achieved the essence of what it failed to accomplish with its original secular marriage law proposal in 1973. The differences between the failed legislative proposal and the doctrine as it has been developed are in the mechanism by which the divorce is actually effected — by means of the husband's court-supervised *talak* — and the symbolic underpinning of the rules. Unlike the marriage law proposal, the asserted basis for the authority of the rules in the Compilation is as Islamic law. By means of the Compilation, the government seeks to transcend the conflict between state and religious lawmaking authority. Although the authority of the rules remains grounded in religion, the state now becomes the authoritative interpreter of the religious tradition. As a result, it is no longer Islamic law, but *Indonesian* Islamic law that regulates intimate social relations.[159] Once a challenge to state lawmaking, Islam now becomes its vehicle.

V. CONCLUSION

The Religious Judicature Act effects an unstable accommodation between two opposing outlooks. On the one hand the Act shows the unmistakable influence of Islamic modernism. Modernist legal theory embraces the use of human reason to reinterpret the original sources of Islamic law in light of contemporary needs and circumstances, but only within defined limits. While modernism rejects the absolute authority of the *fiqh* as the temporal product of a different social and historical context, it insists on a strict, literal enforcement of those doctrines that have a clear textual basis in the primary sources — the Koran and the Hadith.[160]

The more interesting implication from the Act has to do with the Indonesian state. The recent evidence from Islamic law suggests that the adoption by the New Order of a more Islamic demeanor has not significantly tempered the regime's statist impulses. Behind the appearances there is a remarkable continuity in New Order policy toward Islamic law over the course of nearly twenty-five years. In the early 1970s powerful elements within the government perceived a political advantage in weakening or abolishing Islamic courts and marginalizing Islamic doctrine. By the late 1980s a changed political context had induced the regime to change its posture toward Islamic legal institutions.[161] Instead of restricting the scope of Islamic law and curtailing the powers of Islamic courts, a different group of power brokers began enfranchising the religious courts and enforcing Islamic doctrine. Although the government's attitude toward official Islam had seemingly reversed itself, its more basic objective of acquiring control over Indonesian family law remained unchanged. Having settled on a policy of cultivating rather than confronting Islam, the government set about to assert greater influence over Islamic courts and to establish itself as the authoritative interpreter of a distinctively Indonesian Islamic legal tradition. Rather than competing with Islam for legislative authority, the government is seeking to appropriate the power to declare Islamic law. Instead of defeating Islam, the regime has decided to confiscate it.

How far the current accommodation between Islamic modernism and New Order statism can be maintained remains to be seen. There is an inherent tension between a view which believes in and feels entitled to state enforcement of a set of fixed religious doctrines, and the premises of state positivism, which locate an absolute and indivisible legal sovereignty in the lawmaking organs of the state.[162] If my analysis is correct, moreover, the government is nourishing the present *modus vivendi* with Islamic modernism by encouraging, or at least tolerating, a level of misapprehension of its intentions. Insofar as the government has indicated a commitment to enforcing Islamic doctrine as interpreted by the Islamic community, those indications are misleading.[163] Although the government's regulatory efforts are now articulated with a vocabulary supplied by Islam, the regime's basic objective of expropriating control over Indonesian family law remains unchanged.

Notes

1. Research for this article was supported by a grant from Southwestern University School of Law. I also wish to thank the editors and anonymous readers for *Indonesia* who provided valuable comments on an earlier version of this manuscript.
2. The Act is designated as Law No. 7 (1989).
3. Information about the administration of Islamic justice before the advent of European records is scattered and scarce. Anthony Reid has written that by the early seventeenth century, the major Islamic states in the region had established regular institutions for

the implementation of Islamic law, although there is definite evidence for the existence of Islamic courts per se only in Aceh and Banten. See Anthony Reid, *Southeast Asia in the Age of Commerce, 1450–1680, Volume II: Expansion and Crisis* (New Haven: Yale University Press, 1993), pp. 182–84. Martin van Bruinessen has analyzed records from Banten, where the chief Islamic judge was appointed by the Sultan from at least the beginning of the seventeenth century until the office was abolished with the consolidation of Dutch control over the area in the middle of the nineteenth. Though originally an all-purpose religious official, over time the office of chief judge acquired a narrower adjudicative function. From the eighteenth century on, the chief judge exercised jurisdiction over all non-capital cases and administered a hierarchy of subordinate judges who heard cases at the district level. Martin van Bruinessen, "Shari`a court, tarekat and pesantren: Religious Institutions in the Banten Sultanate," *Archipel* 50 (1995): 165, 168–72. Among the Javanese, the administration of Islamic justice was one of several functions performed by the *penghulu* — the chief administrator of the mosque — who conducted judicial proceedings in the portico of the mosque. The *penghulu* were appointed by and closely linked with the local aristocracy and stood in contrast to the other principal religious elite, the heads of Islamic boarding schools, who remained independent of political authority and had large mass followings. Although the reach of the *penghulu*'s jurisdiction and the extent of the influence of Islamic doctrine is uncertain, the *penghulu* were apparently the primary judicial officers for the Javanese. See Daniel Lev, *Islamic Courts in Indonesia: A Study in the Political Bases of Legal Institutions* (Berkeley: University of California Press, 1972), pp. 10–13.

4. The Decree is designated Staatsblad (State Gazette) No. 152 (1882). For a discussion of the enactment see Harry J. Benda, *The Crescent and the Rising Sun: Indonesian Islam under the Japanese Occupation, 1942–1945* (The Hague: W. van Hoeve, 1958), pp. 83–85; Lev, *Islamic Courts*, pp. 13–14; H. Z. A. Noeh and H. A. B. Adnan, *Sejarah Singkat Pengadilan Agama Islam di Indonesia* (Jakarta: Bina Ilmu, 1983), pp. 32–35; and Karel Steenbrink, *Beberapa Aspek tentang Islam di Indonesian Abad ke-19* (Jakarta: Bulan Bintang, 1984), pp. 220–23.

5. Lev, *Islamic Courts*, p. 14.

6. Benda, *The Crescent and the Rising Sun*, p. 84; Steenbrink, *Islam di Indonesia Abad ke-19*, pp. 221–22.

7. Noeh and Adnan, *Sejarah Singkat*, p. 33.

8. Steenbrink, *Islam di Indonesia Abad ke-19*, p. 217. Although the 1882 edict served as the legal charter for Islamic courts in Java and Madura for more than a century, that was probably not the intention of the colonial officials who formulated the law. To begin with, at the time the recommendations for the Islamic courts were forwarded to Den Haag there was substantial support among Dutch officials in the Indies for abolishing Islamic courts altogether. Steenbrink, *Islam di Indonesia Abad ke-19*, p. 220. And while the consensus favored continuation of the courts, some of those who joined the recommendation did so for political reasons with the anticipation that the courts would eventually be abolished. Ibid. More importantly, Harry Benda's assessment that the 1882 decree was not intended to vest *judicial* power in the penghulu is probably correct. Benda, *The Crescent and the Rising Sun*, p. 84. The requirement of an executory decree for the pronouncements of the penghulu's courts to be enforceable meant that, "[s]trictly speaking, the members of these councils were . . . no more judges than they were 'priests,' even in matters pertaining to their alleged jurisdiction." Ibid.

9. Staatsblad Nos. 116, 610, 639 (1937) discussed in Benda, *The Crescent and the Rising Sun*, pp. 83–88 and Lev, *Islamic Courts*, pp. 17–21. The reforms carried out in the 1930s were based on the report of a committee that had been set up in 1922 to study the Islamic courts. The Committee's recommendations were first embodied in a regulation issued in 1931, Staatsblad No. 53 (1931), which was not implemented until 1937 because of budgetary constraints resulting from the depression, Lev, *Islamic Courts*, pp. 17–18.

10. Lev, *Islamic Courts*, p. 64.

11. Lev, *Islamic Courts*, pp. 18–19.

12. Lev, *Islamic Courts*, p. 21. The Mahkamah Islam Tinggi was originally located in Batavia, but was moved to Surakarta during the war where it remained.

13. Staatsblad No. 116 (1937) discussed in Benda, *The Crescent and the Rising Sun*, p. 88 and Lev, *Islamic Courts*, p. 21.

14. For a discussion of the views of the *adat* law scholars as they relate to the Islamic courts, see Benda, *The Crescent and the Rising Sun*, pp. 65–68; and Lev, *Islamic Courts*, pp. 19–29. The ostensible reasons for Dutch support for custom over Islam were philosophical and scientific. Influenced by continental legal science, which viewed law as the organic outgrowth of a society's history and culture, the *adat* scholars promoted indigenous customary law as the only authentic expression of the ethos of Indonesian society. They supported their claims about the secondary place of Islam in the archipelago's legal culture by painstakingly cataloguing local customary practices which, they contended, demonstrated the limited extent to which Islamic rules were observed in fact. Of course, the promotion of local and particularistic customary law over universalistic Islam also served conservative Dutch political interests. Benda, *The Crescent and the Rising Sun*, p. 68.

15. Lev, *Islamic Courts*, pp. 196–97.

16. See e.g. Hazairin, *Hukum Kekeluargaan Nasional* (Jakarta: Tintamas, 1962), pp. 4–5 condemning the reception theory as "a theory of the devil, that defies the faith of Muslims, defies God, defies the Koran, and defies the Traditions of the Prophet."

17. Lev, *Islamic Courts*, pp. 24–29.

18. Ibid.

19. The proposed marriage ordinance is discussed in Benda, *The Crescent and the Rising Sun*, pp. 88–89; Jan Prins, "Adat law and Muslim Religious Law in Modern Indonesia," *Welt des Islams* I (1951): 283, 294–95; and Cora Vreede-de Stuers, *The Indonesian Woman: Struggles and Achievements* (The Hague: Mouton & Co., 1960), pp. 108–10.

20. On the early Indonesian women's movement see Vreede-de Stuers, *The Indonesian Woman*, pp. 89–99.

21. Benda, *The Crescent and the Rising Sun*, pp. 88–89; Prins, "Adat law and Muslim Religious Law," pp. 294–95; and Vreede-de Stuers, *The Indonesian Woman*, pp. 108–10.

22. See generally, Lev, *Islamic Courts*, ch. 2, 3.

23. Lev, *Islamic Courts*, pp. 43–45.

24. Ibid.

25. See generally Lev, *Islamic Courts*, pp. 63–75.

26. Law No. 1 (1951) discussed in Lev, *Islamic Courts*, p. 65.

27. The drafters of the measure suggested that the legislature be consulted about transferring the functions of the Islamic courts to the civil courts. Lev, *Islamic Courts*, p. 65. A 1948 law, never implemented because of events during the revolution, would

have effected the immediate integration of the Islamic courts into the civil courts. Lev, *Islamic Courts*, pp. 64–65; Noeh and Adnan, *Sejarah Singkat*, pp. 53–54.

28. Lev, *Islamic Courts*, p. 65.

29. On the expansion of the court system see Lev, *Islamic Courts*, pp. 75–92.

30. Gov. Reg. No. 45 (1957) discussed in Lev, *Islamic Courts*, p. 89 and Noeh and Adnan, *Sejarah Singkat*, pp. 59–60. A government regulation requires approval by the full cabinet but not the legislature.

31. Gov. Reg. No. 45 Art. 1 (1957).

32. Ibid., Arts. 2, 6.

33. Ibid., Art. 4(1).

34. Lev, *Islamic Courts*, p. 89.

35. Noeh and Adnan, *Sejarah Singkat*, pp. 69–70.

36. The attitude of rivalry and mutual suspicion that has long characterized relations between the Ministries of Justice and Religion resurfaced recently in the controversy over the so-called Juvenile Courts Bill. In November of 1995 the Justice Department introduced a proposal for a new law regulating various legal issues relating to children, including adoption and guardianship. The proposal vested jurisdiction over these matters in the civil courts. See "Rancangan Undang-Undang tentang Peradilan Anak," in *Mimbar Hukum* 25 (1996): 131–55. The Department of Religion and Islamic organizations opposed the proposal on the ground that it derogated from the powers of the Islamic courts. After a long and acrimonious debate, the offending provisions were removed and the bill was finally passed in December of 1996. "Aturan Anak Nakal itu Lahir," *Gatra* (January 4, 1997).

37. Information on the condition of the courts can be found in H. Ichtijanto, "Pengadilan Agama Sebagai Wadah Perjuangan Mengisi Kemerdekaan Bangsa," *Kenang-kenangan Seabad Peradilan Agama di Indonesia* (Jakarta: Dep. of Religion, 1985), pp. 258–80; Lev, *Islamic Courts*, ch. 4; H. Mastur Jahri, "Memperingati Seabad Peradilan Agama yang Jatuh Pada Tahun 1982 ini," *Kenang-kenangan Seabad Peradilan Agama di Indonesia* (Jakarta: Dep. of Religion, 1985), pp. 349–61.

38. H. Ichtijanto, "Pengadilan Agama Sebagai Wadah Perjuangan," pp. 265–66; Lev, *Islamic Courts*, p. 112; H. Mastur Jahri, "Memperingati Seabad Peradilan Agama," p. 359.

39. H. Ichtijanto, "Pengadilan Agama Sebagai Wadah Perjuangan," pp. 265–66.

40. Lev, *Islamic Courts*, pp. 104–12.

41. Law No. 22 (1946) discussed in Lev, *Islamic Courts*, pp. 53–58.

42. Lev, *Islamic Courts*, p. 139; Vreede-de Stuers, *The Indonesian Woman*, pp. 124–40.

43. For brief discussions of Hazairin's views see B. J. Boland, *The Struggle of Islam in Modern Indonesia* (The Hague: Martinus Nijhoff, 1982), pp. 168–70 and Lev, *Islamic Courts*, p. 219. Hazairin's most important works include Hazairin, *Hukum Kewarisan Bilateral menurut Qur'an dan Hadith* (Jakarta: Tintamas, 1958) and Hazairin, *Hukum Kekeluargaan Nasional* (Jakarta: Tintamas, 1962).

44. Boland, *The Struggle of Islam*, pp. 169–70.

45. See generally Lev, *Islamic Courts*, ch. 7.

46. See generally Ruth McVey, "Faith as an Outsider: Islam in Indonesian Politics," *Islam in the Political Process*, ed. James P. Piscatori (Cambridge: Cambridge University Press, 1983), pp. 199–225.

47. See Benedict Anderson, "Old State and New Society: Indonesia's New Order in Comparative Perspective," *Journal of Asian Studies* 42 (May 1983): 477–96, characterizing

the change from the Sukarno to Suharto regimes as entailing a shift in emphasis from "national" to "state" interests.

48. See David Jenkins, *Suharto and His Generals: Indonesian Military Politics 1975–1983* (Ithaca: Cornell Modern Indonesia Project, 1984), pp. 29–32, discussing the "Islam-phobia" of Suharto's inner circle of advisors.

49. McVey, "Faith as an Outsider," p. 208.

50. Jenkins, *Suharto and His Generals*, p. 79. Because positions in the Department of Religion are not attractive to most university graduates, these changes in the leadership of the Department did not necessarily permeate the rank and file.

51. For instance, shortly after Suharto took over, Muslim groups mounted an effort to revive the so-called Jakarta Charter, a constitutional provision imposing an obligation to carry out Islamic law, that had been considered and rejected in 1945. The Suharto government, however, was unreceptive. Allan A. Samson, "Islam in Indonesian Politics," *Asian Survey* 8 (1968): 1001, 1012–13.

52. For a discussion of the terms of the proposal see Mark Cammack, "Islamic Law in Indonesia's New Order," *The International and Comparative Law Quarterly* 38 (1989): 53, 57–65; Muhammad Kamal Hassan, *Muslim Intellectual Responses to "New Order" Modernization in Indonesia* (Kuala Lumpur: Dewan Pustaka dan Bahasa, 1980), pp. 148–56; June Katz and Ronald Katz, "The New Indonesian Marriage Law: A Mirror of Indonesia's Political, Cultural, and Legal Systems," *American Journal of Comparative Law* 23 (1975): 653–81.

53. "RUU Perkawinan, Aksi dan Reaksi," *Tempo*, September 8, 1973, pp. 6–8. See also Leo Suryadinata, *Military Ascendancy and Political Culture: A Study of Indonesia's Golkar* (Athens: Ohio University Center for International Studies, 1989), pp. 76–77.

54. Harold Crouch, *The Army and Politics in Indonesia* (Ithaca: Cornell University Press, 1978), p. 313. This "invisible cabinet" originated with the appointment of a small Presidential "private staff" in 1966. Although the private staff was officially disbanded in 1968 in response to student protests, a changing group of informal Presidential advisors continued to exercise great influence thereafter. Ibid., pp. 243, 307–309; Jenkins, *Suharto and His Generals*, pp. 23–24.

55. Crouch, *The Army and Politics in Indonesia*, p. 313.

56. Katz and Katz, "The New Indonesian Marriage Law," p. 661.

57. Ibid.

58. Cammack, "Islamic Law in Indonesia's New Order," pp. 57–58.

59. For an account of the controversy provoked by the proposal, see Donald K. Emmerson, *Indonesia's Elite: Political Culture and Cultural Politics* (Ithaca: Cornell University Press, 1976), pp. 229–35.

60. "Ada 'Allahu Akbar' dari Luar," *Tempo*, 6 October 1973, pp. 6–7.

61. "Dan Lahirlah UU Itu — Dengan Afdruk Kilat," *Tempo*, 29 December 1973, pp. 5–8. See also Crouch, *The Army and Politics in Indonesia*, pp. 313–14. The meeting was apparently an attempt by General Sumitro, then head of the internal security apparatus, to exploit the marriage law controversy in his simmering rivalry with Ali Murtopo. Suryadinata, *Indonesia's Golkar*, pp. 77–78.

62. Katz and Katz, "The New Indonesian Marriage Law," p. 663.

63. Law No. 1 (1974). An English translation of the statute is contained in B. B. Hering, "A Translation of the Indonesian Marriage Law," ed. B. B. Hering, *Indonesian Women: Some Past and Current Perspectives* (Brussels: Centre D'Etude du Sud-Est Asiatique et

de L'Extreme Orient, 1976), pp. 91–114. For a good summary of the law see Nani Soewondo, "The Indonesian Marriage Law and its Implementing Regulations," *Archipel* 13 (1977): 283–94.

64. See Cammack, "Islamic Law in Indonesia's New Order," pp. 63–65.

65. See *Peradilan Agama dalam Wadah Negara Pancasila: Dialog tentang RUUPA*, ed. H. Zuffran Sabrie (Jakarta: Pustaka Antara, 1990) which contains a collection of several dozen press reports focusing on this issue. The proposal encountered comparatively little serious opposition in the legislature. Initially, Golkar was divided over the Bill. Those opposed to the measure objected that it perpetuated legal dualism in violation of *Pancasila*. "Sebuah RUU dengan Lapang Dada," *Tempo*, 24 June 1989, p. 26. However, when the Golkar faction formally stated its position on the Bill, it came out in favor. The Democratic Party supported the Bill with reservations. Both the Unity Development Party and the Military faction strongly supported it. "Peradilan Agama: Kebutuhan atau Kecemasan," *Tempo*, 24 June 1989, p. 22.

66. The Democratic Party voiced strong public objection to the title of the Act on the ground that it establishes not "Religious" courts but Islamic courts. See e.g. "Pembahasan Judul RUUPA Berjalan Alot," *Jawa Pos*, 26 September 1989. It is fair to assume that the objection was not only to the accuracy of the label but also to the existence of a separate set of sectarian courts.

67. Chap. I, Art. 1(1). Unless otherwise indicated, citations to statutory authorities refer to the 1989 Act.

68. Chap. II, Art. 6.

69. Chap. I, Art. 1(2).

70. Chap. I, Art. 2.

71. Chap. I, Art. 4.

72. Decision of the Minister of Religion No. 6, January 28, 1980.

73. "Peradilan Agama: Kebutuhan atau Kecemasan," *Tempo*, 24 June 1989, p. 24. By 1996 the only provinces without Islamic High Courts were Bali and East Timor. Based on Department of Religion Statistics.

74. Chap. I, Art. 5.

75. Lev, *Islamic Courts*, pp. 95–96.

76. Lev, *Islamic Courts*, pp. 70–75. The Department of Justice supported Religion's effort to retain administrative control over the Islamic courts in order to protect its own prerogative as the administrative head of the civil court system. The Indonesian bar had long advocated placing the civil courts under the auspices of the Supreme Court as a means of promoting their independence, and continues to do so. Lev, *Islamic Courts*, p. 74, n. 15.

77. Lev, *Islamic Courts*, pp. 71–75.

78. Law No. 14, Ch. II, Art. 10(3) (1970).

79. See Cammack, "Islamic Law in Indonesia's New Order," pp. 66–67 and sources cited therein.

80. "Perkembangan Hukum Islam dan Peradilan Agama di Indonesia," in *Kenang Kenangan Seabad Peradilan Agama di Indonesia* (Jakarta: Department Of Religion, 1985), pp. 47–48.

81. Articles 7 and 8 provide that first instance courts are created by Presidential decree and high courts by statute. The first instance courts are to consist of the court "administration" (*pimpinan*) made up of the chair and deputy chair, member judges, clerks, secretarial staff, and the new position of bailiff/huissier (*juru sita*) necessitated

by the courts' new enforcement powers. Chap. II, Arts. 9(1), 10(1). The high courts are made up of the administration, including a chair and deputy, high court judges as members, clerks and secretaries. Chap. II, Arts 9(2), 10(2), (3).

82. Chap. II, Art. 15(1).

83. Chap. II, Art. 13. Appointment as a high court judge includes the same requirements as well as a minimum age and a requirement of at least fifteen years service as a first instance judge. Chap. II, Art. 14. The other statutory employees are all appointed by the Minister of Religion. Chap. II, Arts. 36, 40, 47. None need be civil servants; all are required to be Muslims. Chap. II, Arts. 27–34, 39, 45. With the exception of the bailiff, all statutory employees are required to have some post-secondary education. Chap. II, Arts. 27–34, 39.

84. Lev, *Islamic Courts*, p. 111.

85. See *Standarisasi Pengadilan Agama dan Pengadilan Tinggi Agama* (Jakarta: Department of Religion, 1983), pp. 94–95. See also Cammack, "Islamic Law in Indonesia's New Order," pp. 68–70.

86. Between 1977 and 1985 the number of full time civil servant Islamic judges tripled, rising from 225 to 765. Cammack, "Islamic Law in Indonesia's New Order," p. 69. By 1989 the number of Islamic court judges had risen to over 1200. "Pengadilan Serambi Milik Kita Bersama," *Tempo*, 4 February 1989, p. 76. In 1983, 401 of the total 680 full-time judges were college graduates compared to only 12 college degree holders among all chief judges a decade earlier. Cammack, "Islamic Law in Indonesia's New Order," p. 70.

87. Chap. III, Art. 49.

88. Chap. III, Art. 51.

89. Chap. III, Art. 49(2).

90. Religious Courts Act, Law No. 7, Elucidation to Art. 49(2) (1989).

91. Supreme Court Directive of August 20, 1975. See also Cammack, "Islamic Law in Indonesia's New Order," pp. 65–66 and cases cited therein.

92. Chap. III, Art. 49(3).

93. Chap. III, Art. 50.

94. Lev, *Islamic Courts*, pp. 199–205. See also Mura Hutagalung, "Faktor-Faktor yang Menpengaruhi Mengapa Banyak Orang Menyelesaikan Masalah Kewarisan Melalui Pengadilan Agama," *Hukum dan Pembangunan* 13, no. 5 (September 1983): 409–16.

95. See e.g. "Dua Pasal RUUPA Harus Dihapus," *Serambi Indonesia*, August 5, 1989; "Disepakati Pilihan Hukum," *Suara Karya*, October 5, 1989; "Akhirnya Lancar, Pembahasan Selesai Lebih Cepat Satu Hari," *Kompas*, October 5, 1989; "RUUPA: Bisakah Mandiri?" *Kiblat*, October 23–November 5, 1989.

96. Chap. IV, Art. 54.

97. Chap. IV, Arts. 57(2), (3).

98. Chap. IV, Art. 60.

99. Chap. IV, Art. 62(1).

100. Chap. IV, Art. 65.

101. National Marriage Act, Law No. 1, Art. 39(1) (1974).

102. Gov. Reg. No. 9, Arts. 14–18 (1975).

103. Chap. IV, Art. 66(1).

104. Chap. IV, Art. 66(2). There is an exception to this rule when the wife "intentionally leaves their common home without the petitioner's permission." Ibid.

105. Chap. IV, Art. 67.
106. A list of grounds for divorce is contained in the official elucidation of the 1974 National Marriage Act, Art. 39(2), and also in the government's implementing regulation for the 1974 Act. Gov. Reg. No. 9, Art. 19 (1975).
107. Chap. IV, Art. 68.
108. In order to facilitate the reconciliation function the parties are required to appear personally at this first session unless one of the parties lives out of the country. Chap. IV, Art. 82(2).
109. Chap. IV, Arts. 69, 82(1), (4).
110. Chap. IV, Art. 70(1).
111. Chap. IV, Art. 70(2).
112. Chap. IV, Arts. 70(3), (4). The wife must be notified of the hearing, but the husband or his delegated representative can recite the *talak* in her absence. Chap. IV, Art. 70(4), (5).
113. Supreme Court Circular No. 13, August 19, 1985.
114. Chap. IV, Arts. 73–86.
115. Gov. Reg. No. 9, Arts. 20–36 (1975). In the Regulation the complaint procedure is theoretically available to either husband or wife. The Act makes it clear that it is for the only party to the marriage who would have occasion to use it, that is, the wife. Chap. IV, Art. 73.
116. The substantive law of divorce applied by Indonesian Islamic courts prior to the passage of the Marriage Act is summarized in Lev, *Islamic Courts*, pp. 153–78.
117. See Cammack, "Islamic Law in Indonesia's New Order," pp. 63–65.
118. Chap. IV, Art. 76.
119. Chap. IV, Art. 73(1).
120. Chap. IV, Arts. 82(1), (4).
121. Chap. IV, Art. 80.
122. Chap. IV, Art. 75.
123. Chap. IV, Art. 75.
124. Chap. IV, Art. 81.
125. See Joseph Schacht, *An Introduction to Islamic Law* (Oxford: Oxford University Press, 1964), p. 165.
126. See e.g., "PDI Minta RUUPA Diluruskan," *Media Indonesia*, September 26, 1989; "Tidak Ada Maksud untuk Mengubah Hukum Islam," *Pelita*, October 3, 1989.
127. See H. Achmad Roestandi and Muchjidin Effendie, *Komentar atas Undang-Undang No. 7 Tahun 1989 tentang Peradilan Agama* (Bandung: Nusantara Press, 1991), p. 18 stating that two (unidentified) legislative factions had objected to the *li'an* proposal on the grounds that it was substantive rather than procedural and violated Islamic doctrine. See also H. Munawir Sjadzali, "Landasan Pemikiran Politik Hukum Islam dalam Rangka Menentukan Peradilan Agama di Indonesia," *Hukum Islam di Indonesia: Pemikiran dan Praktek*, ed. Eddi Rudiana Arief (Bandung: PT Remaja Rosdakarya, 1991), pp. 41–67 containing the government's response to objections to the draft in which the Minister of Religion rejects the GOLKAR faction's argument that the matter of divorce on grounds of adultery is fully addressed in the Marriage Act.
128. Chap. IV, Arts. 87, 88.
129. The simple "modernist v. traditionalist" distinction obscures a great deal of diversity of viewpoint within those broad approaches. It is also true that there are other

interpretive traditions that cannot fairly be labeled either modernist or traditionalist. Nonetheless, the basic distinction between those who advocate adherence to the interpretations of the classical era jurists (traditionalists) and those who advocate a return to the original sources (modernists) remains a useful one.

130. See Al Yasa Abu Bakar, "Beberapa Teori Penalaran Fiqih dan Penerapannya," *Hukum Islam di Indonesia: Pemikiran dan Praktek*, ed. Eddi Rudiana Arief (Bandung: PT Remaja Rosdakarya, 1991), pp. 173–208 for a succinct statement of this view by an Indonesian Islamic scholar.

131. Koran xxiv, pp. 6–9. See also Asaf A. A. Fyzee, *Outlines of Muhammadan Law*, 4th ed. (Delhi: Oxford University Press, 1974), p. 166. Modernist influence is more apparent in the recently implemented Compilation of Islamic Law, which is discussed above. The most obvious example of refusal to move beyond the terms of scripture is in the provisions on inheritance. For instance, the chapter that defines intestate shares includes the provision that female children receive one-half the share of male children. Apart from being inconsistent with modern notions of equality, this rule was never widely practised in Indonesia. Its inclusion in the Compilation is explainable only on the modernist principle that there can be no derogation from those legal rules that are clearly stated in the Koran.

132. See e.g. *Polemik Reaktualisasi Ajaran Islam* (Pustaka Panjimas: Jakarta, 1988) containing a collection of responses to the Minister's proposals for inheritance law reform.

133. See Cammack, "Islamic Law in Indonesia's New Order," p. 70. Nur Ahmad Fadhil Lubis has confirmed the basically modernist outlook of the current Islamic judiciary. In a survey of approximately one hundred Islamic court judges conducted in the late 1980s, a large majority agreed that the *fiqh* texts are not always compatible with Indonesian circumstances and agreed on the need for reformation of Islamic institutions to meet changing needs. Nur Ahmad Fadhil Lubis, *Islamic Justice in Transition: A Socio-Legal Study of the Agama Court Judges in Indonesia* (Ph.D. dissertation, UCLA, 1994), pp. 322–23.

134. The Act states the general rule that "Litigation costs for marriage actions are charged to the petitioner or the complainant." Chap. IV, Art. 89(1). Included in the statutory costs are fees for clerks, witnesses, experts, translators, evidentiary reconstructions, and costs of summonses and other official announcements. Chap. IV, Art. 90(1).

135. The chapter is clearly not a comprehensive treatment of the subject. For instance, nothing in this chapter or any other treats the voting rules for the court or even the number of judges required for a court quorum. It was assumed, presumably, that matters not addressed in the statute will be regulated according to prior practice. That which is included in the chapter is not particularly noteworthy. Most often mentioned is the specification of responsibilities of the bailiff/*huissier* in enforcing court orders. This is significant because prior to the passage of the Act, enforcement of Islamic court orders had to be obtained through the civil courts.

136. Chap. VII, Art. 107, 108.

137. Draft Marriage Law, Arts. 40, 41, 42(e) (1973).

138. National Marriage Act, Law No. 1, Arts. 38–40 (1974).

139. National Marriage Act, Law No. 1, Elucidation to Art. 39(2) (1974).

140. In fact the regulations are far from clear. Indeed, there seems to have been a deliberate effort by the drafters to avoid explicitly describing the divorce procedure as a court

sanctioned *talak*. The word *talak* occurs only once, a single reference buried in the elucidation to the regulation. Even that reference seems unnecessarily obscure. It states simply that the procedure laid out in the regulation governs *talak* divorces.

141. Gov. Reg. No. 9, Arts. 14–17 (1975).
142. The popular interpretation of the Marriage Act as essentially a dead letter was advertised around the country in 1985 when Oma Irama, a popular film and music personality, married a second wife without obtaining judicial approval and then divorced his first wife through an extra-judicial *talak*, neither of which is permitted under the Marriage Act. At the time, Oma Irama was easily Indonesia's most popular entertainer and enjoyed wide name recognition throughout the country. His actions and example carried special significance because of his strong identification with Islam. Both his music and films are filled with explicit religious themes.

    News of Oma Irama's having taken a second wife and then divorcing his first made headlines in Jakarta's sensationalist "red press" for months. It was a deep embarrassment to government efforts to assert authority over Muslim marriage practices. Popular opinion of Oma Irama's actions varied. He was criticized for his insensitivity toward his first wife, who was unaware of the polygamous marriage. He was also faulted for not respecting Indonesian law. But there was seemingly universal recognition of the explanation for his actions as an acknowledgment of the ultimate authority of the religious law of marriage and divorce.

143. See Roestandi and Effendie, *Komentar*, 18; "Tidak Ada Maksud untuk Mengubah Hukum Islam," *Pelita*, October 3, 1989; "Masalah Cerai-talak Alot," *Suara Karya*, October 3, 1989.
144. "Tidak Ada Maksud untuk Mengubah Hukum Islam," *Pelita*, October 3, 1989.
145. "Pendapat Akhir Fraksi Persatuan Pembangunan DPR-RI terhadap Rancangan Undang-Undang tentang Peradilan Agama," in H. Achmad Roestandi and Muchjidin Effendie, *Komentar atas Undang-Undang No. 7 Tahun 1989 tentang Peradilan Agama* (Bandung: Nusantara Press, 1991), pp. 213–23.
146. "Pendapat Akhir Fraksi ABRI atas Rancangan Undang-Undang tentang Peradilan Agama," in H. Achmad Roestandi and Muchjidin Effendie, *Komentar atas Undang-Undang No. 7 Tahun 1989 tentang Peradilan Agama* (Bandung: Nusantra Press, 1991), pp. 199–212.
147. Supreme Court Circular No. 2 (April 3, 1990).
148. A description of the project by the Supreme Court Justice who chaired it can be found in Bustanul Arifin, "Kompilasi: Fiqh dalam Bahasa Undang-Undang," *Pesantren* 2, no. 2 (1985): 25–30.
149. Pres. Ins. No. 1 (June 10, 1991).
150. Compilation of Islamic Laws, Chap. XVI, Art. 115.
151. Compilation of Islamic Laws, Chap. XVI, Art. 129.
152. Compilation of Islamic Laws, Chap. XVI, Art. 117 (emphasis added).
153. Compilation of Islamic Laws, Chap. XVI, Art. 123.
154. M. Yahya Harahap, "Informasi Materi Kompilasi Hukum Islam: Mempositifkan Abstraksi Hukum Islam," *Mimbar Hukum* 3, no. 5 (1992): 21–63.
155. Ibid., p. 22.
156. Ibid.
157. Ibid., pp. 29–30.
158. Ibid., p. 52.

159. As Justice Harahap put it, "It is as if Indonesia has created its own doctrine (*fiqh*) and school (*mazhab*), distinct from the schools that have existed in the past." Ibid., p. 37.

160. Clifford Geertz summed up the failure of Islamic modernism or "scripturalism" to escape the constricting influence of textual literalism: "Stepping backward in order better to leap is an established principle in cultural change . . . But in the Islamic case the stepping backward seems often to have been taken for the leap itself, and what began as a rediscovery of the scriptures ended as a kind of deification of them." Clifford Geertz, *Islam Observed: Religious Development in Morocco and Indonesia* (Chicago: University of Chicago Press, 1968), p. 69.

161. Cf. R. William Liddle, "The Islamic Turn in Indonesia: A Political Explanation," *Journal of Asian Studies* 55 (August 1996): 613–34 arguing that the Suharto government's support for the reformist oriented Association of Muslim Intellectuals or ICMI is designed to derive political advantage from the Islamization of Indonesian society. For a different view of the significance of ICMI see Robert W. Hefner, "Islam, State, and Civil Society: ICMI and the Struggle for the Indonesian Middle Class," *Indonesia* 56 (1993): 1–35.

162. See John Henry Merryman, *The Civil Law Tradition: An Introduction to the Legal Systems of Western Europe and Latin America*, 2d ed. (Stanford: Stanford University Press, 1985), pp. 19–22; Gianfranco Poggi, *The Development of the Modern State: A Sociological Introduction* (Stanford: Stanford University Press, 1978), pp. 87–92.

163. Cf. e.g. H. Muhammad Daud Ali, "Soal Anak Sudah Diatur Syariah," *Mimbar Hukum* 25 (1996): 33–38, in which a leading modernist scholar of Islamic law states, in opposing a proposal for a statute governing juvenile courts, that adoption and other matters relating to children are regulated in the original sources of Islamic law, and that state rules contrary to Islamic doctrine will not be obeyed.

7

THE POLITICAL BACKDROP OF THE ENACTMENT OF THE COMPILATION OF ISLAMIC LAWS IN INDONESIA

Ahmad Imam Mawardi

INTRODUCTION

Kompilasi Hukum Islam di Indonesia (KHI), literally translated as the Compilation of Islamic Laws in Indonesia, is one of many vehicles used by the Indonesian Government to unify and codify Islamic law. This codification, utilized by judges in the religious courts, was meant to serve as a reference guide in deciding cases. Before the enactment of the KHI, other efforts to unify and codify Islamic law had been tried out. A government regulation suggesting the use of only thirteen *fiqh* books[1] as judicial references and the enactment of Marriage Law No. 1/1974 and Religious Judicature Act No. 7/1989 are among those efforts.

With respect to the historical perspective, efforts to unify and codify Islamic law in Indonesia may be regarded as an extension and perpetuation of Islamic legal thought expressed throughout the development of Islamic law. Notions of unification, compilation, and codification have occupied jurists from the early days of Islamic history. Ibn al-Muqaffa' (d. 139/756), for example, suggested to al-Mansur (754–775), an Abbasid Caliph, that "the caliph should review the different doctrines, codify and enact his own decisions in the interest of uniformity, and make this code binding on the *kadis*".[2] For this reason, Ibn al-Muqaffa' proposed to al-Mansur

This chapter is derived from the author's Master thesis, "The Socio-Political Backdrop of the Enactment of the Compilation of Islamic Laws in Indonesia" (McGill University, 1998).

to make the *al-Muwatta'* of Imam Malik ibn Anas, the Medinan jurist, the standard juridical work to be used throughout the empire. During his first pilgrimage, al-Mansur met with Imam Malik and repeated al-Muqaffa's proposal to make the *al-Muwatta'* the standardized reference for all juristic questions, and that it be given a prominent place in the *Ka'bah*, with copies circulating in all parts of the empire.[3] However, Imam Malik declined the suggestion,[4] insisting that people should not be forced to adhere to the opinions of a single jurist — opinions, which might possibly be wrong and imperfect.[5]

From the medieval era on, efforts to codify Islamic law, or in the words of Muhammad Hashim Kamali "the introduction of statutory legislation", have been made in most Muslim countries.[6] In the Ottoman Empire, particularly during the Tanzimat period (1839–1879), the government was successful in codifying the provisions of Islamic law and compiling them in the so-called *Majallah al-Ahkam al-'Adliyah*.[7] The Mughal emperor Awrangzib Alamgir (d.1707) ordered the compilation of *fatwa*s known as *Fatawa al-Alamgiriya* or *Al-Fatawa al-Hindiyah*[8] in an attempt to unify legal rulings of his realm. The *Code Morand* or *Avant-Projet de Code du Droit Musulman Algerien*, published in 1916 in Algeria, had a similar purpose.[9] In Indonesia, attempts at the unification, compilation, and codification of Islamic laws have been numerous. The KHI, which was officially issued in 1991 through a Presidential Instruction (*Instruksi Presiden* or *Inpres*), is only the latest so far.

It should be remembered that behind the enactment of any law, the political goal of a government often encounter the demands of society. This frequently happens as Lev notes:

> What law is . . . depends upon what it is allowed to be by conditions of political power and authority, and these conditions in turn are determined by a wide variety of social, cultural and economic forces. When the conditions change, the law must also change, sometimes explicitly but at the very least implicitly.[10]

Or in Joseph Schacht's words:

> Modernist legislation is imposed by a government whenever the modernists have succeeded in gaining its sympathy and the government feels strong enough to overcome the resistance of the traditionalist.[11]

The enactment of *Majallat al-Ahkam al-'Adliyah* and the development of legal codification in Malaysia,[12] the Philippines,[13] and Thailand[14] all concede to Schacht's model as both government and society determined Islamic legal development. The enactment of the KHI is not an exception to this rule. The demands by Indonesian Muslim society for a codified set of Islamic laws and the government's support for this endeavour resulted in the enactment of the KHI. However, this development gives rise to at least two important questions: why was the KHI enacted as late as 1991 when the need for codification had long been felt? To what degree are the contents of the KHI political?

In an attempt to answer these important questions, this chapter provides an analysis of the political backdrop to the emergence of the KHI, a standardized reference by which the religious courts (*Pengadilan Agama*) apply Islamic law in

Indonesia. This analysis will focus on three major themes: first, the historical account that surrounds the issuance of the KHI; second, the relationship between the Indonesian Government and Islam, especially the political policies devised by the government to shape the development of Islamic law; and third, the political rationale behind the enactment of the KHI. All these themes will be discussed in the light of the New Order era when the KHI was enacted. Political content in the KHI in terms of the political aspects and implications of the document will also be explored.

HISTORICAL ACCOUNT OF THE KOMPILASI HUKUM ISLAM (KHI)

It would be difficult to identify, with certainty, the first figure to promote the KHI. Some say the idea was the brainchild of then Minister for Religious Affairs Munawir Sjadzali, who proposed it at a general lecture in the State Institute for Islamic Studies (IAIN) Sunan Ampel Surabaya in February 1985.[15] Others, however, believe the notion came from Professor H. Bustanul Arifin, SH,[16] the Junior Head of Religious Judicial Affairs, who organized a RAKERNISGAB (The Meeting on Co-operative Technical Work) bringing together the Supreme Court, the Department of Religious Affairs, and the High Religious Courts in a co-operative venture to develop Islamic law through jurisprudence.[17] However, a third group declares that Bustanul Arifin's initiative was little more than a response to Ibrahim Hosen's call for the compilation or codification of Islamic law.[18]

In the official history, however, the decision to enact the KHI is attributed to the co-operative efforts of the Supreme Court and Department of Religious Affairs. Together, they concluded that a functional, religio-judicial body must be preceded by two matters: (1) a formal basic foundation to the religious judicature which would ensure legal certainty in procedural law and legal security in terms of material law; and (2) a compilation of Islamic rulings pertaining to marriage, inheritance, and *waqf*, allowing judges, justice seekers, and Islamic society in general to attain legal certainty.[19]

Bustanul Arifin declared that the idea of compiling an Indonesian Islamic law first gained currency two and half years after the Supreme Court had established a judicial technique for religious courts in accord with the demands of Statute No. 14/1970. This statute places the Supreme Court at the apex of all other courts, including the religious courts, and stipulates that the personal, financial, and organizational management of existing courts are to be determined independently. The Supreme Court, however, determines judicial technique.[20] This arrangement was formalized in 1983. The idea of enactment gained wider currency once the Supreme Court had identified certain weaknesses in the religious courts. These weaknesses particularly stemmed from the legal uncertainty perpetrated by the various legal opinions resorted to in each court when ruling on similar cases. Thus, the only way to eliminate these weaknesses was by compiling all legal materials administered under the authority of the religious courts and, then, using it as a standardized reference for all legal arbitration.

In short, it may be said that the notion of compilation first appeared in 1985 as a result of the co-operative efforts of the Supreme Court and the Department of Religious Affairs, which received further impetus when President Soeharto initiated and signed a letter sanctioning co-operative work (known by its Indonesian acronym SKB) between the heads of the two bodies with the aim of launching the KHI.[21] The SKB was initiated on 21 March 1985 in a formal co-operative meeting attended by the head of the Supreme Court and the Minister for Religious Affairs in Yogyakarta.[22] In this meeting, the Minister promoted the event as an opportunity as well as a challenge to the *ulama* who wished to contribute to the application of Islamic law in the country.[23]

SKB No. 07/KM/1985 and No. 25/1985 dated 25 March 1985 stated that: (1) the project is to be headed by Professor Bustanul Arifin, SH, from the Supreme Court, and assisted by two individuals: one from the Supreme Court and the other from the Department of Religious Affairs; (2) the project must be completed within two years of the date of the SKB's commencement; (3) an outline of the schedule and agenda of the project were to keep it true to what had been decided upon; (4) the guarantee of financial support from the government on the basis of the Presidential Decision (*Keputusan Presiden*) No. 191/SOSRROCH/1985[24] and No. 068/SOSRROCH/1987; (5) the project was to begin on 25 March 1985; and (6) a stipulation that the premier aim of the project should be to develop Islamic law through jurisprudence by enacting the KHI. This last stipulation affirmed that the goals of the project were to ascertain the "living" Islamic laws in society and, together with the compilation of regulations derived from various *fiqh* texts, to devise suitable Islamic laws for Indonesia.[25]

To attain these goals the project initiated four stages: the gathering of data; interviews; comparative studies; and a workshop.[26] The first stage — gathering data — entailed the examination of thirty-eight *fiqh* texts[27] and numerous works of jurisprudence. The chosen *fiqh* texts do not only originate from the Shafi'ite *mazhab* (school of thought), but from other *mazhabs* as well. The thirty-eight books are listed here:

1. *Hashiyyah Kifayat al-Akhyar* by Ibrahim ibn Muhammad Al-Bajuri
2. *Fath al-Mu'in* by Zayn al-Din al-Malibari
3. *Sharqawi 'Ala al-Tahrir* by 'Ali ibn Hijazi ibn Ibrahim al-Sharqawi
4. *Mughni al-Muhtaj* by Muhammad al-Sharbini
5. *Nihayat al-Muhtaj* by Al-Ramli
6. *Al-Sharqawi 'Ala al-Hudud* by 'Ali ibn Hijazi ibn Ibrahim al-Sharqawi
7. *I'anat al-Talibin* by Sayyid Bakri al-Dimyati
8. *Tuhfat al-Muhtaj* by Shihab al-Din Ahmad Ibn Hajar al-Haytami
9. *Targhib al-Mushtaq* by Shihab al-Din Ahmad Ibn Hajar al-Haytami
10. *Bulghat al-Salik* by Ahmad Ibn Muhammad al-Sawi
11. *Al-Faraid* by Shamsuri
12. *Al-Mudawwanat al-Kubra* by Sahnun ibn Sa'id al-Tanukhi
13. *Kanz al-Raghibin wa Sharhuhu* by Jalal al-Din Muhammad al-Mahalli

14. *Fath al-Wahhab* by Abu Yahya Zakariyya al-Ansari
15. *Bidayat al-Mujtahid* by Ibn Rushd
16. *Al-Umm* by Muhammad ibn Idris al-Shafi'i
17. *Bughyat al-Mustarshidin* by 'Abd al-Rahman ibn Muhammad al-'Alawi
18. *Aqidah wa al-Shari'ah* by Mahmud Shaltut
19. *Al-Muhalla* by 'Ali ibn Muhammad Ibn Hazm
20. *Al-Wajiz* by Abu Hamid al-Ghazzali
21. *Fath al-Qadir 'Ala al-Hidayah* by Muhammad ibn 'Abd al-Wahid al-Siwasi
22. *Al-Fiqh 'Ala Madhahib al-Arba'a* by 'Abd al-Rahman al-Jaziri
23. *Fiqh al-Sunnah* by Sayyid Sabiq
24. *Kashf al-Qina' 'an Tadmin al-Sana'i'* by Ibn Rahhal al-Ma'dani
25. *Majmu' Fatawa Ibn Taimiyyah* Ahmad ibn Taymiyyah
26. *Qawanin al-Shar'iyyah* by al-Sayyid 'Uthman ibn Aqil ibn Yahya
27. *Al-Mughni* by 'Abd Allah ibn Ahmad Ibn Qudamah
28. *Hidayah Sharh Bidayat al-Mubtadi* by 'Ali ibn Abi Bakr al-Marghinani
29. *Qawanin al-Shar'iyyah* by Sayyid 'Abdullah ibn Sadaqah Dakhlan
30. *Mawahib al-Jalil* by Muhammad ibn Muhammad Hattab
31. *Hashiyat Radd al-Mukhtar* by Muhammad Amin ibn 'Umar Ibn Abidin
32. *Al-Muwatta'* by Malik ibn Anas
33. *Hashiyya al-Dasuqi 'ala al-Sharh al-Kabir* by Ibn 'Arafah al-Dasuqi
34. *Bada'i' al-Sana'i' fi Tartib al-Shara'i'* by Abu Bakr Ibn Mas'ud al-Kasani
35. *Tabyin al-Haqa'iq* by Mu'in al-Din ibn Ibrahim al-Farahi
36. *Al-Fatawa al-Hindiyyah* by al-Shaikh Nizam and other 'ulama'
37. *Fath al-Qadir* by Muhammad ibn Ahmad al-Safati al-Zaynabi
38. *Nihayat al-Zayn* by Muhammad Ibn 'Umar al-Nawawi.

In examining these books, the committee for the project devised questions to be resolved by seven IAINs[28] by referring to the above books. Their conclusions were subsequently discussed by the *ulama* in a separate workshop.

While the thirty-eight books convey a definite bias in favour of the Shafi'ite school of thought,[29] a few books from the other schools, were also taken into consideration. The use of Ibn Qudamah's *al-Mughni* and *Majmu' Fatawa Ibn Taimiyyah* (from the Hanbalite school), Maliki's *al-Muwatta'* and Zaynabi's *Fath al-Qadir* (Malikite school), and *Tabyin al-Haqa'iq* and *Fatawa al-Hindiyyah* which generally follow the Hanafite school, are very important comparative texts. Moreover, the use of books that fall outside the four schools, such as Ibn Hazm's *al-Muhalla* from the Zahirite school and Sayyid Sabiq's *Fiqh al-Sunnah*, which are comparative legal books, was very meaningful to the development of Islamic law in Indonesia, since the promotion of pluralism in Islamic thought has become the new paradigm in Indonesia.[30]

While the books convey a strong grasp of Islamic law and an openness to opinions that fall outside the Shafi'ite *mazhab*, they lack one very important element axiomatic for contextualization of Islamic law — none of these texts include the works or *fatwas* of Indonesian scholars who based their opinions on specifically

Indonesian social phenomena. These include the works of Hasbi Ash-Shiddieqy,[31] Hazairin,[32] and A. Hassan,[33] to name but a few. The KHI failed to consider any of these important works. Fortunately, this imbalance was tempered by the formal use of *fatwa*s issued from the MUI (Majelis Ulama Indonesia, or Council of Indonesian Ulama),[34] the Majelis Tarjih of Muhammadiyah,[35] and the Bahtsul Masa'il of Nahdlatul Ulama (NU),[36] which were included in the gathered data.[37]

Aside from examining the *fiqh* books, the committee also examined jurisprudential works that had been compiled into sixteen books. These can be categorized into the following groups: four books of compiled legal decisions; three books of compiled *fatwa*s; five books of jurisprudence from the religious courts; and four law report books.[38] These were studied by the Directorate of the Establishment of the Bodies of the Religious Judicature (Ditbinbapera).

The second stage of the KHI project consisted of interviews with the *ulama*. One hundred and sixty-six *ulama*, regarded as the representatives of the body of Indonesian *ulama*, were interviewed from across ten cities. In addition, of the 166 *ulama*, some were representatives of Islamic organizations while others were independent *ulama*, especially from among the heads of the *pesantren*s. The interviews were conducted both individually and collectively at a set location where the *ulama*'s opinions were solicited on the problems outlined in the agenda.[39] These interviews proved fruitful in illuminating the Islamic laws to be used by Indonesian Muslim society. Hasan Basri, head of the MUI, commented that this interview process would make the KHI's work "responsive, accommodative, and credible".[40]

The third stage entailed comparative studies with the Muslim countries of Egypt, Turkey, and Morocco, to which Indonesian experts in Islamic law were sent.[41] Morocco was chosen because it followed the Malikite school; Turkey, because it was a secular state and follower of the Hanafite school; and Egypt, because of its geographical position between Morocco and Turkey and its adherence to the Shafi'ite *mazhab*.[42] A question about the choice of the comparative countries is: why was a Hanbalite country, such as Saudi Arabia or Syria, not included in this comparative study when Hanbalite opinions are found in the KHI and in Indonesian society? In this manner, the means by which each of these countries applied Islamic law, particularly in matters related to the KHI's work, could be understood and taken into account in making the KHI.

The last stage comprised a five-day[43] workshop in Jakarta, inaugurated by the head of the Supreme Courts, Ali Said, and the Minister for Religious Affairs. In his speech, the Minister asserted that:

> To place the religious courts on a firm basis, or in stable condition, the New Order government has striven to provide a draft of the bill for the religious judicature . . . [such that] the religious courts will be independent courts . . . The continuous effort that is exerted by the New Order government in improving and establishing a stable religious court is completing and perfecting the material laws used by the religious court. Ideally, new complete regulation should be in the form of law (*Undang-undang*), but for a temporal time, based on

agreement between the Supreme Court and the Department of Religious Affairs, this will be in a form of a Compilation of Islamic Law, that will be a reference or guide for the Religious Courts.[44]

The Minister's choice of words, especially the words "ideally" and "for a temporal time", implied a willingness to promulgate the KHI into law with binding power over the issues brought before the religious courts.

The workshop was attended by 124 persons from every province in Indonesia, including the heads of the provincial MUI, the heads of the High Religious Courts, rectors of IAINs, deans of *Syari'a* faculties, *ulama*, Muslim scholars, and representatives of Islamic and women's organizations.[45] Unfortunately, none of the examiners of the thirty-eight *fiqh* texts were invited to contribute to this workshop and were, as such, unable to present their comments.[46] Three different committees were formed to evaluate the acquired data in the various areas of law: (1) the law of marriage; (2) the law of inheritance; and (3) the *waqf* law.[47] The workshop resulted in the compilation of three volumes of the KHI containing 229 articles: the first volume deals with marriage law; the second one evaluates inheritance law; and the third deals with *waqf* law.

Three years after its completion, the KHI came into legal force through Presidential Instruction (*Inpres*) No. 1/1991,[48] dated 10 June 1991, and followed by the Decision of the Minister for Religious Affairs No. 154/1991,[49] dated 22 July 1991.

GOVERNMENT AND ISLAM IN THE NEW ORDER ERA

President Sukarno's letter to General Soeharto "to take all steps deemed necessary to guarantee the security, tranquility and stability of the government machinery and the process of the revolution",[50] ushered in the New Order era on 11 March 1966, and marked a decisive transfer of political power.[51]

It is widely held that Sukarno's letter was dictated by the political will of ABRI (Indonesian army), which hoped to limit the power and authority of the PKI (Partai Komunis Indonesia, or Indonesian Communist Party) and a large part of society concurred with that judgement. Towards that end, a coalition between ABRI, Muslims, and students was formed as a front against the communist bloc that had gained strength in the last part of the Old Order era. Muslims joined in this endeavour out of a dislike for the ideology of communism and for the style of the Old Order government.[52] In addition, Muslims hoped that the New Order era would bring them a better life[53] and allow them a greater role in civic affairs. They were to be disappointed. Even though they participated in efforts to establish the New Order government, Muslims did not initially gain much in image and position in the New Order system.[54] Instead, the relationship between the state and Islam in the initial period of the New Order establishment was marked by small gain and much discord.

Dody S. Truna differentiates two periods in the relationship between the government and Islam: first, the period from 1966 to 1984, when the relationship was coloured by mutual suspicion and limited accommodation; and, second, the period from 1985 to 1990 when the relationship was more co-operative and mutually supportive.[55] Abdul Azis Thaba segments the same time frame into three periods: first, the antagonistic period from 1966 to 1981; second, a reciprocal and critical period from 1982 to 1985; and the last, the accommodative period from 1986 up to the present.[56] Both writers, however, come to a similar conclusion that the relationship between Islam and the government in the New Order era was always moving towards a better direction.[57] Howard M. Federspiel, however, believes that the political tendencies towards accommodative relationship have occurred since the 1970s.[58] Federspiel's notion appears closer to the fact as in 1974 and 1975, the government began accommodating the Muslim aspirations concerning the law of marriage as evinced by the promulgation of Law No. 1/1974 and Government Regulation No. 9/1975.

The first two decades of the New Order era — the antagonistic period — were marked by high government suspicion of Muslim involvement in building the New Order system.[59] Afan Gaffar[60] provides three reasons for this state of hostile suspicion. The first is that Muslims operated on the premise that an enhanced Islamic role in the state affairs would be preceded by the democratic reforms called for by Islam. Secondly, it was feared that majority of the Muslim population would mobilize to achieve political power and facilitate Islam's penetration into the political realm. And thirdly, Gaffar believes that among Muslims, it was felt that many individuals and groups were inclined to interpret Islam literally and to express strong criticism against the government for not following their conception of just what an "Islamic" government should be.

Aside from the aforementioned, Islam's "image problem" in the eyes of the government and the features of the New Order government itself also contributed to the strained dialogue. Among the Army Ground Forces (ABRI Angkatan Darat), for example, unpleasant memories remained of past experience with some Muslims, such as Kartosuwiryo, Kahar Muzakkar, and Daud Beureuh, who fought to establish an Islamic state and a diminished national Indonesian state. To the armed forces, therefore, Islam remained suspicious and was marked as an ideology of the "extreme right". The New Order government's "authoritarian" and hostile posture towards Islamic political aspiration and Muslim sentiment created antipathy on the part of many Muslims and invited a negative response from the Muslim society.[61]

In the legal field, the New Order government launched an agenda to clarify the type and order of law permitted and regulated by the Constitution of 1945. The People's Assembly, through Decree No. XX/MPRS/1966, determined that Pancasila must be a source of all laws and adopted the following order of laws proposed by the House of Representatives:

a. Constitution (*Undang-undang Dasar*)
b. Decrees of the People's Assembly (*Ketetapan MPR*)
c. Statutes (*Undang-undang*)
d. Government Regulations (*Peraturan Pemerintah*)
e. Presidential Decisions (*Ketetapan Presiden*)
f. Other implementing regulations.[62]

In the first years of the New Order, an effort was undertaken to promote the image of Indonesia as a state based on law (*negara hukum, rechtstaat*). A law upholding the independence of judicial bodies and promoting a better judicial system was promulgated. Law No. 19/1964, which had previously allowed the President to intervene in judicial matters, was thus phased out and summarily replaced by Law No. 14/1970, the Basic Law of the Judiciary.

One important clause in Law No. 14/1970, which addresses the status of the religious court and Islamic law, recognizes the former as equal to other courts. Moreover, it outlines four court systems with a Supreme Court at the apex. These include: a Public Court (*Peradilan Umum*) for civil and criminal matters; Religious Courts (*Peradilan Agama*); Military Court (*Peradilan Militer*); and State Administrative Court (*Peradilan Tata Usaha Negara*).[63]

Theoretically, the religious court is equal to other courts in terms of its standing in the national judicial system. On the practical level, however, equality was elusive as remnants of the colonial administrative system dictated that all decisions rendered by the religious courts were to be ratified by the local civil court in order to be officially enforceable. Even Marriage Law No. 1/1974, which was largely viewed as a concession to Islamic law, stipulated that it was mandatory that all religious court decisions must be approved (*dikukuhkan*) by its counterpart, the Civil Court.[64] This indicates that the religious courts were actually below the civil courts.[65]

Among other indicators of the antagonistic relationship between Islam and government in the period 1966–81 is the government's idea to put *aliran kepercayaan* (literally meaning "the syncretism belief group") into the GBHN (State General Guidelines) as one of the "official religions" of Indonesia, with equal standing to Islam, Christianity, Hinduism, and Buddhism.[66] The members of this group were seen by Muslim community readers as Muslims, despite their adherence to practices and beliefs drawn from traditions other than Islam. Consequently the effort to move them away from Islam was bitterly approved. At the end of the day, however, Muslim protests against this initiative went unheard.

Soon after the *aliran kepercayaan* case, on 16 August 1973, the government brought up another controversy: the Draft of the Marriage Law (RUU Perkawinan) which contained regulations seen by many Muslim scholars as not reflecting some of the nuances of Islamic law. Kamal Hassan mentions that all *ulama*, from Aceh to East Java, from both traditional or modern institutions, opposed this Draft Law.[67] Some critics dubbed this an effort to Christianize Indonesian law, while others argued that the Draft was made without the consultation or involvement of the Department of Religious Affairs, widely regarded as the authoritative institution on the matter. The vehemence of the response prompted the government to compromise by deleting the clauses regarded as problematic and un-Islamic.[68]

The next period, from 1982 to 1985,[69] was characterized by a growing reciprocity between the government and Islam. Over these four years, a balance of accommodation and understanding was struck between the two positions. This period was also marked by government calls for Pancasila to be accepted as the sole ideological basis of political organizations and, later on, of all social organizations.

Muslim reactions varied. Some reacted passively and in the spirit of order, while other reactions were extreme and flouted the new regulation.[70] The more compliant position was taken by the Partai Persatuan Pembangunan (PPP, or United Development Party), an Islamic political party, while the latter was adopted by individual groups critical of the government policy. In the long run, all political and social organizations accepted Pancasila as their sole basis of organization. The PPP was quick to accept it, while the NU became the first Islamic social organization to accept it in its general conference (*muktamar*) in 1982.[71] Muhammadiyah was the last Islamic social organization to accept Pancasila, which it did in its forty-first *muktamar* in December 1985.[72]

In 1986,[73] the accommodative[74] or good relations between Islam and the state were more obvious. In general, this accommodative relationship followed several mutual principles. Federspiel identified five main principles in operation at the time:

1. Worship and ceremonial practices of religion will be encouraged;
2. The state will continue to provide an administrative system for the functioning of certain Islamic communal obligations in education, in family matters, and in support of the pilgrimage, and to provide a mechanism for protecting the general standards of orthodoxy.
3. Religious goals will not be expressed in political terms, nor will religion be used as the primary organizational tool by political group;
4. Religious groups seeking to operate outside the system to achieve their religious goals will be treated as outlaws and punished severely.
5. Muslim leader groups, particularly religious scholars and intellectuals, will support the government's national development policies.[75]

The government regarded these as positive overture and paved the way for co-operative *détente*.[76]

Most scholars agree that the acceptance of Pancasila by Islamic social organizations as the sole ideological basis eased the government suspicion of Islam. In return, the emergence of the Law on National Education,[77] which removes the prohibition on the wearing of Islamic clothes[78] for Muslim students, is regarded as the first positive gesture for the Muslim acceptance of Pancasila as the *asas tunggal* (sole basis).

Soon after the issuance of the Law on National Education, the government again supported the Muslim aspiration by passing the Law on the Religious Judicature,[79] a procedural law that is necessary for the functioning of the religious courts. The issuance of this law, as well as the codification of Islamic law, stems from judicial uncertainty and legal confusion observed earlier in this chapter.[80]

The ratification of this law was much criticized by nationalist Muslims and non-Muslims who remain suspicious of long-term Muslim political aspirations. Some of the critics said that the law was the latest manifestation of the *Piagam Jakarta* (Jakarta Charter), which has been denounced by non-Muslim groups as negatively affecting their status. Others, especially Christians and Hindus, lobbied the government to provide other religious communities with an opportunity to have their own specific law and courts.[81] The controversy ended when President Soeharto publicly declared that the government would not apply the *Piagam Jakarta*.[82]

The promulgation of the KHI in 1991, which is the main topic of discussion of this chapter, is also seen as an extension of the government's accommodative stance towards Muslims, as the fate of the KHI was very much determined by the President and the Supreme Court. The call for the KHI generally came from the middle-class, comprising intellectuals, students, and professionals. This class is always considered the linchpin, to use Lev's term of law-movements.[83] Following Marxist analysis on the role of the middle-class in ushering in fundamental change in Europe, Lev pays great attention to the role of middle classes in promoting law in post-colonial Asia and Africa.[84]

Other government policies viewed as solicitous to the needs and interests of Muslims included the banning of the tabloid *Monitor*,[85] the sending of 1,000 *muballighs* (Islamic preachers) to resettled areas on a Rp100,000 per month stipend, the establishment of the ICMI (Ikatan Cendekiawan Muslim Indonesia, or Indonesian Muslim Intellectuals Association), the establishment of the BMI (Bank Muamalat Indonesia), and the commitment and promise of President Soeharto to finance the building or renovation of religious buildings, by using funds raised privately but distributed by the state through the Yayasan Amal Bakti Muslimin Indonesia (Social Welfare Fund for Indonesian Muslims).[86]

For their part, Muslims responded to the government by providing both direct and indirect support. Afan Gaffar lists three major incidents which show political support for government policies: (1) the show of support by Muslim leaders for Soeharto's re-election as President for the period 1993–98, (2) Muhammadiyah's support of Soeharto for re-election as President, and (3) the "political prayer" for his future success.[87]

Political observers attribute reciprocal support to the position and interests of the respective parties. For the government, Islam is no longer viewed as a threat to national stability and, conversely, can actually be used to rally the support of Muslims. Meanwhile, for Muslims, the accommodative relationship provides greater opportunity for involvement and access to the decision-making process in national policies.

From the end of the 1980s to the early 1990s was an auspicious time to launch the KHI for two main reasons: first, to drum up support for the 1992 election, the government needed to convince Muslim society of its commitment and support to Islamic life; second, the Muslims were aware that the religious courts urgently required the enactment of standardized codification, or compilation, of law to follow up on the application of the Law on the Religious Judicature and to strengthen the position of the religious courts *vis-à-vis* other courts.

The timing of this move towards legal reformation seems to lie outside Lev's theory that, in Indonesia and Thailand, legal reforms "are likely to emerge when a crisis of legitimacy almost inevitably develops between evolving middle strata and political élites".[88] Lev's theory may be appropriate for the political life of the 1970s, but not after 1980, when the relationship between the élite and middle class, including Muslim intellectuals and professionals, improved. After the 1980s, Muslims have not been confrontational in demanding legal reform as can be seen from the non-confrontational approach when faced with the controversial draft of the Law on the Religious Judicature, compared with the response to the enactment of Law No. 1/1974 on Marriage. This harmonious relationship between political élites and the Muslim middle class was also evident when the KHI was enacted.

POLITICAL RATIONALE BEHIND THE KHI

Despite the politico-historical explanation for the emergence of the KHI, which stresses the self-interest of both the government and the Muslims, an examination of the codes themselves illuminates the political rationale behind their enactment. The enactment of any new law must take into account the opinions and interests of the public, as well as the social, cultural, and political norms of the society.[89] The power of a government comes into play when normative rules are translated into a formal system.[90] Islamic law, as a set of regulations or rules, can also be shifted or translated into a formal legal system in Indonesia, as had been done with other regulations arising from other sources of law.

As far as historical perspectives are concerned, the accommodative relationship between the government and Islam, which characterized the early 1980s, has continued to elicit a positive response from the government with respect to the needs and interests of Muslims.[91] Government support to the Muslim life in general and the practice of Islamic law in particular eventually culminated in the promulgation of a procedural and codified law to fulfil the juridical needs of the Islamic courts. On 29 December 1989, the government implemented Law No. 7/1989 on Religious Judicature, after overcoming the criticisms and protests of both Muslim nationalists and non-Muslims.[92] The promulgation of the law was considered as having provided enough incentive for the Supreme Court and the Department of Religious Affairs to enact the KHI, a compilation of material law,[93] without which the Law on Religious Judicature cannot work proportionally.

After the KHI committee completed the draft of this codified Islamic law, its members encouraged the government to give the new code a formal status. However, disagreement as to whether the KHI would be issued as a law/statute, or as a Presidential Decision (*Keputusan Presiden*), soon emerged. Although Muslims wanted it to be circulated at least in the form of a Presidential Decision, the final result was that it was formed and legalized by Presidential Instruction No. 1/ 1991.[94]

The ease with which the government agreed to the KHI's project was also indicative of its willingness to transform Islamic law into national legislation. This intention had been obvious ever since the government issued the Law on Religious Judicature in 1989.[95] The government apparently reasoned that this was legally permitted by the 1945 Constitution, which recognizes Islamic law as the unwritten law of Indonesian Muslim society.[96] A more obvious sign supporting this legal transformation was found in the speech of the Minister for Religious Affairs at the opening session of the workshop on the KHI, which made a strong statement for the KHI to become formal law.[97] In relation to this, Masran Basran states that the KHI, as a formal or positive law, represents the unification of national law as governed by the State General Guidelines (GBHN); the KHI then mediates legitimacy for Islamic law in the national legal arena.[98]

The political rationale of the enactment of the KHI may also be viewed from the stated and assumed goals set out by the committee itself. M. Yahya Harahap,[99] one of the committee members of the KHI project, says that there were at least four goals operative during deliberation: (1) to complete the pillars of the religious judicature; (2) to make legal application uniform; (3) to cement the notion of *ukhuwah* (Islamic brotherhood);[100] and (4) to deter the settling of disputes in a non-formal manner. The three pillars mentioned in the first goal include the existence of a well-organized judicial body, the functionaries (that is, judges and advocates) and the sources of reference. The Islamic court had met the first requirements by being accepted as a state court under the control of the Supreme Court as the highest state court.[101] The second pillar had been fulfilled by the religious courts even before Indonesia gained its independence. But, the third pillar, that is, as a source of reference, generated confusion before the introduction of the KHI. Although the Marriage Law, Government Regulation No. 1/1975, and a few clauses in the Law on Religious Judicature all deal with material law, many matters remained unaddressed. To fill this void, the KHI was conceived and offered as a positive codified law.[102]

As an instrument for uniformity in legal decisions, the KHI was not intended to hamper the creativity of judges, but rather to eliminate disparity in legal decisions in the interest of social justice and of legal certainty. The KHI was also meant to promote *ukhuwah* (brotherhood among Muslims) and to minimize debate and conflict concerning *khilafiyah* (the legal problems which are subject to various opinions and interpretations)[103] on matters of marriage, inheritance, and *waqf*. The many problematic cases and resulting chaos that arose out of *khilafiyah*[104] made this an imperative.

The last goal was to remove the traditional assumption that family law was a personal matter which needed no government intervention. Many Muslim citizens, *ulama,* and even élites still believe that the government should remain aloof from the administration of Islamic law in the areas of private business and personal affairs.[105] Marriage, divorce, and inheritance, for example, are considered the personal affairs of man before his God without requiring any intervention from others. This view was not accepted. Instead, the community obligation was stressed and KHI legitimated government intervention in the application of Islamic law on the basis of social welfare.

As a material law used in the State Islamic court, the support of the government in its enactment is necessary. The involvement of the Supreme Court, one of whose duties is to control the legal application of the Islamic courts, and also the direct support from President Soeharto both indicate the government interest towards the KHI. The KHI offers political advantages both to the government and the Islamic courts. These advantages can be clearly understood through these three points.

First, the enactment of the KHI in the late 1980s and its launch in 1991 are politically very meaningful to the government, that is, to demonstrate better relationship between the New Order government and Islam, and to convince the Muslims that the government is giving considerable attention to Muslim concerns. In turn, the Muslims are expected to give their support to government policies.

Secondly, the goals of the KHI clearly show the political will behind the enactment of the KHI. One goal is to give Islamic courts a stronger position in the Indonesian legal system. Doubt on the Islamic courts as independent courts was refuted soon after the enactment of both the procedural Law on Religious Judicature and the KHI as the material law. Another clear goal is to shift Islamic law along with some *adat* laws, from unwritten law, as mentioned in Article II of the transitional provision in the Constitution of 1945, into the written law. Many scholars suggest that the promulgation of the KHI is the way to ratify Islamic law. Another purpose, although not an absolutely clear one, is to help the Supreme Court in its function to monitor and control the legal practice of the Islamic courts. This is not without complication since, as it is known, only one person among the members of the Supreme Court can read Arabic text. Therefore, the enactment of the KHI in the Indonesian language and in the format of a statute should facilitate the members of the Supreme Court in monitoring and controlling the Islamic courts.

The third point is that many of the provisions in the KHI echo previous regulations and law, particularly the Law on Marriage No. 1/1974, Government Regulations No. 9/1975 and No. 28/1977. There are two reasons behind these similarities: first, the Muslims want to support the existence and application of previous laws and regulations, which also signifies, to some extent, their support of the government; second, they want to put the position of the KHI equal to the laws and regulations whose provisions are adopted by the KHI.

The combinations of these goals constitute general political rationale for the promulgation of the Kompilasi Hukum Islam. Whether this reasoning is actually realized after the enactment of the KHI is another issue which needs further research.

CONCLUSION

The enactment of the Compilation of Islamic Laws (KHI) in Indonesia is the latest effort to keep pace with social development and stay within tradition. The KHI has presented novel regulations on cases which are not previously recognized by Indonesian Islamic law. The use of non-Shafi'ite sources at the official judicial institutional level may be considered a new historical chapter, following legal developments being discussed at the academic level. In addition, the willingness to consider social tradition and custom (*adat*) in choosing the law compiled in the KHI reflects the spirit of the Islamic legal reform, as promoted by many scholars who seek to Indonesianize *fiqh* or indigenize Islamic law. This matter reverses a tradition of simply referring to the regulations stated by *fiqh* classical sources. However, it is unfortunate that the topics taken up by the KHI do not cover all legal trends and new cases in the society. It is right to say that although the KHI has demonstrated very rapid development in terms of the references used, the boundaries of family law do not really go beyond the family law covered by the previous law.

However, the promulgation of the KHI, with its limits and weaknesses, at least, has helped lessen the rigidity of the current Islamic courts in rendering decisions. As a material law that acts as a counterpart to procedural Law on Religious Judicature, the KHI with its Presidential Instruction and Ministry decision is suitable to be the main reference on Indonesian Muslim family law.

The accommodation of KHI to *adat* law does not necessarily mean the end of *adat* law or its replacement by Islamic law. Rather it reunites what has been lost for a long time. Moreover, as the product of many Indonesian *ulama* and scholars, the KHI is a great legal phenomena in terms that the Islamic legal reform and renewal are not promoted by the Islamic side alone but, rather from the standpoint of social consensus and the involvement of the government.

The renewal or reform made by the KHI is actually in line with Islamic legal trends in academic life. In the IAIN, for instance, the voice of Islamic reform and the use of many modern sources as reference of study have been clearly advocated for some time. The study of comparative *mazhab*s (*muqaranat al-madhahib*) in the *Shari'a* faculty is the most apparent development in this matter. Therefore, we may say that the enactment of KHI is, to some extent, an attempt to follow this academic trend.

Notes

1. Those books are *Bughyat al-Mushtarshidin* by Husain al-Ba'lawi, *al-Faraid* by al-Shamsuri, *Fath al-Mu'in* by Zayn al-Din al-Malibari, *Fath al-Wahhab* by Zakariyya al-Ansari, *Kifayat al-Akhyar* by al-Bajuri, *Mughni al-Muhtaj* by al-Sharbini, *Qawanin al-Shar'iyyah* by Sayyid 'Uthman ibn Yahya, *Qawanin al-Shar'iyyah* by Sayyid 'Abdullah Ibn Sadaqah Dakhlan, *Sharh Kanz al-Raghibin* by al-Qalyubi and 'Umayrah, *Sharh al-Tahrir* by al-Sharqawi, *Tuhfat al-Muhtaj* by Ibn Hajar al-Haytami, *Targhib al-Mushtaq*

by Ibn Hajar al-Haytami, and *al-Fiqh 'ala Madhahib al-Arba'ah* by al-Jaziri. These books were used on the basis of the Letter of the Religious Judiacry Bureau (*Surat Edaran Biro Peradilan Agama*) No. 8/1/735, dated 18 February 1958 as a manifestation of Government Regulation (PP) No. 45/1957 regarding the establishment of Religious Court/Mahkamah Syar'iyah outside Java and Madura. The above books are Shafi'ite, except for the last one, *al-Fiqh 'ala Madhahib al-Arba'ah*, which provides comparative opinions from the four famous schools of Islamic law, that is, the schools of Maliki, Hanafi, Shafi'i, and Hanbali.

2. Joseph Schacht, *Introduction to Islamic Law* (Oxford: Clarendon Press, 1986), p. 55. See also N. J. Coulson, *A History of Islamic Law* (Edinburgh: Edinburgh University Press, 1964), p. 52. In Marshal G. S. Hodgson's words, Ibn al-Muqaffa' urged al-Mansur to control any group in the society "by rallying the agrarian classes . . . and tying the religious specialist (*ulama*) to the state". His policy towards the *ulama* was making "the piety minded . . . into an official established order . . . copying such a priestly structure by asserting a final authority in question of law". See *The Venture of Islam* (Chicago: The University of Chicago Press, 1977), vol. 1, pp. 284–85.

3. Mazheruddin Siddiq, Preface to *Muwatta' Imam Malik*, trans. and notes by Muhammad Rahimuddin (New Delhi: Kitab Bhavan, 1989), pp. iv–v.

4. Patricia Crone and Martin Hinds, *God's Caliph: Religious Authority in the First Century of Islam* (Cambridge: Cambridge University Press, 1986), pp. 86–87. See also Joseph Schacht, "Foreign Elements in the Ancient Islamic Law", *Journal of Comparative Legislation and International Law* 32 (1950): 17; Ann Elizabeth Mayer, "The Shari'ah: A Methodology or a Body of Substantive Rules", in *Islamic Law and Jurisprudence: Studies in Honor of Farhat J. Ziadeh*, edited by Nicholas Heer (London: University of Washington Press, 1990), p. 179.

5. Siddiq, Preface to *Muwatta'*, p. v.

6. Muhammad Hashim Kamali, *Principles of Islamic Jurisprudence* (Cambridge: Islamic Text Society, 1991), p. xvii.

7. See S. S. Onar, "The Majallah", in *Law in the Middle East: Origin and Development of Islamic Law*, edited by Majid Khaddury and Herbert J. Liebesny (Washington, D.C.: The Middle East Institute, 1955), pp. 292–306.

8. See Shaikh Nizam and 'Ulama' al-Hind al-'Alam, *al-Fatawa al-'Alamkiriyah al-Ma'rufah bi al-Fatawa al-Hindiyyah*, edited by Ghulam Nabi Tunsawi (Kuitiyah: Maktabah Majidiyah, 1983), 6 vols.

9. See Schacht, *Introduction to Islamic Law*, pp. 94–98.

10. Daniel S. Lev, *Islamic Courts in Indonesia* (Berkeley: University of California Press, 1972), p. 2.

11. Schacht, *Introduction to Islamic Law*, p. 105.

12. See Ahmad Ibrahim, "The Shari'ah and Codification: Malaysia Experience", *Shari'ah Law Journal* (January 1987).

13. See Datu M. O. Mastura, "Shari'ah and Codification: Islamic Legislation in Relation to Legal Reforms in the Philippines", *Shari'ah Law Journal* (January 1987).

14. See Arong Suthasasna, "Shari'ah and Codification: Thailand Experience", *Shari'ah Law Journal* (January 1987).

15. See Abdurrahman, *Kompilasi Hukum Islam di Indonesia* (Jakarta: Akademika Presindo, 1995), p. 31; See also Amrullah Ahmad et al., eds., *Dimensi Hukum Islam dalam Sistem Hukum Nasional: Mengenang 65 tahun Prof. Dr. H. Bustanul Arifin, SH* (Jakarta: Gema Insani Press, 1996), p. 11.

16. See "Sejarah Penyusunan Kompilasi Hukum Islam di Indonesia", in *Berbagai Pandangan Terhadap Kompilasi Hukum Islam*, edited by Tim Ditbinbapera (Jakarta: Yayasan al-Hikmah, 1993), p. 8.

17. See Roihan A. Rasyid, *Kompilasi Hukum Islam (Penelitian Tentang Dasar dan Norma Hukum Serta Aplikasinya di Peradilan Agama)* (Yogyakarta: Fakultas Syari'ah IAIN Sunan Kalijaga, May 1995), pp. 8–9.

18. See Panitia Penyusunan Biografi, *Prof. K. H. Ibrahim Hosen dan Pembaharuan Hukum Islam di Indonesia* (Jakarta: Putra Harapan, 1990), pp. 223–24.

19. Presented by Bustanul Arifin on 16 October 1985 in the opening ceremony of an interview with the *ulama*. See Abdul Chalim Muhammad, "Peradilan Agama dan Kompilasi Hukum Islam sebagai Pranata Hukum Nasional", *Pesantren* VII, no. 2 (1990): 35–36; See also the speech of the Minister for Religious Affairs Munawir Sjadzali in the opening ceremony of the National Seminar on Inpres 1/1991 regarding the socialization of the KHI. He said that the emergence of Law No. 7/1989 and the KHI have made the religious courts equal to other courts in the country, in terms of having procedural law and material law to gain the legal certainty. See Munawir Sjadzali, "Peradilan Agama dan Kompilasi Hukum Islam", in *Peradilan Agama dan Kompilasi Hukum Islam dalam Tata Hukum Indonesia*, edited by Moh. Mahfud et al. (Yogyakarta: UII Press, 1993), pp. 1–2.

20. According to Articles 10 and 11 of Statute No. 14/1970, LN (State Letter) 1970–74, the main stipulations of the judicial authorities are as follows: four kinds of court (Civil Court, Religious Court, Military Court, and State Administrative Court) under the Supreme Court as the highest judicial body, with jurisdiction beyond which there is no appeal (*kasasi*, the highest legal decision on a case), and control over those four courts.

21. See Ismail Sunny, "Kompilasi Hukum Islam ditinjau dari Sudut Pertumbuhan Teori Hukum Indonesia", *Suara Muhammadiyah*, No. 16/76, August 1991, p. 43; For the President's impetus and support, in the final workshop of the KHI, the Islamic leaders and the *kiyai*s asked the Minister Munawir Sjadzali to represent the whole Indonesian Muslim society to thank the President. See Sjadzali, "Peradilan Agama dan Kompilasi Hukum Islam", p. 3.

22. See Masran Basran, "Kompilasi Hukum Islam", *Mimbar Ulama*, No. 105/X, May 1986, p. 12.

23. Bustanul Arifin, "Pemahaman Hukum Islam dalam Konteks Perundang-undangan", *Wahyu*, No. 108/VII, May 1985, p. 47.

24. This financial support came directly from the President, not from the APBN (National Budget). The amount of this support was Rp.230,000,000. See *Panji Masyarakat* No. 502/XXVII, 1 May 1986.

25. For further information about the content of the mentioned SKB, see "Sejarah Penyusunan Kompilasi Hukum Islam di Indonesia", as mentioned in footnote 16 above, pp. 10–12.

26. Ibid., p. 12; Rasyid, *Kompilasi Hukum Islam*, p. 10; Compare to M. Atho' Mudzhar, *Fatwas of the Council of Indonesian Ulama*, bilingual edition (Jakarta: INIS, 1993), p. 39, who says that there are five stages. Mudzhar adds the examination of the previous jurisprudence used by the Religious Court as one stage, but according to the SKB it is included in the gathering of data. However, both are essentially correct. Mudzhar's note is similar to Zarkasih's. See Muchtar Zarkasih, "Hukum Islam dalam Putusan-putusan Pengadilan Agama", Unpublished paper, 1985, p. 10.

27. Mudzhar mentions forty-one *fiqh* books, but according to primary sources, it is thirty-eight. See Mudzhar, *Fatwas of the Council*, p. 39. The list of the thirty-eight *fiqh* texts is available in Abdurrahman, *Kompilasi Hukum Islam di Indonesia*, pp. 39–41.

28. The seven mentioned IAINs are IAIN Syarif Hidayatullah Jakarta, IAIN Sunan Kalijaga Yogyakarta, IAIN Sunan Ampel Surabaya, IAIN Arraniri Banda Aceh, IAIN Antasari Banjarmasin, IAIN Alauddin Ujungpandang, and IAIN Imam Bonjol Padang. The choice of these IAINs is based on the letter of co-operative work between the Minister for Religious Affairs and the Rectors of the IAINs dated 19 March 1986. See, Abdurrahman, *Kompilasi Hukum Islam di Indonesia*, p. 39.

29. The preference for Shafi'ite books here is a reflection of the Shafi'ite *mazhab*'s prevalence in Indonesia. From the list of books used by the project of the KHI, it is surprising that the monumental work of al-Nawawi, *Minhaj al-Talibin*, and that of al-Rafi'i, *al-Muharrar*, are not included as those books are famous and widely used in the *pesantrens* (Islamic boarding schools). The reason for this exclusion may be that commentaries of al-Nawawi and al-Rafi'i, such as *Kanz al-Raghibin* and *Mughni al-Muhtaj* have been included.

30. Compare with the thirteen books used before the KHI. See footnote 1 of this chapter. The use of the opinions of other schools, besides Shafi'ite, is indicative of the KHI's flexible and accommodative nature to Indonesian social needs.

31. T. M. Hasbi Ash-Shiddieqy was an Indonesian scholar who expressively promoted the idea of Indonesianizing *fiqh* (Islamic law). He wrote many books on various aspects of Islam such as Qur'anic exegesis (*Tafsir*), prophetic tradition (*Hadith*), and *fiqh*. Among his *fiqh* works are: *Syari'at Islam Menjawab Tantangan Zaman* (Yogyakarta: IAIN Sunan Kalijaga, 1961); *Pengantar Ilmu Fiqh* (Jakarta: Bulan Bintang, 1967); *Fiqh Islam Mempunyai Daya Elastisitas, Lengkap, Bulat dan Tuntas* (Jakarta: Bulan Bintang, 1975); *Falsafah Hukum Islam* (Jakarta: Bulan Bintang, 1975); *Hukum Antar Golongan dalam Fiqh Islam* (Jakarta: Bulan Bintang, 1971); *Kumpulan Soal-Jawab dalam Post Graduate Course Jurusan Ilmu Fiqh Dosen-dosen IAIN* (Jakarta: Bulan Bintang, 1972); *Dinamika dan Elastisitas Hukum Islam* (Jakarta: Bulan Bintang, 1976); *Pengantar Ilmu Perbandingan Madzhab* (Jakarta: Bulan Bintang, 1975).

32. Hazairin wrote many books on his Islamic legal idea and thought. Among them are *Hukum Kekeluargaan Nasional, Hukum Islam dan Masyarakat, Hukum Kewarisan Bilateral menurut Qur'an dan Hadits,* and *Tinjauan Mengenai UU Perkawinan nomor 1/1974.*

33. A. Hassan was a religious scholar who came to Indonesia from Singapore. He was very active in promoting Islamic purification in Indonesia through educational instruction. See, Howard M. Federspiel, "The Importance of Islamic Law in Twentieth Century Indonesia", Unpublished paper, p. 8; There are many books written on his thought and organization, PERSIS (Persatuan Islam). The most authoritative works specifically dealing with it are that by Howard M. Federspiel, *Persatuan Islam Islamic Reform in Twentieth Century Indonesia* (Ithaca: Modern Indonesia Project, Southeast Asia Program, Cornell University, 1970) and Akhmad Minhaji, "Ahmad Hassan and Islamic Legal Reform in Indonesia, 1887–1958", Ph.D. dissertation, McGill University, Montreal, Canada, 1997. There are many works written by Ahmad Hassan. Among others are *Soal Jawab* (1931–1950, 1956–1958), *al-Burhan* (1933), *al-Fara'id* (1949), *Risalah Zakat* (1955), *Risalah al-madzhab* (1956), and *al-Furqan* (1956).

34. The MUI was established by the government to answer queries regarding Islam in Indonesia. This council is active in issuing *fatwas* concerning Islamic legal practice. The *fatwas* issued by this council tend to support government policies. For further information on this council, see Mudzhar, *Fatwas of the Council*.

35. Majelis Tarjih is an institution within the Muhammadiyah organization which is responsible for answering religious questions. The scope covered matters on Islamic theology, law, ethics, and modern social issues. The Majelis Tarjih's answers of the problems have been compiled into many books. Among these are *Tanya-Jawab Agama I* (n.p.: Penerbit Suara Muhammadiyah, 1990) and *Tanya-Jawab Agama II* (n.p.: Penerbit Suara Muhammadiyah, 1991).

36. Like the Muhammadiyah, the NU also has an institution for discussing various problems raised by its members throughout Indonesia. This institution is called Bahtsul Masa'il (Forum for Discussing Problems). The conclusions of the answers are collected and published into many books, one of which is *Ahkam al-Fuqaha'*.

37. See M. Yahya Harahap, "Tujuan Kompilasi Hukum Islam", in *Kajian Islam tentang Berbagai Masalah Kontemporer* by IAIN Syarif Hidayatullah (Jakarta: Hikmat Syahid Indah, 1988), p. 93.

38. See Ditbinbapera, *Kompilasi Hukum Islam di Indonesia* (Jakarta: Ditbinbapera, 1991/1992), p. 152.

39. See Bustanul Arifin, "Kompilasi: Fiqh dalam Bahasa Undang-Undang", *Pesantren* II, no. 2 (1985): 29; see also Mudzhar, *Fatwas of the Council*, p. 39.

40. Hasan Basri, "Perlunya Kompilasi Hukum Islam", *Mimbar Ulama*, No. 104/X, April 1986, p. 61.

41. These experts were assisted by Indonesian students in those countries. See Harahap, "Tujuan Kompilasi", p. 29.

42. See Sjadzali, "Pengadilan Agama and Kompilasi Hukum Islam", p. 3; see also Seyyed Hossein Nasr, "Islam", in *Our Religions*, edited by Arvind Sharma (New York: Harper Collins, 1993), p. 466.

43. There are many conflicting reports on this workshop. In Presidential Instruction No. 1/1991, it is mentioned that the workshop was held from 2 to 5 February 1988, whereas in Chapter 4 of the enactment of KHI it was written that the workshop was from 2 to 6 February 1988. Rasyid, in *Kompilasi Hukum Islam*, p. 11, said that the workshop was conducted for two days. Abdurrahman in *Kompilasi Hukum Islam di Indonesia* mentions five days from 2 to 6 February 1988.

44. Translated by the author from Menteri Agama RI, *Himpunan Pidato Menteri Agama RI* (Jakarta: Biro Hukum dan Humas Sekretaris Jenderal Departemen Agama, 1988), p. 28.

45. *Sinar Darussalam* No. 166/167, 1988, p. 11; *Tempo*, 4 February 1989, gives more details about the persons who attended this workshop, that is, 13 professors of Islamic law, 46 *ulama*, 21 jurists, some judges of the Supreme Court, and a number of rectors of IAINs.

46. See footnote 12 in Rasyid, *Kompilasi Hukum Islam*, p. 11.

47. Detailed explanation of the structure of the committee can be read in Ditbinbapera, "Sejarah Penyusunan KHI", pp. 158–59.

48. A Presidential Instruction is different from a Presidential Decision in the sense that the former is not included as an Indonesian legal order while the latter is. The second difference is that a Presidential Instruction is to ask or prohibit something and is addressed to a particular individual or individuals, while the Presidential Decision is to draw up or to rescind a law or regulation and is general in terms of its scope and object. Presidential Instruction No. 1/1991, for example, is addressed to the Minister for Religious Affairs and instructs him to disseminate the KHI and to do the instruction correctly and with full responsibility. See A. Hamid S. Attamimi, "Kedudukan Kompilasi

Hukum Islam dalam Sistem Hukum Nasional: Suatu Tinjauan dari Sudut Teori Perundang-undangan Indonesia", in *Dimensi Hukum Islam dalam Sistem Hukum Nasional: Mengenang 65 Tahun Prof. Dr. H. Bustanul Arifin, SH,* edited by Amrullah Ahmad et al. (Jakarta: Gema Insani Press, 1996), pp. 153-54.

49. In a response to the Presidential Instruction No. 1/1991, the Minister for Religious Affairs made a decision addressed to the all instances of the Department of Religious Affairs and other departments dealing with it, to use the KHI as far as possible, in deciding on matters of marriage, inheritance, and *waqf.* Since this Minister's Decision contains instruction rather than a decision *per se,* Attamimi has criticized it for being a Decision of Minister's Instruction rather than a Minister's Decision. Attamimi, "Kedudukan Kompilasi Hukum Islam", pp. 153–54. The consequence of this critique is that the KHI, according to Attamimi, lacks a strong legitimizing power.

50. This is quoted from the English translated text in *Far Eastern Economic Review,* 24 March 1966, p. 550; In Adam Schwarz's translation, it reads: "to take all measures considered necessary to guarantee security, calm and stability of the government and the revolution and to guarantee the personal safety and authority [of Sukarno]. See his book, *A Nation in Waiting: Indonesia in the 1990s* (Boulder: Westview Press, 1995), p. 26.

51. See Marwati Poesponegoro and Nugroho Notosusanto, *Sejarah Nasional Indonesia,* vol. IV (Jakarta: Depdikbud and Balai Pustaka, 1984), p. 406; See also, Michael R. J. Vatikiotis, *Indonesian Politics under Soeharto: Order, Development, and Pressure for Change* (London and New York: Routledge, 1997), pp. ix, 1; See also Schwarz, *A Nation in Waiting,* p. 26.

52. See Donald K. Emmerson, *Indonesia's Elite: Political Culture and Cultural Politics* (Ithaca and London: Cornell University Press, 1976), pp. 22–23.

53. See M. Syafi'i Anwar, "Negara, Umat dan Ijtihad Politik", *Panji Masyarakat* No. 693, 11–21 August 1991, p. 30. See also Abdul Aziz Thaba, *Islam dan Negara dalam Politik Orde Baru* (Jakarta: Gema Insani Press, 1996), pp. 242–43.

54. See Schwarz, *A Nation in Waiting,* p. 31.

55. See his thesis submitted to the Institute of Islamic Studies McGill University, entitled "Islam and Politics under The New Order Government in Indonesia 1966–1990".

56. Thaba, *Islam dan Negara dalam Politik Orde Baru,* pp. 239–354.

57. The categories used by both authors are, however, too broad to account for all significant cases in each category. The enactment of Law No. 1/1974 and the emergence of government regulations concerning marriage in 1975 and 1979 are, for instance, better included in reciprocal era rather than in antagonistic era in which they fall.

58. Howard M. Federspiel, "The Endurance of Muslim Traditionalist Scholarship: An Analysis of the Writings of the Indonesian Scholar Sirajuddin Abbas", in *Toward a New Paradigm in Indonesian Islamic Thought,* edited by Mark Woodward (Arizona: Arizona State University, 1996), p. 193.

59. See M. Nasir Tamara, *Indonesia in the Wake of Islam* (Kuala Lumpur: Institute of Strategic and International Studies, 1986), pp. 15–16.

60. Afan Gaffar, "Islam dan Politik dalam Era Orde Baru, Mencari Bentuk Artikulasi Yang Tepat", *Ulumul Qur'an* IV, no. 2 (1993): 20.

61. Ibid., pp. 20–21.

62. See TAP MPR No. XX/MPRS/1966. See also Nur Ahmad Fadhil Lubis, "Institutionalization and the Unification of Islamic Courts under the New Order", *Studia Islamika* 2, no. 1 (1995): 13, also reproduced as Chapter 4 in this volume; See

also, C. S. T. Kansil, *Pengantar Ilmu Hukum dan Tata Hukum Indonesia* (Jakarta: Balai Pustaka, 1986), pp. 51–58.

63. Lubis, "Institutionalization", p. 23.

64. See Article 63(2) of Marriage Law No. 1/1974. It states: "Every decision rendered by the Religious Court is to be approved by the Civil/Public Court".

65. See T. Jafizham, "Peranan Pengadilan Agama dalam Pelaksanaan Undang-undang Perkawinan", in *Kenang-kenangan Seabad Peradilan Agama* (Jakarta: Depag, 1985), pp. 170–72.

66. See Kamal Hassan, *Modernisasi Indonesia, Respon Cendekiawan Muslim* (Jakarta: LSI, 1987), p. 186.

67. Ibid., p. 190.

68. For complete information, see Amak F. Z., *Proses Undang-undang Perkawinan* (Bandung: Al-Ma'arif, 1976).

69. Thaba broadly discusses this period is in his *Islam dan Negara*, pp. 262–78.

70. See Affan Gaffar, "Islam dan Partai Politik, Bagian Kedua", *Risalah*, No. 7, November 1994, pp. 21–22.

71. See Rusli Karim, *Dinamika Islam di Indonesia, Suatu Tinjauan Sosial dan Politik* (Jakarta: Hanindita, 1985), p. 168.

72. For detailed information, see Lukman Harun, *Muhammadiyah dan Asas Pancasila* (Jakarta: Pustaka Panjimas, 1986). Further information on the acceptance of Pancasila by Muslim organizations can also be read in Faisal Ismail, "Pancasila as the Sole Basis for All Political Parties and for All Mass Organizations; An Account of Muslims' Response" (Ph.D. Dissertation, McGill University, Montreal, 1995); the short version of this dissertation can be read in *Studia Islamika* 3, no. 4 (1996).

73. As mentioned, Dody S. Truna sees 1985, that is a year before 1986, as the start of a more co-operative and supportive relationship between Islam and the government. Unlike Thaba and Truna, Gaffar, in his "Islam dan Politik", tends to generalize the 1980s as the starting point of this accommodative type of relationship.

74. Some disagree with the term "accommodative" because, according to them, Islam did not receive benefit from the government, while the latter used Islam to mobilize the support for the government's political advantage. M. Syafi'i Anwar uses the term "bargaining position" to indicate this relationship. See his "Negara, Umat dan Ijtihad Politik", p. 31.

75. See Federspiel, "The Endurance", pp. 193–94.

76. See Gaffar, "Islam dan Politik", p. 18. Moreover, Gaffar asserts that one of the important factors in this change is the increase in the number of educated Muslims. M. Syafi'i Anwar mentions Nurcholish Madjid, Dawam Rahardjo, Kuntowijoyo, and Jalaluddin Rahmat as among the intellectuals who contributed to the change of the Muslim perceptions about the government. See Anwar, "Negara, Umat dan Ijtihad Politik", p. 31.

77. This law was submitted to the government on 23 May 1988 through the then Minister for Education and Culture, Professor Dr Fuad Hassan.

78. Wearing *jilbab* (veil) in public schools had been prohibited by previous government regulation No. 052/C/Kep/D.82, applied since 17 March 1982. The emergence of this regulation brought about many conflicts among educators, heads of public schools, and the Muslim society in general. However, in the period 1982–87, which is marked as the reciprocal relationship and the beginning of the accommodative period, the government did not address this issue. See *Panji Masyarakat*, 21–30 December 1990, pp. 80–81.

79. The draft of this law was submitted to the House of Representatives on 3 December 1988, and issued in 1989 as Law No. 7/1989. This law regulates the structure and authority of the religious courts, and explains the religious judicature and civil law procedure used in the religious judiciary. The government has submitted the law in implementation of Act No. 14/1970 on the judicial powers in Indonesia. See Tommi Legowo, "Religious Issues in Indonesia", *Indonesian Quarterly*, No. XVII/2, 1989, p. 105.

80. The discussion on this can be found in Mudzhar, *Fatwas of the Council*, and Zuffran Sabrie, ed., *Peradilan Agama dalam Wadah Negara Pancasila* (Jakarta: Pustaka Antara PT, 1990). The lack of a procedural law and a codified law was also a factor in the emergence of Kompilasi Hukum Islam. In addition, see *Panji Masyarakat* No. 722/XXXV, 11–20 June 1992, pp. 53–54, to see the effectiveness of the Law of Religious Judiciary; see also Zainal Abidin Abubakar, "Kebijaksanaan Pelayanan Hukum di Lingkungan Peradilan Agama", *GEMA*, No. 80/XVIII, June 1996, p. 24.

81. The great debate between many writers, politicians, scholars, and religious leaders captured in many newspapers, journals, and magazines is compiled in a book edited by Zuffran Sabrie, *Peradilan Agama*.

82. See Gaffar, "Islam dan Politik", p. 21.

83. Daniel S. Lev, "Judicial Authority and the Struggle for an Indonesian Rechtsstaat", *Law and Society Review* 13, no. 1 (Fall 1978): 40–41.

84. Lev states: "While elites talk about stability and 'development', and lower-class millions appeal for substantive social justice, the growing middle class adds to this security, personal rights and liberties, and political participation via legal and constitutional routes to change." See Lev, "Judicial Authority", pp. 40–41. Since majority of the middle class in Indonesia are Muslims, the demand for Islamic legal reformation or developments is likely to occur. In other countries, however, the strength of the middle classes to conduct fundamental change varies, depending on other classes or other existing variables.

85. The *Monitor* was banned because it published the results of a poll conducted among its readers, which ranked the Prophet Muhammad as only the eleventh most amazing leader, below such people as President Soeharto, Habibie, Sukarno, and, even Arswendo. This poll invited strong protests and demonstrations from the Muslims. See Schwarz, *A Nation in Waiting*, p. 191.

86. See Gaffar, "Islam dan Politik", p. 21; and Thaba, *Islam dan Negara*, pp. 279–304.

87. See Gaffar, "Islam dan Politik", p. 22.

88. See Lev, "Judicial Authority", p. 41.

89. See Ron Shaham, "Custom, Islamic Law, and Statutory Legislation: Marriage Registration and Minimum Age at Marriage in the Egyptian Shari'a Courts", *Islamic Law and Society* 2, no. 3 (October 1995): 258–60.

90. The relationship between law, rule, and power is clearly expressed in Sir Ivor Jennings, *The Law and the Constitution*, 5th ed. (London: The English Language Book Society, 1979), p. 106; See also Schacht, *An Introduction to Islamic Law*, p. 105.

91. The fact that there were demonstrations and protests against some of the government's planning policies is undeniable. However, we cannot generalize that majority of Muslims agreed with these protests. Moreover, whether the government policies are dealing with Islam and the needs of the Muslims must be verified. It is also important to know the government's response towards these demonstrations

and protests. Without intending to ignore some Muslim protests and demonstrations, the term "accommodative relationship" is intended to characterize the general phenomena of the relationship between the government and Islam.

92. For a detailed account on this matter, see Sabrie, *Peradilan Agama*. This book includes fifty-eight articles in favour of and opposing the Law on Religious Judicature.

93. Abdurrahman, *Kompilasi Hukum Islam*, p. 49.

94. See Ismail Sunny, "Kompilasi Hukum Islam", p. 43.

95. Abdul Gani Abdullah, *Pengantar Kompilasi Hukum Islam dalam Tata Hukum Indonesia* (Jakarta: Gema Insani Press, 1994), Chapter III. In this chapter he describes the history and the development of Islamic law as national legislation.

96. Article II (transitional provision) of the 1945 Constitution, which still recognizes Islamic law as one of four existing laws in Indonesia.

97. Menteri Agama RI, *Himpunan Pidato Menteri Agama RI* (Jakarta: Biro Hukum dan Humas Sekretaris Jenderal Departemen Agama, 1988), p. 28.

98. See Basran, "Kompilasi Hukum Islam", p. 10.

99. Harahap, "Informasi Materi Kompilasi Hukum Islam: Mempositifkan Abstraksi Hukum Islam", in *Berbagai Pandangan*, edited by Tim Ditbinbapera, pp. 149–56.

100. Harahap uses the term *"Taqribi Bainal Ummah"* (process of building a close relationship among Muslim community).

101. Article 1 of Law No. 14/1985 and Article 3 of Law No. 7/1989. It is clear from here that the Religious Court is not a private court, but the Public/State Court for Muslim citizens.

102. In his article, "Tujuan Kompilasi Hukum Islam", p. 91, Harahap mentions the desired characteristics of KHI: systemic, national oriented, suited to the religious courts as a reference which provides uniform, and legal certainty.

103. *Khilafiyyah* means disagreement among *ulama* on a given matter. For a description and analysis on some *khilafiyyah* problems and its debate between *kaum muda* and *kaum tua*, see Howard M. Federspiel, *Persatuan Islam: Islamic Reform in the Twentieth Century Indonesia* (Ithaca: Modern Indonesia Project Southeast Asia Program, 1970).

104. Harahap, "Informasi Materi Kompilasi", pp. 154–55.

105. This statement is based on data gathered from interviews with *ulama* by the committee of the KHI and from the responses of other members of society. See Harahap, "Informasi Materi Kompilasi", p. 155.

8

ISLAMIZING CAPITALISM
On the Founding of Indonesia's First Islamic Bank

Robert W. Hefner

> An anthropologist, huh? Then you must agree with what Clifford Geertz had to say about Indonesian Muslims. Do you?

I had just sat down in the waiting room of the newly formed Union of Indonesian Muslim Intellectuals (ICMI), awaiting the arrival of one of the organization's leaders, and I was startled by the unexpected appearance and questioning of this gentleman, a low-ranking officer in ICMI. It was July 22, 1992, my first day in Jakarta. I had traveled to this office among the modern buildings on Jalan Thamrin to interview a high-ranking ICMI officer about his role in the recent establishment of the Bank Muamalat Indonesia (BMI), Indonesia's first official Islamic bank. The officer hadn't arrived yet, so, hot, jet-lagged from my travel, and anxious about the upcoming interview, I sat down, hoping to use the minutes before his arrival to collect my thoughts. Having heard I was an anthropologist, however, this other gentleman, who had entered the waiting room and abruptly sat down beside me, seemed determined to get an answer.

Previously published as "Islamizing Capitalism: On the Founding of Indonesia's First Islamic Bank", in *Toward A New Paradigm: Recent Developments in Indonesian Islamic Thought*, edited by Mark R. Woodward (Arizona: Arizona State University, 1996), pp. 291–322. Reproduced with permission of the author, the editor, and the publisher.

> Well, uh, no, but, uh . . . Geertz said many things about Indonesian Muslims, some important and others perhaps wrong. I guess whether I agree with Geertz really depends on which of his ideas you're talking about.

My interrogator cocked his head to the side with a skeptical smile, obviously unconvinced by my feigned ignorance. He challenged me again:

> Anthropologists believe that Muslims, the government, and the people [*masyarakat*] can never work together. They must always compete, the government fearing Islam, Muslims opposing the government, and the people rejecting Islamic devotion. The purpose of our organization is to prove Geertz wrong. Rather than separate and opposed, as anthropologists believe, we want to demonstrate that the three social groupings [*aliran*] Geertz described — *priyayi*, *santri*, and *masyarakat* — can work together for the development of Indonesia and the growth of the Muslim community [*ummat*]. *Priyayi* [government officials] don't have to fight with *santri* [practicing Muslims], and Islam can work for the betterment of all the people. The Geertz thesis is false, and we will show that anthropology is wrong.

Startled by this criticism of my profession, I made a feeble attempt to explain that anthropologists' views on Indonesian Islam are diverse, and that many foreign scholars, including me, strongly support Muslims' efforts to strengthen their role in Indonesian government, economy, and society.

> "Indeed," I said, "it's because I feel that Muslims' efforts are important and good that I have come to examine their economic initiatives."

As this example illustrates, Westerners' and, especially, Clifford Geertz's understanding of religion, economy, and society in Indonesia was a recurring theme of conversations I had with Muslims during the summers of 1991 and 1992.[1] Though initially surprised by the passion the issue excited, I later appreciated that there are good reasons for Muslim intellectuals' concerns about academic views of Indonesia. Many of the categories developed by social scientists have come to figure in the Indonesian government's policies, sometimes to the detriment of Muslims. More important, perhaps, the 1980s had witnessed the beginnings of an Islamic revival of unprecedented proportions in Indonesian society. Though the impact of this deepening Islamization was apparent in the Javanese countryside and among the urban poor, it was also powerfully evident among the urban middle class.[2] A significant proportion of that class had been educated in the 1970s and 1980s, and in the course of their studies many had been exposed to Western scholars' ideas on Islam and Indonesian society. For many of these people, Clifford Geertz's tripartite division of Javanese society into the categories of government officials (*priyayi*), practicing Muslims (*santri*), and nominally or mystically Islamic Javanists (*abangan*) had disturbing social implications.[3] It seemed to imply that most of the Javanese population, and especially government officials, were hostile to Islamic devotion, and that Muslims, therefore, should resign themselves to being a marginal minority in a nation dominated by a leadership only nominally committed to the Islamic faith.

There was another dimension to this popular interest in the position of Muslims in Indonesian society. The growth of the middle class in the 1970s and 1980s had been facilitated by an economic expansion that began a few years after the founding of the New Order government in 1966.[4] Fueled at first by conservative economic policies and the sudden growth in oil revenues in the aftermath of the 1973 Arab-Israeli war, the expansion faltered in the early 1980s, as oil prices fell to record lows. The government then scrambled to come up with a program for export-oriented growth based on manufactures in addition to petroleum. Eventually, the government's efforts to promote industrial growth led to a loosening of economic regulations. New policies were announced, designed to encourage investment, stimulate competition, and make capital more widely available for small and large enterprise.[5]

One of the most important of these deregulative measures was announced in November 1988, when, for the first time, private and state-run banks were allowed to open branches in the countryside. In the aftermath of deregulation, a banking fever swept the country. Banks offered prizes to new depositors, and businesses availed themselves of new sources of capital. In the first year of deregulation, the banking industry grew by 12.8 per cent, as opposed to 2.8 per cent a year earlier. Total bank assets grew even more spectacularly, rising from Rp32 trillion to Rp50 trillion.[6]

For many Indonesians, however, there was a bittersweet quality to the boom. Chinese Indonesians have long dominated the private banking sector, and their banks were the most successful in responding to the liberalized bank environment. The penetration of Chinese banking into rural Indonesia brought back memories of the monopoly hold on trade that Chinese enjoyed in the colonial era. Thus it heightened fears that, rather than improving the economic position of *pribumi* ("indigenous," i.e., non-Chinese) Indonesians, deregulation would only strengthen Chinese economic dominance.

Chinese Indonesians seemed to benefit from other government measures as well. As business firms competed in the newly deregulated market, Chinese-owned companies, especially the giant, multisector firms known as "conglomerates" (*konglomerat*), seemed to lead the way once again. Though they comprise only 2.5 per cent of Indonesia's population, Chinese Indonesians own an estimated 70–75 per cent of all mid- to large-scale enterprises; deregulation appeared to be rewarding them with an even larger share of the business pie. Without some kind of corrective initiative, many Muslims said, Chinese economic dominance would only increase. The resulting socioeconomic imbalance could damage ethnic relations, threatening Indonesia's long-term growth.[7]

It is against this background, then, that the gentleman at the headquarters of the newly formed Union of Muslim Indonesian Intellectuals queried me on my views on Indonesian politics, economy, and society. As a result of ongoing national developments, a simplified version of Geertz's model of Indonesian society had received extensive media coverage in recent years. For Muslims, the model had come to symbolize much that was wrong with Indonesian economy and society.

Of course Geertz had not meant to slight Muslim sensibilities when he first presented his analysis. Indeed, he identified devout Muslims (*santri*) as the bearers of a market-oriented ethic better suited for modern development that the patrimonial ethos of *priyayi* bureaucrats.[8]

Nonetheless, many Muslim observers felt that Geertz's broader portrayal in some sense legitimated their relegation to the margins of Indonesian economy and society. They also insisted that Geertz's model overlooked the economic privileges and cozy patronage arrangements long enjoyed by some among the country's Chinese minority. Having served as middlemen for the Dutch, the Chinese were well positioned to maintain economic control in the first years of Indonesian independence. They reinforced their position in the New Order period, since the government needed private capital to jump-start the economy, and turned to Chinese Indonesians for help.[9] In the 1990s, as Indonesia moved into a more competitive phase of economic development, Muslim Indonesians inevitably wondered just what was required to ensure that they, too, might finally enjoy the fruits of development.

In the remainder of this chapter, I want to examine one such Muslim response to this question. By "response" I mean not just ideas but a specific program implemented in 1991 and designed to enhance Muslim participation in the national economy. The initiative was the creation of Indonesia's first Islamic bank, the Bank Muamalat Indonesia, a bank designed to operate without using interest payments. In a country whose population is almost 90 per cent Muslim, the establishment of the Islamic bank was an important but surprisingly controversial measure. The timing of its founding reflected changes in Indonesia's political and cultural climate. The practical organization of the bank also reflected a very important, if again controversial, strategy for accommodating the Muslim community to modern Indonesian capitalism. In the long run, the relative success of this and other economic initiatives will influence not only the economic profile of Indonesia Muslims but also their attitudes toward the state, capitalism, and Indonesia's fragile pluralism.

ISLAM AND BANKING

As in most other parts of the modern Muslim world, the question of just what attitude Muslims should take toward the institutions of modern banking has long been controversial in Indonesia. Muslim commentators disagree as to whether the Quranic prohibition on *riba* (lit., "increase": see Sura al-Baqarah 275) bars all forms of interest on loans or, as many liberal Muslims insist, merely those rates that are so high as to qualify as exploitative or usurious.[10] Indonesian *ulama* (Islamic scholars and jurists) have never reached a clear consensus on the issue. In its thirteenth national congress in 1938, Nahdlatul Ulama (NU) affirmed that bank interest was *halal* (allowed) when and if it brings benefit to the borrower, since the benefit itself represents a "return" on the interest. In 1950 NU moved from theory to practice, establishing two banks in Jakarta; a third was established in 1960 in Semarang. All charged interest on loans. Though all three eventually failed, the banks provided a precedent for NU's involvement in conventional banking. This precedent was revived in 1990, with NU's establishment of People's Credit Banks (Bank Perkreditan Rakyat). Despite these historic initiatives, however, NU has never succeeded in allaying concerns about *riba* among its rank and file. To this day, some NU *ulama* condemn all forms of bank interest, and some have bitterly attacked the NU leadership for working with conventional banks.[11]

In its 1936 national congress, Muhammadiyah, the largest and oldest of Indonesia's modernist organizations,[12] lamented the lack of banking institutions for native Indonesians, and sought to elaborate a banking policy that would assist the growth of Muslim businesses. Ultimately, however, the congress failed to reach the consensus necessary to resolve the matter. Bank interest was identified as *mutasyabihat*, a legal issue that is not yet clear and for which additional study is required. A similarly inconclusive decision was reached at the 1968 national congress in Sidoarjo, East Java.

In 1993, a quarter-century later, the Muhammadiyah has yet to formulate a unitary policy on bank interest. Though some leadership liberals approve of it, others condemn the taking of interest in any form. For example, as the Muhammadiyah contemplated establishing its own credit banks in 1990, the former head of Muhammadiyah's East Javanese Majelis Tarjih publicly condemned banks as a "Jewish creation," and insisted that all Muslims involved in initiatives to establish Muhammadiyah banks "were acting like Jews." Though disagreeing with the force of his sentiments, some of the Muhammadiyah leadership agrees with this *alim*'s condemnation of bank interest as *riba*. Not coincidentally in light of this fact, then, Muhammadiyah intellectuals were the single most influential nongovernmental constituency in the creation of the Bank Muamalat.

A recurring debate in the history of modern Indonesian Islam, the topic of bank interest remains controversial among the general Muslim population. For example, a survey of 479 Jakartan residents found that only 34 per cent approved of bank interest. A full 25.9 per cent were "inclined to disapprove" (*kurang setuju*), and almost 40 per cent either "disagreed" (*tidak setuju*) or "strongly disagreed" (*sangat tidak setuju*).[13]

Not surprisingly, the Islamic revival that has swept across Indonesia since the 1980s has had the effect of deepening these reservations and renewing calls for the establishment of an Islamic bank prohibiting all forms of interest. The appeal has been reinforced by international events, including the establishment of the Islamic Republic of Iran (where no banks use interest) and the growing interest among Sunni Muslims in Islamic banking. In 1973 the Saudi government put its considerable influence behind the establishment of no-interest banks, with the founding of the Islamic Development Bank (IDB). The Indonesian government was a signatory to the agreement founding the bank. The IDB provides only a small amount of capital to Indonesia and has no branch in the country; applications for bank capital have to move through the Indonesian Department of Finance. Nonetheless, the bank's founding sent a clear message that the Saudi government was ready to commit its moral and economic resources to the cause of Islamic banking. (At the same time, of course, a large portion of private Saudi wealth continues to be deposited in Western banks.) It also provided both capital and technical advice to countries interested in establishing their own Islamic banks.[14]

EXTRAGOVERNMENTAL INITIATIVES

Despite these international developments, until 1991 banking regulations in Indonesia prohibited the depositing of money in banks without the payment of interest. In other words, Islamic banking was technically illegal. As the Islamic revival swept across Indonesian campuses in the 1970s and 1980s, however, pressures grew for a reversal of the prohibition so as to allow for the establishment of banks conforming with the anti-interest interpretation of Islamic law (*shari'a*).

As in so many other aspects of the university revival, students, faculty, and alumni associated with the Salman Mosque at the Institut Teknologi Bandung pioneered these efforts to develop an alternative Islamic bank. Still barred by government regulations from forming a no-interest bank, the Salman leadership created a "cooperative," taking care to ensure that its operation was in strict compliance with government regulations on cooperatives.[15] In practice, however, the cooperative, which came to be known as the Baitut Tamwil Teknosa or simply Teknosa Cooperative, worked just like an Islamic bank. It took in deposits (called, in accordance with cooperative regulations, "voluntary contributions") from members and outside "contributors," and paid depositors a share of the cooperative's profits according to the amount and duration of the deposit. The bank used these funds to provide capital for joint-venture (*musyarakah*) and equity partnerships (*mudharabah*), as well as credit-purchase arrangements (*murobahah* and *al-bai'u bithaman ajil*) for members of the cooperative in need of money for the purchase of capital goods.

Under the terms of these contracts, no interest is paid on any capital advanced to a borrower. In joint-venture partnerships (*musyarakah*), both a bank (here, the cooperative) and a business partner provide investment capital and then divide profits or losses according to the proportion of capital provided by each partner and the duration of the contract.[16] Similarly, under the terms of equity partnerships (*mudharabah*), a bank provides all working capital while the partner provides management and labor. Profits and losses are then divided, with the bank's share typically being larger than in a joint-venture contract because of the greater value of the investment. Under lease or credit purchasing (*murobahah*), the bank purchases a capital good for an entrepreneur, who then either sells the good(s) or, where the item in question is machinery, uses it in business. The borrower utilizes the profits resulting from his or her activities to reimburse the bank through either a lump-sum payment or an installment plan. In addition to repaying the bank its investment, the borrower pays an overhead charge. This is identified not as interest on capital but a service or markup fee for use of the good.

The Teknosa Cooperative never became very big, and ultimately it collapsed under the weight of several bad investments. At its height, however, its total membership comprised about 500 people and its assets exceeded Rp1.3 billion (about US$600,000). Despite its later collapse, the cooperative represented a milestone in the development of Islamic finance in Indonesia. It demonstrated that Islamic banking was feasible and could operate even while devoting its resources to the kind of small and medium-size businesses that conventional banks had neglected. In November 1988, the Teknosa example was repeated with the establishment of a similar banking cooperative, the Ridho Gusti Cooperative, in Jakarta. Directed by a widely respected Muslim activist, Adi Sasono, Ridho Gusti had a membership of 126 and concentrated its resources on small and mid-size Muslim entrepreneurs.

THE POLITICS OF BANK POLICY: THE FOUNDING OF THE BMI

Ultimately, the breakthrough allowing the establishment of an officially sanctioned Islamic bank resulted not from these isolated efforts but from Indonesia's Islamic revival and changing government attitudes toward Islam that resulted, in part, from disagreements within official circles. The government-sponsored Council of Muslim Indonesian Scholars (Majelis Ulama Indonesia, MUI) played a decisive role in the first phase of the drive to found the bank. Though long regarded by critics of the government as a corporatist mechanism for co-opting Muslim scholars, the MUI has always had a measure of internal diversity and on occasion has shown a willingness to question government policies.[17] According to Muslim activists whom I interviewed in 1991 and 1992, the MUI had already begun to discuss the possibility of establishing an Islamic bank in the mid-1980s, long before the government had indicated any willingness to support such a proposal. As the government's fears of religious Islam (as opposed to Muslim political parties) diminished, and as the fruits of the Islamic revival became more apparent, some MUI *ulama* began to explore the possibility of again putting forward the proposal for an Islamic bank.

After several unsuccessful discussions with government ministers, in 1989 the MUI was finally given the green light to hold a workshop the following year on "The Problem of Interest and Banking." The conference, held in Cisarua Bogor in early August, brought together banking experts and Islamic scholars to discuss principles of Islamic banking. With high-ranking officials from the Bank Indonesia, the Monetary Council, and the Department of Finance in attendance, it was clear to most observers that important segments of the government — and, by most estimates, President Soeharto himself — had already decided to approve a proposal for the formation of an Islamic bank. Now it was a question of time and careful maneuvering to avoid provoking opposition to the scheme, especially from the ranks of the militiary.[18]

A few weeks after the workshop, from August 22 to 24, the MUI held its national congress and approved the formation of a banking team to be headed by

Dr. M. Amin Aziz. Dr. Aziz acted as the liaison between the MUI and the Union of Muslim Indonesian Intellectuals (ICMI). ICMI was still in embryonic form (it was not formally established until December 1990).[19] Like the BMI, government support for the establishment of ICMI represented an important concession to Muslim interests, and was opposed by many in the military. However, several high-ranking Muslim ministers strongly supported the establishment of both institutions, and worked behind the scenes to win the president to their cause. The man who eventually became ICMI's chairman, the popular minister of research and technology, B. J. Habibie, is said to have been especially influential. Habibie's activism was in keeping with his public reputation as a vocal supporter of closer ties between the government and Muslims.[20]

The way forward to the formation of the bank, however, was not yet clear of obstacles. Many senior figures in the army and intelligence services, as well as some secularist technocrats in the Department of Finance, are said to have privately opposed establishment of the bank, regarding it as a dangerous concession to "primordial" sectarianism. Many had similar reservations about the formation of ICMI. Efforts were under way to establish ICMI at precisely the same time that the MUI and pro-Islamic officials in government were making plans to establish the bank. In fact, in some respects the two initiatives were linked. Several of the figures active in the establishment of ICMI were on the steering committee for the BMI, and several of the cabinet ministers who appealed to President Soeharto to support the formation of ICMI urged support for the BMI. The fact that President Soeharto overruled military and technocratic advisers and supported the establishment of ICMI and BMI was seen by many observers as a sign of a growing rift within the ranks of the government. Muslim observers saw both developments as evidence of an official opening to the Muslim community unprecedented in the history of the New Order.[21]

What prompted the president to side with these Muslim activists? According to many high-ranking observers, Soeharto was not unfamiliar with the political implications of the Islamic revival sweeping Indonesia, especially among the urban middle classes. The timing of the president's decision to support the BMI, however, was most immediately influenced by the upcoming (1992) elections for the National Assembly and the presidency (March 1993). Though throughout 1991 and 1992 the president declined to state unambiguously that he would seek a fifth term, he made repeated indirect suggestions that he would. Unhappy with his unwillingness to step aside, some segments of the military sought to mobilize opposition to the president, provoking an intraelite dispute also unprecedented in New Order history.[22] It was in this context that the president moved to court Muslims to his side.

In addition to political obstacles, the drive to establish an Islamic bank faced financial challenges. To meet the Department of Finance's banking requirements, the organizers had to accumulate Rp10 billion (just under US$5 million) for operating licenses. Here again, the president's support proved decisive. In a carefully choreographed sequence of events, the committee charged with exploring the possibility of forming an Islamic bank visited the president on August 27, 1991.

They were accompanied by several cabinet ministers, scholars from the MUI, and officials associated with ICMI. The president had been informed of the contents of the committee's proposal long before their meeting. He is reported to have responded to the proposal for the bank enthusiastically, and immediately offered to provide Rp50 million of his own money (approximately US$25,000) for the purchase of bank shares. More important, he also agreed to use funds from his Yayasan Amal Bhakti Muslim Pancasila — a presidentially established foundation designed to support mosque-building and Islamic proselytization (*dakwah*) — to provide the Rp3 billion required to get the first of two operating licenses. He also promised to work to secure the remaining Rp7 billion by organizing a meeting on November 3 in which government officials and citizens (including wealthy businesspeople) from the province of West Java would be invited to purchase shares in the new Bank Muamalat Indonesia.

As momentum for the formation of the BMI increased, several members of the bank's planning committee, including Chairman Habibie from ICMI, sought to mobilize additional funds by inviting one hundred wealthy entrepreneurs to the (Muslim-owned) Hotel Sahid on October 13, 1991. There they would be asked to purchase "founding shares" in the BMI. Eighty-seven of the one hundred invitees appeared at the event, and eventually Rp86 billion (approximately US$40 million) was pledged toward purchase of the shares.[23] All told, in the first six weeks after its approval, the BMI mobilized an impressive Rp110 billion (more than US$50 million), making it the thirty-fifth largest of some fifty-six Islamic banks in the world.

Impressive as it was, the initiative was not without controversy. Among the Rp10 billion arranged by President Soeharto, Rp2 billion was provided by the government office that manages Indonesia's national sports lottery (SDSB). The SDSB is a legal, government-sponsored gambling operation that has been bitterly condemned by Muslims since its inception; even the government-supported Majelis Ulama Indonesia has opposed it.[24] Though few Muslim leaders wanted to criticize the president directly, many confided in private that the provision of Rp2 billion from lottery funds was clearly intended to help legitimize a still controversial institution. Ten days after receiving the contribution, bank officers returned it to the lottery office. In subsequent publicity, including the BMI newsletter, the bank took great pains to underscore that it had returned the lottery contribution. By the standards of Indonesian political etiquette, this rejection of presidentially supplied funds was an astoundingly bold assertion of Muslim morality and independence.

Another controversy disturbing the otherwise impressive progress toward creation of the bank involved the sale of "founding shares" at the Hotel Sahid. As it turned out, the single largest buyer of shares was the lumber king, Mohammad Bob Hasan, a close confidant of the president. With his pledge of Rp25 billion, Hasan immediately qualified as the largest shareholder in the BMI. As word of his purchase was disseminated in the press, many observers lamented the fact that a bank designed to meet the needs of small and mid-size "indigenous" (*pribumi*) entrepreneurs was subject to the control of a conglomerate kingpin — one who, though Muslim by faith, was ethnic Chinese.[25] The fund-raising event's promoters did their best to defend Hasan's participation, but the impression remained with many observers that the BMI was but one more example of Chinese and governmental collaboration. The bank's defenders countered this charge by pointing out that less expensive, public shares would eventually be sold to the entire Muslim community in West Java.

The final and most serious point of controversy surrounding the bank was continuing opposition from some members of the military. Military officials were caught off guard by the president's sudden announcement of support for the bank in August 1991. Though, as noted above, Muslim scholars from the Majelis Ulama Indonesia had been working behind the scenes for several years to win backing for the program, most military officials expected Soeharto to preserve the New Order's long-established, if unwritten, policy that Islamic banks are unnecessary and only reinforce "sectarian" or "primordial" social interests. Along with liberal technocrats within the government, many military officials feared that establishment of an Islamic bank would only encourage Muslim condemnation of conventional banks, undermining one of the New Order's most important economic institutions. In the eyes of these critics, the government should work to bring Muslims into the conventional banking system, not segregate them in a separate sector of the economy. "The danger," one interviewee told me, "is that the institutions of Indonesian society will split apart along ethnic lines, as has happened in Malaysia."

The military's fears are not without foundation. Several BMI supporters whom I interviewed, for example, bitterly condemned Abdurrahman Wahid, the liberal leader of Nahdlatul Ulama. They faulted him not just for establishing banks that require interest on loans but also for working with wealthy Chinese bankers to provide training and finance for the NU banks.[26] In their view, an Islamic bank not only should avoid interest but also should refuse to cooperate with non-Muslim Chinese.

Sensitive to military suspicions, the BMI directors have repeatedly stressed their support for Indonesia's conventional banking system. Rather than declaring that bank interest is forbidden (*haram*), bank officials take a more cautious tack, emphasizing the practical advantages of Islamic banking. They argue, first of all, that a significant proportion of Indonesia's Muslims are reluctant to approach conventional banks, fearing that banks violate the Quranic prohibition on *riba*. Though many devout Muslims do not regard interest-bearing banks as sinful, defenders of Islamic banking are correct to emphasize that some still oppose conventional banks. From this perspective, then, the BMI is an important innovation, one with the potential of bringing people marginalized from conventional banking into the modern economy. In so doing, an Islamic bank can help to strengthen the small *santri* middle class. On these grounds alone, its supporters were right to regard the establishment of the BMI as a significant, if still limited, step toward the strengthening of Muslim economic interests.

This issue of clientele aside, some bank promoters have gone on to argue that Islamic banks are better on other more specifically operational grounds. In interviews in 1992, for example, numerous supporters of the BMI argued that Islamic banks encourage their clients to develop better management techniques. Because they rely on profit-sharing rather than interest, they said, Islamic banks are obliged to pay more attention to the day-to-day operations of their customers' businesses than a conventional bank. As one interviewee put it:

> Conventional banks don't feel a sense of responsibility toward their customers. The only thing they're interested in is making sure that the customer pays his debt, whether the customer is making a profit or not. As long as the debt is paid, they couldn't care less about the fate of the business. This is something an Islamic bank won't do.

By contrast, because Muslim banks work on the basis of profit-sharing, and thus get returns on their investments only if clients prosper, supporters of Islamic banks believe that they have a direct interest in reinforcing good managerial practices.[27]

In interviews, some supporters of the BMI took this argument one step further. They claimed that the BMI will not require its clients to have collateral to get bank capital. As one man put it, "The bank will just look at the worth of the project and base its decision on that." Freed from collateral requirements, Islamic banks would be better able to service small, capital-poor entrepreneurs. A story on the bank in *Pelita*, Jakarta's Muslim newspaper, made much the same point:

> The meaning of this is that entrepreneurs from underprivileged social groups won't ever again have to go begging to banks that will set their interest rates high. All they'll have to do is present a request for a cooperative venture with an Islamic bank. Because, besides not using interest, such a bank will provide assistance in the field of management.[28]

ECONOMIC PROGRESS VS. THE SYMBOLISM OF COMMUNITY

These and other arguments provide a sense of the high, and often unrealistic, hopes the BMI's founding has unleashed in the Muslim community. Frustrated by the continuing exclusion of *pribumi* Muslims from large-scale enterprise, for twenty years Muslims have sought to enhance their economic position. Whereas fifteen or even ten years ago, many, indeed most, Muslim intellectuals espoused a loosely formulated ideal of Islamic socialism,[29] the majority today are willing to try some kind of market-oriented capitalism, as long as it does not contradict Islamic law. This in itself is a development of real importance for Indonesian Islam and society. But these same intellectuals are deeply — and understandably — worried that the tide that raises some may not, in fact, raise all boats. Not surprisingly, then, the Bank Muamalat has become a symbol not merely of Islamic economics — the economic viability of which seems well proved by the experience of Islamic banks in other parts of the world — but also of Muslim hopes for redistribution and social justice. Indeed, for some of its supporters, the bank has become a symbol of opposition to Chinese economic dominance.

Unfortunately, from an economic perspective, the moral burden being placed on the BMI seems unrealistically heavy. The performance of the Bank Islam Malaysia Berhad, established by government legislation in neighboring Malaysia in 1983, illustrates some of the problems the BMI is likely to face in the near future. Established with much the same goals as the BMI, that is, to implement Islamic law (or, more precisely, an *interpretation* of that law that sees all bank interest as *riba* and thus prohibited) and to elevate the economic standing of Malaysia's indigenous (non-Chinese) population, the BIMB has proved itself fiscally sound and profitable. To maintain its profitability, however, the BIMB has inevitably had to avoid investment in risky, small-scale enterprise, concentrating its resources on larger, more established firms. Smaller firms have a high rate of failure and, particularly in economies in which a large proportion of enterprise occurs in the informal sector, their fiscal operations are difficult to supervise. All this makes implementation of the profit-sharing mechanisms through which Islamic banks operate more expensive and unwieldy than for larger, more established enterprises.[30] The example also indicates that while Islamic banks can quite effectively operate according to different principles of investment and profit-sharing, in the end they cannot avoid the constraints of supply, demand, and institutional viability imposed by the marketplace.

Although, so soon after its founding, it is impossible to evaluate the economic performance of the BMI, preliminary evidence suggests that the BMI is already facing just this tension between popular aspirations for social justice and the fiscal responsibility required to ensure that this symbol of the Islamic community will survive. In interviews with the bank directors in August 1992, I was unable to get detailed reports on their customers (because the bank had been operating only several months), but the bank's director, Zainulbahar Noor, acknowledged quite candidly that since they opened their doors in March 1992, they had been overwhelmed by credit-unworthy customers.

> Many people seem to think that we are a social welfare agency. We wish we could be, but we're not. Our first responsibility is to run profitably, so as to provide return on our shareholders' investments. Yes, the bank is designed to support middle- and small-scale enterprises, and to improve the circumstances of the Muslim community. But over the long run we cannot do that unless we survive, and survival requires us to operate on a sound fiscal basis.

The director noted that because of the difficulty of supervising innumerable small enterprises, the bank has been obliged to put a lower limit of Rp10 million (about US$5,000) on the capital it provides customers. The maximum amount it will provide is US$1 million. Though the figure of US$5,000 is minuscule by international standards, it is effectively beyond the reach of the mass of small-scale entrepreneurs.[31]

There is other evidence to illustrate this difficult tension between the aspiration for social justice and the need for economic efficiency in the bank's operations. Although bank officials were unable to provide figures on applicants, Muslim commentators close to the bank told me that as many as 97 per cent of applicants for bank "investments" (bank officials prefer not to call the capital they provide "loans") have been turned down because they were too risky or lacked sufficient assets. In an interview in the Muslim magazine *Amanah*, the director of credit at the BMI, Maman W. Natapermadi, acknowledged this point. While holding firmly to Islamic principles, he said, the BMI is obliged to respect certain basic economic realities. In particular, he pointed out that "The problem of investment in middle and small enterprise is not an easy matter . . . because those kinds of enterprises require a good deal of management. For the short term, then, the largest portion of our investments will be directed into enterprises of middle-size on up."[32]

Although in the months following BMI's founding the Muslim press was eager to idealize the advantages of Islamic banking, there were other, more sober analysts who pointed out that Islamic banks are not an economic panacea, but face their own peculiar difficulties. In an interview published just before President Soeharto expressed support for the BMI, the respected independent Muslim intellectual M. Dawam Rahardjo made a quite accurate forecast of what has turned out to be one of the BMI's key challenges:

> The administration of Islamic banking is extremely difficult. The Bank Islam has to control so much and the borrower has to be truly honest in acknowledging profit. Borrowers are inclined to underreport their profits, or not report them at all . . . An Islamic bank has to supervise borrowers so directly that that creates enormous administrative costs. The result is high administrative costs and oversight procedures that are extremely complicated.[33]

In my interview in August 1992, Dawam expressed a more upbeat evaluation of Islamic banking, saying that the founding of the BMI was a "positive step" toward the implementation of Muslim social ideals. Nurcholish Madjid, the much-respected liberal founder of the *pembaharuan* movement for Islamic renewal, voiced a similar opinion. He candidly admitted that the experience of Malaysia's Muslim bank does not inspire confidence that the BMI will be an effective vehicle for social equalization; market realities will limit the bank's ability to realize its stated goal of helping small and medium-sized Muslim businesses. Nonetheless, Madjid said, the BMI is important as a "symbol of the Islamic community, and the realization of its goals in Indonesian society."[34]

All this indicates that the BMI has been charged with two difficult and somewhat contradictory tasks: to represent the growing institutional maturity of the Islamic community and to promote social equalization by supporting the development of small and medium Muslim businesses. The first task requires implementation of Muslim — or at least one segment of the Muslim community's — ideals on how banking and business should be conducted, in accordance with a strict interpretation of *shari'a*. To operate effectively, however, the BMI must survive. And to survive, it must acknowledge the rules of the marketplace, making sound investments and safeguarding the profitability of its operations. It is this latter requirement that stands in tension with the Muslim aspiration for a fairer distribution of the country's wealth. Small firms are risky undertakings, with higher overall administrative costs. This generalization already applies to conventional banks. But it is especially true of Islamic banks, where bank earnings on investments are directly determined by borrowers' profits, and profits can be accurately assessed only through vigilant, and thus expensive, supervision.

PARALLEL VENTURES

This tension between symbolism and social justice is a relative, not an absolute, one. It can be diminished through the development of other, complementary institutions that intervene to assist the BMI in three otherwise daunting administrative tasks: locating creditworthy small enterprises, assisting those enterprises in developing more effective managerial techniques, and keeping accurate records of costs and profits so as to guarantee the bank a fair return on investment.

One embryonic initiative that seeks to address all these concerns is the P. T. Manajeman Musyarakah Indonesia (MMI), a managerial project created by the Union of Indonesian Muslim Intellectuals. The idea for the MMI originated with Sri Bintang Pamungkas, the program's director. An American-educated economist and professor at the University of Indonesia, Sri Bintang is a well-regarded Muslim activist renowned for his integrity and bold criticisms of government corruption.[35] Approved by a motion within ICMI in December 1991 and formally established in March 1992, the MMI's goal is to provide an institutional liaison between small enterprises, the BMI, and investors eager to assist the development of small-scale Muslim enterprise. Not itself an owner of capital, the MMI will identify worthy enterprises, selecting from among small businesses and cooperatives. It will then formulate an investment program for each enterprise, focusing on capital improvements and managerial training. Having outlined an investment program, the MMI will approach investors, attempting to sell shares in these joint ventures with small entrepreneurs. It will also seek to mobilize profit-free grants (*hibah*) from donors. In this manner, the MMI will combine sound market incentives with appeals to social equity and Muslim solidarity. In sociological terms, the resulting business ventures will amount to class alliances between affluent investors and poor Muslim entrepreneurs.[36]

In attempting to mobilize this capital, the MMI can rely on more than moral idealism or profit incentives. According to banking regulations promulgated in January 1990 (the so-called Paket Januari or Pakjan), both private and public banks are required to channel 20 per cent of their credit to small enterprises and cooperatives. In addition, regulations applying to state enterprises now require them to channel 1–5 per cent of their profits into small businesses. Not surprisingly, implementation of these regulations has been notoriously difficult — not merely because of resistance to investing in small enterprises (though this is real enough) but also because many large firms have had difficulty identifying small firms that are economically reliable. Acting as an intermediary, the MMI hopes to help in channeling these funds to worthy enterprises, at the same time providing small businesses with assistance in modern managerial techniques.

Another goal of the MMI is to help in the creation of small-scale "People's Shariah Credit Banks" (Bank Perkreditan Rakyat-Shariah). Here again the MMI will act as an intermediary, tapping investment funds from large firms and the BMI to help local entrepreneurs establish small credit banks. Sri Bintang has estimated that Rp200 million (US$100,000) will be needed for each such bank. Once established, the banks will set up savings and credit arrangements identical to those of the BMI, using a variety of profit-sharing arrangements.[37]

Though both of these projects are in too early a stage of development to assess their success, both exemplify the kind of small-scale, hands-on assistance that will be required if Islamic banking is to move from being merely a compelling symbol of Islamic community to a consequential actor in the Indonesian economy. Critical to the success of Muslim banking is the dissemination of managerial and investment skills beyond corporate corridors, into the general Muslim population. In the meantime, it is clear that initiatives like the BMI face continuing practical difficulties. Not the least of them is the task of providing sufficient supervisory input for small enterprises without, as so often happens in Indonesian development programs, degenerating into bureaucratic heavy-handedness. In any case, these initiative are powerful expressions of the institutional maturation of the Islamic community and of its aspiration to elevate Muslim participation in the Indonesian economy.

CONCLUSION

The BMI and MMI initiatives are only two examples of the economic dynamism unleashed among Indonesian Muslims in the 1990s. There were many other initiatives. In 1990, Nahdlatul Ulama — the association of Muslim scholars and Indonesia's largest Muslim organization — set up an ambitious program to establish People's Credit Banks across Indonesia.[38] Although it also seeks to address the needs of small-scale Muslim entrepreneurs, this initiative is quite different from the Bank Muamalat. As with its earlier banking efforts in the 1950s and 1960s, the NU banks apply interest to loans and savings deposits. Also unlike the Bank Muamalat, NU's program is private, not government-sponsored. In addition, rather than concentrating on the establishment of a large central bank, as with the BMI, NU seeks to establish a network of small, locally financed banks, hoping to create a national bank later.

In announcing the plans for this bank program, NU leadership indicated that it planned to establish two thousand credit banks over the next twenty years. However, in the first year and a half of operation, only nine banks have been established, and most observers believe that the figure of two thousand banks is unrealistic. Nonetheless, by most measures, the NU program has already accomplished a good deal. As of August 1992, assets in the nine operating banks were Rp3.4 billion (around US$1.5 million), with each bank having an operating capital of about Rp100 million. Though modest by comparison with the BMI, all these funds were privately generated, and they are being channeled to the smallest and neediest of Muslim entrepreneurs. In two years of operation, the average personal loan provided by the BPR-NU has been Rp200,000 (less than US$100); the upper limit on loans is Rp10 million. However, only three borrowers have taken out loans larger than Rp5 million.

Perhaps the most dramatic difference between these small-scale banks and the BMI, however, has been that the NU banks have welcomed cooperation with private Chinese banks. In its first months, NU worked with the Bank Susila Bhakti; shortly thereafter, it changed to the much larger SUMMA bank, a banking group controlled by the Soerjadjaja family, once one of the wealthiest Chinese-Indonesian families in Indonesia. In 1992 NU's relationship with the SUMMA bank was jeopardized by the latter's collapse (provoked, in large part, by overinvestment in Jakarta real estate and the subsequent decline of the market).[39] This has forced NU to adjust its long-term development plans, and reinforced observers' convictions that the goal of two thousand banks in twenty years is unrealistic. Nonetheless, whatever its current difficulties, the NU program seems likely to survive (or revive) in some form, servicing the neediest of Indonesia's entrepreneurs and providing an alternative model of Muslim banking, in which interest is not regarded as *riba*.

In all these efforts, of course, it is clear that Muslim Indonesians are still far short of realizing their dream of "proving Geertz wrong" by transforming Indonesia's social landscape and enhancing their economic role. What has been accomplished, however, is already important, and provides insight into the growing institutional influence of Muslim organizations and ideals. The government's support for the Bank Muamalat — despite objections from secular technocrats and certain segments of the military — suggests that a quarter-century into the New Order, some in the government recognize that it is time to acknowledge the Muslim community, and to bring it more vigorously into modern Indonesian development. Several government officials with whom I spoke were unusually frank in expressing the practical reasons for this change of heart. "If we don't do this," one high-ranking official said, "if we continue to push Muslims into the opposition, then our future will be like that of Algeria." In the long run, of course, the fate of these initiatives will depend in large part on whether they become the patronage emoluments of a small circle of government-linked *pribumi* or become vehicles for servicing the economic needs of the Muslim community as a whole.

Whatever the government's motivations, the fact is that Muslims are deeply aware of their growing influence in Indonesian society. It is interesting and significant that they are responding to this newfound influence not merely with deepening piety but also with pragmatic measures that seek to address the most pressing of Indonesia's social and economic problems. In this, as in so many aspects of contemporary Islamic development, we see the positive fruits of a strategy of

Islamic renewal that began in the early 1970s under the guiding influence of such figures as Nurcholish Madjid, Dawam Rahardjo, and Abdurrahman Wahid.[40] Rather than focusing on the conventional arenas of earlier Muslims' struggle — party politics and purist disputes over doctrine — these Islamic leaders recognized that however much the New Order circumscribed Muslim political organizations, it also presented new social and economic opportunities. The nature of those opportunities was such, however, that they required Muslims to express their faith not merely through devotional acts or the struggle for an Islamic state but also through education, job training, and the creation of a socially conscious middle class. The fruits of such toils are just now becoming visible, as evidenced in the deepening Islamization of an important segment of Indonesia's middle class.

It is interesting, too, to observe that this development provides a dramatic contrast with the history of secularization in the West. There, at least in this century, the middle classes have tended to be in the secularist vanguard. In Indonesia, like much of the Muslim world, a different process seems to be taking place. Having experimented with various secular nationalist ideologies, a portion of the Muslim middle class is now turning to a refurbished version of their faith, one that seeks to combine the traditionalist appeal of "indigenousness" with the reformist verve of Islamic modernism. Although we have surely not seen the last of secular nationalist ideologies, this development represents a real change in the religious culture of a portion of the middle class. It will likely be an important influence on Indonesian political and social life in years to come.

In economic terms, of course, the Bank Muamalat and NU's banks are still small operations, however compelling their symbolism as indices of Muslim social achievement. They are nonetheless significant first steps, the beginnings of a process of institution-building and economic socialization that must take place if Muslim Indonesians are to be brought into the modern economy. Whether in the long run Muslims succeed in transforming Indonesian social structure will, of course, depend upon much more than a few adjustments in Indonesia's banking system. In the meantime, there are any number of developments that could derail these initiatives. As noted above, the practical effect of the BMI could be diluted by its transformation into a patronage fiefdom. Conversely, the Islamic revival that helped create the BMI may take a less pragmatic turn, especially if there is political repression or some unexpected economic downturn. In this, as in the founding of the BMI, politics and international developments will greatly affect the attitudes and initiatives of the Muslim community. In any case, this much seems clear: Indonesia's continuing economic development will only increase demands that, in any of several possible senses, Indonesian capitalism be given a more Islamic face.

Notes

1. Research was conducted during July and August of those two years, as part of a larger project, "Islam and Capitalism in Indonesia: Entrepreneurial Opportunities, Moral Dilemmas." The research was sponsored by the Institute for the Study of Economic

Culture, Boston University. I want to express my great appreciation to Peter Berger of ISEC for his support, and to Aswab Mahasin and Enceng Shobirin of LP3ES for their help in organizing interviews in Jakarta.

2. Detailed ethnographic analyses of the revival in rural areas are provided for the Magelang region of Central Java in M. Bambang Pranowo's *"Creating Islamic Tradition in Rural Java"* (Ph.D. diss., Monash University, 1991); and for the Pasuruan and Malang regencies in East Java in R. Hefner, "Islamizing Java? Religion and Politics in Rural East Java," *Journal of Asian Studies* 46, no. 3 (August 1987): 533–54. On the revival in urban areas, see M. Nasir Tamara, *"Islam as a Political Force in Indonesia: 1965–1985"* (Cambridge, Mass.: Center for International Affairs, Harvard University, 1986); François Raillon, "Islam et Ordre Nouveau ou l'imbroglio de la foi et de la politique," *Archipel* 30 (1985): 229–61. A fascinating press account of Islamization among the urban middle class is provided in "Dai Dai Baru Bak Matahari Terbit," *Tempo*, April 11, 1992, 14–17.

3. The two most relevant of Geertz's works on this issue are *The Religion of Java* (New York: The Free Press, 1960) and *The Social History of an Indonesian Town* (Cambridge, Mass.: MIT Press, 1965). Koentjaraningrat's "Review of the Religion of Java," in *Madjalah Ilmu Sastra Indonesia*, 1 (1963): 188–91, provides an important Indonesian critique of this typology; Mark R. Woodward's *Islam in Java: Normative Piety and Mysticism in the Sultanate of Yogyakarta* (Tucson: University of Arizona Press, 1987) provides a decisive reassessment from the perspective of an anthropologically informed Islamic study.

4. The best single collection on economic developments under the New Order is Anne Booth and Peter McCawley, eds., *The Indonesian Economy during the Soeharto Era* (Kuala Lumpur: Oxford University Press, 1981). On the politics of capitalist growth, see Richard Robison, *Indonesia: The Rise of Capital* (Sydney: Allen & Unwin, 1986); and Andrew MacIntyre, *Business and Politics in Indonesia* (Sydney: Allen & Unwin, 1990).

5. See M. Hadi Soesastro, "The Political Economy of Deregulation in Indonesia," *Asian Survey* 29 (September 1989): 853–69; and "Paket Mei Enam," *Tempo*, May 17, 1986. In a more recent article, Richard Robison has observed that many of the large monopolies controlled by politically well-connected individuals escaped the brunt of these deregulative measures. See Robison, "Industrialization and the Economic and Political Development of Capital: The Case of Indonesia," in *Southeast Asian Capitalists*, ed. Ruth McVey (Ithaca, N.Y.: Cornell University, Southeast Asia Program, 1992), 74–76.

6. On bank deregulation, see "Esok Penuh Harapan," *Infobank* 124 (April 1990): 32–3; and Baharuddin Darus, "Venture Capital: The Indonesian Experience," in *The Muslim Private Sector in Southeast Asia*, ed. Mohamed Ariff (Singapore: ISEAS, 1991), 160.

7. See the Indonesian press commentary on Chinese economic dominance in "Kapan Menjadi Tuan?" *Prospek*, May 18, 1991, 84–97. Richard Robison's "The Emergence of a Capitalist Class: Chinese-Owned Capital," in his *Indonesia: The Rise of Capital*, 271–322, provides an overview of the breadth of Chinese corporate expansion during the 1970s and 1980s.

8. See, for example, Clifford Geertz, *Peddlers and Princes: Social Development and Economic Change in Two Indonesian Towns* (Chicago: University of Chicago Press, 1963), 28–81.

9. Though its general focus is the opium trade, James R. Rush's *Opium to Java: Revenue Farming and Chinese Enterprise in Colonial Indonesia* (Ithaca, N.Y.: Cornell University Press, 1990) is rich with insights into the culture and social organization of Chinese commerce in colonial Java. Denys Lombard's *Le Carrefour Javanais*, vol. 2, *Les Reseaux Asiatiques*, (Paris: Editions de l'Ecole des Hautes Etudes en Sciences Sociales, 1990),

208–308, provides a comprehensive overview of Chinese cultural and economic influences over a longer time frame. Robison's *Indonesia: The Rise of Capital* provides a comprehensive discussion of the role of Chinese capital under the New Order.

10. See Maxime Rodinson, *Islam and Capitalism* (Austin: University of Texas Press, 1978), 14–19. Dawam Rahardjo has noted that Mohammad Hatta, the great Muslim Indonesian nationalist (and an economist by training), distinguished between "productive" and "consumptive" debt repayment, insisting that the former was not *riba*. Hatta believed that a banking system could not be run without some kind of interest mechanism. See Dawam Rahardjo, "The Question of Islamic Banking in Indonesia," in *Islamic Banking in Southeast Asia*, ed. Mohamed Ariff (Singapore: Institute of Southeast Asian Studies, 1988), 138–39.

11. On NU's involvement in banking, see Eko Budi Supriyanto, "Ketika Kyai Bisnis Uang," *Infobank* 124 (April 1990): 12–13; in the same issue, see the interview with Abdurrahman Wahid concerning the NU bank initiative, 28–29; see also the special issue of *Santri* — 4, no. 1 (1990) — devoted to presenting NU's new credit banks to the NU membership. The bitterest criticism of the NU bank initiative came from Misbach Nustofa, the director of the al-Balal *pesantren* (Islamic boarding school) in Rembang, Central Java. In a book titled *BPR NU Dalam Tinjauan al-Qur'an*, Nustofa condemned the banks as contrary to Islamic law and, in uncompromisingly hostile language, implied that Abdurrahman Wahid was being manipulated by Chinese capitalists. See "Protes Umat Pada Bisnis NU dan Muhammadiyah," *Prospek*, December 1, 1990, 84–87.

12. On the Muhammadiyah's economic views, see B. Wiwoho, ed., *Kebangkitan Pengusaha Muslim* (Jakarta: PT. Bina Rena Pariwara, 1991); on its efforts in the field of banking, see "Protes Umat Pada Bisnis NU dan Muhammadiyah"; and Adek Aiwi, "Uluran Tangan Tanpa Bunga," *Infobank* 124 (April 1990): 14–15.

13. See Didid Rachbini, "Assalamu Alaikum, Kyai Masuk Bank," *Infobank* 124 (April 1990): 7.

14. See Eddy Sampurna, "IDB Dukung Praktek Bank Islami," *Infobank* 124 (April 1990): 16–17.

15. What follows is based on interviews with Sri Bintang Pamungkas, M. Billah, and P. Fahmi Khatib in July and August 1992. For press commentary on early bank initiatives, see Adek Aiwi, "Yang Lahir Karena Bunga" and "Ridho Gusti Bagi Yang Kecil," *Infobank* 124 (April 1990): 20–23.

16. For an Indonesian analysis of the varied forms of profit-sharing and leasing under Islamic banking, see "Risalah Muamalat," *Info Muamalat*, July 1992, 22–27. For a more theoretical overview, see Muhammad Nejatullah Siddiqi, "Islamic Banking: Theory and Practice," in Ariff, *Islamic Banking*, 34–66; and Muhammad Uzair, "Some Conceptual and Practical Aspects of Interest-Free Banking," in *Studies in Islamic Economics*, ed. Khurshid Ahmad (Leicester, U.K.: The Islamic Foundation, 1980), 37–58.

17. An analysis of the MUI's relationship with the government is presented in Mohamad Atho Mudzhar's "Fatwas of the Council of Indonesian Ulama: A Study of Islamic Legal Thought in Indonesia, 1975–1988" (Ph.D. diss., University of California, Los Angeles, 1990).

18. Interviews, July and August 1992. See "Mengapa Baru Sekarang BMI Berdiri," *Prospek*, November 2, 1991, 72–74.

19. See Robert W. Hefner, "Islam, State, and Civil Society: I.C.M.I. and the Struggle for the Indonesian Middle Class," *Indonesia* 56 (October 1993): 1–35.

20. See "Marhaban, ya Habibie," *Tempo*, December 8, 1990, 33.

21. Interviews with M. Dawam Rahardjo, August 3, 1992; M. Imaduddin Abdulrahim, August 6, 1992; and Dr. Wardiman Djojonegoro, August 9, 1992.

22. See R. William Liddle, "Indonesia's Democratic Past and Future," *Comparative Politics* 24, no. 4 (July 1992): 455–57.

23. See "Mengapa Baru Sekarang BMI Berdiri" and "Bank Istimewa, Tanpa Bunga," *Editor* 5, no. 8 (November 9, 1991): 75–76.

24. See "Ganjalan Pada 110 Miliar," *Editor* 5, no. 9 (November 16, 1991): 57–58.

25. On Bob Hasan's extensive business and patronage ties to Soeharto and the military, see Robison, *Indonesia: The Rise of Capital*, 259–60, 347, 354.

26. This was also one of the points raised in the anti-Wahid polemic made by KH Misbach Nustofa. See "Protes Umat Pada Bisnis NU dan Muhammadiyah."

27. For examples of this argument in the popular media, see "Yang Lahir Karena Bunga," *Infobank* 124 (April 1990): 6–12; and Tigor Sihite, "Bank Islam: Kemungkinan Penerapannya di Indonesia," *Pelita*, September 21, 1984, 1.

28. Elvyn G. Masassya, "Masa Depan Bank Islam di Indonesia," *Pelita*, November 15, 1991, 1.

29. Muslim Indonesians' interest in socialist economics goes back to the founders of Sarket Islam. Originally published in 1924 (Jakarta: Bulan Bintang), H. O. S. Tjokroaminoto's *Islam dan Socialisme* remained influential among Muslim intellectuals through the 1960s. See also M. Dawam Rahardjo's intelligent overview of the socialism debate, "Islam, Sailing Between Two Reefs: Socialism and Capitalism," *Prisma* 35 (March 1985): 49–70. Though today a supporter of Muslim market economics, Nurcholish Madjid has also paid homage to the ideal of "religious socialism." His "Prospek Sosialisme-Religius di Indonesia," in his *Islam, Kemodernan dan KeIndonesiaan* (Bandung: Mizan, 1987), 105–13, provides an insightful summary of the theological grounds for Islamic socialism.

30. For a brief history of the Bank Islam Malaysia Berhad, see Zakariya Man, "Islamic Banking: Prospects for Mudharabah and Musharakah Financing," in *Development and Finance in Islam*, ed. Abdul Hasan Sadeq (Petaling Jaya: International Islamic University Press, 1991), 239–51; and "Islamic Banking: The Malaysian Experience," in Ariff, *Islamic Banking*, 67–102.

31. Interview with Zainulbahar Noor, August 4, 1992.

32. See "Tiada Jalan Surut," *Amanah* 152 (May 1992): 18C.

33. See "Riba, Ijtihad, dan Kesejahteraan," *Infobank* 124 (April 1990): 30–31.

34. Interview, July 27, 1992.

35. See Hefner, "Islam, State, and Civil Society."

36. Interview with Sri Bintang Pamungkas, July 22, 1992. Details of how the MMI will operate are summarized in the company's founding document, "Rencana Usaha PT. Manajemen Musyarakah Indonesia" (March 1992).

37. Interview, July 27, 1992.

38. See Eko Budi Supriyanto, "Ketika Kyai Bisnis Uang," *Infobank* 124 (April 1990): 12–13.

39. On the SUMMA crisis, see "Terobang-ambing di Tengah Negosiasi," *Tempo*, July 4, 1992, 62–67; and "Ini Dia Masalah Bank Summa," *Tempo*, February 13, 1993, 88.

40. See Hefner, "Islam, State, and Civil Society." The best general overview of the origins and consequences of the movement for Islamic renewal that began in the 1970s is Fachry Ali and Bahtiar Effendy's masterful *Merambah Jalan Baru Islam: Rekonstruksi Pemikiran Islam Indonesia Masa Orde Baru* (Bandung: Mizan, 1986).

9

FATWA AND POLITICS IN INDONESIA

Nadirsyah Hosen

The aim of this chapter is to demonstrate how Indonesian *fatawa* (plural for *fatwa*) gave response to politics and government policies from 1926 up to 1998. It also shows how political situations influenced the issuance of *fatawa* and, at the same time, how *fatawa* influenced the Indonesian political atmosphere. Until the beginning of the twentieth century, *ijtihad* in Indonesia was performed by individual *ulama*. In the second quarter of the twentieth century, the practice of *ijtihad* as performed by the *ulama* in groups began. In 1926, traditionalist *ulama* founded the Nahdlatul Ulama (NU) organization, and it began issuing *fatawa* as early as during its first congress. The modernist Muhammadiyah organization, which was founded in 1912, did not concern itself with *fatwa* until 1927 when it created a special committee called Majelis Tarjih to deal with religious issues in general and Islamic law in particular.[1]

Although *fatawa* issued by certain individual *ulama* could still be observed, the tendency was for more and more *ulama* to identify themselves with one of those two poles: the NU or Muhammadiyah. A new development emerged when the Council of Indonesian Ulama (Majelis Ulama Indonesia, or MUI) was established in 1975. Both the traditionalist and the modernist *ulama* are represented in the MUI through which they issue joint *fatawa*.[2]

Unlike in Egypt and Saudi Arabia, Indonesia does not have a grand *mufti*. *Fatawa* are issued collectively by Islamic organizations. The characteristics of Indonesian collective *ijtihad (ijtihad jama'i)* are as follows: firstly, before issuing *fatawa*, each organization holds a meeting attended by their *ulama* and — if necessary — other scholars. They discuss the subject, and the conclusion of the meeting is issued as a *fatwa* from that particular organization. Secondly, the characteristics of pluralism, which makes Indonesian *fatwa* unique, can be seen. Indonesia has many

Islamic organizations such as the NU, Muhammadiyah, and the MUI, each of which consists of separate branches in more than twenty provinces. It is possible that a *fatwa* from one organization may differ from those of other organizations. It can also happen that a *fatwa* issued from the national organization is different from one given by the provincial organization. Again, a *fatwa* from one provincial branch may be at variance with a *fatwa* from another province, even though both belong to the same organization. Therefore, it is possible to have many *fatawa* covering one case.

Indonesian *fatawa* cover several matters such as ritual, charity, pilgrimage, economics, politics, and other social problems. However, unlike the case with religious courts, there are no government regulations about *fatwa*. The *ulama* are free to produce *fatawa*. Unlike in Malaysia, *fatawa* from Indonesian *ulama* do not require the approval of the government (or the Sultan in Malaysia's case).[3] The position of *fatwa* in Indonesia is not nearly as strong. Indonesian Muslims consider *ulama* only as principally religious patrons whose advice and exemplary lives are to be followed, but not in the sense of religious obligation or prescription.

The significant thing to note is that the *ulama* do not have the power and cannot force Indonesian Muslims to obey and follow their *fatawa*. Indonesian *ulama* have much authority; but no actual political power. It is not compulsory for people to follow *fatwa* from *ulama*. However, they tend to do so because they recognize certain qualities in the *ulama* and not because the *ulama* are in possession of the instrument of coercion or are in positions of command. The high regard people have for *ulama* persuades them to respect the *ulama*'s positions. However, because *ulama* do not have coercive power, they cannot order sanctions against those who refuse to follow their advice.

ULAMA AND POLITICS

As will be discussed later, *ulama* have wielded considerable political influence through their official *fatawa*. The question is, why should *ulama* play any part in politics? Although Indonesia is not an Islamic state, the idea and culture of Islam heavily influences Indonesian Muslims. The next question is, what do Islamic teachings have to say on this? Firstly, the Qur'an (16 : 43) orders people to "question the people of remembrance (that is religious scholars), if you do not know". One interpretation of this verse holds that Muslims are under an obligation to consult with and seek advice from individuals known to possess knowledge and moral probity, that is, *ulama*.[4]

Secondly, according to al-Syatibi, where a *mufti* exists in a Muslim community, he stands in the same position as the Prophet.[5] The Prophet is regarded not only as a religious leader, but also as a leader of political affairs.

Thirdly, the doctrine of *amar ma'ruf nahi munkar* (command the good and forbid the evil) also contributes to this matter. It is derived from the Qur'an (3 : 104): "Let there become of you a group of people which shall call for righteousness, enjoin the good and forbid the wrong. Such men will surely triumph." This doctrine is used by the *ulama* to justify their role in politics. When they do involve themselves in politics, they claim to be doing so on the basis of this doctrine. The *ulama* feel that it is their duty to guide and show people what is right and what is wrong in politics. Politics, as is known, sometimes conflicts with ethics. Therefore, the *ulama* justify their becoming involved in politics on the ground that politics and the politicians must act in line with Islamic ethics.

Fourthly, the Qur'an (4 : 59) states: "O ye who believe! Obey Allah, and obey the messenger and those of you who are in authority *(ul al-amri)*." One interpretation believes that the words *ul al-amri* refer to both *ulama* and the government *(umara)*.[6] Therefore, *ulama* and the government are equal in position. This is based on the Prophet's saying that there are two groups in a community, *ulama* and *umara* (government); that if they are good, then all in the community will be good; and if they are bad, then all will be bad.[7] However, the *ulama* can refuse to obey the government in matters where the latter departs from Islamic teachings; as mentioned in another saying of the Prophet.[8]

Fifthly is the theory of *maslahah al-'ammah*. This holds that whatever is good in Islamic societies is also good in the eyes of Allah. According to the saying of the Prophet, Muslims will not agree on an error.[9] If there are two options in politics, the *ulama* will choose the safer and more beneficial one, according to their Islamic knowledge and spirituality. *Ulama* often find themselves in an accommmodationist position and sometimes, as the critics say, they adopt a very opportunistic approach.[10]

What do *ulama* do in politics? I have argued elsewhere that *ulama* become involved in politics in manifolds. Apart from the issuing of *fatwa*, which is this chapter's centre of attention, the *ulama* also have appeared in Indonesian political arena in three forms.[11]

The first way *ulama* play a role in politics is by forming political parties. Under the Soeharto government, which allowed only three parties to function, several *ulama* joined these parties, namely, Partai Persatuan Pembangunan (PPP), Golkar (Golongan Karya), and Partai Demokrasi Indonesia (PDI). Following the downfall of Soeharto on 21 May 1998, the government withdrew its restriction on the number of political parties that are able to contest elections. As a result, forty-eight political parties participated in the 1999 election. Twenty are recognized as Islamic parties. It is interesting to note that although KH Abdurrahman Wahid of NU heads Partai Kebangkitan Bangsa (PKB) and Professor Amien Rais formed Partai Amanat Nasional (PAN), both do not describe their parties as Islamic parties. Instead, they argue that their parties are based on nationalism; not religion. Wahid (NU) and Rais (Muhammadiyah) may have different opinions on many things, but they both believe that Indonesia should not be an Islamic state. Whilst the NU and Muhammadiyah still exist as Islamic organizations, most of their *ulama* joined the PKB and PAN respectively.

The second role played by *ulama* in Indonesian politics is by bringing the masses to Islamic ceremonies such as *tabligh akbar* or *istigasah*. For example, in 1992, three months before the election of that year, Wahid had shaken up the normally quiet world of Indonesian politics by hosting a mass rally, which gathered between 150,000 to 200,000 members of the NU at the Senayan Sports Stadium in Jakarta. The ostensible purpose of the rally was a reaffirmation of the Muslim organization's commitment to the state ideology, Pancasila, amid a perceived rising tide of sectarianism and fundamentalism in Indonesia at that time.

The third political role of *ulama* is advising Muslims how to act in political situations. In this regard, it is interesting to note that several weeks before the 1999 election, both the MUI and Muhammadiyah stated that Indonesian Muslims should refrain from voting for any political party which had non-Muslim candidates standing for election. Clearly, this proposal was a negative response to Megawati's party (PDI-Perjuangan), which allegedly about 40 per cent of its candidates are non-Muslims. This is a huge proportion considering that non-Muslims only make up 20 per cent of the Indonesian population. Despite the statements by the MUI and Muhammadiyah, which cost Megawati's party possibly 10 per cent of its vote, it is clear from the result that PDI-P emerged the winner of the election. Professor Ali Yafie of the MUI rejects the consequent interpretation that the success of the PDI-P shows that Muslims did not follow the MUI directive. Rather, he argues that most of the followers of the PDI-P were not strong Muslims anyway. Accordingly, they were not influenced by the MUI's argument.

FATWA ON POLITICS AND GOVERNMENT

KH Hasyim Asy'ari of the NU issued a *fatwa* on the religious necessity of defending Indonesian independence and waging *jihad* against the Dutch Army, which was trying to re-establish its power in Indonesia. It is unfortunate that the date and the full text of the *fatwa* are not known.[12] However, one may look at the content of the decision of thirty religious dignitaries of Yogyakarta, as published in the Indonesian daily newspaper, *Kedaulatan Rakyat,* on 20 November 1945 as follows:[13]

> Thirty religious dignitaries of Djogyakarta came together under the management of KH Fadil and KH Amir at a small mosque of Notopradjan and declared:
>
> 1. To agree to the *fatwa* of KH Hasyim Asy'ari which is summarized as follows: One. The statute which calls for fighting against infidels who obstruct our independence is an individual obligation (*fard 'ayn*) for every Muslim who has the ability even if he is poor.
>
>   Two. The statute which says anyone who dies in the fighting against the NICA [the Netherlands Indies Civil Administration] and its allies is a martyr.
>
>   Three. The statute which says whoever divides our unity is liable to be killed. Regarding that *fatwa,* the religious dignitaries are always ready to fight to the utmost of their strength in order to defend religion and independence.

2. Related to religious practices:
    One.   All the Muslim community is called upon to engage in a prayer for a
    specific wish (*salat al-hajah*) asking for the salvation of God, Allah the Almighty,
    and the continuity of Independence.

    Two.   To augment fasting, during fasting (before breaking it), also to augment
    istigfar (asking forgivenes) and prayers (*al-du'a*).

    Three.   To augment reading the Holy Qur'an (especially *surah al-Baqarah* or
    Alam Nasrah or *Alam Tara.*)

The NU also issued a resolution regarding holy war. It was declared in
Puwokerto, Central Java in March 1946. It gave a statement that the statute of
individual obligation fell on those who lived within a radius of 94 kilometres of
where the infidels invaded. Those who lived outside that radius had a collective
obligation (*fard kifayah*) to expel the infidels. However, if the people within the first
radius were unable to defeat the enemy, inevitably, the people within the second
radius would have the same obligation as the people of the first radius. The
obligation would be to support them as well until the enemy could be subjugated.[14]
This *fatwa* is based on *al-Bujairami 'ala Fath al-Wahab, al-Bajuri, Hasyiyah al-Jamal,
Raudat al-Talibin, Rad al-Mukhtar,* and *al-Hawi al-Kabir.*

Fifty years after the *fatwa* on *jihad,* the NU issued a *fatwa* in 1997 which
influenced the Indonesian political atmosphere. It stated that political demonstration
is allowed in Islam. It could be seen as part of *amar ma'ruf nahi munkar.*[15] This
obviously opposed government policy restricting the rights of political
demonstrations and protests. University students, members of non-government
organizations (NGOs), and workers tend to express their dissatisfaction with the
government by means of demonstrations. The Soeharto government did not look
kindly upon such activity because of its potential to fuel instability in Indonesian
politics. Demonstrations and disturbances in a number of Indonesian cities forced
President Soeharto to resign on 21 May 1998, six months after the NU *fatwa* of
1997. Although that *fatwa* does not mention a holy war nor request Soeharto to
step down, it is clear that directly or indirectly the NU provided a justification for
mass movement during that time.

Regarding *fatwa* on government policies, it should be noted that there are
fatawa that support government policies as well as several *fatawa* that oppose the
government. Examples of both *fatawa* are presented below. Firstly, several *fatawa*
on issues such as the use of condoms in sexual relations between unmarried couple,
mixed marriages, joining a legislative body, and attending Christmas celebrations
can be presented as illustrations of where *fatawa* seem to oppose government
policies. Balanced against these examples is the *fatwa* on family planning which
supports government policy.

The MUI has been involved in a campaign against the acquired immune
deficiency syndrome (AIDS). In November 1991, the Minister for Health,
Adhyatma, said that co-operation with the MUI was important as the council
could help enhance the people's awareness of the dangers of AIDS through a

religious approach.[16] However, KH Hasan Basri, the general chairman of the MUI, expressed his disagreement with an official anti-AIDS campaign recommending the use of condoms in sexual relations between unmarried couple, because this implied that the government condoned the sort of sexual behaviour which was abhorrent to Islam. He said that the policy could incite people to commit adultery.[17]

Muhammadiyah held its *Tanwir* conference from 12 to 16 January 1992 in Jakarta. A total of 200 executive members of the organization from all over the country participated in the conference, which was opened by the Minister for Home Affairs, Rudini, and closed by the Minister for Religious Affairs, Munawir Sjadzali.[18]

The conference concluded that on the issue of "mixed marriage", Law No. 1 of 1974 on Marriage had already regulated marriage clearly and strictly, so that a new regulation or law concerning marriage between partners of different religions was not needed. If anything should be amended, this should only be in the form of a confirmation of, or information added to, the Marriage Law.

This conclusion was clearly a response to the statement of the Minister for Religious Affairs, Munawir Syadzali. On 7 January 1992 (five days before the conference), he stated that Indonesia needed a new formulation of official regulations which would allow people of different religions to marry. According to him, since Indonesia is a heterogeneous society, mixed marriages are inevitable. This idea received negative response, not only from Muhammadiyah, but also from Muslim scholars and the MUI.[19] The latter had already issued a *fatwa* in 1980 that inter-religious marriages are not allowed under Islamic law.[20] Furthermore, the NU issued *fatawa* on this issue in 1962, 1968 and, again, in 1989, confirming the view that inter-religious marriages are not permitted.

The 1992 conference of Muhammadiyah also decided to allow executive members of the organization to become members of a body of people's representation on a national or regional level, unless it was considered that their function hampered the organization, especially in its relations with the government. This was a new step for Muhammadiyah, which since its thirty-eighth *muktamar* in 1971 in Ujungpandang, South Sulawesi had forbidden Muhammadiyah executives from becoming members of the legislative body, except by permission from the Central Board.

The 1992 *Tanwir* conference also urged the government to avoid the subjugation of political decisions to economic requirements. It appealed to the government to be responsive to the social and political aspirations of the people by accelerating the process of democratization.[21]

Another example of *fatwa* which opposes the government can be seen when the MUI issued a *fatwa*, on 7 March 1981, stating that a Muslim's attendance at Christmas celebration was *haram*, and that, therefore, Muslims should not be involved in any such activity.[22] The *fatwa* was issued in response to the custom of inviting Muslims to formal Christmas celebrations. Many Muslims were reluctant to decline such invitations for fear of being accused of intolerance. In their confusion, many Muslims asked the MUI about the legal status of such a practice, and this led the MUI to issue the *fatwa*. The *ulama* took the view that Muslim attendance at Christmas celebrations constituted a step towards Christianization.[23]

The Indonesian government was not very happy with the timing of the MUI's *fatwa*, which was considered disadvantageous to the government's efforts to promote Muslim–Christian harmony after the conflicts of the late 1960s and the early 1970s. The *fatwa* was seen by the government as particularly damaging to its efforts to regain inter-religious harmony, and it regarded the *fatwa* as a reflection of the MUI's inflexibility.[24]

Although the government strongly opposed this *fatwa*, the MUI remained firm. The government went so far as to ask the MUI to revoke the *fatwa*, but was refused. The result is that the *fatwa* still exists today, but the general chairman of the MUI, Professor Hamka resigned from his position because of it. In his letter to the MUI, Hamka wrote:

> The Minister of Religious Affairs, Alamsjah Ratu Perwiranegara, at a meeting with the MUI held on April 23, 1981, expressed his disappointment with the release of the *fatwa* of the MUI [on Muslims' attendance at Christmas celebrations]. The Minister also indicated his being furious [about the matter], and stated his intention to resign from the ministerial office.

> In response to the statement of the minister, I said that it was not he but I who had to resign, for I am the one who is responsible for the release of the *fatwa* which has made the minister intend to resign.[25]

By contrast, family planning provides a good example of how the government has been able to influence a *fatwa*. Indonesia succeeds in its family-planning programme because the MUI, NU, and Muhammadiyah all state that family planning is *mubah* (permissible). Therefore, Muslims are able to lend their support to this programme.

The *fatwa* of the MUI on family planning was not produced by the Fatwa Committee, but at the National Conference of *Ulama* on Population, Health, and Development, held in Jakarta from 17 to 20 October 1983. The main points of the *fatwa* are as follows:

> One.   Islam justifies the practice of family planning exercised for the sake of the health of the mother and the child, and for the interest of the education of the child. The practice must be undertaken by choice, and employ contraceptives that are not prohibited in Islam.

> Two.   Abortion practised in any form and at any stage of pregnancy is forbidden in Islam (*haram*), because it constitutes murder. This includes menstrual regulation by pills. Exception is granted only if the abortion is conducted to save the life of the mother.

> Three.   Vasectomy and tubectomy are forbidden in Islam, except in emergency cases such as to prevent the spread of disease or to save the life of the person undergoing vasectomy or tubectomy.

Four. The use of IUDs (Intra Uterine Devices) in family planning is justified provided that the insertion is carried out by female doctors or, in certain circumstances, male doctors in the presence of other females or the husband.[26]

The issuing of a *fatwa* involves intellectual activity. Thus, it is possible that a *fatwa* — as an intellectual activity — can be opposed by others. This occurred with respect to determining the first day of Syawwal, as the appropriate ending to the fasting month of Ramadhan. The Islamic year is a lunar year, as opposed to a solar year, of approximately 354 days. A new month begins when a new moon is sighted. This is of special importance during Ramadhan and Syawwal to determine the start and end of fasting. Muslims will observe the sky carefully for sign of a new moon. The word "observe" often invites problems.

In 1992, the government determined Sunday, 5 April, as Idul Fitri. The government's decision was supported by the MUI and Muhamamdiyah. However, the NU issued an order from its chairman, KH Abdurrahman Wahid, to stop fasting on Saturday, as the last day of Ramadhan was on Friday, 3 April, but to join the prayers and celebration only on Sunday out of respect for the government's decision. Wahid said that it was *haram* to fast on the first of Syawwal, which according to him fell on Saturday, whereas Idul Fitri prayers are *sunnah*, not obligatory. This apparently caused confusion among Muslims. The confusion was caused by disagreements among religious experts and astronomers about when the month of Ramadhan actually ended.

The disagreements arose because there are two ways to determine the end of Ramadhan, namely by *hisab* (astronomic calculation) and by *ru'yah* (sighting the new moon). Based on *hisab,* the new moon would not be sighted on 3 April 1992. However, a number of *ulama* said they saw the crescent on that day. The government relied on both methods, posting officers all across the archipelago from Ambon, via Manado, West Nusa Tenggara, Semarang, Pelabuhan Ratu, Palembang and Medan to Sabang, to observe the sky for the new moon. However, none spotted the crescent. The Minister for Religious Affairs concluded that the result of *ru'yah* concurred with that of *hisab,* meaning that the fasting month was to last up to Saturday, 4 April. Two well-known *ulama* of the NU, KH Idham Chalid and KH Ali Yafie, were still fasting on Saturday and performed the Idul Fitri prayers on Sunday.[27]

Many Muslims believe that the disagreement was politically engineered by Wahid. Wahid did not support government intervention in religious matters, particularly the activities of ICMI (Ikatan Cendekiawan Muslim Indonesia, or Indonesian Muslim Intellectuals Association) which was headed by Professor B. J. Habibie and strongly backed by President Soeharto. For this reason he opposed the government's decision on the first of Syawwal on principle. However, a certain shifting of his position could be seen in 1997. He became very close to Soeharto's daughter, Siti Hardiyanti Indra Rukmana (known as "Mbak Tutut") during the general election period in 1997.

Since 1997 Amien Rais, chairman of Muhammdiyah, has been critical of the government's policies on law enforcement and the handling of the economic crisis. On 26 January 1988, Australian television network ABC reported that Rais said the administration under seventy-six-year-old President Soeharto had fostered a culture of corruption, collusion, and nepotism.[28] Then, in 1998, Muhammadiyah celebrated Idul Fitri on 28 January, whereas the government, the MUI, and the NU celebrated it on 29 January.

It can be said that the NU had religious argument on its side when, in 1992, it decided to celebrate Idul Fitri a day earlier. The Muhammadiyah also produced religious argument as to why it celebrated Idul Fitri on a different day from the government in 1998. However, many Muslims feel that the shifting political positions of Wahid and Rais, as mentioned above, influenced both decisions on Idul Fitri. Indeed, when they were very close to the government, they tended to support its decisions through their *fatawa*. But when their relationship with the government cooled, they produced somewhat different *fatawa*. Because the MUI tended to support the government's decision on the first of Syawwal, many Muslims began to allege that the council was under the control of the government. The leaders of the MUI, NU, and Muhammadiyah, however, reject the suggestion that their *fatawa* are influenced by political conditions.[29]

According to M. B. Hooker, looking at the period from 1975 to the early 1990s, it is quite clear that the main function of the MUI was to support and, in some cases, to justify government policy and programmes.[30] Some *fatawa*, such as on the breeding of frogs and rabbits for food, are controversial, and several Muslims claim that the MUI tends to legitimize government policies rather than act for the common good.[31]

Ibrahim Hosen, chairman of Fatwa Committee of the MUI, in replying to those critics, said the MUI had a deep understanding of the sayings of the Prophet: "The most reckless of you in issuing *fatawa* is the most sure to go to hell (narrated by al-Darimi)."[32] This indicates that the MUI is serious in performing its duties and always considers many aspects before issuing *fatwa*. Hosen rejects the view that the *fatwa* of the MUI tended to legitimize the government's policies. According to him, the MUI produces a *fatwa* in order to answer questions posed by both the government and society. He points out, for example, that the *fatwa* on vasectomy and tubectomy differs from the government's policies on these issues.[33]

It is interesting to consider the conclusion of M. Atho Mudzhar in his dissertation concerning the independence of the MUI:

> In general it can be said that the *fatwa*s of the MUI have been products of certain sociocultural and sociopolitical settings in which government policy is a part. However, the degree of the impact of the *fatwa*s on society corresponds neither negatively nor positively with the governmental influence. The *fatwa* on the lawfulness of the use of IUDs in family planning which was strongly influenced by government policy may have had as much impact as did the *fatwa* on Muslim's

attendance at Christmas celebrations, which was free from governmental influence or even opposed to government policy.[34]

Moreover, Ali Yafie, Ali Mustafa Yaqub, and Anwar Ibrahim argue that if the MUI tends to support the government view in a negative way — as some scholars have claimed — why does the Fatwa Committee still receive many letters from the public seeking *fatwa* (the *fatwa*-askers)? According to them, this indicates that, firstly, Muslim society still trusts the MUI as a legitimate council for issuing *fatwa*. Secondly, it shows that the MUI is still needed by Indonesian Muslims.[35]

In October 1999, Amien Rais of Muhammadiyah was elected as chairman of the MPR (the House of Representatives), while the general chairman of the NU, Abdurrahman Wahid was elected as the President of Indonesia. This was the first time in Indonesian history that the leaders of the NU and Muhammadiyah have led the country. The important question to be considered in this context is: to what extent does the change from Soeharto to Habibie and now to Wahid influence the development of the *fatwa* in Indonesia? The next question is, what role can be played by *ulama*, by participating in the government, and at the same time, issuing *fatawa*, to aid the emergence of a more democratic Indonesia and the expunging of corrupt, collusive, and nepotistic elements in Indonesia? Certainly, these questions need to be examined more fully in future studies.

CONCLUDING REMARKS

All the above discussions lead to the conclusion that *fatwa* in Indonesia has dealt with Indonesian problems, including politics, for more than seventy years. The *fatwa* has been instrumental in securing the success of government programmes, as shown in the case of family planning. This chapter has demonstrated that although there are some *fatawa* that support government policies, this does not mean that the *fatawa* are not religiously based.

Finally, the issues which are covered by Indonesian *fatawa* are wider than those discussed in the books of *fiqh*. The topics in books of *fiqh* do not cover modern issues such as political demonstration, vasectomy and tubectomy, to name a few, because those books were written hundreds of years ago. Nor do the Qur'an and the *sunnah* mention these things for the same reason. Indonesian *ulama* have used *fatawa* as an instrument to cope with modern developments. The institution of *fatwa* is a viable tool through which a society can adjust itself to internal and external social, political, and economic change.

Notes

1. Mohamad Atho Mudzhar, "Fatwas of the Council of Indonesian Ulama: A Study of Islamic Legal Thought in Indonesia 1975–1988" (Ph.D. dissertation, University of California, 1990), p. 6.

2. Ibid., p. 15.

3. In Malaysia, the Sultan, as head of the Muslim religion, has a great deal of influence on the appointment of religious officials, especially the *mufti*, and the direction of religious affairs in the state. According to Ahmad Ibrahim, *fatawa* which are based on other than the orthodox doctrines of the Shafi'i school require the approval of the Sultan. Under the various state enactments relating to the administration of Muslim law, the power to issue *fatawa* is given to the *mufti*, Fatwa Committee, or the Majelis Ugama Islam. See Ahmad Ibrahim, "The Position of Islam in the Constitution", in *The Constitution of Malaysia: Its Development 1957–1977*, by Tun Mohamed Suffian et al. (Oxford University Press), p. 59.

   In Malaysia, *fatwa* from *ulama* has a strong power. For example, three young Malaysian women were arrested in July 1997 after they took part in the Miss Malaysia Petite pageant at a hotel in Selangor. The arrests were made under 1995 *Syari'ah* enactment allowing for prosecution based on a *fatwa* by the Selangor *Mufti*. (Roger Mitton, "Islam Calling", *Asiaweek*, 18 July 1997, p. 22) *The Economist* reported that they were not themselves from Selangor, and were unaware of the ban, which had not stopped beauty contests in the past. But, ignorance of a *fatwa* is no defence. ("Beauty and the priests: Malaysia", *The Economist*, 23 August 1997, p. 31.)

   The *ulama* in Johor order people to make a report if they see any Muslim who is absent for Friday prayer for three times. Meanwhile, the *Kathi* (Judge) of Muar District, Muhammad Burhanuddin Tibek, says that any Muslim who is absent three times from Friday prayer can be sent to jail for fifteen days based on Article 143 of Administration of Muslim Law Enactment in Johor. ("Ulama Malaysia: Laporkan Muslim yang Absen Shalat Jumat", *Republika*, 23 September 1997.)

4. See Muhammad b. Jarir al-Tabari, *Jami' al-Bayan 'an Ta'wil ay al-Qur'an*, vol. 14 (Cairo: Mustafa al-Babi al-Halabi, 1954), pp. 108–9; Muhammad 'Ali al-Sabuni, *Safwah al-Tafasir*, vol. 7 (Beirut: Maktabah al-Gazali, n.d.), p. 128.

5. al-Syatibi, *al-Muwafaqat fi Usul al-Ahkam*, vol. 4, pp. 224–25.

6. See al-Mawardi, *al-Nukat wa al-'Uyun Tafsir al-Mawardi*, vol. 1 (Beirut: Dar al-Kutub al-'Ilmiyah, n.d.), pp. 499–500; Wahbah al-Zuhaili, *al-Tafsir al-Munir*, vol. 5 (Beirut: Dar al-Fikr), p. 126.

7. This *Hadith* is often quoted by Indonesian *ulama*. Unfortunately, I cannot find the complete text with the full *sanad* and sources in nine primary books of *Hadith* (*kutub al-tis'ah*). I found the text in Jalal al-Din al-Suyuti, *al-Jami' al-Sagir*, *Hadith* Number [HN]: 5047. It is interesting to note that al-Suyuti takes the view that this *Hadith* is weak (*da'if*).

8. There are various texts on this topic. One of them can be found in *Sahih Muslim*, book *al-Imarah*, HN: 3,423.

9. See *Sunan Ibn Majah*, book *al-Fitan*, HN: 3,940.

10. *Maslahah al-'ammah* words are abstract words which can be interpreted by everyone. In other words, *maslahah al-'ammah* is difficult to define precisely, and too easily associated with the arbitrariness of personal opinion. Al-Ghazali tries to define *maslahah* as an expression for "seeking something useful or removing something harmful". He explains that "seeking utility and removing harm are the purposes at which the creation aims and the goodness of creation mankind consists in realising its goals". (Al-Ghazali, *al-Mustasfa min 'Ilm al-Usul*, vol. 1, pp. 286–87).

   Syatibi mentions three characteristics of *maslahah*. Firstly, the purpose of divine law is to establish *masalih* (plural form of *maslahah*) in this world and in the hereafter, but in such a way that they do not disrupt the system of Islamic law. Secondly, Allah intends the *masalih* to be absolute. Thirdly, the reason for the above two considerations is that Islamic law has been instituted to be *abadi* (eternal, continuous), *kulli* (universal), and *'amm* (general) in relation to all kinds of obligations (*takalif*), subjects of law (*mukallafin*), and conditions or states (*ahwal*). (Abu Ishaq al-Syatibi, *al-Muwafaqat*, vol. 2, p. 37.)

The above three characteristics require the *masalih* to be both absolute and universal. The absoluteness means that *maslahah* should not be relative and subjective. Relativity is usually based on equating a *maslahah* with one of the following: personal likings, personal advantages, fulfilment of passionate desires and individual interests.

The *ulama* claim that using *maslahah al-'ammah*, which is for the universal benefit or utility for all Muslims, is one of its criteria in choosing between many different opinions. The question is, how do the *ulama* know that the opinion chosen contains benefit for all Muslims? For example, in 1985, the MUI wrote a letter to the Indonesian Minister for Social Affairs asking for re-evaluation of the Porkas lottery project. The MUI argued that based on reports from the mass media and many *ulama*, the Porkas lottery contained more harm than benefit for the interest of society. By contrast, the government replied that, based on its study, the project contained more benefits and the government believed that it could control the negative effect of the Porkas. It was unfortunate that the MUI accepted, without reserve, what the government said. The MUI does not have institutions to do its own research, in order to compare between mass media reportage and the government's answer. It can be argued that no one — including the government and the MUI — has the right to determine what is of more benefit for the interests of the Muslim society, without first having independent and direct research from the Muslim community.

11. For full account, see Nadirsyah Hosen, "The Role of *Ulama* in Indonesian Politics", Paper presented at the Asia Centre, University of New England, 2 September 1999.

12. See Amiq, "Two *Fatwas* on *Jihad* against the Dutch Colonization in Indonesia: A Prosopographical Approach to the Study of *Fatwa*", *Studia Islamika* 5, no. 3 (1998): 87.

13. Ibid., p. 86.

14. K. H. Azis Masyhuri, ed., *Masalah Keagamaan Hasil Muktamar dan Munas Ulama Nahdlatul Ulama 1926–1994* (Surabaya: PP RMI & Dinamika Press, 1997), p. 197.

15. See *Hasil-hasil Munas dan Konbes Nahdlatul Ulama* (Jakarta: PBNU, January 1998), pp. 35–36.

16. See *Jakarta Post*, 25 November 1991.

17. See *Republika*, 10 April 1993.

18. See *Berita Buana*, 17 January 1992.

19. See *Jakarta Post*, 8 January 1992; and *Kompas*, 8 January 1992.

20. Majelis Ulama Indonesia, *Himpunan Keputusan dan Fatwa* (Jakarta: Sekretariat MUI, 1995), pp. 91–92.

21. See *Kompas*, 13–17 January 1992.

22. Majelis Ulama Indonesia, *Himpunan Keputusan dan Fatwa*, pp. 126–35.

23. M. Atho Mudzhar, "The Council of Indonesian Ulama on Muslims' Attendance at Christmas Celebrations", in *Islamic Legal Interpretation*, by M. Khalid Mas'ud, Brinkley Messick, and David S. Powers (Harvard, 1996), p. 233.

24. Ibid., p. 235.

25. As quoted by M. Atho Mudzhar, ibid., p. 237.

26. The full text of the statement can be found in Majelis Ulama Indonesia, *Himpunan Keputusan dan Fatwa,* pp. 110–12; the quotation and the translation from Indonesian used above are from M. Atho Mudzhar, "Fatwas of the Council of Indonesian Ulama", pp. 227–28.

27. See *Pelita,* 7 and 8 April 1992; also *Tempo,* 18 April 1992.

28. See "The Voice of Real Islam in Indonesia — the Voice of Justice", *Australian Muslim News* IV, no. 2 (1998): 5.

29. Fathurrahman Djamil and Asymuni Abdurrahman (from Muhammadiyah), Azis Masyhuri (from NU), and Ibrahim Hosen (from MUI) strongly reject this analysis. They believe that the decision of each organization is not influenced by any political interest. That decision, according to them, is based purely on religious argument. (Personal interviews with them in Jakarta, Yogyakarta, and East Java in 1998.)

30. M. B. Hooker, "Islam and Medical Science: Evidence from Malaysian and Indonesian *Fatwas*", *Studia Islamika* 4, no. 4 (1997): 16.

31. Allegations that *ulama* tend to support government policies and their *fatawa* are influenced by the political situation emerge not only in the Indonesian situation. Dar al-Ifta in Egypt, for example, has also been the target of similar allegations. See Jakob Skovgaard-Petersen, *Defining Islam for the Egyptian State: Muftis and Fatwas of the Dar al-Ifta* (Brill, 1997.)

32. Abu Muhammad al-Darimi, *Sunan al-Darimi,* book *al-Muqaddimah,* HN: 152.

33. Ibrahim Hosen, "Sekitar Fatwa Majelis Ulama Indonesia", *Mimbar Ulama,* No. 230, October 1997, pp. 10–16.

34. Mudzhar, "Fatwas of the Council", p. 260.

35. Personal interviews with: Professor Ali Yafie in Jakarta on 12 January 1999, Professor Ali Mustafa Yaqub in Jakarta on 30 December 1998, Dr M. Anwar Ibrahim in Jakarta on 31 December 1998. In contrast, other scholars and *ulama* — such as Said Aqil Husein Siradj — went further to ask the MUI to dismiss itself, since they feel that quite often the MUI acts as a confederation of Islamic organizations. Moreover, they do not want the MUI to be so powerful that it could jeopardize their status with the Muslim masses.

10

ZAKAT ADMINISTRATION IN POLITICS OF INDONESIAN NEW ORDER

Arskal Salim

INTRODUCTION

It has been argued in the literature on Islam and politics in Indonesian New Order that the early phase of the regime was marked by antagonism towards Islam, while the last phase was characterized by a more accommodative approach. Abdul Aziz Thaba has further subdivided the New Order regime into three phases.[1] He refers to the first phase (1967–82) as the antagonistic period. During this time, the regime systematically frustrated Muslim aspirations to power. The second phase (1982–85) is described as having been marked by reciprocal criticism. During this time, the regime imposed Pancasila as the sole basis for the Muslim political party (Partai Persatuan Pembangunan, or PPP) and almost all Muslim organizations, a move that was initially met with some resistance. The third phase (1985–94) on the other hand was a period of active accommodation. Realizing that political Islam was no longer a threat, the state began to build a Muslim base of support through a number of policies thought to agree with Islamic socio-cultural and political interests, for example, the passing of the Religious Judicature Law (1989), the founding of Ikatan Cendekiawan Muslim Indonesia (ICMI, or Indonesian

A preliminary brief version of this article in Bahasa Indonesia was published in *Kompas*, 14 January 1999, "Politik Zakat Pemerintah Orde Baru". Republished with permission of the author and the publisher. The author wishes to thank the Pusat Penelitian IAIN Jakarta for its support as he pursued the research that led to this article, and Amru for his help in gathering data from the National Library of Jakarta and Indonesian National Archives. The views expressed in this chapter are the author's own.

Muslim Intellectuals Association) (1990), the compilation of Islamic law (1991), the issuance of the Joint Ministerial Decree on guiding *zakat* administration or BAZIS (1991), the holding of an Islamic cultural festival (1991), the establishment of the Islamic Bank (1992), and the annulment of the national lottery (1993).[2]

It must be remembered, however, that these divisions are simply heuristic devices that should not be interpreted literally. During the antagonistic period, for example, there was a policy on *zakat* that accommodated Muslim religious concerns. When President Soeharto delivered his official speech on the occasion of the *Isra' Mi'raj* celebration on 26 October 1968, he declared that he, as "a private citizen", was willing to take charge of the massive national effort of *zakat* collection and to submit annual reports on its collection and distribution.[3] Following that declaration, he then officially instructed three high-ranking military officers, one of them being General Alamsyah, who was a Minister of the State Secretariat at that time, to make all necessary preparations for a nation-wide *zakat* collection drive.[4] These initiatives, of course, raise many questions. Why did such a favourable policy occur during a period of general antagonism? How did Muslims respond to this policy? What was the impact?

In my own opinion, Soeharto's policy indirectly, but deliberately, suspended the regulations issued by the Minister for Religious Affairs on the establishment of the *zakat* committee (Peraturan Menteri Agama No. 4 tahun 1968), henceforth referred to as "PMA *zakat*". However, some of the studies[5] that have been conducted on *zakat* in Indonesia did not realize that the two policies were in conflict. So the question to be asked is, since it was impossible for Soeharto to deliver a speech declaring his readiness to oversee *zakat* without knowing that there already existed a policy on *zakat* issued by the Ministry of Religious Affairs (MORA), what was his motive in doing so? Clearly, if it was not his intention to abolish existing policy, then all he had to do was to remain silent on this topic.

This study investigates the social and political implications of Soeharto's policy on *zakat*. Whether the *zakat* policy in 1968 actually addressed a major issue in the Muslim political agenda or if it was merely a political manoeuvre designed to placate a minor concern in order to distract the Muslim community from more profound issues is discussed. In addition, the study also verifies whether Thaba's theory regarding the three phases of Indonesian New Order policy towards Islam is still valid. Since *zakat* represents a test case in the complicated relationship between the religious/social duties of Muslim citizens and the non-religious character of the Pancasila state, it is a topic worth investigating in some detail.

In wider perspective, this chapter deals with the problematic issue of Islam in politics of the New Order regime.[6] This chapter argues that while political Islam had been marginalized during the New Order era, Islamic politics had still been given attention by the New Order regime. However, its attention towards Islam could hardly be considered as significant, since it did not reflect sincerity and even indicated subordination. Thus, the chapter asserts that the New Order regime had treated both political Islam and Islamic politics almost in similar ways.

THE INSTITUTIONALIZATION OF *ZAKAT* IN INDONESIA

It is not surprising to learn that there is little information on Indonesian *zakat* practices, particularly from before the New Order regime. The genesis of the central government's interest in *zakat* collection and distribution can, however, be traced back to the nineteenth century, when the Netherlands Indies Government realized that the misuse of *zakat* by its own appointed officials might, in the end, be detrimental to its authority.[7] According to Snouck Hurgronje, in nineteenth-century Banten (West Java) *zakat fitrah* was for the most part paid to religious teachers, either *kyai*s or village Qur'an teachers. In East Java, as opposed to most of West Java, *zakat maal* fell under the jurisdiction of the *kyai* and other *ulama*. *Zakat fitrah*, on the other hand, was presented to village religious functionaries, such as *khatibs* (preachers) and other mosque officials. Since neither *zakat maal* nor *zakat fitrah* in East Java was channelled through any *amil* agency, the misuse of these religious contributions was very rare. In West Java, on the other hand, specially appointed religious functionaries exercised the role of *amil*, and these were in turn under the direct supervision of the so-called native chiefs in their respective administrative division. It was from these regions that the government received most reports of misuse of *zakat* funds.[8]

It was for the above reason that the government of the Netherlands Indies issued a regulation (in 1893) to prevent the misuse of *zakat* by appointed religious officials (*penghulu, naib,* etc.) and their supervisors-cum-partners, the native officials. In 1905, the government issued another regulation (Bijblad 6200), which specifically forbade native officials (the *priyayi* and members of the *binnenlands bestuur*) to intervene in *zakat* management. Thus Dutch government policy towards *zakat* management did attempt to make a clear distinction between the state and the Muslim community's affairs in religious matters.[9]

It was during the Japanese Occupation that an attempt was made to get the government more directly involved in *zakat* collection. The Majlis Islam A'la Indonesia (MIAI), the pre-war federation of Islamic political parties and mass organizations revived by the Japanese, took the initiative of establishing a Java-wide Baitul Maal in 1943. The MIAI hoped that it could regain its influence after the Japanese military administration had changed its Islamic policy. Despite the rather lukewarm attitude of the Japanese, the MIAI managed to establish several branches of the *Baitul Maal* all over Java. But it wasn't long before the MIAI itself was dissolved (in late 1943). This attempt to involve the government in *zakat* management thus ended in failure.[10]

After Indonesia won its independence, MORA was established in January 1946. This ministry had initially been proposed to take the place of the Dutch colonial "Office for Native Affairs" and the *Shumubu* of the Japanese period.[11] MORA later issued an announcement (*Surat Edaran* No. A/VVII/17367) on 8 December 1951, declaring that it was the ministry's position not to interfere in the collection and distribution of *zakat fitrah*. MORA's task was simply to encourage people to fulfil their obligation of paying *zakat* and of ensuring that it was distributed properly in accordance with religious teachings.[12] This announcement was the first sign of the Indonesian government's stand towards *zakat*. It shows that, at least at the very beginning, the government never intended to interfere in religious affairs (*zakat*), due to the fact that it was based on the Pancasila.

In 1967, immediately after Indonesia had overcome the attempted communist *coup d'etat*, the central government showed increased interest in the promotion of *zakat* collection. KH Saefuddin Zuhri, Minister for Religious Affairs at that time, presented a draft of *zakat* law to the provincial parliament (officially called Mutual Help People's House Representative, or DPRGR) on 5 July 1967. Moreover, MORA also sent this draft to the Ministries of Finance and of Social Affairs to obtain feedback. Although the latter never responded, the Minister for Finance replied with a suggestion that *zakat* management would be better regulated by ministerial regulations instead of by law.[13] It was perhaps because of this that the provincial parliament chose not to pursue discussion of the draft *zakat* law, which had been presented by MORA. It might have inspired MORA, under the leadership of KH Mohammad Dahlan, to issue regulations concerning the foundation of the Badan Amil Zakat or *zakat* committee (No. 4/1968) (henceforth called PMA *zakat*) and the Baitul Maal or Islamic treasury agency (No. 5/1968) in July 1968. These regulations implied that the foundations would operate at all administrative levels (both district and subdistrict) and throughout Indonesia.

THE CLASH OF POLICIES

There is no evidence that either regulation had been previously discussed with President Soeharto. Accordingly, both had to be set aside as MORA issued a ministerial instruction for the deferment, if not revocation, of both regulations in January 1969. Why was such a "deferment" decided on? What factors accounted for that action?

Abdullah,[14] Dawan Rahardjo,[15] and Bahtiar Effendy[16] explain that the PMA *zakat* was suspended because the Minister for Finance rejected the idea of legislating *zakat*, drafted a year earlier by MORA. This explanation is, however, unsatisfactory since it is not in accord with the other facts. This is why, to some extent, Effendy was astonished that the decision on deferment was taken even though the Minister for Finance had suggested that a ministerial decision was sufficient to regulate the administration of *zakat*.

It is my opinion, however, that PMA *zakat* was forcibly deferred due to Soeharto's speech on *zakat* during the *Isra' Mi'raj* celebration on 26 October 1968. The speech was clearly a veiled criticism of the prevailing local or subdistrict-based organization for collecting *zakat*, considering that Soeharto had offered to take over responsibility on a personal basis as a "private citizen". Had Soeharto wanted to endorse the existing system, he could easily have done so in his speech. His offer to set up a centralized system, despite the absence of any open criticism of PMA *zakat* policy, was nothing less than a roundabout way of announcing impending changes to the mechanism that was already in place.

Nonetheless, MORA seemed not to catch on immediately to the implications of Soeharto's speech; thus only two days later the ministerial instruction (No. 16/1968) on the guidance of the application of PMA *zakat* was reissued. MORA only came to the realization that Soeharto objected to PMA *zakat* after receiving a letter (No. B-3732/Setkab/12/1968) from the Cabinet Secretary on 16 December 1968. It can be concluded that this letter had a strong influence on the decision to suspend the policy (PMA *zakat*). Looking carefully at the ministerial instruction (No. 1/1969) on the suspension of PMA *zakat*, there were at least two reasons for its suspension that suggest themselves. First, the collection of *zakat* as defined in PMA *zakat* was seen by the Cabinet Secretary as the exclusive concern of MORA itself, without co-ordinating with other departments. Second, it was expected that, following his speech, Soeharto would issue regulations (such as *Keppres* or *Inpres*) concerning the collection of *zakat*. The feeling at MORA was that a high-level directive to this effect would be preferable even to any rules issued by the ministry. Such regulations, however, were never issued. The follow-up to Soeharto's speech consisted in nothing more than a command letter (*surat perintah*) and announcement letter (*surat edaran*), neither of which had any essential or legal implications.

This naturally leaves a number of questions still unresolved. What needs to be investigated is, why did Soeharto deliver such a speech, in which he declared himself ready to take on the role of the *zakat* agency? Didn't he know that PMA *zakat* had been issued three months earlier? Was Soeharto trying to interfere in the operation of PMA *zakat*? Were there political motives behind his speech?

Abdullah explains that Soeharto's speech was a response to an appeal by eleven influential Jakarta *ulama* stressing the importance of *zakat*, both as a religious obligation and as a means towards social amelioration.[17] Maybe this was so. But looking carefully at the letter sent by these *ulama,* we see that Soeharto had many options available to him. There are two suggestions and one hope expressed in the letter that was presented by those eleven *ulama*. First, they asked President Soeharto as "a Head of the State" to urge Islamic adherents, particularly those living in the capital city of Jakarta, to comply with this religious obligation (*zakat*). Second, they asked the President to advise the governors of all provinces to take initiatives in co-ordinating the collection and distribution of *zakat*, "in accordance with the principles of *zakat* law and in keeping with the instructions and directions of the Minister for Religious Affairs and Minister for Home Affairs". The ulama also hoped that President Soeharto would be willing to set an example by paying his zakat obligation, as a Muslim faithful to Islamic religious precepts.[18]

Both the suggestions and the hope mentioned had been unsuitably responded by Soeharto's speech. Soeharto neglected the first suggestion by presenting his offer in his capacity as a private Muslim citizen, not as Head of the State. Furthermore, Soeharto not only ignored the appeal to involve governors and ministerial instructions, but went a step further in offering to centralize *zakat* collection altogether. Yet in spite of these considerations, it seems fair to say that President Soeharto exploited the appeal by the eleven *ulama* as an excuse to pronounce on this topic and thus indirectly abrogate PMA *zakat*. The question is, why should this have been the case?

POLITICAL CLIMATE: JAKARTA CHARTER

The explanation can perhaps be traced to the political circumstances of the post-Sukarno era. It can be said that Muslim demands for the legalization of the Jakarta Charter as an integral part of the preamble to the 1945 Constitution had forced the political élite to be cautious in taking any initiative regarding Islam.

Boland explains the political circumstances at that time:

> In this situation Muslims turned once again to the Jakarta Charter of 1945 and its famous "seven words".[19] Apparently a new discussion on the Jakarta Charter in the June–July session of the People's Congress (MPRS) of 1966 was prevented because it was spread about in the lobbies beforehand that the army would not allow such a debate. A new attempt was made during the session of February–March 1967, when the only point on the agenda was the deposition of President Soekarno and the appointment of General Soeharto as Acting President. But the attempt to add some Muslim demands to the agenda was rejected. Once again the Muslims struggle of NU [Nahdlatul Ulama] members as well as Partai Muslimin followers to give the Jakarta Charter an official status during the session of the MPRS in March 1968 was unsuccessful.[20]

The rejection of Muslim demands for the legalization of the Jakarta Charter in the MPRS did not discourage them from pursuing their goals. On 29 June 1968, celebrations commemorating the Jakarta Charter were held in Jakarta (*Kiblat*, 3/XVI/1968). The purpose of this event was to re-emphasize the position of the Jakarta Charter with regard to the 1945 Constitution, particularly after President Sukarno's decree on 5 July 1959, announcing a return to that Constitution. In this ceremony, two speeches were delivered, one by KH Mohd Dachlan, Minister for Religious Affairs, and the other by General A. H. Nasution, the chairman of MPRS. In his speech, KH Mohd Dachlan declared that the commemoration was important, since certain political groups had attempted to deny the significance of the Jakarta Charter in Indonesian history. Dachlan argued that the Jakarta Charter internalized the Constitution of 1945 as well as automatically stood as a source of law.[21] Dachlan offered two pieces of evidence to support his statements. First, it was clearly mentioned in Article 10 of the memorandum of the DPRGR to the MPRS on the sources of law and its hierarchies, that the Jakarta Charter was to be regarded as a source of law. Second, he cited the post-decree government's replies to the question of Ahmad Syaikhu, a member of parliament, to the effect that:

> The acknowledgement of the Jakarta Charter as a historical document of Indonesia directly implied to its influence toward the Constitution of 1945.

So, it not only influenced the preamble of the 1945 Constitution, but also article 29 of the same document, which would serve as a foundation of law in religious life. The word "Belief in God" in the preamble thereby could be interpreted as "Belief in God, with the obligation for adherents of Islam to practise Islamic law. For this reason, the specific law for Muslims in accordance to the *shari'a* might be legalized.[22]

Meanwhile, Nasution in his speech took a different line. He tried to give the Jakarta Charter a wider understanding, one that involved a relationship between the state and all its citizens, not just Muslims. Nasution said:

> If we read the Jakarta Charter with the spirit of the Pancasila and the 1945 Constitution as a whole, it should be interpreted that the Republic of Indonesia requires its citizens to acknowledge the God, and thus to do all God's commands and to avoid His prohibitions in this life, personally or socially, in accordance with their respective religions.[23]

If we explore Nasution's speech further, recorded in full in *Kiblat* magazine, we find that he never correlated the Jakarta Charter with the application of Islamic law. Although he mentioned Islamic law in several places, he nonetheless added that there were some who were wary of the Jakarta Charter on this score. Even though he explained that the government aimed to make its citizens more devout, he implied that this was not in the Jakarta Charter's framework.

The above illustration shows that Nasution was not in line with Dachlan concerning the Jakarta Charter. Their different focal points can be seen in the case of *zakat* management in particular. On the one hand, Dachlan tried to ground all the government's efforts in the religious field on the Jakarta Charter's framework. Dachlan asserted:

> The implementation of the Jakarta Charter consistently would make us able to organize all kinds of *zakat* obligation, without neglecting the rights of the poor, in the interest of development. Such an undertaking could also attract the participation of citizens to be sources of power for the success of the Five Years Development Plan (REPELITA).[24]

Nasution, on the other hand, never made such a connection and thought that religious development in Indonesia depended more on how it was fostered by the religious awareness of its adherents, not because of government impositions. Nasution emphasized that the practice of *zakat* in the first place stems from Muslims' willingness to realize it and is then reinforced by "government guidance", whether legislative or executive. He further explained what he meant by "government guidance", that is, the stipulations imposed by the government to supervise the *zakat* agency and prevent misuse of the funds.[25] Nasution's speech furthermore clarifies the position of the government towards the Jakarta Charter, that is, that it would not be proactive in endorsing the achievement of some practices relating to Islamic law. Its position on the application of Islamic law (the Jakarta Charter) was passive and its function simply facilitative.

Because of this different interpretation of the Jakarta Charter, it may have led to a misunderstanding on Dachlan's part. The latter seemed to perceive that the presence of Nasution and his willingness to deliver a speech in such a ceremony signified that Nasution supported the idea of *zakat* management, thus giving MORA a green light to issue ministerial regulations regarding *zakat*. This perception may have laid the foundation for MORA's issuance of PMA *zakat* two weeks after the celebration.

At that time it was believed that the legalization of *zakat* law was the first step in implementing the Jakarta Charter. KH Mohd Saleh Suaidy, one of the eleven influential ulama who signed the appeal to President Soeharto, remarked that to implement the Jakarta Charter wholeheartedly would require a great effort to compose regulations regarding the collection, distribution, and utilization of *zakat*. He adds, "For the first step, we should be able to manage (*zakat*) internally in our area in accordance to our religious consciousness. Later on, we should strive either to enact legislation on *zakat* law or to strive in the provincial parliament to ratify the same matter".[26] This statement indicates a perception that the implementation of the Jakarta Charter was equivalent to government legalization of certain Islamic rules.

Given the political climate described above, the issue of PMA *zakat* would certainly have been seen as corresponding to the Jakarta Charter issue. For this reason, it is likely to have had an influence on Soeharto's speech, which, though it sounded very accommodating to Muslims aspirations, constituted an indirect effort to reject the implementation of the Jakarta Charter through PMA *zakat*. Thus it is clear that there was a political reason behind Soeharto's speech.

For further verification, it is necessary to observe the atmosphere of MORA in the early New Order era. It could be said that the New Order regime in its early phase was less powerful. This was perhaps due to the fact that almost all departments in New Order cabinets (*Kabinet Ampera*) were still cultivated by political parties wanting to protect their interests, a political realism which derived from Sukarno's regime. Nahdlatul Ulama (NU), for instance, one of several political parties at that time, was in control of MORA. Through KH Mohammad Dachlan, who was the chairman of NU during 1954–57 and then became Minister for Religious Affairs (1968–71), the NU operated MORA in accordance with its political agenda. This can clearly be seen in some policies of MORA, which did not conform with the political agenda of the New Order regime, which sought political consolidation at that time.[27] Seen from this perspective, the clash between PMA *zakat* and Soeharto's ambitions appear to have been inevitable.

TOWARDS A NEUTRAL INTERPRETATION

It can therefore be argued that the New Order's policy regarding Islam was antagonistic at that time. The problematic issue here is who makes the interpretation. If it is those who were involved, it might be seen as a "black or white" or "win or lose" issue. A neutral interpretation, which avoids taking sides in the dispute is preferable, especially to analyse the various religious phenomena which have political undercurrents. This kind of interpretation is very useful not only because it helps to clarify historical facts, but also because it avoids any presumptions.

A good example of this is Thaba's theory, which defines the early phase of the New Order as antagonistic to Islam, but fails to take into account the general trend of policy of the New Order regime towards Islam. His theory of antagonism suggests that the New Order policy towards Islam included strategies designed to weaken the power of Islam in a thoroughly repressive manner, such as by limiting freedom of expression, trampling human rights, or limiting public access by securing the capital and assets accumulation, such as in the case of *zakat*. Since *zakat* is a tool for securing capital, it has the potential of advancing the economic power of Muslims. According to this reasoning, the New Order regime sought to control *zakat* in order to keep the Muslim community from becoming a strong contender and a serious threat to the power of the New Order regime. This kind of interpretation, which Kuntowijoyo classifies as conspiracy theory, is difficult to rely on because of its speculative tendency. How could this theory explain why Soeharto was ready to take over *zakat* agency in the period of antagonism (1968), whereas in the accommodative period (1991) he rejected such a position?[28] To another fact in 1973–74, this theory also fails to explain why a draft of a marriage law (*RUU Perkawinan*), which was initially very "secular", was transformed and eventually made to conform with the Muslim aspirations. Wasn't the New Order regime capable of imposing whatever marriage law it wished to at that time? If Soeharto disagree to such a marriage law, we will never see it exist in Indonesian history of New Order. Thaba's theory of three phases in the New Order's policy towards Islam, especially with regard to *zakat,* clearly deserves to be questioned.

What is the neutral interpretation? It is a factual analysis, an interpretation based on logical observation of the evidence and without any foregone conclusions. If we utilize this approach in observing the issues surrounding *zakat* in 1968 as well as in 1991, we will find that President Soeharto deliberately tried to demonstrate the government's responsibility in the religious field, as required by Article 29 of the 1945 Constitution. However, this offer was made not in its capacity as a religious institution but in that of a political institution. This can be seen by Soeharto's phrase which he offered his services "as a Muslim private citizen but not as the Head of State". This was because it was impossible for President Soeharto, as the Head of State, to act as the *amil* for *zakat* purposes under Pancasila ideology, which makes a clear distinction between state and religion.[29] So, it can easily be understood that Soeharto intentionally phrased his speech in order to avoid accusation that he was straying into unconstitutional waters.

The willingness of Soeharto to become *amil* in 1968 and his rejection of the position of *amil* in 1991 show the general attitude of the Indonesian New Order regime towards *zakat*. Since *zakat* collection was a religious duty, the

New Order regime consistently viewed that the government would not assist in its implementation. Effendy has also made a similar assessment. He says:

> The state neither shared the necessity to legislate zakat into a law, nor acknowledged the urgency of instituting its officials to function as national or regional *amil* of *zakat*. As suggested by Munawir Sjadzali (Minister of Religious Affairs during 1983–93), the state has no intention to regulate or manage *zakat*. Instead, the state confines its role to the extent that it simply supervises and guides the implementation of *zakat*.[30]

CONCLUSION

It may be inferred from the above discussion that the New Order regime never changed its policy towards *zakat*. What has been perceived as a different attitude in the policies of the New Order regime towards *zakat* is in reality perfectly consistent. Both Soeharto's speech in 1968 and the Joint Decree of the two ministers in 1991 were hardly significant either as political accommodation or developments of Islamic teachings. Both seemed more of cases of moral support rather than of structural assistance on the part of the government. However, as Abdullah notes, the most important achievement of the *zakat* drive in Indonesia, particularly under the New Order regime, was the growing awareness of the Muslims of their *zakat* obligations.[31] This is perhaps what led the post-Soeharto government of which B. J. Habibie presented a draft of *zakat* law to the parliament (DPR), subsequently concurred on 14 September 1999 (*Suara Pembaruan*, 15 September 1999). Nevertheless, this *zakat* law seems little more than an extended version of the Joint Decree with several complementary sections.

Notes

1. Abdul Aziz Thaba, *Islam dan Negara dalam Politik Orde Baru* (Jakarta: Gema Insani Press, 1996).
2. Ibid., p. 287.
3. The full text of Soeharto's speech can be found in Ditjen Bimas Islam dan Urusan Haji Depag RI, *Pedoman Zakat* (Jakarta: Proyek Pembinaan Zakat dan Wakaf, 1992/1993), pp. 403–9.
4. Taufik Abdullah, "Zakat Collection and Distribution in Indonesia", in *The Islamic Voluntary Sector in Southeast Asia*, edited by Mohammed Ariff (Singapore: Institute of Southeast Asian Studies, 1991), p. 51; Andi Lolo Tonang, "Beberapa Pemikiran tentang Mekanisme Badan Amal Zakat", in *Zakat dan Pajak*, edited by B. Wiwoho (Jakarta: PT Bina Rena Pariwara, 1992), p. 264.
5. Some studies have been conducted on *zakat* in Indonesia. Several scholars such as Abdullah (1991), Permono (1993), Mas'udi (1991), Rahardjo (1987), Fadlullah (1993), and Tonang (1992) have devoted their study to *zakat* normatively and empirically, but they have been infrequent in discussing such a theme concerning the political approach. Although Abdullah (1991), Rahardjo (1986), Tonang (1992), and Fadlullah (1993) quoted PMA *zakat* together with the speech of President Soeharto, they abandoned the correlation

of each other, and hence, could not notice the contradiction between the two. This also happened to Effendy (1998), who studied the relationship between religion and the state in New Order era. Despite observing through a political approach, he did not probe deeper the reasons beyond the suspension of PMA *zakat*.

6. It is important to note that this chapter distinguishes the term "political Islam [*Islam politik*]" from "Islamic politics [*politik Islam*]". The former refers to the vertical mobilizations which are run by the Islamic groups or Islamic institutions, while the latter means the attempt by a person or institution who pays attention or is interested in striving Islam or Muslim interests within Indonesian public realm. In other words, if political Islam is manifested within Islamic political parties, Islamic politics can be seen through any initiatives or activities done, even by non-Muslims, for the purpose of Islam or Muslim interests. In short, political Islam is not inherent with Islamic politics.

7. Abdullah, "Zakat Collection", p. 57.

8. Ibid.

9. Ibid.

10. Ibid., pp. 57–58.

11. B. J. Boland, *The Struggle of Islam in Modern Indonesia* (The Hague: Martinus Nijhoff, 1982), pp. 9–10.

12. Tonang, "Beberapa Pemikiran", p. 262.

13. Tonang, "Beberapa Pemikiran", p. 264; Abdullah, "Zakat Collection", p. 58.

14. Abdullah, "Zakat Collection", p. 58.

15. Dawam Rahardjo, "Zakat dalam Perspektif Sosial Ekonomi", *Pesantren* III, no. 2 (1986): 40.

16. Bahtiar Effendy, *Islam dan Negara: Transformasi Pemikiran dan Praktek Politik Islam di Indonesia* (Jakarta: Paramadina, 1998), pp. 297–98.

17. Abdullah, "Zakat Collection", pp. 50–51.

18. Ibid., p. 51. The full text of this letter can be found in Cholid Fadlullah, *Mengenal Hukum ZIS dan Pengamalannya di DKI Jakarta* (Jakarta: BAZIS DKI, 1993).

19. The seven words in Bahasa Indonesia are "*dengan kewajiban menjalankan syariat Islam bagi pemeluk-pemeluknya*", which translate to "with the obligation to practise Islamic law for its adherents".

20. Boland, *The Struggle of Islam*, p. 159.

21. KH. Mohammad Dachlan, "Piagam Djakarta Sumber Hukum Mendjiwai U.U.D. 1945" [The Jakarta Charter is the source of law that inspires the 1945 Constitution], Speech delivered at the Commemoration of Jakarta Charter Day Celebration in Jakarta on 29 June 1968. Full transcripts published in *Kiblat* XVI, no. 3 (1968).

22. Ibid.

23. Abdul Haris Nasution, "Tuntutan Persatuan Umat Islam perlu Dilembagakan Djadi Madjelis Permusjawaratan Islam yang Permanen" [The demand for the unity of the Muslim community has to be permanently institutionalized as a Muslim Congress], Speech delivered at the Commemoration of Jakarta Charter Day Celebration in Jakarta on 29 June 1968. Full transcripts are published in *Kiblat* XVI, no. 4 (1968).

24. Dachlan, "Piagam Djakarta".

25. Nasution, "Tuntutan Persatuan".

26. Mohd. Saleh Suaidy, "Mari Kita Laksanakan Piagam Djakarta", *Kiblat* XVI, no. 4 (1968).

27. Ali Munhanif, "Mukti Ali: Modernisasi Politik Keagamaan Orde Baru", in *Menteri-Menteri Agama RI: Biografi Sosial Politik*, edited by Azyumardi Azra and Saiful Umam (Jakarta: INIS-PPIM-Balitbang Depag RI, 1998), p. 288.

28. Prior to issuing the Joint Decree between the Minister for Religious Affairs and the Minister for Home Affairs on the establishment of *zakat* agency (BAZIS), Munawir Sjadzali (Minister for Religious Affairs) and KH. Hasan Basri (Chairman of Indonesian Council of Ulama), on one occasion in 1991, consulted with President Soeharto. In that meeting, both requested President Soeharto to issue a presidential decision (*Keppres*) or a presidential instruction (*Inpres*) on *zakat* management and asked if Soeharto would be able to act as national *amil* (*zakat* agency). Soeharto refused this request and said that it would be better to be administered in the Joint Decree of the two ministers, and to let Muslims themselves manage *zakat*. So, Muslims perform the obligation while the government facilitates its operation. See *Pedoman Pembinaan BAZIS: Hasil Pertemuan Nasional I BAZIS se-Indonesia tanggal 3–4 Maret 1992* (Jakarta: Dirjen BIUH Departemen Agama RI, 1992), p. 83.

29. Mohamed Ariff, "Resource Mobilization through the Islamic Voluntary Sector in Southeast Asia", in *The Islamic Voluntary Sector in Southeast Asia*, edited by Mohamed Ariff (Singapore: Institute of Southeast Asian Studies, 1991), p. 33.

30. Effendy, *Islam dan Negara*, p. 300.

31. Abdullah, "Zakat Collection", p. 79.

11

ISLAMIC VALUES, LAW AND EXPECTATIONS IN CONTEMPORARY INDONESIA

Howard Federspiel

In the latest era of Indonesian history, from the mid-1960's to 1998, known as the New Order Era, leaders from the army, key technocrats, and agents of other nationalist-oriented groups control the Indonesian government. These leaders have not challenged the basis of the state that was inherited from the preceding Sukarno era (1945–1965); it rests on the 1945 Constitution, the philosophic slogan of the Five Principles (Pancasila), and the personality of President Suharto (b. 1921) as national guide and leader. This elite has provided political stability — welcome after a lengthy period of turmoil (1942–1966) — and it has constructed a national consensus for a policy of economic development. All other considerations are subordinate to the twin policies of political order and economic development; the place and role of Islam is no exception. (Hooker, Virginia M. 1993, 1–19; Vatikiotis 1993, 1–6, 191–205)

Prior to and throughout this era Muslims leaders, spokesmen and activists have spoken of the importance of Islamic values in the life of the Muslim community and in the operation of the Indonesian state. It is not surprising that such a call should be made, since it is a historical Muslim contention that Islamic values

Previously published as "Islamic Values, Law and Expectations in Contemporary Indonesia", *Islamic Law and Society* 5, no. 1 (February 1998): 90–117. Reproduced with permission of the author and the publisher, Koninklijke Brill N.V.

should be paramount wherever Muslims live; the modern call emphasizes that in Islam there is no separation between religion and state. Within this context it is possible to identify a large number of general and specific values. Most important for our purposes are *syariah*, the immutable and transcendent law of God, which all Muslims are enjoined to obey, and *tauhid*, the concept of God's unity, which is to be honored and, whenever possible, applied in belief and behavior — both private and communal. Most other values are subsidiary to these two paramount concepts and they serve as a central reference point for the Muslim community of Indonesia. (Voll 1991, 23–33; Faruqi 1980, 76–89, 264–79)

A. ISLAMIC STANDARDS AND THE GOVERNMENT

With these statements about elite concerns and Islamic values in mind, the relationship among contending and coexisting groups can be explored to ascertain an understanding of the position of Muslims and Islam in the Indonesian state and its society. One way of doing this is to compare the world views of four sets of government agencies and ministries.

1. "The Guardians"

The first set includes the presidency itself, the security forces (armed forces and the police), and the Coordinating Ministry of Public Order, which have been the heart of the New Order political system. We call this group the "guardians," for they decide the basic interests of the New Order and focuses on threats and how to handle them. Until now it has had the final authority on all state matters of any consequence. The cornerstone of the guardians' power rests on the "dual-function" (*dwi-fungsi*) principle, in which the armed forces claim to have the interrelated roles of providing both public security and political stability for the nation. This has been further refined to focus on two primary concerns: protection from new upheavals from the left, i.e., movements arising from the ashes of the Indonesian Communist Party exterminated in the late 1960's, and threats from the right, that is, extremist Muslim groups threatening the religious status quo of the Indonesian state. Periodic arrests have been made to forestall threats from these two "enemies" as well as from other groups, such as former military officers calling for reform, student leaders calling for wider participation in government policy, and an autochthonous cultural personality and his associates who called for change on the basis of portents and omens. The guardians propound the "Pancasila State," based on a philosophic slogan dating to 1945 with its themes of "Belief in God," "humanitarianism," "nationalism," "democracy," and "social justice." This slogan, with the attendant policies based on it, are featured as providing a framework for the unity of all racial, ethnic, religious, and social groups within the country and as transcending any cracks, ruptures or strains in the social fabric of the population. Within this *weltanschauung*, religion is regarded as important to the population and to the state itself, providing the moral fibre necessary for the nation to attain its goals and, afterwards, to enjoy the results of its economic development in a modern society exhibiting the highest moral and ethical standards. Under the New Order regime, only five religions are recognized — Islam, Catholic Christianity, Protestant Christianity, Hinduism and Buddhism. All the Indonesian followers of these religions are expected to reflect the values of Indonesia itself, while eschewing allegiances with other regions of the world (i.e. Islam with the Middle East and Christianity with the West). Islam, as the religion of the majority of the population, is regarded as the foremost actor in this effort. This view of the position and responsibility of religion relates directly to general East Asian models apparent in Japan, Korea, Taiwan, Thailand and Singapore. (Aqsha 1995, 158–79; Crouch 1994, 122–45; Jenkins 1984, 255–65)

Beyond illegal Muslim threats, the guardians have been suspicious of Muslim political activity, regarding it as the instrument of a counter-elite and as the leading edge of a system of political rule, i.e., the Muslim state, inimical to the interests of the New Order and the Indonesian way of life in general. Consequently the guardians placed severe limits on Muslim political activity, even while recognizing the value to the general population of Muslim morals, ethics and religious life style. This concern was clearly apparent in government policy throughout the 1970's and 1980's when the political system was managed so that Muslim political efforts were essentially ineffective and Muslim representative strength in parliament was weakened. In a dramatic about-face at the turn of the decade, about 1990, the Suharto presidency, with only limited support within the ruling elite, allowed a new Muslim organization to come into being that, while not technically a political organization, has increasingly taken on a political outlook. So, there is now some division among the guardians, but, there still seems to a consensus that religious groups are not to become politically powerful. (Rasyid 1995, 150–54; Abdullah, Taufik 1996, 1–19)

Within this guardian group nationalist outlooks prevail and Islamic identification is viewed as a communal matter for those who are Muslim. Islamic law is seen in this context, i.e. relating to communal obligations, and, as such the state provides only facilitative institutions for that purpose. A special Muslim court system, inherited from the colonial period, is allowed to deal with marriage and inheritance in cases in which all parties in such litigations are Muslim. This is regarded as a special concession to the Muslim population as the majority group, but is carefully described so that only Muslims are served by the system and then, only for very special cases. Through new legislation and administrative enactments in the late 1980's and early 1990's this court system was streamlined and brought into administrative harmony with the regular national system of justice. Significantly the Muslim elites regarded the reorganization as a positive step by government in reaffirming the importance of Islamic law in the Indonesian state and allowing the continued use of certain traditional law texts as a source of law for some types of cases. This court system is discussed in another context below. (Soeharto 1976, 51–79; Cammack 1996, 66–67; Hooker, M. B. 1995, 13–26)

But, if the guardians are willing to allow the Muslim community to have limited access to Islamic law as matter of self-identification, they are also inclined to use interest in Islamic law to further the New Order state. This can be seen in the establishment of the Religious Scholars Council (Majlis Ulama Indonesia) as a quasi-government agency. It is modeled after similar councils existing in the Dutch colonial period, which were themselves taken over from the early Southeast Asian Muslim sultanates. Indonesian mass organizations in the early twentieth century also used such councils to interpret Islamic law on matters under dispute among believers. In structure the Council is part of a two-tier system with provincial councils handling questions of religious standards at the local and provincial levels, with matters of broad concern addressed by the Council itself. The Council has issued only a small number of recommendations, usually on contentious matters of procedure in religious rites, ceremonies and exercises in an attempt to buttress Sunni orthodoxy. But alongside those matters some issues of wide social concern have been considered, such as *in vitro* fertilization, family planning and the place of a national lottery in Indonesian society. Appointments to the council are made by the government and includes religious scholars of learned reputation and several lay members representing the guardian group itself. In its public relations efforts, particularly in the international Muslim community, the Indonesian government — in this case the guardians — portrays the Council as its chief point of contact with religious leaders and ascribes much of the New Order's success in mobilizing Muslims in support of its development plans as a by-product of the work of the Council. Observers have responded that the government is selective in the policies it brings before the Council and the Council itself has been overly careful in its deliberation, not wishing to offend either the government or the Muslim population. (Majelis 1984; Mudzhar 1990, 119–26; Aqsha 1995, 196–214)

2. "The Technocrats"

A second set of ministries, consisting of the Ministry of Planning (Bappenas) and the Ministry of Finance are controlled by economists and management specialists who are devoted to the construction of a modern national infrastructure based on technical and economic knowledge transferred from the West and adapted to the Indonesian environment. We call the people in this group the "technocrats," a term with which they themselves identify. Many of this group were educated in the West, often in the United States, and the rest are drawn from the major Indonesian national universities, which also are under heavy Western influence in curriculum and teaching emphasis. These two ministries work closely with a consortium of Western nations which underwrites the Indonesian foreign debt and gives advice on how to improve and expand the Indonesian economy's ability to absorb Western investment and products, while improving Indonesia's own productive capacity. The ministries also work with local financial conglomerates composed of Indonesian businessmen, many of them of Chinese descent and others tied to prominent families and important military commanders. These two sources provide the local economic funds and labor mobilization for development projects, turnkey projects and expansion of the general economy. Despite severe problems of uneven development and continuing low levels of per-capita income in comparison with Indonesia's neighbors, these ministries receive high marks from international economic agencies, such as the World Bank and the International Monetary Fund, for the considerable work that has been done in developing a solid economic infrastructure for the Indonesian nation. Many of the high- and middle-level members of these ministries are Christian and other non-Muslims, as well as people whose upbringing has not put an emphasis on Muslim values and world view. The civil service supporting the ministries are nationally oriented in their outlook and see religion as little involved with state matters except to extend its support to the state and provide a strong sense of ethics and morality for the general population. That viewpoint is sometimes portrayed as "secular," but is not so easily pigeonholed in the Asian context where reciprocating duties and responsibilities are viewed as creating a mutually supporting relationship. This view is not necessarily at odds with that of the guardians, but, overall within these ministries, Islamic standards and Islamic law receive almost no attention and attitudes exist toward serious Islam that vary from low-level distrust to benign indifference. (Habir 1993, 161–82; Robison 1986, 211–49; Pangestu 1993, 277–80)

Non-concern for Muslim sensitivities can clearly be seen in the case of capital formation used by the technocrats. This is accomplished through large-scale borrowing from international development banks and a national banking system the technocrats themselves have structured; both are based on interest earnings and payments. These economic practices have not been challenged by Muslim groups, despite Syafi'i school writings that label such funding practices as either "reprehensible" or "forbidden." Indeed, among Muslim mass organizations in Indonesia a consensus has not developed on this issue, with some groups arguing that traditionalist views on usury still stand and others arguing that contemporary banking practices are not really at odds with standard Islamic values. Still, there has been a growing feeling among devout Indonesian Muslims in the past decade that "alternative" banks should exist in Indonesia for the use of those Muslims who wish to avail themselves of institutions built on specific Islamic criteria. As a result several have come into existence, usually with one of the Indonesian mass organizations as sponsor, but one bank, the Bank Muamalah Indonesia has Indonesian government backing. Usually such Muslim banks become co-investors in enterprises, rather than serving simply as lenders of capital, so that rates of return are from profits, not from interest. There have been few suggestions from the Muslim community, however, that the normal banking system be abandoned as contrary to Islamic law. This development suggests that while the technocrats may wish to create guidelines that bypass religious considerations on the grounds of the technical nature of the issues they face, they probably cannot escape the demands of a predominately Muslim society that ultimately those guidelines be subject to Islamic standards, even to Islamic law itself. (Hefner 1995, 26–29; Aqsha 1995, 184–87, 193–95)

3. "The Educators"

The third set of government agencies consists of the Department of Education and Culture and related departments in the Social Welfare sector. The Department of Education and Culture has been the primary mover in promoting Bahasa Indonesia as a functioning national language despite the past identification of large parts of the population with important regional languages. Mostly this has been accomplished through a national education system spanning the teaching range from primary school through university, which also ranks as a contribution to national unity and identity. Significantly, while the education system is centralized, it has mobilized people in all sections of the country, of various ethnic groups, religious affiliation, and social outlook to build a common national outlook that can be used to socialize pupils and students attending the school system. Despite their concern for using a national language and their devotion to promoting Indonesian national norms, these people remain closely identified with their own primordial groups for their personal and social values. We call the people in this sector the "educators," but the term probably does not do justice to their role as cultural brokers who socialize young people from regions into national culture. (Indonesia 1989, 200–03; Muhaimin 1987, 28–42)

While Christians are prominent throughout the education system, Muslim presence is strong and has been influential in the work of education and culture. Since the education system utilizes the schools established by private institutions for much of the primary and secondary instruction, both Christian and Muslims have contributed schools, administrators, teachers and pupils. Of the Muslim groups the modernist mass organizations, such as the Muhammadiyah, have profited the most by associating their educational efforts with it, much more than the Traditionalist groups, which, until recently, concentrated on purely religious education under the aegis of the Department of Religious Affairs. In the Department of Education religious education is part of the curriculum, with the amount and content varying according to the type of school that is receiving a government subsidy. In the reformed madrasah, for example the amount of Islamic education is quite high, approximately 40 per cent of the course offerings. Sectarian values are important considerations and the attitudes of participants vary according to the discipline, the school, and the affiliation that each has. Some educators identify quite strongly with the importance of Islamic values, including Islamic law; this is discussed further in the section on popular views of Islam. In higher education educators in public universities tend toward Pancasilaist definitions of religious obligation, while, not surprisingly, in private Muslim universities Muslim obligations are viewed more sympathetically. Within disciplines in higher education, those in the sciences and technologies are more likely to be outspoken Pancasilaists and those in the arts more likely to see Islamic values as important. Overall among the educators the concept of the Pancasila state receives high attention and general recognition, but it is nowhere as strong as among the guardian and technocrat groups described above. Rather, the sense of individual and group identity is more recognized, and such identity includes religion.

4. "The State Islamicists"

The fourth set of government agencies centers on the Department of Religious Affairs and its subsidiary agencies, which oversee religious matters in general, provide registers for marriage, divorce and family matters, operate a pilgrimage service, and provide for a system of religious courts. Significantly the Department also oversees religious schools and operates a system of fourteen institutes dealing with Islamic Studies at the university level. We will call the people identified with this sector "state Islamicists." The primary clientele for this ministry is largely rural, generally outside the economically developing sector and conservative in religious and social values, but still heavily nationalistic. The main institution in this system is the Islamic boarding school (*pesantren*), a religiously-oriented school using Arabic as one medium of instruction and the famed "yellow books" (*kitab kuning*) of the classical scholars of Islam as texts. These texts include several on Syafi'i *fiqh*. Most operate at the primary and secondary level and a few have course work reaching to the university. (Meuleman 1996, 1–9; Van Bruinessen 1990, 226–37)

Supplemental to the boarding school system is the National Islamic Studies Institutes (Institut Agama Islam Negara — IAIN) which trains young men and women for positions teaching Islamic education in public and private schools, for work in the Department of Religious Affairs and for jobs benefiting from general Muslim education. Some of the last group are found in journalism, for example. In this ministry and associated institutions Islam is of high priority and its values are constantly lauded and put forward as worthy for the state and nation as a whole to follow. Like its counterparts in Brunei and Malaysia, the Department operates a revivalist (*dakwah*) program, and there are also services for strengthening the performance of ritual and belief throughout Indonesia. (M. Ali 1987, 71–73; Departemen Agama 1985, 63–68)

While there is strong identification with the Indonesian nation-state, these state Islamicists believe that accommodation can be made by the state with Islamic values and that it would be possible to have Islamic law operating in Indonesia. Here the *weltanschauung* relates clearly with Middle Eastern notions of the importance of Islam to the operation of personal, communal and national life, even though there is concern that a high level of Indonesia culture be retained in that identity. To offset this Middle Eastern bias, ministry leaders have attempted to bring more Western-trained Islamicists into its midst, particularly in the IAIN system, and has sent nearly 100 young staff members to the West — primarily Canada and the Netherlands — for advanced training. Evidence indicates that while such trainees like their sojourns in the West and profit from their training, especially in use of methodology, they do not desert their fundamental belief that Islamic values are important in the definition of

Indonesian public policy. Still the number of graduates from Middle Eastern programs of learning — at Cairo, Mecca and other sites — easily outnumbers those participating in Western sponsored training programs. That keeps the emphasis on Islamic values much the same, despite the changed training efforts. (Aqsha 1995, 104–5)

Among these state Islamicists Islamic law has a special context not apparent elsewhere in the Indonesian government, for the terms "sacred law" (*syariah*) and "unity" (*tauhid*) are important principles for Muslim personnel in the ministry. Compelled by tradition and political circumstance to accept and promote the Pancasilaist view of religion, the personnel attempt to reconcile standard Sunni Islam with state objectives. Hence the religious courts, mentioned above, are viewed as providing vital services for the Muslim community within the context of traditional Sunni ways of thinking, since their decisions are mostly based on Syafi'i *fiqh* rulings from personnel trained as religious scholars. In 1989 and 1991 a long-awaited overhaul of the religious justice system was undertaken which clearly recognized the religious courts as courts of the first instance for Muslims in family matters (i.e. marriage, divorce and reconciliation) and certain other matters (i.e. pious endowments and some cases of inheritance). But whereas the earlier rulings of the religious courts were regarded by the civil courts as merely advisory, i.e., as *fatwas*, the new law specifies that within their competence the decisions of the religious courts will be regarded as binding. Final appellate jurisdiction, however, rests with the Indonesian Supreme Court.

An important part of this review of the religious courts was the attempt to codify the law that was to be used by the courts. In the work of compilation, previous Indonesian legislation and administrative regulations were combined with former colonial statutes and jurisprudence from some of the traditional Sunni Islamic legal texts in use by the Muslim jurists in the religious court system over the past fifty years. The new compilation covered only the areas of marriage, inheritance and pious foundations, that is, those matters over which the religious courts have jurisdiction. The compilation was seen by some observers as formulating Islamic law on the basis of consensus of the scholars, the fourth source of authority in the formulations described in classical Islamic law, which may be challenged by some religious scholars not included in the discussions. Still, at present, there does not appear to be very much opposition to such law formulation, either among the state Islamicists or those outside of government. (Aqsha 1995, 93–98; Hisyam 1996; Lubis 1995, 24–27, Cammack 1996, 67.)

But there is also belief among state Islamicists that the range of religious law in Indonesian courts could be expanded. A clear example is available in the efforts of a former Minister for Religion, Munawir Sjadzali (b. 1925), who held that office from 1982 to 1992. During his tenure he spoke nationally and internationally about the importance for Muslims to be ruled by Islamic law (*syariah*) and that such law could be used in Indonesia. Arguing the point made by several important Muslim scholars ahead of him, such as Hazairin (d. 1975) and T. M. Ash-Shiddieqy (d. 1975), he contended that standard *fiqh* from the historical Middle East should not be used in Southeast Asian since culture and geography are different; rather, he stated, it is the principles of Islamic law that should be extracted and used according to the conditions of whatever region they are applied. This attempt to institute an "Indonesianized" Islamic law compatible with Sunni standards, but not identical with established schools, received a mixed reception among Indonesian Muslims. There was considerable dissent from those supporting Traditionalist values, because they believed that the Syafi'i formulation of law would be lost in this effort. Muslim intellectuals, on the other hand, usually associated with Modernist and Neo-Modernist approaches, were more open to this position, although their views toward structuring a modern jurisprudence were quite diverse. In general the proposal has not generated widespread enthusiasm nor did it create an important opening toward establishment of Islamic law in Indonesian society. Still, it is reflective of the point of view of many state Islamicists. (*Panjimas* 403, 66–71; Sjadzali 1985; Hazairin 1957)

A further example of the attitude of state Islamicists can be found in the construction of curriculum at the national Islamic studies institutes, where the study of Islamic law occupies an important place. One of the major disciplines is Islamic Law (*syariah*) and students in that program deal in depth with the history of Islamic law, its principles, and the major texts employed by Muslim jurists throughout Islamic history. Such a course of study is intended to provide personnel for the Islamic court system, but equally to provide general scholars for the public educational system. It is not an effort to train officials for the large-scale application of Islamic law in Indonesia. At a more general level, however, efforts have also been made to inculcate ethical and moral standards in all students attending the institutes. The effort is reminiscent of Ismail Faruqi's (d. 1986) call for all Muslim university students to complete a course in Muslim religion and civilization, but is not as ambitious. An example of this effort is provided in the writings of Fatchurrahman (b. unk.), a faculty member at the Yogyakarta institute, which outlines an entire set of Muslim obligations based on the Qur'an and selected Traditions of the Prophet. The topics are reflective of the themes used historically in the writings of Muslim jurists, starting with the categories of "intention" and "sincerity" and including, on one side, "showing respect to elders" and "unity and brotherhood" among Muslims on another. But nationalist themes are not forgotten, for allegiance to nation and respect for national leaders are important points of these teachings. Such courses, which emphasize the obligations and correct attitude Islam demands of its followers, are found throughout the Indonesian Islamic school system. Fatchurrahman's course is important because it deals with the university level and fortifies state Islamicist viewpoints among the new elite of religious leaders the Indonesian government hopes will emerge from these institutes. (Fatchurrahman 1966, I, vii.)

B. ISLAMIC VALUES AND LAW IN INTELLECTUAL THOUGHT

Outside of government there are important intellectual groups involved with literature, the arts and the writing of history. Intellectual groups made substantial contributions to the pre-colonial princely courts of Indonesia, gave direction and inspiration to the nationalist movement earlier in the century and have acted as an important contributor to national life since independence at mid-century. One particular group, relating to the educator class, and allied to the guardians, has given Indonesia a particular view of national history, in which the classical empires of Majapahit (1294–1527) and Sriwijaya (700–1400) are seen as prototypes for the modern Indonesian state. All events since then relate to the creation and retention of the national Indonesian state, including the Muslim mass organizations founded in the early twentieth century, which are seen as part of the nationalist movement. Another group, prominent in literature in the 1940's and 1950's, wrote extensively reflecting the values of an Indonesian society in transition from a colonial to an independent state. Today the descendants of that group reflect themes that are nationalistic and relate to reconsideration of older, usually Javanese themes within Indonesian society. They tend to be non-Muslim in orientation and treat Islam as a cultural influence on the Indonesian scene, but not as the dominant theme. A contemporary group, associated with the "Technocrats" is found in the Centre for Strategic and International Studies (CSIS), a think-tank working on Indonesian foreign policy, particularly its relationship to other Southeast Asian nations and on policy decisions concerning future national development; it consists of the most distinguished Indonesian intellectuals of the contemporary era. (Poesponegoro 1984, 5v; *Indonesian Quarterly* 23, 2, inside cover)

Muslims themselves have long been active as intellectuals within their own self-identified groups, promoting Islam as the dominant concept in Indonesian communal life. An important cadre of such intellectuals existed in the 1920's and 1930's around Agus Salim (d. 1954) and during the 1940's and 1950's around Mohammad Natsir (d. 1991). An important Indonesian Muslim intellectual movement developed in the 1970's and 1980's concerned about the progress of the Indonesian state, society and economy. In the 1990's the movement has been partially absorbed in a new government-affiliated association, mentioned earlier, name the Indonesian Scholars Association (ICMI), which has pulled together all scholars wishing to take part in such considerations. Some government officials, most notably B. J. Habibie (b. 1936), the Minister for Research and Technology, are convinced that Muslim intellectuals can be more closely harnessed to assist in the government's efforts to improve the economic conditions of the country through its development plans. Muslim intellectuals, in general, favor that association, although a few prominent personalities have not yet associated with that new organization. (Ramage 1995, 74–121; Aqsha 1995, 261–76)

The original group of Muslim intellectuals at work before ICMI's formation consisted of young and middle aged men, most of whom attended advanced institutions in the West, such as the University of Chicago, the University of Illinois and Cornell University. They reflected a highly intellectual approach to Islam, which combined firm personal commitment with the analytical methods they gained in the West, compatible with Muslim Neo-Modernism. The themes of "fear of God" (*taqwa*) and "unity of God" (*tauhid*) was central and sacred law was seen as an important feature of the obligations of the believer. In this they reflected values that were common at the time, whether one is talking about the Revivalist movement, about Neo-Fundamentalism or about Post-Modernist Muslim thought. Still, to them contemporary Muslim scholars living in the West, like Fazlurrahman (d. 1990), Ismail Faruqi (d. 1986), Muhammad Arkoun (b. unk.) and Seyyid Hossein Nasr (b. 1933), were more relevant than scholars of the Muslim past. Accordingly these Indonesian scholars introduced the methods of evaluation and general intellectual approaches learned from Muslims in the West into Indonesia and applied them to national problems there. Through numerous seminars and writing they presented new perceptions about Indonesian history, the structure of Indonesian Muslim society, and the nature and goals of economic and political development. Their successors in ICMI continue this tradition, but in a less coherent matter, since they have been mixed with large groups of educated Muslims — many from the technocrats mentioned above — whose concerns and views are not well focused at this current juncture. Meanwhile individual scholars of the old grouping, such as Nurcholish Madjid (b. 1939), Dawam Rahardjo (b. 1942), and Amin Rais (b. 1944), continue to set their own particular directions in intellectual thinking and have considerable followings of their own. (F. Ali 1986, 167–295; Barton 1995, 5–71)

Almost universally this group of thinkers accepts the contemporary state ideology as basic to Indonesian civic life, but they do argue for greater inclusion of Muslim values to describe that ideology more fully. Islamic law is viewed as a means of regulating Muslim contemporary life, relying on contemporary development suitable to the needs of Muslims in a given cultural area. For many, such law could easily be national law itself, so long as Islamic standards are used in constructing the law. Several writers, notably T. Abdullah (b. 1936) and D. Noer (b. 1926), have suggested that the development of Indonesia's current legal system qualifies as "Islamic" since it was developed by Muslims who were simply following a secular approach, but still used Islamic principles in structuring the system. Others, such as N. Madjid and A. Wahid (b. 1940), urge greater accommodation of Islamic principles and state policy to bring Indonesia and Islam into a new understanding with each other. Nasikun's (b. unk.) intellectual analysis of the "legal" sections of the Qur'an and their implications for formal law represents an approach to extraction of specific principles from religious sources themselves. (Federspiel 1992, 92–97, 187–89)

Alongside this group of Western-trained intellectuals is another group trained in the Middle East, who see Muslim standards and particularly the *syariah* in more conventional terms, even though their views of the importance of a national Indonesian state and its development policy are not issues of contention. They too draw on Fazlurrahman and other "Westernized" Muslim intellectuals, but less so than members of the first group and they cite Egyptian writers, such as Ahmad Syaltout (d. 1964), al-Maraghi (d. 1945) and al-Aqqad (b. unk.). The leading intellectual in this "Middle Eastern" educated group is M. Quraish Shihab (b. 1944), whose writings on the Qur'an iterates the obligations of Muslims to God and the corresponding views Muslims are to have regarding society, nation and the world in general. Islamic law is seen as an obligation of Muslims, but little specific discussion is made of the subject itself. (Shihab 1996, 253–73)

Among both groups of intellectuals there are some who see the continued relevance of the Syafi'i code in contemporary society. Z. Dhofier (b. 1941) warns that care must be taken by present-day Muslims lest they take statements from scripture out of context. Accordingly, he warns, it would be wise to consider what earlier scholars have had to say, particularly those of the Syafi'i school. Ahmad Saefuddin (d. 1940), while not specifically calling for a reinstitution or redevelopment of the historical Muslim jurisprudence codes, still finds the principles in those codes valuable for revealing Muslim standards of ethics in various areas of living. In particular, he uses those values to examine modern economic structure, operation and theory. This reflects the approach of Saudi scholars who promoted the viewpoint at a conference held in the late 1970's. (*Panjimas* 403, 52–53; Saefuddin 1987, 113–25)

C. ISLAMIC VALUES AND LAW AMONG THE GENERAL POPULATION

If four general attitudes toward Islamic values exist in government and intellectual groups have several different interpretations, it is not surprising that there are differing attitudes toward these matters in the general population. First, some fifteen to twenty per cent of the population is non-Muslim and usually against any efforts that would promote the interests of Islam to any more favored position in the nation and society than already exists. There was strong opposition to the concepts of Islamic law and Islamic state from these non-Muslims in 1945 at the preparatory meetings for declaring Indonesian independence and at the 1956 Constituent Assembly sessions; it has been voiced again in the 1990's in the wake of Islamic revivalism. This feeling is strongest among Christians, but exists among the Hindus and Buddhists as well. Throughout the history of the republic since 1945 there has been suspicion and recrimination among some Christian and Muslim groups about the rights and prerogatives of religious communities, particularly in regard to conversion. At times, as in the 1966 to 1970 period and again in the early 1990's, some Muslim groups were incensed about Christian missionary activities that had success among nominal Muslim groups. Rough verbal reaction from important Muslim spokesmen and civil demonstrations against some Christians led to further defensiveness among Christians about their position in a state in which Muslims were the majority. (Aqsha 1995, 96; Boland 1970, 224–42)

But even among Muslims the feelings about intensification of Islamic values and the adoption of Islamic law depends largely on the social class, ethnic identity, educational background and political identity of different individuals and people.

For example, feeling about Islamic obligation is high among Acehnese, while much more relaxed among the Javanese. Rural populations near Islamic boarding schools (*pesantren*) relate strongly to Islam, while urban dwellers often have less intense identification. Customary regulations (*adat*), so prominent in the early part of the century, remain significant in regional cultures, particularly in life-cycle ceremonies, i.e., marriage, birth, puberty, death and inheritance. The national court system bases parts of its civil jurisdiction on the culture and custom of regions, continuing the century-long concern for conformity with "the living law" of particular ethnic groups. This has an impact on Muslims since standard Islamic practice conflicts with these cultural mores in many ways. A frequently cited example is the matrilineal inheritance patterns existing in Minangkabau, among some Bataks and among some Acehnese groups and the bilateral forms among some Javanese. All of these conflict with Syafi'i *fiqh* which prescribes a modified patrilineal form of inheritance. Historically most Muslims have accepted the cultural norms but recently there has been challenge by some Muslims who find the dictates of Islamic law to have higher priority. Naturally there is resentment to such "literalness" by other members of the group favoring the status quo. (Koentjaraningrat 1990, 316–23; Hooker, M. B. 1978, 1–8, 145–51)

An important case involving a population with nominal ties to Islam occurred in the 1980's. At that time the government, i.e., the guardian group, assigned administrative oversight of the Javanese mystical orders to the Department of Interior with instructions that their practices were to be nurtured as a feature of Javanese culture worthy of preservation for the entire nation. These groups had long accepted the general designation of being Muslim, but without much attention to Sunni rites and practices; instead their real attention focused on unspecific mystical practice, in part drawn eclectically from pre-Islamic forms and part taken from religious and moralistic systems finding their way into Central Java over time. The change in administrative responsibility was seen by observers as removing the mystical orders from purist Muslim control in the Department of Religion, where they were regarded as aberrant Muslim groups in need of retraining to conform with orthodox Sunni Muslim teachings. Such "corrective" action would have, of course, destroyed the sects themselves, which the purist Muslims regarded as manifestation of polytheism unacceptable to Islam. Government action aimed at buttressing the tradition of an important region and assisted people who were opposed to such Muslim operations, as well intentioned as they may have been. Actually, many Javanist groups have accepted Sunni teachings willingly in recent years, but others have resisted for perpetuation of their own particular beliefs and practices. (Hefner 1987, 533–54)

The difference in *weltanschauung* between pious and nominal Muslims in East and Central Java has produced a historical rivalry which has resulted in bloodshed on several important occasions. The rivalry was an important factor behind harsh treatment by communist forces against Muslim political activists in a bloody incident at Madiun in 1948; the communists drew heavily for members from among the nominal Muslim Javanese. The situation was reversed in 1965 and 1966 when

Muslim activists hunted down and killed supposed communist members and sympathizers in the aftermath of an abortive communist coup attempt in Jakarta; in this case the nominal Muslim Javanese were the primary target. Thirty years later these incidents still have repercussions that spell out relationships among Indonesians with different views of Islam. The guardians insist that the situation must always be closely monitored and that only within the Pancasilaist state can all groups exist without discord. (Ricklefs 1981, 217, 274)

Politically as well, many Indonesians find it comfortable to follow the lead of the guardian group and associate with the political organizations intended to mobilize the population for supporting the Pancasilaist state. Mostly this involves joining or supporting Golkar, the political party organized to support the New Order. All government employees, including those in the Department of Religion, are obliged to belong to Golkar and are expected to support its candidates in elections. In general Golkar does not speak in religious terms; in fact, on many matters it comes across as non-Islamic — if not actually anti-Islamic — in support of government policy, particularly on matters of development. Hard-core Golkar membership approaches fifty per cent of the population by some estimates, indicating a strong non-Islamic bias that is suspicious of Muslim attempts to attach Islamic institutions to government policy or to make them more operative in society. However, it does appeal to Muslims by promoting a mosque building program, sponsoring Qur'an reciters in the annual competition, and organizing collection drives for *zakat* during the fasting month of Ramadan. Among Golkar activities, these programs for Muslims are minor in its overall operation and political decisions are not made on the basis of any sort of a Muslim agenda. Islamic law is not even discussed. (Suryadinata 1989, 49–58)

There is also a significant number of Indonesian Muslims who have generally regarded their religious teachings as an important part of their earthly obligations along with being Indonesian citizens. These are the counterparts of the state Islamicists. They are often identified by their affiliation or sympathy with one or another mass Islamic organization — the Muhammadiyah and the Nahdlatul Ulama are the largest and most famous. Among this sector Islamic teachings are studied carefully and proper Muslim conduct is regarded as important. Organizations on the model of the Muhammadiyah with its "middle class," accommodationist approach to society, have centered on creation of an "Islamic society," with its emphasis on education, social welfare and community institutions. Religiously such organizations aim toward correct forms of worship, toward fulfillment of Islamic obligations and good attitudes toward Islamic teachings. While Islamic law is an important part of Islamic teachings, it has been approached by these organizations as resting on an updated interpretation of the Qur'an and firm Traditions of the Prophet, and the effort to produce new findings fitting with contemporary conditions has been important as well. Hence, in this approach Islamic law lacks unification and its principles are applied piecemeal in rulings concerning the particular problems that are confronted. For example the history of such review has led to a consideration of a long line of issues, beginning with the ruling to have the Friday sermon in Indonesian, to a ruling to allow medicine to be taken by a sick Muslim during Ramadan, and to the recent effort to form Islamic-style banks not employing interest as a financial tool. Those groups following the model of the Nahdlatul Ulama are involved with Islamic principles based on a time-honored tradition, but most of it is involved with the learning of Arabic and the intensification of teaching in the old revered texts, i.e., the "yellow books" mentioned earlier. Principles of Islamic law are an important part of the teachings and it is expected that Muslims will attempt to make their own behavior conform to that set by the Syafi'i school, primarily through interaction with a guiding *alim*. For assistance in this effort there are translations of numerous Arabic legal texts in Indonesian such as the *Al-Umm* of Syafi'i (d. 820) and the *Riyadlush Shalihin* of Al-Nawawi (d. 1278). The two important Islamic law texts of the late colonial era, the *Tuhfat* of Ibn Hajar al-Haitami (d. 1567) and the *Nihayah* of al-Ramli (d. 1596), are not in widespread use in translation, although both texts are available in Arabic versions and are used among Indonesian *ulama* in that form. The Nahdlatul Ulama regards its own organizational rulings to be under guidance of the principles laid down by previous Syafi'i *ulama*, such as its decision in 1986 to accept Pancasila as its primary organizational principle, based on the legitimacy of the present Indonesian government as determined by the Indonesian *ulama* at its early meetings in independent Indonesia. (Jainuri 1995, 44–49; Rosyidi 1989, 148–62; Nahdlatul Ulama 1985, 110–14; Wahid 1986, 179–83)

The Revivalist (*dakwah*) movement has convinced many Indonesian Muslims to take their Islamic obligations more seriously than was the case in the past, especially in matters of worship. Consequently, attendance at mosques, attention to fasting, performance of the pilgrimage and other indications of religious association have increased dramatically over the past fifteen years. Included in such revitalized Islamic activity has been greater attention to Qur'an recitation and Tradition study. Such intensification of Islamic practice has produced concern among worshippers about proper fulfillment of other Muslim obligations. Significantly, Indonesian Muslims, in the main, have not followed the lead of some Malaysian Muslims and several other Islamic populations in some parts of the Middle East and North Africa in adopting militant political attitudes and actions to further their Islamic agenda. Many factors are at work in this attitude, but mostly it relates to government concerns and policies, outlined earlier, and consequent societal caution. One of the most pronounced influences of Revivalism on Indonesian society has manifested itself in the popularity of Tradition study, the literature concerning the actions and speech of the Prophet Muhammad. There are a wide number of primers, each presenting inspirational anecdotes concerning the Prophet, designed to strengthen the reader in his belief and in his performance of religious obligation. These writers regard the promotion of faith and character, aside from the formality of a religious law, as a beneficial expression of Islamic identification. While certainly different in scope and emphasis than classical jurisprudence, this new stress on behavior covers the same subject areas and may be a means for addressing the same issues as Islamic law, without formally calling it that. (Federspiel 1993, 3–5)

Aside from the new-found popularity of certain Muslim practices, there is another sector of the population that seeks to observe the tenets of Islamic law in their individual lives and in their family settings. This is a fairly small sector of the population. The continued popularity of two texts — *Sual-Jawab* and *40 Masalah Agama* — both written in earlier eras, and similar writings drawn from readers' columns in Muslim newspapers and magazines for questions concerning Muslim belief and behavior, indicate that this trend is substantial and is not yet diminishing. *Sual-Jawab*, written in the 1930's and 1950's by the fundamentalist Indonesian writer Ahmad Hassan (d. 1958) lays out, point by point, a pious life in all behavior, with nearly all important decisions in life subject to measurement against standards from the Qur'an and firm Traditions of the Prophet. The American anthropologist John Bowen notes the use of that text among pious Muslims in the Gayo Highlands. My own field notes tell of a rector of a national Indonesian university who regarded himself a disciple of Ahmad Hassan, and daily judged himself against the standards set in *Sual-Jawab*, even to those decisions made on behalf of the university. *40 Masalah Agama*, written by Sirajuddin Abbas (d. 1980) in the 1960's and 1970's, is only slightly less pervasive in its application of Islam principles to the lives of believers but draws these principles from the Syafi'i school of *fiqh*. This text produces a less puritanical outlook than that of Hassan, but is no less thoroughly Islamic in its outlook. Observations show this text in wide use in Indonesia and in neighboring countries where Malay is used, particularly northeastern Malaysia and southern Thailand. The collection consists of a lengthy discussion of topics ordinarily addressed by pious Muslims, which the author asserts are in the tradition of the Syafi'i school of jurisprudence. He covers most areas of worship and general behavior, emphasizing piety and close attention to nuances of worship and other religious practice. But there is also attention given to current developments. He urges that modernization not be merely an imitation of Western culture, but an adaptation of technology to improve Indonesian skills, while Islamic teachings reinvigorate society itself. Letters written to *Al-Muslimun*, an Islamic magazine published in Bangil, East Java, provides an illustration of the concern by some ordinary Muslims for following guidelines they believe are reflective of the *syariah*. The editors of *Al-Muslimun* are known for their thorough and uncompromising approach to Islamic teachings they define in fairly narrow terms. It must be realized that other approaches exist as well that are less exacting on specifics and these can be found in other magazines and newspapers. (Bowen 1993, 53, 61–62; Hassan, 1985; Abbas 1972; *Al-Muslimun* 1995–96)

D. COMPARISON WITH OTHER COUNTRIES

In the Islamic world Indonesia can be compared easily with any number of Muslim countries, but three seem to have special relevance: Turkey, Iran and Pakistan, each for a different reason. Like Turkey, Indonesia has been under the leadership of an elite that pushed Islam into the background as it developed a modern political nation. Like Iran, Indonesia has undertaken an ambitious economic development plan which has been disruptive of traditional values and social order. Like Pakistan, Indonesia is composed of diverse ethnic and regional groupings, with a tradition based on pre-Islamic Indic civilization. A brief examination of these factors will place Indonesia's situation into better international perspective.

The case of Turkey is well known for the attempt of Ataturk and his successor Inönü from the 1920's to the 1950's in establishing a republic, based on Westernization, secularism and Turkish nationalism. These policies led to a deliberate severing of state and religion with a greatly diminished role for religion in important matters of the country. The viewpoint behind this policy was that Islam as practiced in the Ottoman empire was pre-modern in attitude and was best jettisoned from public life as useless cultural baggage. New law was brought in from Europe that replaced Ottoman law in most legal sectors and, while not completely successful in removing all vestiges of its earlier dominance, little that concerned Islam survived in the legal system. Of course, care must be taken to not overemphasize the Ataturk changes, since the process of copying Europe was an important feature of the later Ottoman governments as well. But under Ataturk even matters related to worship were "reformed," such as the call to prayer in Turkish and other restrictions on the use of the Arabic language. Government policy discouraged religious piety and close identification with Islam. As the result of a vigorous campaign against Islam and a corresponding campaign to promote civic values based on nationalism, identification with Islam was seriously undermined. The religion survived mostly in popular Islamic practices and associations, largely connected with the mystical brotherhoods (*tarekat*), which had little concern for Islamic law. Consequently, as Islam has reasserted its identity among Turks since the 1960's, the concept of Islamic law has not been very prominent, except among some fundamentalists. Turkish Muslim intellectuals, for example, have been far more concerned with reestablishing the importance of the Qur'an to Turkic Muslims, than they have been with the more complex matter of the *syariah*. In Indonesia, by contrast, the series of nationalist elites that have dominated government have never attempted to destroy or diminish the faith of Islam, although they have attempted to curtail and control its political manifestations. This follows the general tenet of Snouck Hurgronje in late nineteenth-century Netherlands Indies that differentiated between Islamic matters of worship and those actions belonging to politics; it permitted the former and disallowed the latter. Consequently, the institutions of Islam — the mosque, the religious scholar, the boarding school — have never come under state attack and, in fact, most have been encouraged and, frequently, coopted. Also, unlike Turkey, Indonesian Muslims retained a measure of Islamic law in government sanctioned courts and mass organizations of the Muslim community have likewise provided a forum for the discussion and promotion of Islamic law. Further, Muslim intellectuals in Indonesia have been concerned with a very complex mix of Muslim obligations that clearly moves beyond that of their Turkish counterparts, and that discussion includes Islamic law. In general, while "secularizing" governments existed in both countries, the attack on Islam in Turkey destroyed many of the institutions of Islam, while in the case of Indonesia Muslim institutions outside of those active politically were not much harmed and often assisted by government. Islamic law, in one basic form, was included in those permitted activities. (S. Ayata 1996, 42–48; U. C. Sakallioglu, 1996, 242; M. Meeker, 1991, 189–216; Starr, 1992, 220–25)

The Iranian comparison is compelling to some observers since Iran underwent a long tutelage period with Western countries from the 1950's to the 1970's when economic development and schemes of modern nation-building were considered paramount. Those efforts resemble Indonesia's efforts more recently. In the case of Iran political power was centralized in the monarchy and its institutions and all other possible sources of political strength were systematically weakened or destroyed. The religious scholars, also under state attack, were able to survive, with some members willing to form a political opposition to the government, and became one of the few alternatives to the ruling elite itself. At the same time Shiah beliefs, practices and behavior were not challenged in the main, although certainly the influence of Shiah legal principles was often jettisoned in the Shah's efforts to build a "modern" legal system based on Western concepts. Personal identification with Islam was not really attacked, although many Westernized Iranians turned aside from observation of the principles and admonitions of Shiah *fiqh* as not relevant to a modern lifestyle. While by-passing the possibility of Indonesia experiencing an Iranian-type revolution, it can be said that there are some significant differences between pre-Revolutionary Iran and Indonesia at the present time. The religious scholars of Indonesia have never been the standard bearer of the political opposition, and seldom have been seriously alienated from the government. The Indonesian *ulama*, in fact, have always attempted to bring themselves into conformity with government expectations, whether that was in the political realm when they accepted Pancasila as the primary source of its organization at the government's insistence, or in the field of education when the government insisted that the boarding schools should be revised to upgrade rural learners in non-religious subjects. But, like Iran, the religious scholars have kept alive the theme of the *syariah* as an important goal of the Muslim community. Unlike their Iranian counterparts, Indonesian religious scholars have been in no great hurry to assure that Islamic law replace national law; in fact, there is little evidence that they want immediate action on that front; their goal on this matter favors gradualism. (Abrahamian 1993, 39–59; Hooglund 1986, 74–83; Zubaida 1989, 55–62)

The Pakistan case has more similarities with Indonesia than is immediately apparent, although again there are significant differences. Specifically in the matter of Islamic law, both inherited religious courts from their respective colonial pasts that became part of their government structure and both used law that was developed during the colonial past itself, even if different in the two cases. In Pakistan it was a case-precedent system, termed Anglo-Muslim law, while in Indonesia it was an attempt to use Muslim codification of *fiqh* in specific cultural settings. Early in their respective histories as independent nation-states, both societies, each heavily Muslim, were concerned about the use of Islamic institutions to shape and direct their political destinies. In both countries Islamic law was discussed as the core element in the establishment of such Islamic states. Pakistan went on to consider several possibilities and ultimately applied one particular form of the *syariah* as a feature of its governing style. Indonesia, on the other hand, eschewed the Islamic state for a different political model that uses Indonesian nationalism as the driving force, where Islamic values are considered supportive, but in no way paramount. As we have seen in the discussion above, the Indonesian state has continued the application of Islamic law only in the limited area of marriage matters, *waqf* and inheritance, even while some of its Muslim population urges greater stress on Islamic law and some people apply its principles to their own personal lives. (R. Mehdi, 1994, 205–19; Nasr 1993, 261–83; Voll 1982, 233–40, 324–28)

Each of the three comparisons shows similarities with the Indonesian case, but considerable differences as well. What emerges from this discussion is the uniqueness of nation-states within the Islamic world, as indeed, is the case elsewhere in the world as a whole. Concern for Islamic values also differ in time and place and certainly the definition of "*syariah*" is appreciably different in the four countries reviewed here, although probably all Muslims would hold with a statement that the *syariah* ought to be operative in a good Muslim society. Beyond that, different perceptions of just what the *syariah* is, how it is to be instituted and the degree to which it should be applied would differ substantially, even though some politically motivated Muslim groups would minimize such differences.

E. SUMMARY STATEMENT

In concluding discussion about the New Order Era, it can be stated that Indonesia is in the midst of modernizing itself economically and that much of the supporting political and societal structure is being changed with it. As elsewhere in most of East Asia, formal religion has not suffered from economic modernization, but it has had to undergo considerable alteration to allow its members to meet national policy goals.

Indonesian national life is regulated by secular law and the remnants of customary regulations, with religious law having only a small jurisdiction in family and inheritance matters. While there has been greater emphasis in recent times on fulfilling Muslim obligations, this has only partially translated itself into concern for application of Islamic law. The most striking feature that emerges from this study is the change in perception among Indonesian Muslim intellectuals and activists about the manner in which Islamic values and Islamic law are to manifest themselves in society and nation. From relatively simple notions of Islamic law early in the century, these intellectuals and activists have come to regard the values and mores of Indonesian culture as important and as necessary to consider in any establishment of Islamic law in the country. There is considerable feeling that

Islamic law has to be indigenized to be applicable and defensible. In addition the nationalist movement, with its concern for Western, East Asian and other non-Islamic methodologies and approaches to modern living has described a context for the operation of any value system, including Islam, that wishes to operate in Indonesia. Hence, to be successful Islamic law must be expressed and understood in contemporary terms, i.e., as modern. This still has not been done. Beyond this the general population is certainly not committed to political Islamization so that the experiment can take place, even though Islamic identification and religious practice is popular among large sections throughout the nation.

The major question to be asked is whether the recent trend toward religiosity and greater concern with Islamic forms will lead ultimately to an "Islamic revolution," with the full imposition of Islamic laws, as in Iran. That is not impossible. Still it is likely that other societal forces in Indonesia that have checked Islam in the past — some of them described above — will continue to exert influence and prevent any transformation into an Islamic state. But, even without such wholesale Islamization, Islamic law is apt to remain an important issue for Indonesian society.

The Indonesian Muslim community is faced with a great choice: to follow the government's lead and continue on the path to modernization and Westernization or to reflect the growing Muslim restlessness elsewhere and move toward greater concern with Islamic religiosity. The pattern over the past twenty years has been toward both goals and, while the room for maneuvering between the two aspirations has narrowed considerably, both can still be accommodated at the present time. This means that any thinking about religious law will have to be cognizant of this context to have any chance of being considered seriously. Indonesian Muslims have been doing this with Islamic law for fully 600 years. Undoubtedly the pattern will continue.

12

EPILOGUE
Shari'a in Indonesia's Current Transition: An Update

Arskal Salim

The collapse of the New Order regime in May 1998 has ushered in some new hopes for the application of *shari'a* (Islamic law) in Indonesia. Numerous Muslim groups and Indonesian figures consider this a golden opportunity to struggle for a fuller incorporation of *shari'a* into Indonesian legal systems. These aspirations are actually gaining in significance because, with the political liberalization in the wake of Soeharto's fall, each individual or group is free to express their goals and interests. In addition, the political shift from an authoritarian to a more democratic order, including some amendments to the 1945 Constitution (Undang-undang Dasar, or UUD 1945), has given the Indonesian people a fresh beginning for rebuilding the nation and consolidating upon existing legal systems. Triggered by demands for legal reform, the place of Islamic law and its institutional presence in Indonesia constitute an important issue. Now that Indonesia is undergoing a transition, there have been numerous interesting developments in the application of Islamic law in Indonesia.

Since most of the preceding chapters in this book were written during the New Order period, there is no analysis of the latest developments regarding *shari'a* in Indonesia, particularly during the terms of both President Habibie (May 1998–October 1999) and President Abdurrahman Wahid (October 1999–July 2001). Thus, this closing chapter will attempt to bring the book up to date. A number of remarks will also be made concerning some points made in previous chapters. It will be argued that political change in the post-New Order period has offered an opportunity for incorporating more *shari'a* elements into Indonesian legislation and has opened the gate for increasing demands for the local application of *shari'a* in certain regions in the country.

This chapter begins with a discussion of Indonesia's political transition, during which the political and social make-up of religious institutions has been realigned structurally. As the Supreme Court (Mahkamah Agung, or MA), the House of Representatives (DPR), and the Indonesian Bank (BI) have become more independent bodies, certain Islamic institutions such as the Islamic court and the Islamic Bank have also gained a more advantageous position and an increased capacity. The administrative and legal improvements in the handling of both the *zakat* and the *hajj* are another outcome of this political transition. Discussion will then turn to the rising aspirations for *shari'a* implementation in certain regions as the Indonesian nation undergoes processes of decentralization. Finally, attention will be given to the formal enactment of *shari'a* law in Aceh, as regulated by the special autonomy laws passed in the past few years.

As noted in the preceding chapters by Hooker and Lubis, the 1945 Constitution contains conditions that make authoritarianism possible. In fact, the 1945 Constitution has been widely criticized for being very "executive-heavy", with too much power being concentrated in the hands of the President. If one considers the content of the 1945 Constitution prior to any amendments, it can be found that fourteen of the thirty-seven articles therein deal with the executive power of the government, including one on the Supreme Advisory Council (DPA) and one on state ministries. Only eleven deal with the sovereignty of the people, through such institutions as the DPR and the People's Consultative Assembly (MPR). Indeed, only one article deals with judicial power in the original Constitution. So, even though the status of executive, legislative, and judiciary are outlined in the 1945 Constitution, this bears no resemblance to the theory of *Trias Politica* developed by Montesquieu, a theory which advocates a separation of powers between these three branches of government. In fact, during the New Order era the President assumed a leading role in the legislation process and often intervened upon judicial decisions. And though the 1945 Constitution states that the President's power is not unrestricted, in reality Soeharto could do whatever he wanted.

During Habibie's period of office many serious attempts were made to remove the dependency of government and military institutions upon the presidency, a dependency that had developed under the authoritarian structures put in place by Habibie's predecessors. It is worthwhile emphasizing that Habibie did adopt measures to remove a great number of political powers that had accrued to the executive branch of the government. There had long been widespread demands that the President be denied absolute power. Many Indonesians believe that the legislative and the judicial institutions should be freed from executive interference, particularly when upholding the law. It was in this era that the DPR proposed new laws on this issue. With such amendments to the Constitution, the President could no longer appoint or dismiss a high-ranking police or military officer without prior consultation and approval from the House of Representatives. In short, the

Habibie era was marked by a shift from "executive-heavy" rule to "legislative-heavy" rule. This trend developed further during Abdurrahman Wahid's term.

How has this new balance of power affected the implementation of Islamic law at the national level? To some extent, the increased independence of the parliament, the Supreme Court, and the central bank, to name just a few, has also fostered the development of some Islamic institutions. The Islamic court, the Islamic Bank, the *Zakat* Committee, and the *hajj* service have become important concerns, and these concerns have led to significant developments in the legal system.

THE ISLAMIC COURT

As a follow-up to the MPR Decree (TAP No. X/MPR/1998), which went part of the way in establishing the MA as an independent body, Habibie proposed a bill of law for the reorganization of all courts under the auspices of the MA. This bill, which introduced the so-called "single roof system", was passed by parliament on 30 July 1999 (Law No. 35/1999), effectively an amendment to Law No. 14/1970 on the Fundamental Rules of Judicial Power. The amendment allowed for MA supervision of special courts such as the Islamic court and the military court, institutions previously responsible to the Ministry of Religious Affairs (MORA) and the Ministry of Defence and Security respectively.

Unfortunately, it seems the attempt to release the Islamic court from executive interference (via MORA or otherwise) has failed. The proposal to position the Islamic court under the control of the MA has raised criticisms. During parliamentary discussions, the bill was protested by the Indonesian Ulama Council (MUI). The MUI sent an official letter to President Habibie requesting that the Islamic court be exempted from the "single roof system" under the MA. Malik Fadjar, Minister for Religious Affairs in Habibie's government, was reluctant to accept such a proposal. This was a clear signal that fundamental disagreement persisted among ministry officers on this issue.[1] Malik Fadjar's reluctance is understandable. Although the idea of a "single roof system" was popular among judicial officers, Islamic judges, and court clerks, the proposal was met with stiff opposition from Muslim figures considered "outsiders" of the Islamic court — this includes some bureaucrats from MORA and several key figures from the MUI.[2]

The exclusion of the Religious Court from MA supervision seems to have gained more support nowadays. Stemming from a number of protests by Muslim citizens, especially from members of the MUI, Law No. 35/1999 was adjusted so that those courts under the "single roof" would be given five years to progressively adjust their administrative and financial organization in accordance with MA procedures (Article 11A, point 1). The adjustment period for the Religious Court was deliberately left unspecified (Article 11A, point 2). Thus, so long as this readjustment is delayed, the Religious Court remains under the management of MORA.

Interestingly, the main reason for refusing the "single roof system" appeared to be nostalgia. According to the research conducted by the Religious Court

Directorate of the Ministry of Religious Affairs in 2000, in co-operation with the Faculty of Syariah at the State Institute for Islamic Studies (IAIN) Syarif Hidayatullah Jakarta, most of the respondents who disagreed with the proposal were wary of losing the historical values of the Religious Court. Given the long-standing relationship between the Religious Court and MORA, anxiety centred upon how a disruption of this relationship would affect the special status of the Religious Court.[3] This demonstrates that the Religious Court, like MORA, has become an important icon for Indonesian Muslims to identify themselves within the non-Islamic state of Indonesia.

How will the political reform agenda for the separation of powers function when one court remains under the control of the executive for an indefinite period of time? Many are pessimistic, but not Muladi, Minister for Justice during the Habibie government. He was of the opinion that the MPR Decree (TAP No. X/MPR/1998) plainly required the separation of power between the judiciary and the executive, and that the law really does not acknowledge exemptions for particular courts. He insisted that sometime in the future all courts would come under the administrative and financial control of the MA.[4] In my opinion, Muladi might have been too optimistic. As long as there are still strong sentiments for the exclusive position of the Religious Court in the eyes of Indonesian Muslims, it is difficult to predict when the Religious Court might come under the auspices of the MA. This is partly because the very idea is considered by some a threat to the existence of Islamic law in the country. Thus, the agenda for separating the different branches of government, particularly in terms of judicial independence, will be no simple matter.

THE ISLAMIC BANK

As Hefner points out in Chapter 8 of this book, the fate of the non-interest Indonesian Bank (Bank Muamalat Indonesia, or BMI) is still an issue for Indonesian Muslims — whether such banks can survive the triumph of capitalism. Hefner's chapter, completed in 1994, should be followed up with some discussion of Bank Muamalat in the aftermath of the economic crisis that has affected Indonesia in the past five years. This section offers a brief look at recent developments within the Islamic Bank in Indonesia and its response to the economic downturn since 1997.

The survival of the Islamic bank during the crisis, which began in 1997, stemmed from its rejection of interest rates. In the mid of bank collapses, the Islamic Bank (Bank Muamalat Indonesia) was performing strongly, mostly because they applied the *shari'a* system (a profit and loss sharing principle) rather than interest. For some, this system has fewer burdens than the interest model, which is the standard for non-*shari'a* banking systems. The Islamic Bank prohibits interest on loans and deposits, and this saved it from collapse with the onset of a crisis of confidence in the banking sector. As the confidence of bank depositors and creditors dropped sharply, the real sector started to feel the impact since banks clamped down on lending, thereby contributing to a dramatic rise in lending rates. As had been depicted by Baharuddin Darus, a Professor of Economics from the University of North Sumatera, Medan, the Indonesian Bank (BI) fixed the interest rate at 45 per cent from 22 per cent before lifting it up to 50 per cent per annum on 21 April 1998. This rate was eventually raised to 58 per cent, effective from 7 May 1998. Indeed, the banking sector experienced further predicaments, especially given the fact that at least seventy banks collapsed, sixteen closed due to insolvency, seven frozen, and another seven taken over.[5]

It is interesting to note that Bank Muamalat's survival was also due to the support of Bank Islam Malaysia Berhad (BIMB) which took over 49 per cent of Bank Muamalat's total shares.[6] On 16 June 1998, the overall value of these shares was US$15 million or Rp150 billion. This transaction was made because Bank Muamalat itself had to deal with a problem of liquidity. An extraordinary general meeting of the Bank Muamalat's stockholders had been arranged to discuss the possibility of these shares being listed on the Jakarta Stock Exchange (BEJ) in order to gain greater financial support, but BIMB intervened. Was this a deliberate move for Bank Muamalat's survival? Would have Bank Muamalat survived if BIMB did not buy almost 50 per cent of the shares? This move was important since the public reputation of Islamic banking would have declined significantly, thereby threatening the failure of a genuine attempt to facilitate an economic alternative to capitalism.

The position of the Islamic Bank in Indonesia has been further strengthened by the new status of the Bank of Indonesia (BI) under the reformed political system. The BI is now more independent from executive interference. Two new laws (UU No. 10/1998 and UU No. 23/1999) have given the BI the authority to arrange *shari'a* banking without prior consultation with the executive. So, not only has the Islamic Bank been formally legalized for the second time, the laws also give technical directions to non-Islamic banks, including state-run banks, on how to open a special branch in accordance with *shari'a* principles or even complete conversion into an Islamic bank. It is worth noting that state-run banks, such as Bank Mandiri, Bank BNI, and a private bank, Bank IFI, have already established special branches, in accordance with such *shari'a* principles. Antonio noted that in February 2000 a great number of banks had already set up or considered setting up *shari'a* branches, namely, Bank IFI, Bank Niaga, Bank BNI, Bank BTN, Bank Mega, Bank BRI, Bank Bukopin, BPD West Java, and BPD Aceh.[7]

ZAKAT MANAGEMENT

The discussion of *zakat* in my earlier chapter in this book mostly focuses on New Order policy and does not cover the period of the post-New Order. I wrote that there had been no significant progress in *zakat* management throughout Soeharto's rule of more than three decades. On the contrary, *zakat* was often used for the political interests of his regime. Although Soeharto's government gave lip service to support *zakat* collection in Indonesia, in reality this regime was ambiguous at best. Soeharto's readiness to assume the responsibilities of *amil* (collecting and distributing *zakat*) in his early years of office and his approval for *zakat* management via joint ministerial decisions rather than statute (UU) or governmental regulations (PP) in the early 1990s formed part of this ambiguous stance. It is no wonder, therefore, that many Muslims regarded Law No. 38/1999 on Zakat Management (passed by Habibie) as an important political achievement.

The *zakat* law appears to have been hastily drafted to meet triangular interests: to conform with the *shari'a*, to satisfy Muslim constituents, and to advance the government's political interests. The first and second interests were evident from the wording of the law, but the last interest was more subtly veiled. Few would deny that by enacting laws such as this, the Habibie government sought to attain broader political support from Muslims, especially in the lead-up to the presidential election.

Several important aspects concerning the legal process and enactment of the Law on Zakat Management need to be highlighted here. First, MORA was solely responsible for drafting the bill and conveying it to the parliament for approval. MORA was wary of any criticisms directed by Muslims or others towards the bill. For example, MORA tried to restrict the participation of certain prominent figures such as Masdar F. Masudi[8] and Eri Sudewo[9] from contributing their views on *zakat* administration in Indonesia. In a seminar on the dissemination of the bill in Treva Hotel, Jakarta, on 19 August 1999, Masdar said that Malik Fadjar, Minister for Religious Affairs for the Habibie government, had asked him personally to refrain from criticizing the bill.[10] This effectively muzzled his public criticisms of the bill. Likewise, Eri Sudewo was confused by MORA's invitation for him to discuss the bill on 14 May 1999, without attaching a copy of the proposed law. When he finally obtained the draft a day before the meeting, after persistently requesting a copy from MORA, there was not much he could offer the public in terms of informed criticism.[11] Furthermore, Eri was astonished to receive a telephone invitation to address a parliamentery discussion of the bill just a day before the meeting with legislative members on 25 August 1999. This was a very strange procedure for such an important meeting. Eri is therefore convinced that MORA sought to dominate the enactment of this law without much consultation, especially from those private institutions with a sound record in *zakat* administration, such as the Institute of *Zakat* Management (IMZ).[12] This clearly shows that non-governmental elements were deliberately bypassed for the implementation of this law on *zakat* administration in Indonesia.

Among others, MORA may have wanted the bill to empower the role of BAZ (Badan Amil Zakat or Government Amil Zakat Board) over and above LAZ (Lembaga Amil Zakat or other informal/private institutions for *amil zakat*). In fact, out of the thirty-three articles mentioned in Decree No. 581/1999 by the Minister for Religious Affairs, which was issued as detailed regulation, only four dealt with LAZ. Furthermore, MORA had long anticipated such a law on *zakat*. This would constitute the sixth bill on *zakat* passed in Indonesia.[13] The first such bill was presented to parliament (DPR-GR) in 1967, and the latest had been passed in 1999.

Secondly, the enactment of *zakat* law took place amid fierce political manoeuvring by certain political groups and parties, and as a result many people failed to notice its enactment. The hot issues of the day were the referendum for East Timor and the Bank Bali scandal. The widespread protest that surrounded the bill concerning the Religious Court in 1989, were practically non-existant during parliamentary discussions of the *zakat*. Even the Indonesian Democratic Party faction (F-PDI), known for its fiercely secularist platform, was strangely quiet on the bill. In fact, F-PDI spokesperson Sajid Soetjoro said, "Muslim citizens have long awaited for the *zakat* to function as a religious institution that efficiently and effectively enhances the prosperity and welfare of the people."[14] Without any significant resistance it is no wonder that the parliament took less than one month to pass the bill.

Finally, the law has repositioned the previous regulation on *zakat* to a higher level (from a joint ministerial decision into statute), introduced some new rules, such as the "deductible tax"[15] (Article 14, point 3), and added some innovative *zakat* payments such as earnings and fisheries (Article 11, point 2). However, there is a further problem which resulted from its hasty construction, that is, the law still lacks a proper implementing framework. There has been a decree issued by the Minister for Religion (KMA No. 581/1999) for the rule's implementation, but such regulation is not adequately appropriate since the law implies the involvement of three departments, Ministry of Interior Affairs, Ministry of Finance, and MORA. So what is needed, according to Eri Sudewo, is a guideline that has greater significance than a ministerial decree, that is, a governmental regulation covering interdepartmental institutions.[16] Although it is stated in law that further instructions will be sufficiently directed by ministerial decree (Articles 7, 10, 15, and 16), there is a number of issues that were beyond the authority of the Minister for Religious Affairs, such as the "deductible tax" and decentralization, that may affect the *zakat* law. Certainly, in order to apply the law successfully there needs to be governmental regulations (PP) dictating interdepartmental policy implementation.

It is interesting to note that with the introduction of the *zakat* law in 2002, a law allowing Muslim individuals and corporations to deduct the amount of *zakat* they have paid from their net taxable income, a number of criticisms have arisen concerning discrimination in the application of the law. A *Jakarta Post* editorial fiercely questioned "why the government has singled out the Muslim community when it is well aware that followers of other creeds also pay religious donations".[17] Abdul Munir Mulkhan, a sociologist of religions at the IAIN Yogyakarta, strongly advocates that the government extend the same policy to followers of other religions since other religions also have sacred duties to collect charitable donations from their community.[18]

However, Komaruddin Hidayat, a Muslim scholar and acting Director of Islamic Higher Education at the MORA, said that the policy was in no way discriminatory since all religions were free to draw up similar schemes. He remarked, "(t)here are

Directorates General for Christians and other religions in the Ministry of Religious Affairs. They can also submit similar ideas. Why not?".[19] It seems obvious that the government could not immediately meet such aspirations. Minister for Religious Affairs in Megawati's government, Said Agil Husein Al Munawar, clearly stated that before it considers applying the tax deductible *zakat* policy on similar kinds of alms-giving from other religions, the government will focus on administering the *zakat*. Reassuring other religious groups, Al Munawar said, "God willing, we will arrange it later . . . We will do this one by one".[20] In this respect, it is clear that Islam has been given more priorities than any other religions in Indonesian socio-political life over the past few years.

It is supposed that the tax deductible policy would boost participation levels and increase the amount of *zakat* payment from Muslim in an effort to eradicate poverty. But for some, this appraisal sounds too optimistic. M. Ikhsan, a reader of the *Jakarta Post*, wrote an open letter in which he suggested that because the self-assessment principle for tax restitution is not applied in Indonesia, where tax officers must audit all bookkeeping procedures, business people would not really respond to this policy. In other words, if tax deduction is introduced as a procedure for *zakat*, it is hard to imagine this policy encouraging the involvement of business people and corporations.[21] Indeed, given the real problems with tax restitution in Indonesia, this policy is not likely to be successful in the short term. Perhaps, attention should first be given to improving the efficiency of the tax restitution system.

THE *HAJJ* SERVICES

Little attention has been given to the politicization of the *hajj* (pilgrimage to Mecca) services in Indonesia's New Order. The only direct discussion known to the writer is Deliar Noer's monograph.[22] One chapter in his monograph highlighted the problem of government monopoly over the *hajj* services. Noer suggested that two regulations (Presidential Decree no. 22/1969 and Presidential Instruction No. 6/1970) issued by President Soeharto effectively prevented any private companies from organizing *hajj* services, in spite of their sound record in this regard.

Noer highlighted the success of one private organization, the Association of the Indonesian Muslim Businessmen (HUSAMI) in the administering of *hajj* services. As chairman of this organization, Syafruddin Prawiranegara, former governor of the Bank of Indonesia (BI) and a minister under Sukarno, made every endeavour to challenge and criticize government monopolization of *hajj* services. Noer noted that "Syafruddin believes any monopoly could easily lead to corruption and inefficiency", and it could "deprive Muslims the choice of agents who might offer better service at lower cost". Syafruddin was therefore in favour of private companies competing with the government, although there must be an institution established to supervise such competition. Because of the monopoly system, he believes, above all, that MORA was acting more like a commercial enterprise rather than an institution serving the public interest.[23] Despite many criticisms from within the Muslim community, the New Order government showed little sign of concern and maintained their monopoly over *hajj* services.

Law No. 17/1999 on Hajj Services, signed by President Habibie on 3 May 1999, effectively ended government monopoly of *hajj* services. Although administration of the *hajj* is considered a national duty and a government responsibility via MORA, qualified private companies can now organize *hajj* services as well (Article 6). The objective of this legislation was to offer the best direction, service, and security for those Muslims making the pilgrimage to Mecca in accordance with Islamic precepts, and so that pilgrims can independently perform the *hajj* rituals to obtain God's reward (Article 5). It is clear from this article that the government is concerned with how Muslim people can successfully undertake their religious duties. The law is not concerned with devotion since that is something beyond governmental authority. Accordingly, there are no punishments mentioned for those who are physically and financially capable to perform the pilgrimage but are reluctant to do so.

The promulgation of the Hajj Services Law by the DPR provided an indication of how the parliament was gaining in political strength. It was the first time after nearly three decades that the DPR had initiated a bill, even if this was its right as the highest legislative body. This also reflected the declining influence of the executive branch over such processes. Throughout the New Order era, parliament was subordinated to the power of the President. Ramlan Surbakti came up with Table 12.1 that indicates how the DPR had no real influence over legislative processes from 1966 to 1995.[24]

What encouraged the DPR to propose this bill concerning the *hajj* services? Was it driven by the DPR's ambition to demonstrate its rebirth as the real legislative power after a long period as a "rubber stamp"? Indeed, one may confidently presume that gaining independence from the executive branch was a prime motive. The opportunities that arose in the reform era following the downfall of the authoritarian Soeharto regime also encouraged the DPR to convince the people

TABLE 12.1
Laws Passed by the Indonesian Parliament, 1966–95

DPR Period	Laws Proposed		Laws Passed	
	By Government	By DPR	Government-initiated	DPR-initiated
1966–71	98	25	81	7
1971–77	43	—	43	—
1977–82	59	—	55	—
1982–87	46	—	46	—
1987–92	55	—	55	—
1992–97 (95)	60	—	60	—
Total	361	25	340	7

Source: Surbakti 1999, p. 69.

that parliament was now more articulate and communicative. In fact, the enactment of the Hajj Services Law by the DPR can be considered one of the great attempts to even up the balance of power between the executive and legislative bodies.

Viewed from a political perspective, however, the DPR remains susceptible to the allegation of facilitating the political interests of the incumbent government. By enacting this law President Habibie could improve his image among Muslims, to show that he was concerned with their needs and their political aspirations. Muslim people were expected to constitute a majority vote in the June 1999 elections. In this regard, it is no wonder that the Hajj Services Law, initiated by the DPR on 18 February 1999, was gladly approved by President Habibie three months later on 3 May 1999.

SHARI'A IN THE ERA OF DECENTRALIZATION

In response to political reform agendas, Habibie's government passed two very important laws to promote regional autonomy. The first was Law No. 22/1999 on Regional Government, and the second, Law No. 25/1999 on balancing finances between the central and regional governments. These legislations established a revolutionary model for extending broad regional autonomy within the existing unitary constitution. Law No. 22/1999 on Regional Government emphasizes that there are two basic levels of governance, that is, the central government headed by the President and autonomous local governments at the *kabupaten* (districts) and *kotamadya* (cities) levels, headed respectively by the *Bupati* (regent) or *Walikota* (mayor). This law clearly implies that this division of power and responsibility is not strictly hierarchical. The law delegates at least eleven areas of authority to the local governments. This includes land matters, agriculture, education and culture, employment (manpower), health, environment, public works, transportation, trade and industry, capital investment, and co-operative enterprise (*koperasi*). These areas of authority are entrusted with the 300 or so districts throughout Indonesia, and not to the provinces.

Foreign affairs, defence, security, justice, monetary and fiscal policy, religious affairs, and other fields are not mandated to the regions under the autonomy policy. The central government retains responsibility for the administration of religious matters. Many believe religious decentralization could provoke national disintegration. In fact, it is widely presumed that some regions would seek to re-establish themselves along religious lines, whether they are Islamic districts, Catholic regencies, or Hindu municipalities for example. Such notions are common among policy-makers and many members of the wider Indonesian community. The MUI provides an example of one major political grouping that resorts to this view.

Implementation of regional autonomy was begun in January 2001, but many problems have since arisen. For instance, there are concerns over the rising aspiration for the full implementation of *shari'a* in particular region, especially Aceh, South Sulawesi, Cianjur, Tasikmalaya, Banten, West Sumatra, and South Kalimantan.[25]

Although religious matters do not come under regional authority, it appears that since local governments are allowed to enact regional regulations or by-laws (*Peraturan Daerah*), such processes are imbued by local cultures and religious values that basically derive from Islamic law. According to Mutammimul Ula, a legislative member from the Justice Party, a number of articles in the Law on the Regional Government actually provide the authority for the Head of Regions to pass by-laws. So not only does the regional government have political, economic, and cultural autonomy, but legal autonomy as well.[26] In short, while religious affairs are not mandated to the local governments, legal autonomy gained through decentralization has provided avenues for the autonomous implementation of *shari'a* throughout Indonesia.

With such legal autonomy, regional leaders and local legislatures can pass by-laws endorsing some matters prescribed by the *shari'a*, or can order people to refrain from doing anything prohibited in accordance with Islamic law. The local legislature of West Sumatra, for instance, has proposed a by-law on the prohibition and the eradication of immoral deeds (*maksiat*). This bill states, "an adult woman is not allowed to be outside her home between the hours of 10 p.m. and 4 a.m. unless accompanied by a close relative (*muhrim*) or if she must engage in something protected by law".[27] The logic underlying this rule is that by prohibiting women from leaving the home at night, all activities that violate God's law will eventually disappear. The bill has raised many criticisms from locals and human rights activists. One feminist activist in the seminar on "Women and the Islamic *Shari'a*: Indonesian perspectives", held in Jakarta in June 2001, asked why this bill was more concerned with prohibiting women, not men.[28] The bill was considered a denial of women's rights, and was criticized for unfairly placing the blame on women for an apparent rise in immoral acts in the city of Padang.

Another example of an Islamic law implemented during the era of decentralization is the by-law produced in Martapura that placed bans on eating and drinking in public places during the fasting month of Ramadhan. As reported in the *Jakarta Post*, the District Court of Martapura, the capital of the Banjar regency in South Kalimantan, has imposed fines on anyone caught eating and drinking in public places during Ramadhan. "Two residents of Danau Salak village were fined Rp15,000 (US$1.50) each for eating, drinking and smoking, and two others from Sungkai were fined the same simply for smoking. [In addition,] the court fined two Sungkai villagers Rp60,000 (US$6) and Rp50,000 (US$5) for opening their food stalls." So far, Banjar is the only regency in South Kalimantan that has such a by-law. The regency only began enforcing the by-law in the second week of Ramadhan and, in the first week, they had warned people about the consequences of eating and drinking in public places.[29]

It is interesting to note that amid the debate over the arrangement to locally implement the *shari'a* in Aceh, the province of South Sulawesi has been triggered to demand a similar scenario. The so-called Komite Persiapan Penegakan Syariat Islam (Preparatory Committee for the Implementation of Islamic Law, or KPPSI) has composed a draft bill for special autonomy and the application of *shari'a*. In

December 2001, they held their second congress in Makassar, during which they finalized the draft to be conveyed to the DPR for implementation.

All these cases suggest that while the formal implementation of *shari'a* at the national level is encountering many structural obstacles, its supporters nevertheless attempt to apply Islamic law at the regional level, especially in Muslim-majority districts. Instead of expecting the ratification of *shari'a* through a top-down process, the strategy has now changed to begin implementation from the local level. Ula suggests there are two formal ways to implement *shari'a* in Indonesia — constitutional amendment and legislation. Ula says the former is much more difficult to achieve. Indeed, every attempt to reinsert the "seven words" of the Jakarta Charter (with the obligation to carry out the *shari'a* for its adherents) into the 1945 Constitution, which would have given *shari'a* constitutional status, has faced strong resistance. Through the legislative process, particularly if it is carried out in the form of a by-law, the application of *shari'a* would be much easier.[30]

It is worth noting the other problem on *hajj* service here in order to accentuate the types of jurisdictional disputes arising between the local governments and the central administration. Some regional governments have demanded the right to organize *hajj* services for their own constituents.[31] These demands stem from a belief that the closer the provider of public services is to the client, the better the services will be made available to the community. Furthermore, the advantages of the decentralized *hajj* service will not only go to local governments but also to the pilgrims. The regional governments of Riau and East Java, for example, suggested that through a decentralized *hajj* service costs would naturally decrease, service improve, along with the creation of additional revenue for the local government.[32] But such dreams might not be realized since the Law on the Hajj Services has fixed the organization of *hajj* as a national prerogative undertaken by MORA.

THE APPLICATION OF *SHARI'A* IN ACEH

The application of *shari'a* in Aceh has been initiated recently with the promise of two laws: Law No. 44/1999 on the Administration of the Specificity of Aceh as a Special Province passed by the Habibie administration and Law No. 18/2001 on the Exclusive Autonomy for the Special Province of Aceh as Nanggroe Aceh Darussalam Province, signed by President Megawati on 9 August 2001. It is hoped that discussion of several important questions will provide an adequate portrayal of the fierce and ongoing debate concerning the application of *shari'a* in Aceh.

What could the central government expect from implementation of *shari'a* in Aceh? Is it true that this has been done to satisfy the demands of the Acehnese themselves, or does it merely distract the Acehnese from other grievances that form a major part of their insistence to separate from Indonesia? To answer these questions we should briefly consider the General Explanation for Law No. 44/1999 concerning the Administration of the Specificity of Aceh as a Special Province, with particular attention to historical relations between Aceh and Indonesia.

Many Acehnese believed their prominent role during the national revolution — they provided financial support to the young Indonesian Government — would be recognized in the new Indonesian state, but they were eventually disappointed. At first, in return for Acehnese support for Indonesian independence, on 17 December 1949, the central government offered Acehnese special treatment by declaring Aceh an autonomous province beyond the domain of the North Sumatra province. But one year later, Aceh was incorporated into the larger province of North Sumatra, thereby souring relations between the centre and many Acehnese who felt their autonomy and identity had been threatened. This led to resistance movements, and by 1953 armed confrontations between the so-called Darul Islam movement and Indonesian military forces (TNI) took place.

A temporary ceasefire was achieved in 1959 when Deputy Prime Minister Hardi, proposed a special region status for Aceh, thereby allowing the Acehnese self-governance in the fields of religion, customs, and education. But this offer was never realized during the Old Order era (1959–66) or even in the New Order era (1966–98). In fact, during the New Order period the concentration of power in the hands of the Soeharto government only exacerbated problems for many Acehnese. For these reasons, and in line with the advice given by his advisers, Habibie enacted the long-overdue law. It appears the central government believed the widespread dissatisfaction in Aceh could be overcome through the provision of greater local authority over religious life, customs, and education and by strengthening the role of *ulama* (Islamic scholars) in the creation of regional policy (Articles 2–9 of Law No. 44/1999). Through this offer, it was expected that Aceh province would remain happily within the fold of the unitary state of Indonesia.

In my opinion the central government's offer to Aceh was inappropriate for a number of reasons. First, the issue of self-governance for religion, customs, and education is no longer the sole concern in Aceh. Rather, concern has markedly shifted to the problems of welfare and security. For decades, particularly under the New Order, the Acehnese have seen a rise in the exploitation of their natural resources, mostly oil and natural gas, and the profits have been channelled to the central government with little redistributed back to Aceh. In addition, the re-emergence of the Acehnese resistance movement in the late 1970s, formally manifested as the Free Aceh Movement (GAM) during the proclamation of the independent state of Aceh in 1976, prompted the central government to send more troops to Aceh. In fact, between 1989 and 1998 Aceh was placed under direct military rule, where special army units engaged in the routine torture and murder of suspected GAM members. In this regard, the Acehnese are actually less concerned with the application of *shari'a* law than economic inequality and human rights abuses.

One can assume that the central government's attempt to impose the *shari'a* in Aceh will only distract international attention upon human rights abuses, since it is assumed that the predominantly secular make-up of the international community would be concerned about the possible rise of Islamic fundamentalism with the implementation of *shari'a*. In addition, a number of initiatives to implement *shari'a* in Aceh have only aggravated the situation. In the lead-up to the official application of *shari'a* in Aceh, a young man accused of adultery was punished in accordance with Islamic law — he was whipped one hundred times in public. Meanwhile, because she was pregnant, the penalty for the woman implicated in this affair was to be deferred until she had given birth.[33] In another case, four prostitutes, one of their patrons, and a thief had their hair completely shaved in view of the public gathered in the yard of the Great Mosque of Banda Aceh. They were then paraded around the city.[34] So, lacking any detailed regulations and by-laws on *shari'a*, the euphoria of its application has led to fears and suspicion about the possibility of increased Islamic fundamentalism in Aceh.

The central government's initiative to implement *shari'a* in Aceh has invited a number of criticisms. Hasballah Sa'ad, an Acehnese and a former Minister for Human Rights, said that the implementation of *shari'a* is not the solution to the problems in Aceh.[35] Likewise, Imam Suja', chairman of the Aceh branch of Muhammadiyah, is pessimistic about whether the *shari'a* could guarantee the eradication of bloody conflicts in Aceh. For Imam, the application of *shari'a* is a contradiction, because while the central government imposes the *shari'a* in Aceh, civilian killings and tortures by the state security apparatus continue. He regards the application of *shari'a* in Aceh as an effort to absorb the political thought of the Acehnese and to conceal the crimes committed by the Indonesian state in the past.[36] According to A. M. Fatwa, a chief deputy of the DPR, the application of *shari'a* is one matter and the finalization of problems in Aceh is something else. For him, the application of *shari'a* in Aceh is no more than an offer for psychological effect.[37] If these responses are taken to reflect the *status quo* it would appear that the central government's offer to apply *shari'a* in Aceh has no real correlation with the troubles and difficulties currently faced by the Acehnese.

By and large, it may be said that the application of *shari'a* in Aceh has become a political commodity for the élites. For one thing, it enables certain political parties to show off their artificial commitment to the Acehnese. Notably, the National Awakening Party (PKB), under the leadership of former President Abdurrahman Wahid, has exploited the issue at the expense of others. During discussions of the bill for Law No. 18/2001 on the Exclusive Autonomy for the Special Province of Aceh as Nanggroe Aceh Darussalam Province, Soetjipto, General Secretary of the Indonesian Democratic Party of Struggle (PDI-P), the party which had gained most seats in the 1999 election, remarked that his party wanted the bill to be in line with the principle of the unitary state of Indonesia and the state philosophy of Pancasila.[38] This statement was immediately interpreted as a PDI-P refusal for the application of Islamic law in Aceh, thereby prompting many negative responses from members of the DPR.

In a separate press conference, Ali As'ad and Yusuf Mohammad, both PKB leaders, expressed their party's standpoint that "the application of *shari'a* in Aceh is the solution for ending the conflicts taking place. Such application does not only correspond with Aceh's history, it does not contradict the spirit of the Indonesian unitary state or the 1945 Constitution". In other words, "the PKB is not in the position to question the application of *shari'a* in Aceh".[39] In a presidential remark for the commemoration of *Waisak* (Buddha's birthday), President Wahid further commented on this issue saying that he was astounded that some still opposed the plan to apply *shari'a* in Aceh, whereas Law No. 44/1999, which had been passed by Habibie, allowed for such application. He stated firmly, "like it or not, the Law is already there and we are obliged to implement it".[40] The PDI-P was forced to clarify its stance, saying that it agreed with the application of *shari'a* in Aceh so long as it would not weaken the principle of national unity.[41] The PKB's political manoeuvre in relation to Soetjipto's statement had placed the PDI-P in a difficult position, particularly in the eyes of the Acehnese. One can be sure that this manoeuvre was taken by the PKB since the PDI-P had given full support to the censures that the parliament had imposed upon President Wahid for the "Buloggate" case in which it was alleged Wahid had engaged in corrupt dealings.

For another thing, the vague conceptions of how the *shari'a* would be implemented eventually disappointed the Acehnese. According to the law signed by President Habibie on 4 October 1999, the application of *shari'a* in Aceh was not specific and may include the original penal punishments. Article 4 of Law No. 44/1999 states, "the performance of religious life in Aceh is conducted in accordance with the *shari'a* for all Muslim citizens". Over time, however, some have reached the standpoint that national law should also be adhered to alongside *shari'a*. In this regard, Marzuki Darusman, Attorney General under President Wahid's government, said that the "implemented *shari'a* would only cover civil law [family law and Islamic banking], whilst the national penal law was still applicable".[42] Meanwhile, President Wahid said "*shari'a* has broad meanings and can be used any time and in any place". Referring to Asmawi, the former Chief of the Supreme Court of Egypt, he pointed out "the most important thing is that the term *shari'a* should comply to the underlying principles rather than its physical content".[43]

For many, President Wahid's comments were vague and therefore required some clarification in order not to confuse many people. In response to President Wahid's plan to declare Islamic law in Aceh during his visit to the region in December 2000, Andi Mallarangeng, an adviser to the government on regional autonomy, said that "it is still very unclear what model this *shari'a* law is based upon — a Saudi Arabian model or even that of the Taliban in Afghanistan . . . We need clearer definitions . . . to avoid misunderstandings".[44] Nurcholish Madjid, a prominent Indonesian Muslim intellectual, reminded President Wahid that to "implement the *shari'a* in Aceh effectively, the President must explain to the people what Islamic *shari'a* is". Furthermore, Madjid doubted whether the *shari'a* in Aceh will be successfully implemented if it is only considered a governmental experiment, because in his view, "it might be heavy for one to pronounce, but it is heavier still to carry it out".[45]

Since it is still unclear what form the *shari'a* would take in Aceh, there is very little optimism among the Acehnese themselves. Whereas the previous law (Article 4 of Law No. 44/1999) has invited the unconditional application of *shari'a* in Aceh, the latest enactment stipulates that *shari'a* law should not contradict or clash with the national legal system (Article 25 of Law No. 18/2001). Thus, any by-law (*qanun*) regarding specifics for the implementation of *shari'a* should comply with the national legal system of Indonesia. Otherwise, the central government has the right to annul them. In addition, the DPR have not passed a number of proposed changes on the court system based on *shari'a*. For instance, appeals must still be conveyed to the Supreme Court of Indonesia (Article 26). This means that there is really no substantial difference between the legal implementation of *shari'a* in Aceh and that in other regions in the country. This provides a very clear indication of how the application of *shari'a* in Aceh was watered down by the central government. The Acehnese, once again, could only be disappointed.

CLOSING REMARKS

In the wake of the New Order government's collapse, public appeals for the implementation of *shari'a* in Indonesia have returned to the fore dramatically. The discourse is by no means a new issue, since there have been several parallel episodes. This might be traced back to the early days of Independence when some Muslim leaders attempted to introduce the Jakarta Charter into the 1945 Constitution. Similar disputes arose during the sessions of the Constituent Assembly (1957–59). It re-emerged in the MPRS between 1966 and 1968. One may wonder why the call for the implementation of *shari'a* appears strongly during periods of political transition. This is partly due to the fact that the interim governments are often weakened by the strong pressures imposed by numerous factions and interest groups. In addition, since the call for *shari'a* is always considered as a non-structural issue and supposed to be containing an explosive political risk, it tends not to become priorities and even avoided or left with an air of uncertainty. Given that the issue has never been properly resolved, some Muslim politicians take the advantage of the transition period to raise the issue of *shari'a* implementation.

The state's response towards the growing demand of the application of *shari'a* in Indonesia's current transition seems to be dissimilar from one government to another. It can be said that although Habibie's term in office was shorter than Wahid's, most initiatives for the formal implementation of Islamic law occurred during the Habibie presidency. The Laws on Hajj Services, Zakat Management, Islamic Banking, and the initial offer for the application of *shari'a* in Aceh, were initiated during President Habibie's period of office. In contrast, very few measures were taken in relation to *shari'a* during President Wahid's term. However, Wahid did issue two presidential decrees on *zakat* management and *hajj* services — Decree No. 22/2001 concerns the management of funds from *hajj* services, while Decree No. 8/2001 outlines the National Zakat Committee set-up to co-ordinate *zakat* administration throughout the country. These decrees, unrelated to concerns for the application of *shari'a*, appear to have been made because further regulations were needed for the practical implementation of *zakat* and *hajj* management.

What is worth noting from the current administration is that President Megawati has taken up the policies initiated by her two predecessors, particularly in relation to *zakat* management. While Habibie and Wahid laid the legal foundations, President Megawati has had the pleasure of officially launching the "Zakat Awareness Movement" and inaugurated the National Zakat Management Agency (BAZNAS) in December 2001. President Megawati provided a symbolic beginning by paying her *zakat* to the Agency.[46] Although Megawati's support might appear merely ceremonial, it has become an official (and therefore political) example of her Islamic piety.

It is obvious that MORA has a significant role to play in the ongoing development and incorporation of *shari'a* into national law or governmental regulations. Very few people would deny that MORA has played an important role in the development of Islam and the Muslim community in Indonesia since Independence. To cite Boland (1982), the existence of MORA proves the positive attitude of the Indonesian state towards Islam, for it has been the most effective agent for the translation of the principle of the Belief in the One Almighty God into the practical lives of Indonesian Muslims. Boland calls it "religious dirigisme", meaning that, to some extent, the government regulates and promotes almost every aspect of religious activity through official bodies. The process of the Hajj Services Law and the Zakat Management Law demonstrates MORA's initiative in the expansion and strengthening of a unified Islam in Indonesia. It seems that the short-term agenda of MORA will be the enactment of the laws on *waqf* (charitable foundation) and Islamic inheritances. The *waqf* rules were originally introduced by Government Regulation No. 28/1977, while Islamic inheritance has been effected by Presidential Decree No. 1/1991. MORA believes these regulations need to be raised to a higher legal standing, such as statute, in order to provide them with a stronger legal basis.

It is important to emphasize here that these latest legislations on Islamic tenets such as *hajj*, *zakat*, and Islamic bank are merely in the sense of procedures and administrative manner. It is not compulsory for Indonesian Muslims to make a pilgrimage to Mecca, pay *zakat* contributions, or participate in an Islamic bank. The laws on *hajj* services, *zakat* management, and Islamic banking have been enacted in order to facilitate the efficient performance of religious duties for Muslim citizens. No punishment will be meted out to those who decline to perform such religious duties. However, this is not the case at local level. It is observable that in this era of decentralization, some sorts of *shari'a* rules with particular Islamic punishments are implemented. Martapura regency, for example, has passed a by-law for the punishment of those caught eating or drinking in public places during the fasting month of Ramadhan. Furthermore, the recent controversy over the stoning (*rajam*, a punishment for those who have committed adultery) by Laskar Jihad in Ambon, provides another example of this trend.

The increasing aspirations for the application of *shari'a* particularly at local level have also ushered in an equally passionate counter movement. It is unfortunate that neither sides appears to seek a consensus on many of the more significant issues at stake. In fact, the trend is that both sides doggedly maintain their views, with physical confrontations often the result. The November 2001 clashes between Laskar Jihad and the Ngawi branch of the PDI-P in East Java provides a warning for those who would seek to apply a "hard" version of *shari'a* at the macro level.[47] In this respect, Indonesia should learn from the Nigerian experience in the application of *shari'a*, a process that has triggered bloody riots and created splits in certain provinces of Nigeria. The aftermath of *shari'a* implementation in some northern provinces of Nigeria should demonstrate to Indonesians that failure to openly engage with the more sensitive aspects of such a process will only lead to political instability.

Finally, as the extensive demand for the application of *shari'a* locally (Islamic by-laws) and nationally (amendment to Article 29 of the 1945 Constitution) is on the rise, full attention is needed to avoid the seeds of disintegration finding their fertile soils by looking at the possible compromises. Both the Jakarta Charter of 22 June 1945 and the Presidential Decree of 5 July 1959, which have been obscure underpinnings in favour of *shari'a* for several decades, must be immediately ended. It must be a great concern of both the opposed argument concerning the application of *shari'a* to reach a lasting consensus of specific interpretation and implementation of *shari'a* in the Constitution, and to ascertain the precise levels of *shari'a* that can be implemented in a plural political space like Indonesia. Once the limits can be ascertained in the Constitution, it goes without saying that every proposal for the implementation of *shari'a* must be submitted within such a constitutional framework. This, at any rate, would seem to be the only realistic option for the future of Indonesian religious pluralism and the only and the best alternative to a complete abandonment of the notion of a legal system based on *shari'a*.

Notes

1. "Menag Soroti Penggabungan PA dengan MA" [Minister for Religious Affairs evaluates the incorporation of the Religious Court into the Supreme Court auspices], *Media Indonesia*, 28 July 1999.
2. M. Amin Suma et al., "Respon Hakim, Panitera, Karyawan Pengadilan Agama dan Masyarakat Muslim terhadap UU no. 35 tahun 1999" [The responses of Judges, Clerk of the Religious Court and Muslim community towards the enactment of the Law no. 35 of 1999], *Research Report* (Jakarta: Proyek Pengembangan Penelitian Ditbinbapera Depag RI, 2000).
3. Ibid.
4. "Kebebasan MA minus Peradilan Agama" [The Independence of the Supreme Court minus the Religious Court], *Pelita*, 3 August 1999.
5. Baharuddin Darus, "Tingkat Bunga Super Ribawi dan Runtuhnya Sendi Perekonomian" [The most excessive interest rate and the collapse of economic pillars], *Republika*, 24 July 1998.
6. Ibid.
7. M. Syafi'i Antonio, *Bank Syariah: Suatu Pengenalan Umum* [Shari'a Bank: A general introduction]. (Jakarta: Tazkia Institute, 2000), pp. 239–40.

8. Masdar F. Mas'udi, Director of Perhimpunan Pengembangan Pesantren dan Masyarakat (P3M), is popular for his controversial book on *zakat* issues. In this work, entitled *Risalah Zakat (Pajak) dalam Islam* (Jakarta: Pustaka Firdaus, 1991), Masdar argues that *zakat* and tax are indistinguishable according to Islamic doctrine.

9. Eri Sudewo, chairman of the *Zakat* Forum (FOZ), is well known for his efforts to collect and distribute *zakat* through the Dompet Dhuafa Institute, an institute that aims to provide economic empowerment for lower income Muslims in Indonesia.

10. Masdar F. Mas'udi, an oration delivered in a seminar on the Dissemination of the Bill of Zakat Laws at Treva Hotel, Jakarta on 19 August 1999.

11. Eri Sudewo, "Ahlan Wa Sahlan, UU Zakat" [Welcome the Zakat Law], *Neraca*, 4 August 1999.

12. Eri Sudewo, "Menyoroti Implementasi UU Zakat dan UU Pajak" [Examining the Implementation of the Zakat Law and the Tax Law], *Republika*, 27 October 2000.

13. Ahmad Sutarmadi, a remark delivered in a seminar on the Dissemination of the Bill of Zakat Laws at Treva Hotel, Jakarta on 19 August 1999.

14. "RUU Pengelolaan Zakat Disetujui Menjadi UU" [The Bill of Zakat approved], *Pikiran Rakyat*, 15 September 1999.

15. A taxpayer who pays his *zakat* may lodge for a deduction when paying tax to the government.

16. Sudewo, "Menyoroti Implementasi".

17. "Zakat Plan Questioned", *Jakarta Post*, 1 December 2001.

18. "Tax Deduction of 'Zakat' Must Apply to Non-Muslims", *Jakarta Post*, 29 November 2001.

19. "Noted Religious Scholars Welcome Ruling on Zakat", *Jakarta Post*, 1 December 2001.

20. "Govt Wants to Focus on 'Zakat' First: Minister", *Jakarta Post*, 3 December 2001.

21. M. Ikhsan, "Tithe and Tax Reduction", *Jakarta Post*, 5 December 2001.

22. Deliar Noer, *The Administration of Islam in Indonesia*, Monograph Series no. 58 (Ithaca, New York: Cornell Modern Indonesia Project, 1978).

23. Ibid., pp. 57–58.

24. Ramlan Surbakti, "Formal Political Institutions", in *Indonesia: The Challenge of Change*, edited by Richard W. Baker et al. (Singapore: Institute of Southeast Asian Studies, 1999), p. 69.

25. "Gairah Syariat Islam di Berbagai Daerah' [Calls for *shari'a* in various regions], *Suara Hidayatullah*, July 2000.

26. Mutammimul Ula, "Peluang dan Tantangan Penerapan Syari'ah Islam" [The opportunity and challenge of *shari'a* application], *Journal Politik Akses* I, no. 1 (2001): 18–19.

27. "Jam Malam bagi Wanita Akan Berlaku di Sumbar" [Night-time restrictions to be applied for women in West Sumatra], *Media Indonesia*, 30 June 2001.

28. "Otonomi Daerah dan Rentannya Posisi Perempuan" [Decentralization and the vulnerability of women's position], *Kompas*, 18 June 2001.

29. "Martapura Enforces Ban on Eating in Public Places", *Jakarta Post*, 4 December 2001.

30. Ula, "Peluang dan Tantangan", pp. 18–19.

31. "Tarik Menarik Mengurus Tamu Allah" [Tug-of-war in managing pilgrims], *Gamma*, 21 July 2001.

32. "Jawa Timur Minta Otonomi Haji" [East Java asks for decentralized *hajj* services], *Media Indonesia*, 26 June 2001.

33. "Seorang Pezina Dicambuk 100 kali di Aceh" [An adulterer whipped 100 times in Aceh], *Media Indonesia*, 30 November 1999.
34. "Hukum Rajam bagi Pezinah dan Pencuri di Aceh" [The stoning of adulterers and thieves in Aceh], *Republika*, 6 December 1999.
35. "Penegakan Syariat Islam Bukan Berarti Aman di Aceh" [The application of *shari'a* does not necessarily imply peace in Aceh], *Kompas*, 12 December 2000.
36. "Deklarasi Syariat Islam di Aceh Harus Ikhlas" [The enactment of *shari'a* in Aceh must be done sincerely], *Kompas*, 11 December 2000.
37. "Pemberlakuan Syariat Islam di Aceh Hanya Seremonial" [The enactment of *shari'a* in Aceh is only ceremonial], *Kompas*, 13 December 2000.
38. "PDI-P Inginkan RUU Aceh Sesuai dengan Pancasila" [PDI-P wants the Bill of Aceh to be in line with Pancasila], *Kompas*, 5 May 2001.
39. "PKB Tak Permasalahkan Syariat Islam di Aceh" [PKB has no question over the application of *shari'a* in Aceh], *Kompas*, 8 May 2001.
40. "Syariat Islam Hanya Berlaku untuk Kaum Muslimin" [*Shari'a* applies only to Muslim], *Kompas*, 8 May 2001.
41. "PDIP Tak Keberatan Syariat Islam Diterapkan di Aceh" [PDI-P has no objection over the application of *shari'a* in Aceh]. <http://www.detik.com/peristiwa/2001/05/08/200158-185728.shtml>. Retrieved on 8 May 2001.
42. "Syariat Islam Hanya Berlaku untuk Kaum Muslimin".
43. Ibid.
44. "Critics Slam Plans to Launch Islamic Law in Aceh". <http://news.indiatimes.com/apit/08worl24.htm>. Retrieved on 12 January 2001.
45. "Presiden Harus Jelaskan Dulu Syariat Islam" [President should first explain what *shari'a* is], *Kompas*, 9 May 2001.
46. "Megawati Bayar ZIS saat Nuzulul Qur'an" [Megawati pays *zakat* during the Commemoration of the Revelation of the Qur'an], *Pikiran Rakyat*, 27 November 2001.
47. "Ngawi Mencekam, Kader PDI-P Diculik" [Ngawi in tense, PDI-P activist kidnapped], *Kompas*, 2 December 2001.

APPENDICES

Appendix I

THE LAW OF THE REPUBLIC OF INDONESIA NUMBER 1 OF THE YEAR 1974 ON MARRIAGE

BY THE GRACE OF GOD ALMIGHTY
THE PRESIDENT OF THE REPUBLIC OF INDONESIA

Considering:

Whereas in accordance with the philosophy of Pancasila and the aspirations to promote national law, it is deemed essential that there shall be a Law concerning Marriage to be in force for all Indonesian nationals.

Pursuant to:

1 Article 5 paragraph (1), Article 20 paragraph (1), Article 27 paragraph (1) and Article 29 of the 1945 Constitution; 2. Decision of the People's Consultative Assembly Number IV/MPR/1973.
With the concurrence of the House of People's Representatives.

HAS RESOLVED
To sanction: LAW ON MARRIAGE
CHAPTER I
FOUNDATIONS OF MARRIAGE

Article 1.

Marriage is a relationship of body and soul between a man and a woman as husband and wife with the purpose of establishing a happy and lasting family (household) founded on belief in God Almighty.

Sources: *The Compilation of Islamic Laws in Indonesia*, (1996/1997). Project for Religious Law Counseling Development Directorate for Religious Courts, the Directorate General for Development of Islamic Institutions. Jakarta: Department of Religious Affairs of Republic of Indonesia.

Article 2.

(1) A marriage is legitimate, if it has been performed according to the laws of the respective religions and beliefs of the parties concerned.

(2) Every marriage shall be registered according to the regulations of the legislation in force.

Article 3.

(1) In principle in a marriage a male person shall be allowed to have one wife only. A female person shall be allowed to have one husband only.

(2) A court of law shall be capable of granting permission to a husband to have more than one wife, if all parties concerned so wish.

Article 4.

(1) If a husband desires to have more than one wife, as referred to in Article 3 paragraph (2) of this Law, he shall be required to submit a request to the Court of Law in the region in which he resides.

(2) The Court of Law referred to in paragraph (1) of this article shall grant permission to a husband wishing to have more than one wife if:

a.   his wife is unable to perform her duties as wife;

b.   his wife suffers from physical defects or an incurable disease;

c.   his wife is incapable of having descendants.

Article 5.

(1) In order for a request to be submitted to the Court of Law as referred to in Article 4 paragraph (1) of this Law, the following requirements shall be obtained:

a.   the approval of the wife or wives;

b.   the assurance that the husband will guarantee the necessities of life for his wives and their children;

c.   the guarantee that the husband shall act justly in regard to his wives and their children.

(2) The approval referred to in paragraph (1) under the letter a of this article shall not be required of a husband if it is impossible to obtain the approval of his wife or wives and if she or they are incapable of becoming partner or partners to the contract, or if no information is available with respect to his wife or wives for the duration of at least 2 (two) years, or on account of other reasons requiring the Judgement of a Judge on the Court of Law.

CHAPTER II
PREREQUISITES FOR MARRIAGE

Article 6.

(1) A marriage shall be founded upon an agreement between both the aspirant bride and the aspirant bridegroom.

(2) In order to enter into matrimony a person who has not attained the age of 21 (twenty one) years shall obtain the consent of both parents.

(3) If one of the two parents has died or finds himself or herself in a condition of being incapable of stating his or her will, the consent referred to in paragraph (2) of this article

shall suffice to be obtained from the parent still living or from the parent who is capable of stating his or her will.

(4) If both parents have died or find themselves in a condition of being incapable of stating their will, the consent shall be obtained from the guardian, the supporter or a family member having a blood relationship ascending in a straight line, as long as they are still living and in a condition of being capable of stating their will.

(5) In the case of a difference of opinion prevailing among the persons referred to in paragraphs (2), (3) and (4) of this article, or one or more persons among them having made no statement of opinion, the Court of Law in whose territorial jurisdiction the person wishing to enter into matrimony resides, at the request of the person referred to, can grant permission after having previously heard the persons referred to in paragraphs (2), (3) and (4) of this article.

(6) The provisions referred to in paragraph (1) through paragraph (5) of this article remain in force as long as the laws relating to the respective religions and beliefs of those concerned have not provided otherwise.

Article 7.

(1) Marriage shall be permitted only if the male aspirant has reached the age of 19 (nineteen) years and the female aspirant has reached the age of 16 (sixteen) years.

(2) In the case of deviation from the provision in paragraph (1) of this article a request for dispensation can be submitted to a Court of Law or another functionary designated by both parents of the male aspirant as well as the female aspirant.

(3) The provisions relating to the condition of one of the parents or both parents referred to in Article 6 paragraph (3) and (4) of this Law, are equally applicable in the case of a request for dispensation referred to in paragraph (2) of this article without prejudice to the provision in Article 6 paragraph (6).

Article 8.

No marriage shall be allowed between two persons who:

a. have either an ascending or descending line of blood relationship;
b. have a lateral line of blood relationship, i.e. between brothers and sisters, between a person and a brother or sister of either parent and between a person and a brother or sister of any grandparent;
c. have a relationship by marriage, i.e. parent-in-law, step child, daughter or son-in-law and step mother or step father;
d. have a foster relationship, i.e. foster-parent, foster-child, foster-sister or foster-brother, and foster-aunt or fosteruncle;
e. have a sibling relationship with a wife or as an aunt or niece of a wife, if a husband has more than one wife;
f. have such relationship as being prohibitive for marriage by any religion or other regulations in force.

Article 9.

A person joined in matrimony with another person shall not enter into another marriage, except in cases as provided for in Article 3 paragraph (2) and Article 4 of this Law.

Article 10.

In the case of a husband and a wife who have been divorced and who have been married again to each other and have been divorced again for the second time, no marriage between them shall be performed again, insofar as the law of their respective religions and beliefs does not provide otherwise.

Article 11.

(1) For a woman whose marriage has been dissolved there shall be applicable a waiting period.

(2) The length of the waiting period referred to in paragraph (1) shall be regulated in a subsequent Government Regulation.

Article 12.

The procedure relating to the implementation of marriages shall be regulated in separate legislative provisions.

CHAPTER III
PREVENTION OF MARRIAGE

Article 13.

A marriage may be prevented in the case of any party not meeting the prerequisites for the performance of the marriage.

Article 14.

(1) Those who may prevent a marriage are the family members in a straight line of either ascendancy or descendancy, siblings, marriage guardian, guardian, supporter of either the aspirant bride or aspirant bridegroom and any interested parties.

(2) Those referred to in paragraph (1) of this article also have the right to prevent the performance of a marriage if either the aspirant bride or, the aspirant bridegroom is under the care of a supporter, and if consequently the marriage would indeed result in misery for the other aspirant who has a relationship with persons as referred to in paragraph (1) of this article.

Article 15.

Whosoever on account of a marriage is still bound to either one of the two parties, by virtue of the existence of such a marriage, may prevent a new marriage, without prejudice to the provisions in Article 3 paragraph (2) and Article 4 of this Law.

Article 16.

(1) The appointed official shall be obliged to prevent the performance of a marriage if the provisions in Article 7 paragraph (1), Article 8, Article 9, Article 10 and Article 12 of this Law have not been fulfilled.

(2) With respect to the appointed official referred to in paragraph (1) of this article further regulations shall be adopted in legislative provisions.

Article 17.

(1) The prevention of a marriage shall be submitted to the Court of Law in whose territorial Jurisdiction the marriage will be performed, while at the same time the official keeper of the marriage register shall also be notified.

(2) The aspirant bride and bridegroom shall be notified of the request to prevent the marriage as referred to in paragraph (1) of this article by the official keeper of the marriage register.

Article 18.

The prevention order of a marriage may be revoked by the decision of a Court of Law or by withdrawal of the request to prevent the marriage from the Court of Law by the party who has submitted the request.

Article 19.

A marriage shall be incapable of being performed if its prevention order has not been revoked.

Article 20.

The official keeper of the marriage register shall not be allowed to perform or assist in the performance of a marriage if he is aware of infractions against the provisions in Article 7 paragraph (1), Article 8, Article 9, Article 10 and Article 12 of this Law even if there is no appeal for prevention of marriage.

Article 21.

(1) If the official keeper of the marriage register is of the opinion that: there is a prohibition against a marriage according to this Law, he shall refuse to perform such a marriage.

(2) In the case of such a refusal, at the request of one of the parties desiring to perform a marriage, the official keeper of the marriage register shall issue a written certificate concerning the refusal, setting out the reasons for such a refusal.

(3) The parties whose marriage performance has been refused have the right to submit a request to the Court of Law in whose territorial jurisdiction the official keeper of the marriage register who has made the decision is stationed, accompanied by the submission of the certificate of refusal referred to.

(4) The Court of Law shall deal with the case by summary procedure and shall decide either to support the refusal or to issue directives with a view to the performance of the marriage.

(5) This decision shall cease to be in force, if the obstacles resulting in the refusal referred to disappear and the parties desiring to marry may repeat the notification of their intention.

CHAPTER IV
DISSOLUTION OF MARRIAGE

Article 22.

A marriage may be dissolved should the parties fail to fulfil the prerequisites for the continuance of the marriage.

Article 23.

The request for the dissolution of the marriage may be submitted by:
a.   the family members in a straight line of ascendancy of the husband or of the wife;
b.   the husband or the wife;
c.   authorized officials as long as the marriage has not been dissolved;
d.   the appointed official referred to in paragraph (2) of Article 16 of this Law and anybody who has a direct legal interest with respect to the marriage, however only after the marriage has failed

Article 24.

Whosoever on account of a marriage is still bound to either one of the two parties, by virtue of the existence of such a marriage, may submit a request for the dissolution of the new marriage, without prejudice to the provisions of Article 3 paragraph (2) and Article 4 of this Law.

Article 25.

The request for the dissolution of a marriage shall be submitted to the Court of Law in whose territorial jurisdiction the marriage has been performed or at the location of the domicile of both husband and wife; of the husband or of the wife.

Article 26.

(1) A marriage which has been performed before an unauthorized official keeper of the marriage register, an illegal marriage guardian or which has been performed without the presence of 2 (two) witnesses may be requested to be dissolved, by the family members in a straight line of ascendancy of the husband or of the wife, the public prosecutor and the husband or the wife.

(2) The right of dissolution by the husband or by the wife by virtue of the reasons in paragraph (1) of this article shall be forfeited if the parties have been living together as husband and wife and are able to produce the certificate of marriage issued by the unauthorized official keeper of the marriage register and the performance of marriage shall be repeated with a view to rendering it legal.

Article 27.

(1) A husband or a wife may submit a request for the dissolution of a marriage if it was performed under illegal threat.

(2) A husband or a wife may submit a request for the dissolution of a marriage if at the time of the performance of the marriage there was misinformation with respect to the person of the husband or the wife.

(3) If the threat has ceased to exist, or the party who has been misinformed has become aware of the situation and subsequently during a time period of 6 (six) months the parties concerned have continued living together as husband and wife and the right to submit a request for the dissolution of the marriage has not been used, such right shall be forfeited.

Article 28.

(1) The dissolution of a marriage starts at the moment the judgement of the Court of Law has become final and comes into force from the moment of the performance of the marriage.

(2) The judgement shall have no retroactive force with respect to:

a. the children born of the marriage referred to;

b. the husband of the wife who has been acting in good faith, except with respect to joint property, if the dissolution of the marriage has been by virtue of the existence of a previous other marriage.

c. other third parties not included in a and b insofar as they have obtained rights in good faith previous to the moment that the judgement concerning the dissolution of the marriage became final.

CHAPTER V
MARRIAGE CONTRACT

Article 29.

(1) At the time or before the performance of marriage, both parties by mutual consent may enter into a written contract that has been legalized by the official keeper of the marriage register, subsequent upon which act the contract shall also come into force with respect to third parties insofar the interests of those third parties are involved.

(2) The marriage contract shall not be capable of being legalized if it is in violation of legal, religious and moral limits.

(3) The marriage contract shall come into force as from the moment of the performance of the marriage.

(4) The marriage contract shall be incapable of being modified for the duration of the marriage, except in case both parties have agreed to the modification and such modification will not be prejudicial to the interests of third parties.

CHAPTER VI
RIGHTS AND RESPONSIBILITIES OF HUSBAND AND WIFE

Article 30.

Husband and wife shall bear the lofty responsibility of maintaining a household which constitutes the fundamental basis of the structure of society.

Article 31.

(1) The rights and responsibilities of the wife are equivalent to the rights and responsibilities of the husband in the life of the household and in the social intercourse in society.

(2) Either party to the marriage has the right to conduct legal actions.

(3) The husband is the head of the family and the wife is the mother of the household.

Article 32.

(1) Husband and wife shall have a permanent residence.

(2) The domicile referred to in paragraph (1) of this article shall be determined jointly by husband and wife.

Article 33.

Husband and wife shall love and respect each other, be faithful to each other and give each other physical and moral support.

Article 34.

(1) The husband shall have the responsibility of protecting his wife and provide her with all the necessities of life in & household in accordance with his capabilities.

(2) The wife shall have the responsibility of taking care of the household to the best of her ability.

(3) If either the husband or the wife has neglected his or her respective responsibility either one of them may submit a claim to a Court of Law.

CHAPTER VII
PROPERTY DURING MARRIAGE

Article 35.

(1) Property acquired during marriage shall become joint property.

(2) Property brought in by the husband or the wife respectively and property acquired by either one of them as a gift or an inheritance shall be under the respective control of either one of them, provided the parties have not decided otherwise.

Article 36.

(1) With respect to joint property either the husband or the wife may act by virtue of an agreement between both parties.

(2) With respect to property brought in by the husband and the wife respectively, the husband and the wife have the fullest right to conduct legal actions in regard to their respective individual property.

Article 37.

In the case a marriage has been dissolved on account of a divorce, the joint property shall be dealt with according to the respective laws.

CHAPTER VIII
DISSOLUTION OF THE MARRIAGE AND ITS CONSEQUENCES

Article 38.

A marriage may be dissolved for the following reasons:
a.   death, b. divorce and c. by virtue of a judgement by a Court of Law.

Article 39.

(1) A divorce shall be carried out only before a session of a Court of Law after the Court concerned has endeavored and has been unsuccessful in bringing about a conciliation between the two parties.

(2) In order to carry out a divorce sufficient reasons shall be present indicative of the incompatibility of the husband and the wife living together in harmony.

(3) The procedure of divorce before a session of a Court of Law shall be provided in separate legislative provisions

Article 40.

(1) A claim for divorce shall be submitted to a Court of Law.

(2) The procedure of submitting a claim as referred to in paragraph (1) of this article shall be provided in separate legislative provisions.

Article 41.

The consequences of the dissolution of a marriage on account of a divorce are as follows:

a.   The mother as well as the father shall continue to have the responsibility of maintaining and educating their children, solely by virtue of the interests of the children; in the case of a dispute concerning the custody of the children, a Court of Law shall render its judgement.

b.   The father shall be accountable for all the expenses relating to the maintenance and the education needed by the children; in the case of the father being in fact unable to discharge his responsibility a Court of Law may decide that the mother shall share the burden of the expenses referred to.

c.   A Court of Law may confer the obligation upon the ex-husband to pay alimony and/or determine an obligation on the part of the ex-wife.

CHAPTER IX
POSITION OF THE CHILDREN

Article 42.

A legitimate child is a child born in or as a consequence of legitimate marriage.

Article 43.

(1) A child born out of wedlock shall have civil law relations with its mother and the family of its mother only.

(2) The position of a child referred to in paragraph (1) aforementioned shall be further provided in a Government Regulation.

Article 44.

(1) A husband may contest the legitimacy of a child born of his wife if he is able to furnish evidence that his wife has committed adultery and that the child is a consequence of such an adultery.

(2) A Court of Law shall render judgement concerning the legitimacy of a child upon request of the interested party.

CHAPTER X
RIGHTS AND RESPONSIBILITIES BETWEEN PARENTS AND CHILDREN

Article 45.

(1) Both parents shall be responsible for the maintenance and education of their children to the best of their ability.

(2) The responsibility of the parents referred to in paragraph (1) of this article shall be in force until the children are married or are able to support themselves and shall continue to be in force notwithstanding the marriage between both parents having been dissolved.

Article 46.

(1) The children shall honour their parents and obey their just wishes.

(2) When the children have attained maturity, they shall have the responsibility of maintaining to the best, of their ability their parents and the members of the family in a straight ascendancy line, if they are in need of such assistance.

Article 47.

(1) A child who has not attained the age of 18 (eighteen) year or who has never been married shall be in the custody of its parents as long as it has not been removed from their custody.

(2) The parents shall represent the child in all legal actions before or outside of a Court of Law.

Article 48.

The parents shall not be allowed to transfer a right or to mortgage immovables possessed by a child of theirs who has not attained the age of 18 (eighteen) years or who has never been married, except if the interest of the child so requires.

Article 49.

(1) The custody by one of the parents or by both parents over one of their children or more than one of their children may be revoked for a specified period of time upon the request of another parent, a family member of the child in a straight line of ascendancy and a sibling who has attained maturity or an authorized official, by a judgement of a Court of Law in the following cases:

a.   Gross negligence of responsibility towards the child;

b.   Very bad behaviour.

(2) Notwithstanding the custody of the parents has been revoked, the parents remain responsible for pro-living expenses for the child.

CHAPTER XI
GUARDIANSHIP

Article 50.

(1) A child who has not attained the age of 18 (eighteen) years or who has never been married, and who is not in custody of its parents, shall be in custody of a guardian.

(2) Such guardianship shall apply to the person of child as well as its property.

Article 51.

(1) A guardian may be designated by a parent exercising parental custody, prior to his or her demise by last will and testament in writing or orally before 2 (two) witnesses.

(2) A guardian shall be selected preferably from among the family members of the child or another adult person who is of sound mind, just, reliable and of good behaviour.

(3) A guardian shall have the responsibility of taking care of the child in his custody and its property to the best of his ability and shall respect the religion and belief of the child.

(4) A guardian shall make a list of the property of the child in his custody at the time he starts to assume his function and shall record all the changes affecting the property of the child or the children.

(5) A guardian shall be accountable with respect to the property of the child under his guardianship and any losses due to his faults or negligence.

Article 52.

Article 48 of this Law shall be applicable to the guardian.

Article 53.

(1) The authority of the guardian may be revoked in cases such as referred to in Article 49 of this Law.

(2) If the authority of a guardian has been revoked as referred to in paragraph (1) of this article, another person shall be appointed by a Court of Law.

Article 54.

A guardian who has been the cause of losses sustained by the property of a child under his guardianship, after having been sued by the child or the family of the child resulting in a judgement by a Court of Law, may be obliged to pay compensation for the losses incurred.

CHAPTER XII
MISCELLANEOUS PROVISIONS
First
First Section
Evidence of parentage of the child

Article 55.

(1) The parentage of a child shall be able to be proved only by an authentic certificate of birth, issued by an authorized Official.

(2) In the absence of a certificate of birth referred to in paragraph (1) of this article, a Court of Law may pass an award with respect to the parentage of a child subsequent to a careful investigation having been conducted founded upon admissible evidence.

(3) By virtue of the provisions of the Court of Law referred to in paragraph (2) of this article, the functionary for the registration of births present in the territorial jurisdiction of the Court of Law concerned shall issue a certificate of birth for the child concerned.

Second Section
Marriages outside Indonesia

Article 56.

(1) A marriage performed outside Indonesia between two Indonesian nationals or between an Indonesian national and a foreign national shall be legitimate if carried out according to the laws in force in the state wherein the marriage has been performed and if insofar as the Indonesian national is concerned, the marriage is not in contravention with the provisions of this Law.

(2) Within a period of 1 (one) year subsequent to the return of husband and wife to Indonesian territory, their certificate of marriage shall be registered with the Office of the Marriage Registrar at their place of residence.

Third Section
Mixed Marriages

Article 57.

In this Law a mixed marriage shall be understood to be a marriage between two persons who in Indonesia are subject to different laws due to a difference in nationality and one of the parties is a foreign national while the other party is an Indonesian national.

Article 58.

Persons with different nationalities who have performed a mixed marriage may acquire the nationality of the husband or wife and may also lose their nationality, according to procedures provided in the Law of nationality of the Republic of Indonesia in force.

Article 59.

(1) The nationality acquired due to a marriage or to the dissolution of a marriage shall determine the law in force with respect to public law as well as civil law.

(2) A mixed marriage performed in Indonesia shall be carried out according to this Law of Marriage.

Article 60.

(1) No mixed marriage shall be performed prior to proof having been furnished of fulfillment of the marriage prerequisites provided by the law in force for the respective parties.

(2) As proof of the prerequisites referred to in paragraph (1) having been fulfilled and consequently of the absence of obstacles to the performance of a mixed marriage, those who

according to the law in force for the respective parties are authorized to register marriages shall issue an affidavit confirming the fulfillment of the prerequisites.

(3) In case of refusal by the official concerned to issue an affidavit, upon request of interested parties, the Court of Law shall pass judgement without right of appeals in regard to the question whether the refusal to issue an affidavit has proper foundation or not.

(4) In case the Court of Law decides that the refusal has not been properly founded, the award of the Court shall become a substitute for the affidavit referred to in paragraph (3).

(5) The affidavit or the award in lieu of an affidavit shall no longer be in force should the marriage not have been performed within a period of 6 (six) months subsequent to such an affidavit having been issued.

Article 61.

(1) A mixed marriage shall be registered by the authorized official.

(2) Whosoever performs a mixed marriage without prior exhibit to the authorized official registrar the affidavit or the award in lieu of an affidavit referred to in Article 60 paragraph (4) of this Law shall be sentenced by imprisonment for a maximum period of 1 (one) month.

(3) The official registrar of marriages who registers a marriage while being aware that the affidavit or the award in lieu of an affidavit is absent, shall be sentenced by imprisonment for a maximum period of 3 (three) months and by administrative penalty.

Article 62.

In a mixed marriage the position of a child shall be regulated according to Article 59 paragraph (1) of this Law.

Fourth Section
Courts of Law
Article 63.

(1) In this Law a Court of Law shall be understood to mean:
a.   a Religious Court for those having Islam as religion;
b.   a General Court for all others.

(2) Every decision of a Religious Court shall be confirmed by a General Court.

CHAPTER XIII
TRANSITIONAL PROVISIONS

Article 64.

Marriages and anything relating to marriages which took place prior to this Law having come into force which had been carried out according to the old regulations, shall be legitimate.

Article 65.

(1) In case a husband has more than one wife according to either the old law or by virtue of Article 3 paragraph (2) of this Law the following provisions shall be operative:
a.   The husband shall furnish equivalent means of living to all his wives and their children.

b. The second and subsequent wives shall have no right upon the joint property extant prior to the marriage with the second and subsequent wives.

c. All wives have equal rights upon joint property acquired subsequent to their respective marriages.

(2) Provided the Court of Law which has granted permission to take more than one wife according to this Law has not decided otherwise, the provisions in paragraph (1) of this article shall be in force.

CHAPTER XIV
FINAL PROVISIONS

Article 66.

With respect to marriages and anything related to marriages by virtue of this Law by the coming into force of this Law the provisions contained in the Civil Code (Burgerlijk Wetboek), Ordinance on Christian Indonesian Marriages (Huwelijks Ordonnantie Christen Indonesiers, S. 1933 No. 74), Regulation on Mixed Marriages (Regeling op de gemengde Huwelijken, S. 1898 No. 158), and other regulations containing provisions in regard to marriages, insofar as have been regulated in this Law, shall be declared rescinded.

Article 67.

(1) This Law shall come into force on the date of its promulgation and its effective implementation shall be further regulated by Government Regulation;

(2) Matters in this Law requiring implementary regulation shall be further regulated by Government Regulation.

In order that everybody may take cognizance of this Government Regulation, its promulgation is herewith ordered through publication in the State Gazette of the Republic of Indonesia.

Promulgated in Jakarta
On January 2nd, 1974
Minister/State Secretary of the
Republic of Indonesia
sgd.
SUDHARMONO SH
Major General TNI

Sanctioned in Jakarta
On January 2nd, 1974
The President of The
Republic of Indonesia
sgd.
SOEHARTO
General TNI

State Gazette of the Republic of Indonesia of the year 1974
number 1

CLARIFICATION OF
THE LAW ON MARRIAGE
OF
THE REPUBLIC OF INDONESIA
NUMBER 1, 1974

General Clarification

1. For a State and Nation like Indonesia the existence of a marriage Law on a National basis is imperative, a Law which simultaneously incorporates the principles and legal basis which thus far have been observed and which have come into force in the various groupings in our community.

2. At this stage various marriage Laws are operative amongst the different groups of citizens and found in different regions as follows:

    a. For indigenous Indonesians of the Moslem Religion the Religious Law is applied which is excluded in the Customary Law;

    b. For other indigenous Indonesians the Customary Law is applied;

    c. For indigenous Indonesians of Christian Faith the Marriage Ordinance for Indonesian Christians is applied (S. 1933. No. 74);

    d. For Orientals of Chinese origin and Indonesian subjects of Chinese descent the regulations in the Civil Code are in force with a few minor changes;

    e. For other Orientals of non-Chinese origins and Indonesian subjects of non-Chinese descent their own Customary Law is in force;

    f. For Europeans and Indonesian subjects of European descent the regulations in the Civil Code are in force.

3. True to the basic philosophy of Pancasila and the 1945 Constitution this Law should on the one side, realize the principles embodied in Pancasila and the 1945 Constitution but at the same time should accommodate the living realities that are found in our present society, on the other. This Marriage Law contains already all the elements and regulations of the Law of their respective religions and beliefs.

4. This Law embodies the basic principles of marriage and all other regulations which have any bearing on the consummation of marriage and are already adapted to progress and the demand of time. The foundations or principles contained in this Law are as follows:

    a. The aim of marriage is to establish a happy and lasting family. To this end husband and wife must support and supplement each other to develop themselves towards spiritual and material wellbeing.

    b. It is stated in this Law that a marriage is valid if contracted according to the respective Law of Religion and Faith and apart from that it is required that each marriage should be registered according to the regulations of existing Laws. The registration of marriage is similar to the registration of important events in the life of an individual, like birth and death as stated in public announcements, in formal documents as well as in civic registration lists.

    c. This Law follows the principles of Monogamy unless it is otherwise desired by those concerned, according to the provisions of the Law and Religion they adhere to, in which case a husband is allowed to take more than one wife. Nonetheless the marriage of a husband with more than one wife, even if so desired and agreed upon by the respective parties can only be performed if certain requirements can be met and if it is determined by the court.

d. This Law holds that the aspirant husband and wife must be mentally & physically mature to be allowed to perform their marriage in an ideal and lasting form without ending in a divorce for the sake of healthy off-spring. It is therefore necessary to prevent the marriage of aspirant husbands and wives who are still under-age.

Apart from that the problem of marriage is closely related to the problem of population. It appears that a lower age limit for women to marry brings about a higher birth rate compared with a higher age limit. Because of this the Law holds that a good minimum age limit for the contraction of marriage for men and women is respectively 19 years and 16 years of age.

e. Since the ideal of marriage is to create a happy, lasting and prosperous family, this Law pursues a principle of making divorce most difficult. For divorce to be granted it must be supported reasons that are warranted and only through a process before a Court hearing.

f. The rights and status of the wife are the equivalent of the right and status of the husband both in their own household and in their social intercourse so that all matters in the family can be jointly discussed and decided between husband and wife.

5. To guarantee the certainty of legitimacy, a marriage, including everything evolved therein, which took place before this Law came into force and performed according to existing regulations, is declared valid. Likewise if for a certain matter this Law does not provide the required regulations then automatically the existing regulations are applicable.

CLARIFICATIONS OF ARTICLES

Article 1.

As the State is based on the Principles of Pancasila, the First Principle being 'Belief in God Almighty', so marriage is also closely related to religion and spiritual values. It does not only possess a physical value but a mental value as well which plays a vitally important role. The establishment of an ideal marriage is closely connected with phenomenon of birth which is the essence of marriage so that the care and education of the offspring are the responsibilities of the parents.

Article 2.

With the formulation in Article 2, paragraph 1, it is established that there is no marriage contracted beyond the Law of the respective Religions and Beliefs, in line with the 1945 Constitution.

What is meant by the Law of the respective religions and beliefs also incorporates regulations valid for the followers of those religions and beliefs as long as they do not run counter to this Law or are not otherwise decided therein.

Article 3.

(1) This Law adheres to the principle of Monogamy.

(2) The Court in giving decision should, apart from checking if the requirements as contained in Articles 4 and 5 are already met, examine if the rules of the marriage law allow for polygamy on the side of the prospective husband.

Article 4.

Sufficiently clear.

Article 5.

Sufficiently clear.

Article 6.

(1) Since the aim of marriage is to ascertain that husband and wife can build up a happy and lasting family in conformity with fundamental human rights, the marriage must be agreed upon by both contracting parties without any pressure from whatever source. The provisions in this article are not, meant to lessen the terms of marriage according to the existing rules of marriage law as long as they do not run counter to the provisions in this Law as already explained in Article 2 Paragraph 1 of this Law.
(2) Sufficiently clear.
(3) Sufficiently clear.
(4) Sufficiently clear.
(5) Sufficiently clear.
(6) Sufficiently clear.

Article 7.

(1) To ensure the health of husband-wife and offspring it is necessary to determine age limits for marriage.
(2) With this Law coming into force, the provisions which grant dispensations for marriage as explained in paragraph (1) regulated according to the Civil Code and the Marriage Ordinance for Indonesian Christians (S. 1933 No. 74) are declared void.
(3) Sufficiently clear.

Article 8.

Sufficiently clear.

Article 9.

Sufficiently clear.

Article 10.

Since the aim of marriage is to establish a lasting family for husband and wife it is therefore necessary that any step which may give rise to the termination of a marriage must really be given throughout consideration first.

This provision is made to avoid the recurrence of marriage and divorce so that husband and wife can really appreciate and value each other.

Article 11.

Sufficiently clear.

Article 12.

The provisions in article 12 will not disparage the provisions as contained in Law no. 22 of 1946 and Law no. 32 of 1954.

Article 13.

Sufficiently clear.

Article 14.

Sufficiently clear.

Article 15.

Sufficiently clear.

Article 16.

Sufficiently clear.

Article 17.

Sufficiently clear.

Article 18.

Sufficiently clear.

Article 19.

Sufficiently clear.

Article 20.

Sufficiently clear.

Article 21.

Sufficiently clear.

Article 22.

The term may in this article implies that marriage may be dissolved or may not be dissolved according to the alternatives provided by the rules of the Law of the religion concerned.

Article 23.

Sufficiently clear.

Article 24.

Sufficiently clear.

Article 25.

Sufficiently clear.

Article 26.

Sufficiently clear.

Article 27.

Sufficiently clear.

Article 28.

Sufficiently clear.

Article 29.

What is meant by agreement in this article does not include Taklik-Talak.

Article 30.

Sufficiently clear.

Article 31.

Sufficiently clear.

Article 32.

Sufficiently clear.

Article 33.

Sufficiently clear.

Article 34.

Sufficiently clear.

Article 35.

If marriage is dissolved the joint property mentioned will be regulated according to the respective laws.

Article 36.

Sufficiently clear.

Article 37.

What is meant by their law is the law of their respective religion, customary law and other laws.

Article 38.

Sufficiently clear.

Article 39.

(1) Sufficiently clear.
(2) Reasons that can be used as a basis for divorce are:
    a.   If one of the parties commits adultery, becomes a drunkard, an opium addict, a gambler, or addicted to other vices which are hard to cure.
    b.   One of the parties has left the other for two consecutive years without the other's consent and without legitimate reasons or because of reasons over which the first one has no control.
    c.   One of the parties has to undergo a jail sentence of five years or more after marriage is performed.
    d.   One of the parties resorts to violence or ill treatment that can endanger the safety of the other.
    e.   One of the parties develops an incurable disease or a disability which prevents the consummation of marriage between husband and wife.
    f.   If constant quarrels and heated arguments develop between husband and wife which preclude the desired compatibility.
(3) Sufficiently clear.

Article 40.

Sufficiently clear.

Article 41.

Sufficiently clear.

Article 42.

Sufficiently clear.

Article 43.

Sufficiently clear.

Article 44.

The court demands that the interested parties take their oath.

Article 45.

Sufficiently clear.

Article 46.

Sufficiently clear.

Article 47.

Sufficiently clear.

Article 48.

Sufficiently clear.

Article 49.

What is meant by custody in this article does not include the power as the wali-nikah (marriage guardian).

Article 50.

Sufficiently clear.

Article 51.

Sufficiently clear.

Article 52.

Sufficiently clear.

Article 53.

Sufficiently clear.

Article 54.

Sufficiently clear.

Article 55.

Sufficiently clear.

Article 56.

Sufficiently clear.

Article 57.

Sufficiently clear.

Article 58.

Sufficiently clear.

Article 59.

Sufficiently clear.

Article 60.

Sufficiently clear.

Article 61.

Sufficiently clear.

Article 62.

Sufficiently clear.

Article 63.

Sufficiently clear.

Article 64.

Sufficiently clear.

Article 65.

Sufficiently clear.

Article 66.

Sufficiently clear.

Article 67.

Sufficiently clear.

SUPPLEMENT OF THE STATE GAZETTE
REPUBLIC OF INDONESIA
OF THE YEAR 1974 NUMBER 1

Appendix II

THE LAW OF THE REPUBLIC OF INDONESIA NUMBER 7 OF THE YEAR 1989 ON THE RELIGIOUS JUDICATURE

PRESIDENT OF THE
REPUBLIC OF INDONESIA

LAW OF THE REPUBLIC OF INDONESIA
NUMBER 7 OF THE YEAR 1989
RE
RELIGIOUS JUDICATURE

BY THE GRACE OF GOD THE ALMIGHTY
THE PRESIDENT OF THE REPUBLIC OF INDONESIA,

Considering: a. whereas the Country of the Republic of Indonesia, as a legislated state which is based on the Philosophy of Pancasila and the Constitution of the 1945, aiming at realizing a life of a nation which is prosperous, secure, peaceful and order;

b. whereas in order to realize the aforementioned life order and to guarantee the equilibrium of each citizen before the law, measures to uphold justice, truth, order and the law enforcement which are able to protect the people of Indonesia are in need;

c. whereas one of the efforts to uphold the aforementioned justice, truth, order, and law enforcement is by means of Religious Judicature as it is stated in the Law number 14 of the year 1974 re the Basic Regulations of the Judicial Authorization;

Sources: *The Compilation of Islamic Laws in Indonesia*, (1996/1997). Project for Religious Law Counseling Development Directorate for Religious Courts, the Directorate General for Development of Islamic Institutions. Jakarta: Department of Religious Affairs of Republic of Indonesia.

d.   whereas the regulation on the structure, authority, and lawsuit procedure within the Religious Jurisprudence in which so far is still in vary due to the references of:

1.   The regulation on the Religious Judicature in Jawa and Madura (Staatsblad of the year 1882 Number 152 related to the Staatsblad of the year 1937 Number 116 and 610):

2.   The regulation on the Qadi's deliberation and Great Qadi's deliberation (religious leaders) for some parts of South and East Kalimantan Regencies (Staatsblad of the year 1937 Number 638 and 639);

3.   Government Regulation Number 45 of the year 1957, re the Establishment of Religious Court/Syari' at Court outside Jawa and Madura. (State Declaration of the year 1957 Number 99),

That all needs to be ended anule for the sake of the establishment of the unity in law which regulates the Religious Judicature in the framework of the national system and law order based on the Pancasila and The Constitution of 1945;

e.   whereas in relation with the above consideration, and to activate the Law number 14 of the year 1970 re the Basic Regulation of the Judicial Authorization it is deemed necessary to determine a law that regulates the structure, the authority and the Court Law Procedure within the Religious Judicature.

Attending: 1.   Article 5 point (1), Article 20 point (1), Article 24, and Article 25 of The Constitution of 1945;

2.   Law Number 14 of the year 1970 re Basic Regulation of the Judicial Authorization (State Declaration of the year 1970, Number 74, Additional State Declaration number 2951);

3.   Law Number 14 of the year 1985 re Supreme Court (State Declaration of the year 1985 Number 73, Additional State Declaration number 3316)

With the Agreement of
THE HOUSE OF REPRESENTATIVES OF
THE PEOPLE OF INDONESIA

TO DECIDE:

To pass: THE LAW OF THE RELIGIOUS JUDICATURE

CHAPTER I
GENERAL CONDITIONS

Part One
The Definition

Article 1.

The definition used in this law for some terminology are as follows::

1. The Peradilan Agama (Religious Judicature) is a judicature for those who embrace Islam religion.
2. The courts are The Religious Court and The High Religious Court within the Religious Judicature.
3. The Judges are the Judge in the Religious Court and the Judge in The High Religious Court.
4. Pegawai Pencatat Nikah (the Marriage Registrar Official) is the Marriage Registrar Official at the Office of Religious Affairs.
5. The Confiscation Officer and the Substitute Confiscation Officer is the Confiscation Officer and The Substitute Confiscation Officer at the Religious Court.

Part Two
The Status

Article 2.

The Religious Judicature is one of the executives of the Judicial Authority for justice seekers who embrace Islam religion upon certain civil cases which are regulated in this Law.

Article 3.

(1) The Judicial Authority within the Religious Judicature is held by:

a. Religious Court;
b. High Religious Court;

(2) The culminating authority point of The Judicial Authority within the Religious Judicature goes to the Supreme Court as the highest state level of Court in Indonesia.

Part Three
The Location

Article 4.

(1) A Religious Court is located in a regency or the capital of a district, and its jurisdiction territory covers the regency or the district.

(2) A High Religious Court is located in the capital city of a province, and its jurisdiction territory covers an area of the province.

Part Four
The Maintenance

Article 5.

(1) The development of technical judicature for the Religious Court is to be done by the Supreme Court.

(2) The development of the organization, administration and financial affairs are to be done by the Minister of Religious Affairs.

(3) The development and supervision as it is meant in point (1) and point (2) is not to reduce the freedom of the Judges in processing as well as finalizing cases.

CHAPTER II
THE ORGANIZATION OF THE COURT
Part One
General

Article 6.

The Court consists of:
(1) The Religious Court which serves as the First Level Court;
(2) The High Religious Court which serves as the Appeal Level Court.

Article 7.

A Religious Court is established based on a Presidential Decree.

Article 8.

The High Religious Court is established by Law.

Article 9.

(1) The structure of a Religious Court consists of; a Head, Member Judges, Clerk of the Court, Secretary, and the Confiscation Officer.

(2) The structure of a High Religious Court consists of; a Head, Member Judges, Clerk of the Court and Secretary.

Article 10.

(1) The head of the Religious Court consists of a Chairman and a Vice Chairman.

(2) The head of the High Religious Court consists of a Chairman and a Vice Chairman.

(3) Member Judge of the High Religious Court is Senior (first class) Judge.

Part Two
Chairman, Vice Chairman, Judge, Clerk of the Court
and Confiscation Officer
Paragraph 1
Chairman, Vice Chairman, and Judge

Article 11.

(1) The Judge is an officer who performs the duty of judicial authority.

(2) The requirements and the procedure of appointment, resignation as well as the execution of the Judge duties are regulated in this regulation/law.

Article 12.

(1) General control and supervision to the Judge as civil servants is carried out by the Minister of Religious Affairs.

(2) The control and supervision as it is meant in point (1) is not to lessen the freedom of the Judge in processing as well as finalizing cases.

Article 13.

(1) To be appointed as Judge in a Religious Court one must meet the following criteria:
a.   a citizen of Indonesia;
b.   Muslim;
c.   devoted to God the Almighty;
d.   Loyal to Pancasila the State Ideology and the Constitution of 1945;
e.   free from involvement of the banned organization of Indonesian Communist Party, any mass organization under it, and must not be the one involved directly or indirectly in the "contra revolution movement of 30 September/PKI", or other banned organizations;
f.   government official;
g.   a graduate of syari'ah or law faculty majoring Islamic Law;
h.   minimum age is 25 (twenty five) years old;
i.   dignity, honest, impartial, and flawless conduct.

(2) To be appointed as the Head or Vice Head of a Religious Court a minimum 10 years experience as a Judge in Religious Court is required.

Article 14.

(1) To be appointed as a Judge in a High Religious Court, one must meet the following criteria:
a.   requirements as stated in article 13 point (1) letters a, b, c, d, e, f, g, and i;
b.   minimum age requirement is 40 (forty) years old.
c.   a minimum of 5 (five) years experience as a Head or Vice Head of a Religious Court or 15 (fifteen) years as a Judge in a Religious Court.

(2) To be appointed as the Head of a High Religious Court, a minimum of 10 (ten) years experience as a Judge in a High Religious Court, or a minimum of 5 (five) years experience

as a Judge in a High Religious Court and experienced as a Head of a Religious Court is needed.

(3) To be appointed as a Vice Head of a High Religious Court, a minimum of 8 (eight) years experience as a judge in a High Religious Court is needed, or a minimum of 3 (three) years is needed for a judge in a High Religious Court who experiences as a Head of a Religious Court.

Article 15.

(1) A Judge is appointed and resigned by the President as a Head of State proposed by the Minister of Religious Affairs based on the approval of the Head of the Supreme Court.

(2) The Head and the Vice Head of a Religious Court is appointed and resigned by the Minister of Religious Affairs based on the approval of the Head of the Supreme Court.

Article 16.

(1) Prior to holding the positions, the Head, The Vice Head and the Judge are obliged to take an oath in Islamic version with wording as follows:

"By the name of Allah, I swear that I, to take this position, directly or indirectly, using any names or whatever means, will not give or promise anything to anyone."

"I swear, that I, to do or not to do something in this position, will never accept directly or indirectly from anyone a gift or any promise."

"I swear, that I will be loyal and defend as well as apply the Pancasila as a state foundation and ideology, the Constitution of 1945, and any law or other regulations valid in the country of Indonesia.

"I swear, that I will always carry out my duty honestly, thorough, and impartial and will behave and do my best as should be conducted by a Head, a Vice Head, and a Judge of a Court who are honest and ethical in upholding law and justice."

(2) The oath of the Vice Head and the Judges of Religious Court is taken by the Head of the Religious Court.

(3) The oath of the Vice Head and the Judges of a High Religious Court and the Head of a Religious Court are taken by the Head of a High Religious Court.

(4) The oath of the Head of a High Religious Court is taken by the head of the Supreme Court.

Article 17.

(1) Except determined otherwise, or based on the law, a Judge may not double his position as:

a. an executor of a Court sentence;

b. wali, representative, or any position related to the case he/she is working on.

c. a businessman/businesswoman.

(2) A Judge cannot at the same time be a lawyer.

(3) Positions that cannot be doubled by a Judge other than mentioned in point (1) and point (2) will further be regulated by the government bill.

Article 18.

(1) The Head, The Vice Head and the Judges are dismissed honorably from his/her position due to the following reasons:
a. his/her own initiative to resign;
b. chronic physical or non-physical illness;
c. reaching the age of 60 (sixty) for the Head, the Vice Head, and The Judges, in Lower Religious Court, and 63 (sixty three) for the Head, the Vice Head and the Judges in a High Religious Court;
d. being incapable in performing the duty.

(2) The Head and the Vice Head and the Judges who die will automatically be dismissed from his/her position by the President as The Head of State.

Article 19.

(1) The Head, the Vice Head and the Judges are dismissed not-honorably from his/her position due to the following reasons:
a. imprisoned due to found guilty of committed crime;
b. doing disgraceful things;
c. continuously neglecting his/her duty;
d. violating the oath;
e. violating the regulations stated in article 17.

(2) Appeal of dismissal not-honorably with reasons as stated in point (1) letters 'b' to 'e' is to be forwarded after the person concerned was given an ample opportunity to defend him/herself before the Honorable Judge Council.

(3) The establishment, structure, and the working procedure of the Honorable Judge Council as well as the procedure of self-defending is to be determined by the Head of the Supreme Court in cooperation with the Minister of Religious Affairs.

Article 20.

A Judge who is dismissed from his/her position, will not automatically be dismissed from his status as a civil servant.

Article 21.

(1) Prior to the dismissal with honor as stated in article 19 point (1), the Head, the Vice Head, and the Judges may be temporarily freed from the position by the President as the Head of State upon the proposal of the Minister of Religious Affairs based on the approval of the Head of the Supreme Court.

(2) To the proposal of the temporary dismissal as stated in point (1) above, the regulation of that stated in article 19 point (2) is also implied.

Article 22.

(1) Should there be a warrant arrest to a Judge and followed by detainment to the Judge concern, the Judge will automatically be dismissed temporarily from his position.

(2) If a Judge is put on trial in a court for the involvement in a crime as stated in article 21 point (4) of Law number 8 of the year 1981 re Criminal Code in which he is not detained, he can be dismissed temporarily from his position.

Article 23.

Further regulation on the procedure of dismissal with honor, dismissal not with honor, and the temporary dismissal with the rights of the dismissed official, will be regulated by the Government Regulation.

Article 24.

(1) The protocol status of a Judge is regulated by a Presidential Decree.
(2) Allowances and other rights for a Head, the Vice Head, and the Judge is regulated by a Presidential Decree.

Article 25.

The Head, the Vice Head, and the Judge can only be arrested with arrest warrant issued by the Supreme Attorney with the approval of the Head of the Supreme Court and the Minister of Religious Affairs except in the following cases:
a.   caught red-handed while doing a crime, or
b.   allegedly committed a crime which is threatened with capital punishment, or
c.   allegedly committed a crime which endangers the safety of the country.

Paragraph 2
The Clerk of the Court

Article 26.

(1) In each Court there must be a Clerical position chaired by a Clerk of the Court.
(2) In carrying out the duty, a Clerk of a Religious Court is assisted by a Vice Clerk Several Junior Clerks, several Substitute Clerks, and some Confiscation Officers.
(3) In carrying out the duty, a Clerk of a High Religious Court is assisted by a Vice Clerk, Several Junior Clerks, and some Substitute Clerks.

Article 27.

To be appointed a Clerk in a Religious Court, a candidate must meet the following criteria:
a.   a citizen of Indonesia;
b.   a Muslim;
c.   devout to God the Almighty;
d.   loyal to Pancasila the State Ideology and the Constitution of 1945;
e.   a graduate of minimum Bachelor degree from the Syari'ah faculty or a Bachelor of a Law faculty mastering Islamic Law.
f.   a minimum of 4 (four) years experience as a Vice Clerk or 7 (seven) years as a Junior Clerk of a Religious Court, or had a position as a Vice Clerk of a High Religious Court.

Article 28.

To be appointed a Clerk in a High Religious Court one must meet the following criteria:
a.   meets the conditions as stated in article 27 letters a, b, c, and d;
b.   graduate of Syari'ah faculty or law faculty mastering Islamic Law;

c.   a minimum experience of 4 (four) years as a Vice Clerk or 8 (eight) years as a Junior Clerk of a High Religious Court, or 4 (four) years as a Clerk of a Religious Court.

Article 29.

To be appointed a Vice Clerk of Religious Court a candidate must meet the following criteria:

a.   Conditions as stated in article 27 letters a, b, c, d, and e;

b.   having a minimum of 4 (four) years experience as a Junior Clerk or 6 (six) years as a Substitute Clerk in a Religious Court.

Article 30.

To be appointed a Vice Clerk of a High Religious Court, a candidate must meet the following criteria:

a.   conditions as stated in article 27 letters a, b, c, and d;

b.   graduate of faculty of Syari'ah or Law mastering Islamic Law;

c.   a minimum of 4 (four) years experience as a Junior Clerk or 7 (seven) years as a Substitute Clerk of a High Religious Court, or 4 (four) years as Vice Clerk of a Religious Court, or as a Clerk of a Religious Court.

Article 31.

To be appointed a Junior Clerk in a Religious Court a candidate must meet the following criteria:

a.   conditions as stated in article 27 letters a, b, c, d, and e.

b.   a minimum of 3 (three) years experience as a Substitute Clerk of a Religious Court.

Article 32.

To be appointed a Junior Clerk of a High Religious Court, a candidate must meet the following criteria:

a.   conditions as stated in article 27, letters a, b, c, d, and e.

b.   a minimum of 3 (three) years experience as a Substitute Clerk of a High Religious Court, or 4 (four) years as a Junior Clerk or 8 (eight) years as a Substitute Clerk of a Religious Court, or as a Vice Clerk of a Religious Court.

Article 33.

To be appointed a Substitute Clerk of a Religious Court, a candidate must meet the following criteria:

a.   conditions as stated in article 27, letters a, b, c, d and e;

b.   a minimum of 5 (five) years experience as a civil servant in a Religious Court.

Article 34.

To be appointed as a Substitute Clerk of a High Religious Court, a candidate must meet the following criteria:

a.   conditions as stated in article 27, letters a, b, c, d and e;

b.   a minimum of 5 (five) years experience as a Substitute Clerk of a Religious Court or 10 (ten) years as a civil servant in a High Religious Court.

Article 35.

(1) Except determined otherwise, or based on law, a Clerk cannot double the position of being 'wali', guardian, or any position having relation with the case where he takes the position as the Clerk.

(2) A Clerk cannot be at the same time a Lawyer.

(3) Other position that cannot be taken by the Clerk other than the ones mentioned in point (1) and point (2) will further be regulated by the Minister of Religious Affairs with the approval of the head of the Supreme Court.

Article 36.

The Clerk, Vice Clerk, the Junior Clerk, Substitute Clerk of a Court are to be appointed and resigned by the Minister of Religious Affairs.

Article 37.

Prior to holding the position, the Clerk, the Vice Clerk, the Junior Clerk, and the Substitute Clerk will be taken an oath in Islamic version by the Head of the Court where they are stationed.

The oath will be as follows:

"By the name of Allah, I swear, that I, for this position will not directly or indirectly, by the name or any other way give or promise anything to anybody."

"I swear, that I, to do or not to do something in this position, will never accept directly or indirectly from anyone a gift or any promise."

"I swear, that I will be loyal and defend as well as apply the Pancasila as a state foundation and ideology, the Constitution of 1945, and any law or other regulations valid in the country of Indonesia.

"I swear, that I will always carry out my duty honestly, systematically, and impartial and will behave and do my best as should be conducted by a Clerk, a Vice Clerk, and a Junior Clerk, and a Substitute Clerk of a Court who are honest and ethical in upholding law and justice."

Paragraph 3
Confiscation Officer

Article 38.

In any Religious Court there must be a position of Confiscation Officer and a Substitute Confiscation Officer.

Article 39.

(1) To be appointed a Confiscation Officer one must meet the following criteria:
a.   a citizen of Indonesia;
b.   Muslim;
c.   devout to God the Almighty;
d.   Loyal to the Pancasila and the Constitution of 1945;
e.   at least a graduate of Senior High School;
f.   a minimum of 5 (five) years experience as a Substitute Confiscate Officer.

(2) To be appointed a Substitute Confiscation Officer one must meet the following criteria: a. conditions as stated in point (1) letters a, b, c, d and e; b. a minimum of 5 (five) years experience as a civil servant in a Religious Court.

Article 40.

(1) A Confiscation Officer is appointed and resigned by the Minister of Religious Affairs based on the request of the Head of Religious Court.

(2) A Substitute Confiscation Officer is appointed and resigned by the Head of the Religious Court.

Article 41.

Prior to holding the position, the Clerk, the Vice Clerk, the Junior Clerk, and the Substitute Clerk will be taken an oath in Islamic version by the Head of the Court where they are stationed.

The oath will be as follows:

"By the name of Allah, I swear, that I, for this position will not directly or indirectly, by the name or any other way give or promise anything to anybody."

"I swear, that I, to do or not to do something in this position, will never accept directly or indirectly from anyone a gift or any promise."

"I swear, that I will be loyal and defend as well as apply the Pancasila as a state foundation and ideology, the Constitution of 1945, and any law or other regulations valid in the country of Indonesia.

"I swear, that I will always carry out my duty honestly, systematically, and impartial and will behave and do my best as should be conducted by a Confiscation Officer, and a Substitute Confiscation Officer of a Court who are honest and ethical in upholding law and justice."

Article 42.

(1) Except determined otherwise, or based on the law a Confiscation Officer cannot double his position as 'wali', guardian, or any position related to the case where he himself has a vested interest.

(2) A Confiscation officer cannot at the same time be a Lawyer.

(3) Other positions that cannot be taken by the Confiscation Officer other than those mentioned in point (1) and point (2) will further be regulated by the Minister of Religious Affairs with the approval of the Head of the Supreme Court.

Part 3
The Secretary

Article 43.

In each Court there must be a secretariate which is chaired by a Secretary and assisted by a Vice Secretary.

Article 44.

The Clerk of the Court also functions as the Secretary of the Court.

Article 45.

To be appointed a Vice Secretary of Religious Court, a candidate must meet the following criteria:
a. a citizen of Indonesia;
b. moslem;
c. devout to God the Almighty;
d. loyal to Pancasila and the Constitution of 1945;
e. graduate of at least a bachelor of Syari'ah, or law faculty mastering Islamic law or bachelor in Administration.
f. experience in court administration.

Article 46.

To be appointed a Vice Secretary of a High Religious Court, a candidate must meet the following criteria:
a. conditions as stated in article 45 letters a, b, c, d, and f;
b. graduate of Syari'ah or Law faculty and mastering Islamic law.

Article 47.

The Vice Secretary of a Court is appointed and resigned by the Minister of Religious Affairs.

Article 48.

Prior to holding his position, Vice Secretary is taken an oath in Islamic version by the Head of the Religious Court where he is stationed.

The oath will be as follows:

"By the name of Allah, I swear: that I, to be in the position of Vice Secretary will be loyal and thoroughly obedient to Pancasila and the Constitution of 1945, the Country and the Government; that I, will follow all regulations valid in this country and perform the duty that I am assigned dedicatively, conscientiously and full of responsbility; that I, will always respect the dignity of the country, the Government and the integrity of a Vice Secretary and will always prioritze the government interest over my own, individual or group; that I, will keep a secret of something which by nature or under command is to be kept in secret; that I will work honestly, orderly, meticulously, and enthusiastically for the interest of the country."

CHAPTER III
THE AUTHORITY OF THE COURT

Article 49.

(1) The Religious Court has the responsibility and is authorized to process, sentence, and settle cases on the first level between the Muslim people in the subjects of:
a. marriage;
b. inheritance, will, and 'hibah' (present), that are done based on the Islamic stipulation;
c. 'waqaf' and 'shadaqah';
(2) In the subject of a marriage as mentioned in point (1) letter a is the matters that are regulated in or based on the existing and valid marriage law.

(3) In the subject of inheritance as mentioned in point (1) letter b is in determining who are the heirs, determining the left property, determining the portion of each heir, and to execute the division of the left property concerned.

Article 50.

In the case there is a dispute concerning the property right or other civil cases in the cases as mentioned in article 49, the subject of the dispute must be first processed and sentenced by a court of a Public Judicature.

Article 51.

(1) The High Religious Court performs and authorized to preside over the case which is under the authority of the Religious Court in the level of appeal.

(2) The High Religious Court also performs and authorized to preside over the case in the first as well as final level which is in dispute among the Religious Court within its Judicial territory.

Article 52.

(1) The court may give an explanation, recommendation and advice about Islamic law to any government institution within its judicial territory if required.

(2) Beside the task and authority as stated in article 49 and article 51, the Court may be given a task and authority by or based on the law.

Article 53.

(1) The Head of the Court performs supervision and monitoring on the job and the behavior of the Judge, the Clerk, the Secretary, and the Confiscation Officer within his Judicial territory.

(2) Besides the task as stated in point (1), the Head of the High Religious Court within his Judicial territory performs the supervision on the practice of trial in the level of the Religious Court and keeps the court sessions conducted thoroughly and properly.

(3) In carrying out the supervision as stated in point (1) and point (2), the Head of the Court may give guidance, reprimand, and warning if it is deemed necessary.

(4) The supervision as stated in point (1), point (2) and point (3), may not by any means reduce the authority of the Judge in processing and presiding over a case.

CHAPTER IV
CODE OF LAW

Part One
General

Article 54.

The code of law which is valid in the Court within the Islamic Judicature is the Civil Code of Law which is valid in the court within the Public Court, except those which are specifically regulatged in this law.

Article 55.

The trial of a case begins after a request or a suit from the disputed parties accepted and the parties are called through a proper procedure of summon.

Article 56.

(1) The Court cannot refuse to preside over a case with an excuse that the case has no clear ground of law. The court is obliged to put it into a trial and preside it properly.

Article 57.

(1) Justice is done BY THE JUSTICE BASED ON GOD THE ONE AND ONLY.

(2) Every decision and sentence begins with the recitation of a sentence of BISMILLAHIRRAHMANIRRAHIM followed by BY THE JUSTICE BASED ON GOD THE ONE AND ONLY.

(3) Court session is to be carried out in simple way, fast, and at low cost.

Article 58.

(1) The Court puts a lawsuit according to legal manner without discriminating people.

(2) The Court helps the justice seekers and make the best efforts in overcoming constraints to realize a trial which is simple, fast and low cost.

Article 59.

(1) Court session is open for public, except that the law decide otherwise or the Judge with some important reasons which are noted down in the official report decides that the court should be totally or partly be done in a closed session.

(2) Not complying with the regulation as stated in point (1) can cause the whole trial with its sentence void according to law.

(3) Judge deliberation meeting is by nature a secret.

Article 60.

The decision and sentence of a Court is valid and has a firmness in law only if it is declared in an open session.

Article 61.

Upon the decision and sentence of the Religious Court the disputing parties may appeal to the higher courts except the law decide otherwise.

Article 62.

(1) Every decision and sentence of a Court, beside quoting the reasons and the basis must also quote certain articles from the related regulations or other unwritten legal sources which is used as a basis of the trial.

(2) Every decision and sentence of a Court is to be signed by the Head and the Judges who imposed the sentence and the Clerk who joined the session in which the decision and the sentence is imposed.

(3) The Official report of the Court's session is signed by the Head and the Clerk who joined the session.

Article 63.

Upon the decision and sentence of the High Religious Court an appeal can be pursued to the Supreme Court by the disputing parties.

Article 64.

The decision and sentence of the Court which is appealed to the higher level of Courts enables the court to postpone the execution of the sentence for the sake of justice, except that if in the sentence it is stated that the decision or the sentence can be excecuted right away even if there is a counter effort, or appeal to higher level courts.

Part Two
The Trial of a Dispute in Marriage
Paragraph 1
General

Article 65.

Divorce can only be done before a Court session after the Court conducts some efforts and cannot resolve both parties.

Paragraph 2
The Divorce

Article 66.

(1) A Muslim husband who intends to divorce his wife proposes the request to the Court to open a session to witness the 'iqrar talaq'.

(2) The request as stated in point (1) is proposed to the Court which the Judicial territory covers the domicile of the wife except if the wife intentionally left the place where they used to live together without the permit of the husband.

(3) In the case that the domicile of the wife is in a foreign country, the request is to be forwarded to the Court that its Judicial territory covers the place of the husband.

(4) In the case that the couple live in a foreign country, the proposal is to be forwarded to the Court that its judicial territory covers the area where their marriage was conducted or to the Religious Court of Central Jakarta.

(5) Request on taking the charge over children, children funding, the wife allowances, and the joint property may be proposed at the same time as the divorce proposal or after the 'iqrar talaq' is pronounced.

Article 67.

The request as stated in article 66 includes:
a.   the name, age, the domicile of the men (husband) and the woman (the wife);
b.   reasons that based the talaq divorce.

Article 68.

(1) An examination on the talaq divorce proposal is to be done by the Council of Judges within 30 (thirty) days at the latest after the document of the proposal is registered to the Clerk.

(2) The examination of the talaq divorce proposal is done in a close session.

Article 69.

In the trial of the talaq divorce the regulations of article 79, article 80 point (2), article 82, and article 83 are to be applied.

Article 70.

(1) When the Court comes to the conclusion that the couple can by no means be reconciled and there are ample evidences to divorce the Court will decide that the request is accepted.

(2) Upon the decision as stated in point (1) the wife may propose an appeal.

(3) After the sentence/decision obtains the law firmness, the Court will decide the day of the talaq divorce witnessing, by inviting the husband and wife or their representatives to attend the session.

(4) In the trial the husband or his representative who is given the mandate in an authentic note to utter the iqrar talaq will declare the iqrar talaq witnessed by the wife or her representative.

(5) In case that the wife, who has been legally and properly invited, does not come nor send the representative, the husband or his representative may read the iqrar talaq without being attended by the wife or her representative.

(6) If the husband, within the tolerated period of 6 (six) months since the determination of the day of witnessing of the iqrar talaq, does not come by himself or send his representative even though there is a valid or proper summon the determination of the witnessing day is void and the request talaq proposal cannot be retried based on the same reason.

Article 71.

(1) The Clerk of the Court will take notes on everything happens during the session of the talaq divorce.

(2) The Judge issue a sentence containing that the marriage is broken off from the time the iqrar talaq is pronounced and for this decision/sentence there will be no appeal.

Article 72.

For the decision/sentence as stated in article 71 the regulations in article 84 point (1), point (2), point (3), and point (4), and article 85 are to be applied.

Paragraph 3
Claimed Divorce

Article 73.

(1) Claim of a divorce is propsed by the wife or her mandatory to the Court which the Judicial territory covers the area of the domicile of the wife, provided that the husband left the area place of their living together without the permission of the wife.

(2) In the case that the wife lives in a foreign country, the claim of divorce is proposed to the Court which its judicial territory covers the area of the husband's domicile.

(3) In the case that the husband and the wife both live in a foreign country, the claim is to be proposed to the Court that its judicial territory covers the area where the marriage was conducted or to the Religious Court of Central Jakarta.

Article 74.

If the claim of divorced is based on the fact that either party is sentenced to jail, to get the divorce decision/sentence, as an evidence the wife may just submit the copy of the sentence of the Court that tried the husband together with covering letter which stated that the sentence has obtained the fixed law firmness.

Article 75.

If the claim of divorce is based on the reason that the husband is physically invalid or other invalidity that cause him not able to perform his task as a husband, the Judge can order the husband to check himself to a doctor.

Article 76.

(1) If the claim of divorce is based on the reason of 'syiqaq', to get a decision/sentence there must be a hearing session of the witnesses who come from the family or people who close to the husband and the wife.

(2) The court after hearing the explanation of the witnesses on the character of the dispute may appoint one or more persons from both families or outsiders to become the 'hakam' (Jury).

Article 77.

Within the period in which the claim divorce is occurring, based on the request of the wife or the husband or in consideration of the danger that might happen, the Court may allow that the husband and the wife do not live together at the same house.

Article 78.

Within the period in which the claim divorce is occurring, based on the request of the wife, the Court may:
a.   decide the allowance to be paid by the husband;
b.   decide the necessities needed for taking care of the children and their education;
c.   decide the necessities needed for taking care of their joint property or the property of the husband or the property of the wife.

Article 79.

The claim of divorce voids if the husband or the wife die before the sentence of the court.

Article 80.

(1) The examination of the claim of divorce is done by the Council of Judges within 30 (thirty) days at the latest after the document of claim is registered at the Clerk Office.

(2) The session of the claim of divorce is done in a closed session.

Article 81.

(1) The Court Sentence over the claim of divorce is to be read in a court session which is open for public.

(2) A divorce occurs with all legal effects commented from the day it obtained a fix legal firmness.

Article 82.

(1) On the first day of the session of the claim of divorce the Judge will try to resolve both parties.

(2) In the mentioned resolving session, both the husband and the wife must come by themselves except when either party lives in a foreign country and cannot come in person, he may appoint somebody who is specially assigned to represent him on this matter.

(3) If both parties live in a foreign country, the wife must come in person during the resolving day.

(4) Before the sentence is pronounced, the act of resolving can be carried out in every session of the courts.

Article 83.

Should there be a settlement of the problem, there can never be a new claim based on the existing reason which have been known by the husband before the settlement happened.

Article 84.

(1) The Clerk of the Court or other appointed official of the Court is obliged within at least 30 (thirty) days to send one copy of the duplicate of the Court sentence that has obtained a fix legal firmness, without a duty stamp to the Pegawai Pencatat Nikah (Marriage Registrar Official) whose Judicial territory covers the domicile of the mentioned couple, in order to register the divorce in a list that specially prepared for the purpose.

(2) If the divorce is done in a region different from the one of the Marriage Registrar Official where the marriage was conducted one copy duplicate of sentence as mentioned in point (1) which has obtained a fixed legal firmness without duty stamp is sent to the Marriage Registrar Official of the place where the marriage was conducted by whom it is then written a note on the sideline of the marriage note.

(3) If the marriage was conducted in a foreign country one copy of the duplicate as mentioned in point (1) is sent to the Marriage Registrar Official where the marriage was registered in Indonesia.

(4) The Clerk is obliged to issue a divorce act as a proof evidence of divorce to both parties within at least 7 days commencing from the day the sentence that has obtained a fixed legal firmness notified to the concerning parties.

Article 85.

Dereliction in sending the copy of the sentence as stated in article 84, will be the responsible of the Clerk of the appointed Court official, if such a negligence causing lost to the ex-husband or wife or both.

Article 86.

(1) Claims on the control over children, allowance for the children, allowance for the wife, and the joint property of the husband and wife may be proposed together with the claim of divorce or after the sentence of divorce obtained the fixed legal firmness.

(2) Should there be a claim of a third party, the Court may postpone about the joint property issue until there is a sentence of a Court within the Jurisdiction of the Public Court concerning the matter.

Paragraph 4
Divorce Due To Reason of Adultery

Article 87.

(1) If a request or a claim of divorce is proposed due to either of the party committed adultery, while the one who claims fails to provide evidence and the one who is claimed refuse the accusation and the Judge believes that the claim is not at all un-founded and the proved evidence is impossible to obtain either from the one who claims or the one who is claimed, the Judge based on his authority may request the one who claims to pronounce an oath.

(2) The one who is claimed is also to be given a chance to firm the refusal on the same way.

Article 88.

(1) If the oath as stated in article 87 point (1) is done by the husband, the administration can be done by way of "li'an".

(2) If the oath as stated in article 87 point (1) is done by the wife, the administration can be done by the existing code of law.

Part Three
The Cost of the Court Session

Article 89.

(1) The cost of the court session is liable to the one who proposes the claim.

(2) The cost of the decision or the Court sentence which are not final decision will be taken into account at the final decision.

Article 90.

(1) The cost of the court session as stated in article 89 includes:
a. the secretarial cost and the duty stamps needed for the case;
b. the cost for the witnesses, an expert team, translator, and the oath taking needed for the case;
c. the cost that needed to do the spot investigation and other activities needed for the case;
d. the cost for inviting, acknowledging, and so on based on the instruction of the Court that trying the case.

(2) The amount of the cost is to be regulated by the Minister of Religious Affairs with the approval of the Supreme Court.

Article 91.

(1) The amount of the cost for the case as stated in article 90 must be written in the document of the decision or the Court sentence.

(2) The amount of the cost which is charged by Court to either party in the case which is to be paid to the opponent in this matter must also be included in the document of the decision or the Court sentence.

CHAPTER V
OTHER REGULATIONS

Article 92.

The Head of the Court regulates the job division of the Judges.

Article 93.

The Head of the Court hands all the documents or other letters related to the case that is proposed to the Court to the Council of Judges to process.

Article 94.

The Head of the Court decides the turn of the case in numerical order. However, if there is a certain case due to its impact to the public interest must be given a priority he will treat the matter in a specific order.

Article 95.

The Head of the Court is obliged to observe the execution of the sentence or the decision of the Court that has obtained a fixed legal firmness.

Article 96.

The Clerk of the Court is obliged to perform the administration of the case and regulates the duty of the Vice Clerk, the Junior Clerk and the Substitute Clerk.

Article 97.

The Clerk, the Vice Clerk, the Junior Clerk, and the Substitute Clerk assist the Judge by means of attending and making the minutes of the Court session.

Article 98.

The Clerk performs the duty of executing the decision or the sentence of the Court.

Article 99.

(1) The Clerk is obliged to make a list of all cases accepted by the Secretariat of the Clerk.

(2) In providing the list as stated in point (1), each case is given numerical order and added with the short note about the case.

Article 100.

The Clerk makes a duplicate copy of the decision and the sentence of the Court in accordance with the existing and valid law.

Article 101.

(1) The Clerk is responsible for the administration of the case, the sentence or the decision, the document, the acts, registration book the cost of the case, the money from the third party that should be kept, valuable or commercial letters, evidences, and other letters that kept in the secretariat.

(2) All lists, notes, stories, official reports, and all the documents of the case cannot be taken out of the Secretariat, except with the permission of the head of the Court based on the existing regulation.

(3) The procedure of issuing original letters, copies or duplicate of the Court decision or sentences, stories, official reports, acts, and other letters are to be regulated by the Supreme Court.

Article 102.

The task and responsibility as well as the working procedure of the Clerical job of a Court are to be regulated further by the Supreme Court.

Article 103.

(1) The Confiscation Officer performs the duties as follows:

a. to execute any instruction from the chairman of the session;
b. to address the announcements, reprimands, and informing the decision or sentence of the Court in a way that has been regulated by law;
c. to confiscate property under the command of the Head of the Court;
d. to provide an official report of the confiscation and send the duplicate/copy to the concerning parties.

(2) The Confiscation Officer is authorized to conduct his job within the judicial territory of the Court where he is assigned to work.

Article 104.

Further regulation of the job description of the Confiscation Officer will be regulated by the Supreme Court.

Article 105.

(1) The Secretary of the Court organizes/carries out the general administration of the Court.

(2) The Tasks and responsibilities, the organizational structure, and the working procedure of the Secretariat will further be regulated by the Minister of Religious Affairs.

CHAPTER VI
TRANSITIONAL REGULATION

Article 106.

By the time this Law is in effect:

(1) any existing Religious Judicature Institution is officially declared as the Religious Judicature Institution of this Law;

(2) any existing working regulation concerning the Religious Judicature is declared as valid as long as the new stipulations based on this Law is not yet issued and that the existing regulations are not in contradictory with this Law.

CHAPTER VII
THE CONCLUDING PROVISIONS

Article 107.

By the time this Law is in effect:

a. the regulation on the Religious Judicature in Jawa and Madura (Staatsblad of the year 1882 Number 152 and Staatsblad of the year 1937 Number 116 and number 610);

b. the Regulation on the Great Qodi's Deliberation for the part of South and East Kalimantan Regency (Staatsblad of the year 1937 Number 638 and number 639);

c. the Government Regulation Number 45 of the year 1957 re the establishment of the Religious Judicature/Syari'ah Court outside Jawa and Madura (State Gazetten of the year 1957 Number 99), and

d. regulations as stated in article 63 point (2) Law number 1 of the year 1974 re Marriage (State Declaration of the year 1974 Number 1, Additional State Gazetten number 3019), is declared as void.

(2) Regulations as stated in article 236a the renewed Reglemen Indonesia (RIB), Staatsblad of the year 1941 Number 44, re the request for help in dividing the non-disputed left property within the Muslim community which is done based on the Islamic Law is to be processed by the Religious Court.

Article 108.

This Law shall come in to effect as of the date of promulgation. To let every citizen know, it is ordered to place this Law in the State Gazette of the Republic of Indonesia.

To be promulgated in Jakarta
on 29 December 1989

The President of
The Republic of Indonesia

SOEHARTO

Appendix III

THE PRESIDENTIAL INSTRUCTION OF THE REPUBLIC OF INDONESIA NUMBER 1 OF THE YEAR 1991 ON THE COMPILATION OF ISLAMIC LAWS

BOOK I
MARRIAGE LAW

CHAPTER I
GENERAL CONDITIONS

Article 1.

The Definitions

a. *Peminangan* (proposal) is an effort toward a realization of a marriage between a man and a woman.

b. *Wali hakim* is a person who gives the marriage appointed by the Minister of Religious Affairs or other official appointed by him, who has the right and authorized to act as a *wali nikah*;

c. *Akad Nikah* is a series of *ijab* (words of delivery) pronounced by the *wali* and *kabul* (words of acceptance) pronounced by the groom or his representative on the presence of two witnesses;

d. *Mahar* is a gift from the groom to the bride in the form of goods, money or service which do not contradict to Islamic law;

e. *Taklik-talak* is a kind of promise read by the groom after an aqad nikah and printed in the Marriage Document. It is a kind of promise guaranteed to a certain condition that might happen in the future;

Sources: *The Compilation of Islamic Laws in Indonesia*, (1996/1997). Project for Religious Law Counseling Development Directorate for Religious Courts, the Directorate General for Development of Islamic Institutions. Jakarta: Department of Religious Affairs of Republic of Indonesia.

f.   Properties in the marriage or *syirkah* are possessions which are obtained either individually or by both spouse during the marriage life and hence it is called as joint possessions no matter whose name the registration is on behalf;

g.   Children care or *hadhonah* are activities of nursing, looking after, educating offspring until the age of adolescence or able to self sustain;

h.   *Perwalian* is a mandate or an authority given to a certain person to exercise a legal action as a representative for the interest of and on behalf of an orphan or alive parents who are not capable to perform a legal action;

i.   *Khuluk* is a divorce from the demand of the wife side by submitting ransom or *iwadl* to and agreed by the husband;

j.   *Mut'ah* is a gift from an ex-husband for a wife who has been divorced in a form of goods or money, etc.

CHAPTER II
PRINCIPLES OF MARRIAGE

Article 2.

Marriage in Islamic law is a *nikah,* namely the very strong contract (aqad) or *miitsaaqoon gholiidhan* to obey Allah's command and to do it means an *ibadah* (worship).

Article 3.

Marriage has a goal in realizing A family life which is *sakinah* (serenity) mawaddah (prosperous) and *rahmah* (blessed).

Article 4.

Marriage is legal when it is done based on the Islamic Law under Article 2 Verse 1 Law no. 1 of 1974 re Marriage.

Article 5.

(1) To make a marriage orderly, in Islamic society every marriage must be registered.

(2) Registration of marriage as stated in point (1), is done by the Pegawai Pencatat Nikah (Marriage Registrar Official) as it is regulated in Law No. 22 of the year 1946 jo Law no. 32 of the year 1954.

Article 6.

(1) To meet the requirement in article 5 every marriage should be carried out in the presence or under supervision of the 'Marriage Registrar Official'.

(2) Marriage done without the presence or not supervised by the official is considered invalid.

Article 7.

(1) A marriage can only be proved by an existence of 'marriage document' made by the *Pegawai Pencatat Nikah.*

(2) In a case where a marriage cannot be proved by marriage document, the '*itsbat of the nikah*' (a substitute document of marriage) can be claimed to the *Pengadilan Agama* (Islamic Court).

(3) The 'Itsbat Nikah' which can be claimed to the Islamic Court is restricted to the case of;

a.   a marital status for the purpose of divorce;
b.   lost of the Marriage Document;
c.   an ambiguity upon the validation of one of the conditions in the marriage;
d.   a marriage done before the issuance of Law no. 1 of 1994 and;
e.   a marriage done by those who are not in problem according to Law No. 1 of 1994.

(4) Those who have the right to claim the 'Itsbat Nikah' are among others; husband or wife, their offspring, the 'wali nikah' and other parties who have the interest in the marriage concerned.

Article 8.

The breakdown of a marriage other than of death reason, can only be proved by a divorce document issued by the Islamic Court in the form of divorce verdict, ikrar talak (statement of divorce from a husband), khuluk, and the verdict of the taklik talak.

Article 9.

(1) If evidence as mentioned in article 8 is not available due to the loss or other reasons, a copy can be obtained from the Islamic Court.

(2) In the case that an evidence as mentioned in point (1) is not available, a request for it can be put forward to the Islamic Court.

Article 10.

Reconciliation can only be proved by a quotation of the Reconciliation Registration Book issued by the 'Marriage Registrar Official'.

CHAPTER III
THE PROPOSAL

Article 11.

A Proposal can be directly done by a person who intends to have a spouse, or by a trustworthy mediator.

Article 12.

(1) Proposal can be forwarded to a single woman/bachelor or to a widow who has completed her 'iddah' (a period of 40 days absence of her husband).

(2) A woman who has been divorced and still in the period of 'iddah raji'ah', is absolutely forbidden to be proposed.

(3) A woman is not allowed to be proposed while she is still under a proposal of another man and the woman has not uttered her decision on the first man's proposal.

(4) A proposal of a man is broken off due to a statement of breaking off from the man, or the man with no reason avoids the proposed woman.

Article 13.

(1) A proposal has no consequences in law. Each party has the rights to break off the proposal.

(2) A freedom to break off a proposal ought to be done in a proper way in accordance with the Islamic teaching and the local tradition/norms, so that a mutual respect and social harmony can be maintained.

CHAPTER IV
CONDITIONS AND REQUIREMENTS OF MARRIAGE

Part One
Conditions

Article 14.

To conduct a marriage there must be:
a.   A bride
b.   A groom
c.   'the wali nikah'
d.   2 (two) witnesses and
e.   Ijab and Kabul (a delivery and acceptance)

Part Two
The Bride and The Groom

Article 15.

(1) For the sake of the prosperity of a family a household, a marriage can only be done by the bride and the groom who have come to the age as determined in Article 7 of Law No. 1, 1974 i.e. the groom is not less than 19 years old and the bride is not less than 16 years of age.

(2) A groom who is under 21 years of age should ask a permit as it is regulated in article 6 point (2), (3), (4) and (5) Law No. 1, 1974.

Article 16.

(1) A Marriage is based on the agreement of both parties (the bride and the groom).

(2) Agreement of the bride can be manifested in a distinct and clear statement either written, orally or by gestures; or it can also be in silence as far as there is no clear refusal.

Article 17.

(1) Before the wedding ceremony the Marriage Registrar Official is to ask the approval of both the bride and the groom in the presence of two witnesses.

(2) In a case that one party has an objection, the marriage cannot be proceeded.

(3) For the deaf or mute bride and groom an approval can be expressed in eligible gestures or writing.

Article 18.

Both the bride and the groom are not in constraints as regulated in Chapter VI.

Part Three
The 'Wali Nikah'

Article 19.

The 'Wali Nikah' in a marriage is a condition to be fulfilled by the bride who will act to give the marriage.

Article 20.

(1) The one who perform the function as the Wali Nikah is a man who is qualified according to Islamic Law, namely a Moslem, mentally healthy and grown up.

(2) The Wali Nikah can be;

a. *Wali Nasab* (the one who has a blood relationship with the bride)

b. *Wali Hakim* (person other than the above qualification).

Article 21.

(1) The Wali Nasab can be classified into four classes which are orderly arranged according to the status. One class is over the other depends on how close is his relationship with the bride;

Firstly   :   a group of vertical family line, namely; father, grandfather from father's side, etc.

Secondly   :   a group of blood brothers, or half brothers from the line of the father and their male offspring.

Thirdly   :   a group of uncles, i.e. blood brothers from father, or half brothers from father's line and their male offspring.

Fourth   :   blood brothers of grandfather and his half brothers from his father's line and their male offspring.

(2) If within one group there are more than one persons who deserve the right to be the 'wali', the priority should be given to the one whose relationship in the family tree is the closest to the bride.

(3) Blood brothers deserve the right to be the 'wali nikah' more than half brothers from father.

(4) If within one group there are persons who are of the same level of degree in relationship either blood brothers or half brothers, priorities should be given to the elderly one or the one who is more qualified in the requirement of being the wali.

Article 22.

Should the most deserve 'wali nikah' is not qualified to become the 'wali' or because he is deaf or mute or aging, the right to be the 'wali' descend to the one whose turn is next to him.

Article 23.

(1) The 'Wali Hakim' can only takes over the position of the 'wali nikah' if the 'wali nasab' is not available or it is impossible to present him or whose address is unknown or disappeared or "*adlal*" or reluctant.

(2) In the case of the 'wali adlal' or reluctant the 'wali hakim' can only perform his task as the 'wali-hakim' upon the verdict of the Islamic Court concerning the matter.

Part Four
The Witness of the Nikah

Article 24.

(1) Witness in a marriage is a condition to fulfil in of the 'Aqad Nikah'

(2) A marriage is to be witnessed by at least two witnesses

Article 25.

Those who deserve to be the witnesses in the 'Aqad Nikah' are Moslems, impartial, mature, mentally healthy, not deaf or mute.

Article 26.

The witness must be in the place of the ceremony and directly witness the 'aqad nikah' and put their signatures on the marriage document at the time and the place where the 'aqad nikah' happens.

Part Five
The 'Aqad Nikah'

Article 27.

The 'Ijab and Kabul' between the 'wali' and the groom must be distinct, orderly and uninterrupted, nor a pause.

Article 28.

'Aqad Nikah' can be performed personally by the Wali Nikah, or the Wali Nikah may delegate to other personnel.

Article 29.

(1) The one who deserves to utter the 'kabul' (acceptance) is the groom in person.

(2) In certain cases the utterance of the 'kabul' can be represented by other person provided that the groom gives a mandate which stated very clearly that the person perform the task merely for the groom.

(3) In the case that the bride or 'wali' has the objection upon the representation of the 'kabul' by the groom the marriage cannot be proceeded.

CHAPTER V
THE MAHAR (THE GIVING)

Article 30.

A groom must pay a 'mahar' to the bride in which the amount, the form, and the kind is to be agreed by both parties.

Article 31.

The agreement of the 'mahar' is to be based on the simplicity and availability which is recommended in the teaching of Islam.

Article 32.

'Mahar' is submitted directly to the bride and from then on it becomes her personal possession.

Article 33.

(1) The delivery/submission of the 'mahar' is not to be delayed.

(2) Upon the agreement of the bride, the delivery of the 'mahar' can be delayed wholly or partly. The delayed 'mahar' is a debt of the groom.

Article 34.

(1) An obligation of 'mahar' delivery is not a condition of a marriage.

(2) An absence of mentioning the type and the amount of the 'mahar' during the Aqad Nikah does not have the effect of the failure of a marriage. Neither does in the case of the delay of the mahar invalidates the marriage.

Article 35.

(1) A husband who divorces the wife before sexual intercourse is deemed to pay half price of the agreed mahar.

(2) If a husband dies before the first sexual intercourse the whole mahar becomes the full possession of his wife.

(3) If a divorce happens before the first sexual intercourse yet the amount has not been decided, the husband is to pay 'mahar mitsil'.

Article 36.

If the 'mahar' is lost before it is submitted, it can be substituted by other kinds of goods in which the type and the form is similar or by other things having the same values or by money of the same amount as the price of the lost 'mahar'.

Article 37.

Should there be a dispute upon the type and the value of the agreed 'mahar', it can be settled through the Islamic Court.

Article 38.

(1) If the submitted 'mahar' is defected or insufficient, but the bride insist on accepting it without any condition, the submission of the 'mahar' is considered as valid.

(2) If the bride refuse the 'mahar' due to the defect, the groom should change it with the not defective one. As long as the substitute has not been submitted, the 'mahar' is considered as a debt.

CHAPTER VI
PROHIBITION IN MARRIAGE

Article 39.

A man is prohibited to marry a woman due to the followings:
1. A blood family relationship.
    a.   with a woman who gives a birth to him or her mother or her offspring;
    b.   with a woman who is from the same father or the same mother;
    c.   with a niece (brother's or sister's daughter)
2. In-law families.
    a.   with the wife's mother or ex-wife's mother;
    b.   with a woman who used to be his father's wife;
    c.   a daughter from his wife or ex-wife, provided that his ex wife was divorced before sexual intercourse;
    d.   a woman who used to be his offspring's/children's wife.
3. Breast-fed relationship.
    a.   with a woman who used to breast feed him and all her up-line offspring;
    b.   with a fellow breast-fed and all her down-line offspring;
    c.   a sister of a fellow breast-fed and her nieces;
    d.   an aunt of the fellow breast-fed and her great aunt;
    e.   a woman that used to be breast-fed by his wife and all her offspring.

Article 40.

A Moslem man is prohibited to marry a woman in the following situations:
a.   the woman is still married with another man;
b.   a woman who is still in the period of 'iddah' with another man;
c.   a non-moslem woman.

Article 41.

(1) A man is prohibited to marry a woman who has a blood relationship or breastfed with his wife:
a.   blood relationship of the same father or the same mother and their offspring;
b.   her aunt or her niece.

(2) Prohibition as mentioned in point (1) is valid though the wives have been divorced by 'talak raj'i' but still in the period of 'iddah'.

Article 42.

A man is prohibited to marry a woman while he still has four wives, and all four of them are still legally married or still in the period of 'iddah upon the talak raj'i', or one of them is still in the status of married while the other is still in the period of 'iddah upon the talak raj'i'.

Article 43.

(1) A man is prohibited to marry a woman in the following conditions:

a. he has divorced her with three times 'talaks';

b. his ex-wife who has been 'given the 'li'an'.

(2) The prohibition as noted in point (1) letter 'a' void, if the mentioned ex-wife had married other man and then divorced after sexual intercourse and completed her 'iddah' period.

Article 44.

A moslem woman is prohibited to marry a non-moslem man.

CHAPTER VII
AGREEMENT IN MARRIAGE

Article 45.

Both the bride and the groom have the right to establish an agreement in the form of:

1. 'Taklik talak' (reasoning for divorce)

2. Other agreement not contradicting to Islamic teachings.

Article 46.

(1) The content of the 'TAKLIK TALAK' is not to contradict with Islamic Laws.

(2) If a certain situation as mentioned in the 'taklik talak' comes to exist, the talak (divorce) will not automatically come to effect. To conform the 'talak' a wife ought to claim it to an Islamic court.

(3) The agreement of 'taklik talak' is not an obligatory in a marriage, however, once a 'taklik talak' is agreed it cannot be withdrawn.

Article 47.

(1) During or before the wedding both the bride and the groom may fix a written agreement which is validated by the Marriage Registrar Official upon the status of ownership of wealth during the marriage life.

(2) The agreement as in point (1) may comprise the mixing of personal properties and the separation of the individual income/earning so long as it does not contradict to Islamic Laws.

(3) Beside the above regulations, point (1) and (2) there is a possibility that the agreement allows an authorization of each party to agree on mortgage guaranteed for the private possession or joint possession or 'syirkah'.

Article 48.

(1) Should there be an agreement upon the separation of the 'syirkah' possession, it does not by any means putting aside the obligation of a husband to fulfill the living allowance for the household.

(2) If the agreement made does not meet the requirement as in point (1) it is considered that there is a separation of the joint possession and the husband is responsible to fulfill the household needs.

Article 49.

(1) The mixing of private possession may comprise any types of wealth, either their property prior to the marriage or the property each individual obtains during the marriage life.

(2) With no intention of reducing the agreement as in point (1) a kind of agreement where the mixing of private property can be limited to possession brought before the marriage, thus the mixing does not cover the personal income during the marriage life or vice versa.

Article 50.

(1) A marriage agreement concerning the property binds all parties as well as the third party start from the day of the wedding in front of the Marriage Registrar official.

(2) An agreement concerning the property can be broken off by the agreement of both parties and to be reported officially to the office where the marriage is registered.

(3) From the day of the withdrawal the agreement is effective to the married couple, however for the third party the withdrawal become effective after the married couple announced publicly through the local mass media.

(4) If within the period of 6 (six) months no announcement is made by the married couple, the withdrawal of the agreement is void and no commitment of the third party.

(5) The withdrawal concerning the property should not inflict a loss which was formerly made with the third party.

Article 51.

The breech of the agreement descent the right of the wife to ask the cancellation of the *nikah* or make use of it to sue the divorce to the Islamic Court.

Article 52.

At the time a man is having a wedding with the second, the third or the fourth wife, agreement may be made upon the residential, the turning and the household allowances for the wife he is going to marry.

CHAPTER VIII
MARRIAGE DURING THE PREGNANCY

Article 53.

(1) A woman who is pregnant from the premarital sex, may legalize her marriage with a man who caused her so.

(2) The marriage with the pregnant woman as stated in point (1) can be immediately carried out without waiting for the baby to come.

(3) Organizing a marriage for a pregnant woman means that there will not need to be re-wedding ceremony after the child is born.

Article 54.

(1) Someone who is in the 'ihram' condition he/she is not allowed to carry out a wedding neither can be a 'wali nikah'.

(2) A marriage of someone who is in the 'ihram' condition or the 'wali nikah' who is in 'ihram' condition is not valid.

CHAPTER IX
THE POLYGAMY

Article 55.

(1) Polygamy is limited up to four wives at the same time.

(2) The main requirement of a man to marry more than one women is the ability to be justice to his wives and children.

(3) If the person concern is not able to fulfill the requirements as in point (2) polygamy is strictly forbidden for him.

Article 56.

(1) A man who wants to marry more than one woman must ask a permission to an Islamic Court.

(2) A proposal of a permit as stated in point (1) is to follow the procedure as regulated in Chapter VIII Government Regulation No. 9 of the year 1975.

(3) A marriage with the second, the third and the fourth wife without a permit from the Islamic Court is considered as illegal.

Article 57.

The Islamic Court can only issue a permit to someone to do the polygamy in the following cases:
a.   the wife cannot perform her duty/function as a wife,
b.   the wife suffers from the physical malfunction or any incurable illness.
c.   the wife fails to do the reproduction.

Article 58.

(1) In addition to the main requirement as stated in article 55 point (2), in order to get a permit from the Islamic Court, other requirements are also stated in article 5 Law No. 1 of the year of 1974, namely:

a.   there is an approval of the wife;

b.   there is an assurance of the husband that he is really capable of providing allowances for the wives and their children.

(2) Without decreasing the degree of the requirement in article 41 point 'b', the government regulation No. 9 of the year 1975, the approval of the wife or wives can be in the form of written statements, nevertheless the written statements should be confirmed with oral statements of the wives in an Islamic Court session.

(3) The approval as stated in point (1) letter 'a' is not a necessity for a husband in the case that the approval seem to be likely improbable from the wife or wives and cannot be a party in the agreement or the absence of the news of the wife or wives for at least 2 years or other consideration that needs to be taken by the Judge.

Article 59.

In the case that a wife is reluctant to give a permit, and the proposal to have a polygamy based on the reason regulated in article 55 point (2) and 57, an Islamic Law may issue a permit after scrutinizing and hearing the wife concerned in an Islamic Court session, and for this verdict a wife or a husband may propose an appeal to higher level of Islamic Court.

CHAPTER X
CANCELLATION OF A MARRIAGE

Article 60.

(1) Prevention of a marriage is aimed at preventing a marriage which is prohibited by Islamic Law and Regulation concerning Law.

(2) Prevention of a marriage can be applied in the case that a bride or the groom does not meet the qualification of a marriage as allowed in accordance with the Islamic Law or regulation concerning Law.

Article 61.

Being in different belief is not a legal reason to prevent a marriage, except if the difference is on the religion or 'ikhtilaafu al dien'.

Article 62.

(1) The ones who have the rights to prevent a marriage are those who are in vertical line in the family tree, brothers and sisters, the wali nikah and the 'wali pengampu' (a person who acts as the wali of the bride) from either party of the couple.

(2) A father who never fulfills his obligations to the family does not loss his right to prevent a marriage that will be done by another 'wali'.

Article 63.

Prevention of a marriage can be exercise by a husband or a wife who is still married to the husband or the wife who is getting married.

Article 64.

The official who is appointed to supervise the marriage is obliged to cancel the marriage should the conditions and requirements are not fulfilled.

Article 65.

(1) Cancellation of a marriage can be requested to an Islamic Court within the jurisdiction territory where the marriage will be conducted by notifying the Marriage Registrar Official.

(2) The bride and the groom ought to be notified on the cancellation of the marriage, as pointed out in point (1) by the Marriage Registrar Official.

Article 66.

A marriage cannot proceed unless the cancellation is withdrawn.

Article 67.

The cancellation of a marriage can be invalidated by the withdrawal of the cancellation request to the Islamic Court by the one who requests or by the verdict of the Islamic Court.

Article 68.

A Marriage Registrar Official is not allowed to conduct or assist a marriage if he knows that there is a violation of conditions of Article 7 point (1), Article 8, Article 9, Article 10 or Article 12, Law No. 1 of the year 1974 though there is no cancellation request.

Article 69.

(1) If the Marriage Registrar Official considers that there is a prohibition on the marriage according to the conditions in Law No. 1 of 1974 he will refuse to conduct the marriage.

(2) In the case of refusal, the request of either party will be replied in written upon the refusal provided with the reasons by the Marriage Registrar Official.

(3) Both parties of the couple whose marriage is denied/turned down may appeal to the Islamic Court within the jurisprudence of the Marriage Registrar Official, by submitting the letter of refusal.

(4) The Islamic Court will examine the case in a brief session and announce the verdict whether or not the marriage may proceed.

(5) The verdict is ineffective if the constraints affecting the refusal are eliminated and the both parties may renew the marriage proposal.

CHAPTER XI
THE ANNULMENT OF A MARRIAGE

Article 70.

Marriage is invalid in the case that:

a. a husband conducting a marriage while he has no right to do the aqad nikah because he still has four wives even though one of the wives is still in the period of 'iddah talak raj'i';
b. a husband to marry his ex wife who has been 'given the 'li'an'.
c. a husband to marry his wife who has been divorce with three times 'talaks', provided that she married to another man and divorced after sexual intercourse with that man and she has completed her period of 'iddah';
d. a marriage happens between members of the same family or having blood relationship, in-law family, a fellow breast-fed up to a certain degree which forbids the marriage according to Article 8 of the Law No. 1 of 1974, namely:
   1. blood family relationship in vertical line of family tree either up or down.
   2. blood family relationship in horizontal line of family tree, i.e. brother or sister, with a brother/sister of parents and brothers/sisters of grand parents.
   3. in-law family such as; parents in law, step children, children-in-law, step mother or step father.
   4. breast fed relationship, i.e. woman who breast fed him, children of the same breast fed woman, aunt or uncle of the same breast fed.
e. the woman who is the blood sister of his wife or aunt or niece of his wife or wives.

Article 71.

A marriage can be invalidated if:

a. a husband is doing the polygamy without the permission of the Islamic Court;
b. the woman he married is still in the status of married with another man who is 'mafqud'
c. the woman he married is still in the period of 'iddah' from her previous husband;
d. the marriage is done by the couple who are under the age as regulated in Article 7 Law No. 1 of 1974;
e. the marriage is done without a 'wali' or the illegal 'wali';
f. the marriage is done under pressure.

Article 72.

(1) A husband or a wife may appeal for the cancellation of the marriage if the marriage is done under the threat which is against the law.

(2) A husband or a wife may appeal for the cancellation of the marriage if there is a deceit or misjudgment upon the husband or the wife.

(3) If the threat is gone, or the one who misjudges realizes the fact within 6 months and they still in the marriage, while they do not exercise their rights to appeal for the cancellation, their rights are void.

Article 73.

Those who deserve to request for the marriage cancellation are:

a. Members of the family tree in vertical line either upward or downward from the husband or the wife;
b. the husband or the wife;
c. The official who is authorized to supervise the wedding/marriage under the law;
d. The concerned parties who notice the defect in the conditions or requirements in marriage according to Islamic law and the Regulations on law as mention in article 67.

Article 74.

(1) The request for marriage cancellation can be forwarded to the Islamic Court where the marriage couple live or the place where the marriage is going to be done.

(2) The annulment of a marriage becomes effective on the date when the verdict of the Islamic Law is sanctioned and valid from the date of the marriage.

Article 75.

The decision of the marriage cancellation does not effect back dated on:

a. broken off marriage due to the fact that one of the couple is converted to other religion;
b. the offspring born from the marriage.
c. the third party so long as they have the rights with good intention, before the verdict of the marriage cancellation is to be sanctioned.

Article 76.

The marriage cancellation shall not have any effect on the legal status between the children and the parents.

CHAPTER XII
THE RIGHTS AND RESPONSIBILITIES OF
HUSBAND AND WIFE

Part One
General

Article 77.

(1) Husband and wife bear the noble responsibility to maintain the household which is 'sakinah, mawaddah and rahmah', which serves to be the basis of the social structure.

(2) Between the husband and wife are to love each other, mutually respect, loyal and help each other materially and spiritually.

(3) Husband and wife bear the responsibility of looking after their children, i.e. physically, spiritually mentally/intelligence and their religion education.

(4) Husband and wife are to uphold their integrity.

(5) In the case that the husband or the wife neglects the responsibility each party may sue to the Islamic Court.

Article 78.

(1) Husband and wife should have a permanent residence.

(2) The residence as mentioned at point (1) is determined by the couple concerned.

Part Two
Position of Husband and Wife

Article 79.

(1) Husband is the head of the family and wife is the housewife.

(2) The right and status of the wife is equal to the right and status of the husband in the family affairs and so is their role in the community.

(3) Both party have the rights to exercise legal acts.

Part Three
The Responsibility of the Husband

Article 80.

(1) A husband is the leader to his wife and the whole family, nevertheless the important matters about family affairs are to be decided together.

(2) A husband must patronize the wife and fulfill the whole needs of the household according to his capability.

(3) A husband must educate his wife on the religion and give her chances to get knowledge and skills that enables her to dedicate to the religion, country and the nation.

(4) Within his capability in earning, the husband are obliged to provide:

a.   basic needs, 'kiswah' and shelter for the wife;

b.   household needs, health care and maintenance for wife and children;

c.   education funds for the children.

(5) The obligation of a husband to his wife as stated in point (4) letters 'a' and 'b' is effective upon the completeness of 'tamkin' from the wife.

(6) A wife may relieve the husband from the obligation stated in point (4) letters 'a' and 'b'.

(7) The obligation of the husband as stated in point (5) void in the condition that the wife is 'nusyuz'.

Part Four
Residential

Article 81.

(1) A husband is obliged to provide shelter for his wife and children or his ex-wife who is still in the period of 'iddah'.

(2) The shelter is to be a proper place for the wife within the period of marriage, or 'iddah' of divorce, or 'iddah' of death.

(3) Shelter is provided in order to guarantee the safety of the wife and children from the external threats, thus they feel safe and sound. A shelter is also to be functioned as a place to store the wealth/property, as a place where they can put and organize the household equipment.

(4) A husband is obliged to provide shelter for his family in accordance with his capability and to be appropriate with the surrounding in terms of either the household equipment or other supporting equipment.

Part Five
Obligation of a Husband With More Than One Wives

Article 82.

(1) A husband who married to more than one wives is obliged to provide shelter and living cost to each wife equally in accordance with the size of the family of each wife provided that there is an agreement prior to the marriage.

(2) In the case that the wives are willing or have no objection, a husband may place them in one house.

Part Six
The Obligation of the Wife

Article 83.

(1) The primary obligation of a wife is to dedicate physically and spiritually to the husband in as much The Islamic Law allows.

(2) A wife organize and manage the daily activities of the household with her best ability.

Article 84.

(1) A wife can be considered as 'nusyuz' upon the negligence of the obligation as stated in article 83 point (1) provided there is a legal reason.

(2) Upon the 'nusyuz' wife, the obligation of the husband to the wife as stated in Article 80 point (4) letters 'a' and 'b' is void except on the interests of the children.

(3) The obligation of the husband as stated in point (2) above become effective again as the wife is no longer 'nusyuz'.

(4) The decision whether or not a wife is 'nusyuz' must be proved with legal evidences.

CHAPTER XIII
PROPERTY IN MARRIAGE

Article 85.

The existence of the joint property does not by any mean reject the possibility of the individual property for the husband or the wife.

Article 86.

(1) Principally there is no mixture of the husband's possession and the wife's possession due to the marriage.

(2) The property of the wife will always be the possession of the wife and she hold the total control over it, and so will the property of the husband in which he hold the total control over his possession.

Article 87.

(1) The property of each party obtained before the marriage and the property that they gain after the marriage from the gift or inheritance is fully under the ownership of each individual provided that both party decide other in the marriage.

(2) A husband or a wife has the full rights upon their individual property for the legal action that they intend to do concerning their property, namely 'hibah', gift, charity and others.

Article 88.

Should there be a dispute between the husband and the wife upon the joint property, the case is to be settled through the Islamic Court.

Article 89.

A husband is responsible to protect the joint property, the property of his wife as well as his own property.

Article 90.

The wife also bears the responsibility to protect the joint property or her husband property in her own supervision.

Article 91.

(1) The joint-property as mentioned in article 85 may take the form of tangible or non tangible assets.

(2) The tangible joint-property may comprise the fixed assets, mobile assets and securities.

(3) The intangible joint-property may take the form of rights as well as responsibilities.

(4) The joint-property may be offered as collateral article by either party under the agreement of the respective spouse.

Article 92.

Provided with agreement of either party, one is not allowed by any means to sell or transfer the ownership of the joint-property.

Article 93.

(1) Any consequences upon the debt of the husband or the wife shall be liable to each assets respectively.

(2) Any consequence upon the debt for the household's expenditure shall be liable to the joint-property.

(3) In the case where the joint-property is not sufficient to pay the debt, the responsibility goes to the husband assets.

(4) In the case that the husband's asset is not sufficient, the responsibility goes the wife's asset.

Article 94.

(1) The joint property of a marriage of a husband who has more than one wife shall be treated separately and independently.

(2) The ownership of a joint-property of the marriage of a husband who married more than one wife as referred to point (1) is counted in commenting on the day of the second, the third or the fourth 'aqad' (wedding).

Article 95.

(1) Without abridging the regulation of Article 24 point (2) letter 'c' Government Regulation No. 9 of 1975 and article 136 point (2), a husband or a wife may request the Islamic Court to condemn the joint property in the absence of divorce request, if either of the party endangers the joint property, such as gambling, drunk, prodigal and the like.

(2) Within the status of condemnation the joint property may be sold for the needs of the family with the permission of the Islamic Court.

Article 96.

(1) If either party passes away, half the joint property belongs to the survived spouse.

(2) The division of the joint property for the missing husband or wife is to be postpone until there is a definite news on the death of the husband or the wife or the death is legally acknowledge based on the verdict of the Islamic Court.

Article 97.

The divorce and divorcee have equally half of the joint property except there is a certain agreement in the marriage.

CHAPTER XIV
CHILDREN CARE

Article 98.

(1) The are to age limit for a child to be able to self sustain is 21 provided that the child is mentally retarded or physically handicapped or not yet married.

(2) The parents represent the child mentioned at point (1) for every legal act inside or outside the court.

(3) The Islamic Court may appoint a close relative to do the task in the case that the parents are incapable.

Article 99.

The legal children are:
a. Those who are born from the legal marriage;
b. The legal external insemination from the sperm and ovum of the husband and the wife who are legally married and born by the wife.

Article 100.

The child who is born from the extra marital couple shall only have a family relationship with the mother and her family.

Article 101.

A husband who denies the legality of a child while the wife does not object to his denial may confirm his denial with 'li'an'.

Article 102.

(1) A husband who wants to deny a child born by his wife, may put the lawsuit to the Islamic Court within 180 days from the birth of the child or 360 days after the marriage broken off or as soon as the husband knows that his wife deliver a baby and at the place where he might be able to put the lawsuit to the Islamic Court.

(2) The denial proposed exceeding the above mentioned time is unacceptable.

Article 103.

(1) The history of a child can only be proved by birth certificate or other evidence.

(2) In the case of the absence of the birth certificate or other evidence as stated in point (1) The Islamic Court can issue the decree of the history of a child after the careful examination based on the proof evidences.

(3) Based on the decree of the Islamic Court as stated in point (2) the Birth Registration Office within the jurisdiction of the Islamic Court concern can issue a birth certificate for the mentioned child.

Article 104.

(1) All cost spent for breast feeding shall be the responsibility of the father. If the father dies the cost is to be taken over by the person who is in charge of giving the living cost to the father or the foster parent.

(2) Breast feeding may last up to the maximum of 2 years, and can be stop within the period of less than 2 years by agreement of the father and mother.

Article 105.

Should a divorce happen:

a.   Children under 12 years old (before mumayyiz) is to be the right of the mother;

b.   Children after the 'mumayyiz age' may decide whether he will be under the care of the mother or the father.

c.   The cost of bringing up the children will be the responsibility of the father.

Article 106.

(1) Parents have the responsibility of taking care and develop the property of the children who are under adolescence or under care, and cannot in any way transfer or pawn it except for the emergency situation that the children are in badly needs or a fact that they cannot avoid in so doing.

(2) Parents are responsible for the loss caused by the negligence of the obligation as stated in point (1).

CHAPTER XV
PERWALIAN (GUARDIANSHIP)

Article 107.

(1) Guardianship is only for person under 21 years old or not yet married.

(2) Guardianship comprises protection on personnel aswall or their property.

(3) In the case that a guardian is incapable or neglect his guardianship obligation, the Islamic Court may appoint one of the relatives to act as a guardian on the request of the relative mentioned.

(4) Guardian should be as good as possible taken from the child's family or other person who is adult, mentally healthy, justice, honest and having a good conduct, or a legal board.

Article 108.

Parents can make a testimony to someone or a legal board upon the authorization to do the guardianship on the person and property of their children when they die.

Article 109.

The Islamic court may revoke the right of guardianship of someone or a legal board and gives it to other person upon the request of the relatives in the case that the guardian is a drunk, gambler, wasteful, mad or neglect or misuses the right and authority as the guardian for the sake of the prosperity of the children concerned.

Article 110.

(1) The guardian is obliged to manage the person and the property of the children under his custody at his best ability and is obliged to give guidance on religion, education and other skills for the future of the children under his care/guardianship.

(2) The guardian is prohibited to pawn, burden and flight the property of the children under his guardianship, provided that his action will give the benefit to the person under his guardianship or if it is considered as a fact which is unavoidable.

(3) The guardian is responsible for the property of the person under his guardianship, and repay the loss caused by the negligence or the misuse.

(4) Without lessening the regulation as stated in article 54 point (4) Law No. 1 of 1974, the responsibility of the guardian as stated in point (3) should be proved by a balance statement audited once a year.

Article 111.

(1) The guardian must deliver the whole property of the person under his guardianship after the person concern has come to the age of 21 or married.

(2) Upon the ending of the guardianship the Islamic Court is authorized to settle the dispute between the guardian and the person under his guardianship upon the property that he delivered.

Article 112.

The guardian may use the property of the person under his guardianship as far as it is needed by him of some proper amount or 'bil maíruf should the guardian is destitute.

CHAPTER XVI
DISSOLUTION OR BROKEN OFF A MARRIAGE

Part One
General

Article 113.

A marriage can be broken off for the reasons of:
a. death
b. divorce, and
c. the judgement of the court of law.

Article 114.

The broken off marriage due to a divorce may happen because of the 'talak' or a divorce lawsuit.

Article 115.

A divorce can only be done in a trial of an Islamic Court after the Court failed to settle the dispute of the couple.

Article 116.

A divorce may take place from the reason(s);
a. either one of the party committed adultery or drunkard, drug addicted, gambler and the like that are unrecoverable;
b. either one of the party leaves for the period of 2 (two) years in succession with no valid permission of the other party or other things beyond his ability;
c. either one of the party is imprison for 5 (five) year or other severer prison after the marriage;
d. either one of the party does a cruelty or heavy ill treatment which endangers the other party;
e. either one of the party suffer from an illness that unable him or her to perform his/her duty as a husband or a wife;
f. between the husband and the wife there are endless quarreling which cannot guarantee for the achievement of the harmonious life as a family;
g. a husband violates the 'taklik talak';
h. religious conversion that causes the disharmony of the family life.

Article 117.

'Talak' is a promise of a husband in an Islamic Court trial which causes one of the reasons of the breaking off a marriage, in a manner as stated in article 129, 130 and 131.

Article 118.

'Talak Raj'i' is the first or the second divorce statement in which a husband has the right for a reconciliation within the period of 'iddah' of his wife.

Article 119.

(1) The 'Talak Ba'in Sughraa' is a sort of 'talak' that cannot be reconciled but can be remarried by the husband even though the wife is still in the period of 'iddah'.

(2) The 'Talak Ba'in Sughraa' as stated in point (1) is:

a.   talak that happens before intercourse;

b.   talak with redeem or 'khuluk';

c.   talak sanctioned by the Islamic Court.

Article 120.

'Talak Ba'in Kubraa' is a sort of 'talak' that happens for the third time. This kind of 'talak' can neither be reconciled nor re-married, except in a condition that the ex-wife married to someone else and divorced after the sex intercourse and completed her period of 'iddah'.

Article 121.

'Talak sunny' is a permissible talak, namely 'talak' that is given to the wife who is still in the 'non-period' condition.

Article 122.

'Talak Bid'i' is not a permissible one, namely 'talak' that is given to the wife who is still in the period, or the wife might be in a non-period but an intercourse has been done within this time.

Article 123.

A divorce is effective from the time that the divorce is announced in a court trial.

Article 124.

'Khuluk' must be biased on the reason of divorce corresponds to the rules as stated in Article 116.

Article 125.

'Li'an' causes the broken off of a marriage between a husband and a wife forever.

Article 126.

'Li'an' happens when a husband accuses a wife of doing an adultery and or denying a child in a pregnancy or that was born by his wife, while the wife refuses the accusation and or the denial mentioned.

Article 127.

The procedure of 'li'an' is arranged as follows:

a. a husband pronounces an oath repeated four times on the accusation of adultery or the denial of the child, followed by the fifth oath with the phrase "a curse of Allah will be on me if the accusation or the denial is of a lie".

b. the wife rejects the accusation and or the denial with four times pronouncing oath with phrase "the accusation and or the denial is not true" followed by the fifth phrase "the curse of Allah will be on me if the accusation and or the denial is true".

c. the procedure on letter 'a' and 'b' above is an integrated procedure and inseparable;

d. if the procedure in letter 'a' is not followed with the one on letter 'b', the 'li'an' is considered as invalid.

Article 128.

"li'an" is only valid if it is done in an Islamic Court trial.

Part Two
The Procedure of Divorce

Article 129.

A husband who intends to divorce his wife shall propose either orally or written to the Islamic Court on the Jurisdiction territory of his wife together with reasons for it and request for a trial for the purpose.

Article 130.

The Islamic Court may accept or refuse the proposal, and for the sentence an appeal can be forwarded to the Higher Courts.

Article 131.

(1) The Islamic Court concerned will have a study on the proposal as stated in Article 129 and within 30 days at the latest it will invite the couple to ask for a clarification on everything in relation to their proposal.

(2) After the Islamic Court fails to advise them and there are ample evidences for a 'talak', besides, the possibility for the concerned husband and wife to live a harmonious life is impossible, the Islamic Court releases its decision to allow the husband to declare the 'talak'.

(3) Upon the acceptance of the fix legal decision the husband may declare his 'talak' in a session of the Islamic Court on the presence of his wife or her mandate/lawyer.

(4) If within the period of 6 (six) months commented from the day of issuance of his permission to declare the 'talak' and he does not do it his right to divorce his wife is invalid and he is still in the status of legally married.

(5) Upon witnessing the trial on 'talak', the Islamic Court issues the a letter of confirmation about the happening of 'talak' in four copies as an evidence for the ex-husband and ex-wife. The first page of the letter is sent to the Marriage Registrar Official where the husband and the wife domicile for the purpose of registration, the second and the third page go to the husband and the wife concerned and the fourth page is filed by the Islamic Court.

Article 132.

(1) Divorce claim is proposed by the wife or her mandatory to the Islamic Court within the jurisdiction of her domicile provided that the wife left the domicile without permission of the husband.

(2) In the case the husband lives in a foreign country, the head of the Islamic Court notify the claim through the embassy of Indonesia or consulate of Indonesia.

Article 133.

(1) A divorce claim that caused by the reason stated in article 116 letter 'b', may be proposed after a period of 2 (two) years from the time the accused left home.

(2) The claim can be accepted if the accused accepts it and shows an attitude that negate the possibility of going back home.

Article 134.

The divorce claim due to the reasons stated in article 116 letter 'P can be accepted when the Islamic Court is well informed about the reasons or the source of the dispute or quarrel and after hearing sessions with the relatives or close contact with people around the husband and the wife concerned.

Article 135.

For the case of divorce due to imprisonment of the husband for 5 (five) years or more severe sentence as stated in article 116 letter 'c', a wife may use a copy of the verdict of the court which conducted the trial of her husband's case enclosed with the letter of statement of the court saying that the verdict has a fix legal firmness.

Article 136.

(1) During the process of divorce upon the request of the husband or wife and based on the consideration of the safety of either of them the Islamic Court may allow them not to live in the same house.

(2) During the process of divorce upon the request of either party, the Islamic Court may:

a. decide the living cost that should be undertaken by the husband;
b. take some necessary actions to secure or guarantee the joint property of the husband and the wife or the property of the husband or the property of the wife.

Article 137.

A divorce lawsuit becomes void if either party dies before the verdict of the Islamic Court concerning the matter.

Article 138.

(1) In any session of the Islamic Court dealing with the divorce lawsuit, either the husband or the wife or their mandatory will be invited to attend the session.

(2) Letter of summon to attend the session as stated in point (1) is carried out by the official assigned by the Head of The Islamic Court.

(3) The summon is to be accepted in person. If the person concerned is not available, the summon may be addressed through the head of the village or the official of the same level.

(4) The summon as stated in point (1) is to be delivered in a proper manner and is to be accepted by the person or their mandatory at least 3 (three) days before the court session.

(5) The summon to the accused is enclosed with the copy of the lawsuit document.

Article 139.

(1) Should the place of domicile of the accused cannot be traced, or the accused has no permanent place, the summon is done by means of posting the divorce lawsuit on the announcement board of the Islamic Court and announce it in one or several newspaper or other kinds of mass media as advised by the Islamic Court.

(2) The announcement through a newspaper(s) or other mass media as stated in point (I) is to be done 2 (two) times within the period of one month from the first announcement.

(3) The tolerable period between the last announcement as stated in point (2) and the court session is at least 3 (three) months.

(4) Had the summon as stated in point (2) been done and the accused or the mandatory does not show, the lawsuit is accepted without the presence of the accused, provided that the lawsuit has no right or has no reason.

Article 140.

In the case that the accused is in the condition as stated in article 132 point (2), the summon is proceed through the Indonesian Embassy or Consulate.

Article 141.

(1) The scrutiny of the lawsuit document is to be done by the Judge at least 30 (thirty) days upon the acceptance of the divorce lawsuit.

(2) In determining the court session on the divorce case the court should consider the time of the dispatch of the summon and the acceptance from either party or their mandate.

(3) Should the accused in a condition as stated in article 116 letter 'b', the court session on divorce lawsuit is determined at least 6 (six) days commenting from the date of the acceptance of the divorce lawsuit by the Islamic Court Administration.

Article 142.

(1) In a court trial of divorce, both the husband and the wife should come in person or represented by the designated person to represent them.

(2) In the case that the husband and the wife send their representatives, the Judge may request the husband and the wife to come by themselves should a certain condition requires so.

Article 143.

(1) During the period of scrutiny or case examination on divorce the Judge seek the possibility of reconciling the disputed parties.

(2) Before the court comes to a final decision efforts in reconciliation should be sought in any chance during the sessions.

Article 144.

Should a reconciliation comes to exist, there would be no new divorce suit based on the reasoning used before the reconciliation which are known by the wife by the time the reconciliation happened.

Article 145.

If reconciliation is not achieved, the court session on divorce should be organized in a closed court session.

Article 146.

(1) The sentence of the divorce trial is declared in an open court session.

(2) A divorce is considered as valid with its effects from the day of the sentence of the Islamic Court and has a fix legal firmness.

Article 147.

(1) Following the sentence of the court, the clerk of the Islamic Court is to pass a copy of the sentence to the husband and the wife or their representatives and at the same time withdrawing the Enclosure of the Marriage Document from both parties.

(2) The clerk of the Islamic Court is obliged to send a copy of the sentence of the Islamic Court which has fix legal firmness with no seal to the Marriage Registrar Official in the same jurisdictive territory with the wife for the purpose of registration.

(3) The clerk of the Islamic Court send letter of notification to the husband and the wife or their representatives that the sentence as stated in point (1) has already been legally fixed and they may use it as an evidence of the divorce document.

(4) The clerk of the Islamic Court will make a note on the space provided in the Marriage Document saying that they have divorced. The note also includes the date, the place, the number and the date of the letter of decision and the signature of the clerk.

(5) In the case that the Marriage Registrar Official whose jurisdiction territory covers the domicile of the wife differs from the Marriage Registrar Official where they got married one copy of the Islamic Court sentence as mentioned in point (2) is sent to the Marriage Registrar Official where the marriage is done, and if the marriage is done in a foreign country the copy is sent to the Marriage Registrar Official in Jakarta.

(6) Failure of sending the copy as stated in point (1) is to be the responsibility of the clerk, should the matter causes the loss of the ex-husband and the ex-wife.

Article 148.

(1) A wife who sues the divorce by 'khuluk', shall propose the suit to the Islamic Court whose territory covers the place of her domicile.

(2) The Islamic Court within at least 1 (one) month will invite the wife and the husband to have explanations on the matter.

(3) During the hearing session the Islamic Court will explain the negative effects of the 'khuluk', and should give the advice.

(4) When both parties agree on the amount of the 'iwadl' or the redeem, the Islamic Court will issue a decree for the husband to declare the 'talak' in front of the Islamic Court session. For the decree there will be no appeal to the higher level courts.

(5) The follow up steps is to be undertaken as regulated in article 131 point (5).

(6) In the case that there is no agreement on the amount of the 'iwadl' or redeem, the Islamic Court will examine and decide it as in an ordinary case.

CHAPTER XVII
THE CONSEQUENCES OF A BROKEN OFF MARRIAGE

Part One
The Consequences of 'Talak'

Article 149.

If a marriage is broken due to 'talak', the ex-husband is obliged to:

a.   submit a proper amount of 'mut'ah' to his ex-wife either in a form of goods or money, except the divorce takes place before an intercourse.
b.   provide a living cost, 'maskan' and 'kiswah' to his ex-wife during the period of 'iddah', except when the wife is divorced by 'talak ba'in' or 'nusyuz' and not in the pregnancy;
c.   pay off the whole credited 'mahar', or in half if the divorce happens before the intercourse.
d.   provide the 'hadhanah' allowances for his children who are under 21 years old.

Article 150.

The ex-husband has the right to do the reconciliation with his wife within the period of 'iddah'.

Article 151.

The ex-wife, within the period of 'iddah', is obliged to take care of herself in terms of not accepting a proposal or getting married to another man.

Article 152.

The ex-wife has the right of having the 'iddah' allowance from her husband provided that she was 'nusyuz'.

Part Two
The Waiting Period

Article 153.

(1) For a woman who breaks her marriage there must be a waiting time or 'iddah' period, except when she has not done an intercourse and the broken off marriage is not due to the death of the husband.

(2) The waiting period of the woman is regulated as follows:

a.   If the marriage is off due to the death of the husband, even before an intercourse, the waiting time is determined as 130 (one hundred thirty) days;

b.   If the marriage is broken off due to the divorce, the waiting time for those who are still in the 'period' is determined as long as three times cycles with at least 90 (ninety) days;

c.   If a marriage is broken off due to the divorce, while the wife is still in pregnancy, the waiting time for her is up to the delivery;

d.   If a marriage is broken off due to the death, while the wife is still in pregnancy, the waiting time for her is up to the delivery;

(3) No waiting time is imposed for the divorce husband and wife before they have intercourse.

(4) For the marriage that is broken off due to the divorce, the waiting time commences from the date of the legal validation of the Islamic Court sentence, while for the broken off marriage due to the death the waiting time commences from the date of the death of the husband.

(5) The waiting time for the wife who once had a period but then absence from the cycle during the 'iddah' due to breast feeding, her iddah period is to be three time cycles.

(6) In the condition as stated in point (5) but not in breast feeding period, the iddah is one year, however if, within the one year period she has the cycle, her iddah is three times cycles.

Article 154.

If a wife is given the talak raj'i, and within the period of iddah as stated in point (2) letter b, point (5) and point (6) article 153, her ex-husband died, her iddah period becomes four months and 10 days commenting from the date of the ex-husband's death.

Article 155.

For the woman whose marriage is broken off due to 'khuluk', 'fasakh' and 'li'an', the 'iddah talak' can be applied.

Part Three
The Consequences of Divorce

Article 156.

The consequences of a broken off marriage due to divorce are:

a.   children who are not 'mummayiz' (grown up) has the right to have the 'hadhanah' (education) from the mother, provided that the mother died, her right falls to:
   1.   women in vertical up the line from the mother;
   2.   the father;
   3.   women in vertical up the line from the father;
   4.   sisters from the aforementioned children;
   5.   women of the same blood of the horizontal line of the mother;
   6.   women of the same blood of the horizontal line of the father.

b.   the grown up children have the right to choose whether they have the 'hadhanah' from the father or the mother.

c.   if the bearer of the 'hadhanah' right cannot guarantee the safety of the children either physically or spiritually, although materially or financially is adequate, the Islamic Court upon the request of the relatives of the children may transfer the right of the 'hadhanah' to other relative who also bears the right of 'hadhanah';

d.   the whole cost of the 'hadhanah' and living cost of the children are the responsibility of the father within his capability, at least up to the time when the children grown up and able to manage themselves (i.e. 21 years old).

e.   should there be a dispute on the 'hadhanah' and the living cost of the children, the Islamic Court issues the decision based on the ones in letters (a), (b), (c) and (d);

f.   the court may also, by considering the ability of the father, to decide the amount of funds needed for the maintenance and education of the children who do not live with him.

Article 157.

The joint property may be distributed in accordance with the regulations as stated in article 96, 97.

Part Four
The Mut'ah

Article 158.

Mut'ah is 'obligatory' for the ex-husband with the conditions as follows:

a.   the 'mahar' has not been determined for the wife after intercourse happens.

b.   the divorce is initiated by the husband.

Article 159.

Mut'ah is a 'sunnat' (not obligatory but suggested strongly) given by the ex-husband with no conditions as stated in article 158.

Article 160.

The amount of 'mut'ah' should be proper and based on the capability of the husband.

Part Five
The Consequences of Khuluk

Article 161.

Divorce by means of 'khuluk' will reduce the number of talak and cannot be reconciled.

Part Six
The Consequences of 'Li'an'

Article 162.

In the divorce case of 'li'an' the marriage is broken off forever and the child in the pregnancy belongs to the offspring of the mother, while the husband is free from the obligation of giving the living cost.

CHAPTER XVIII
RECONCILIATION

Part One
General

Article 163.

(1) An ex-husband may reconcile his ex-wife who is still in the period of 'iddah'.

(2) Reconciliation may be done in the cases that:

a.   the marriage which is broken off due to talak, except that the talaks have been given three times or the talak happens before intercourse;

b.   the marriage is broken off due to the sentence of the Islamic Court with reason or reasons apart from adultery and khuluk.

Article 164.

A woman in the period of 'iddah talak raj'i' has the right of objection to the reconciliation request of her ex-husband in the testimony of the Marriage Registrar Official witnessed by two persons.

Article 165.

Reconciliation arranged without the agreement of the ex-wife, can be declared as invalid by the decision of the Islamic Court.

Article 166.

Reconciliation must be proved by a quotation from the Reconciliation Registration Book and if the evidence is lost or damage so that it can no longer be used, the duplicate can be requested from the institution that first issued the document.

Part Two
The Procedure of Reconciliation

Article 167.

(1) A husband who intends to reconcile his wife should come together with her to the Marriage Registrar Official or Assistant of Marriage Registrar Official whose territory covers the place of the domicile of the husband and the wife and bring along the document stating about their divorce with other pertinent documents.

(2) Reconciliation is to be done with the agreement of the wife under the testimony of the Marriage Registrar Official or an Assistant of the Marriage Registrar Official.

(3) The Marriage Registrar Official or the Assistant Marriage Registrar Official will study and examine the case whether the husband who wants to reconcile is really reliable or meet the criteria of reconciliation according to 'munakahat' law, or whether the reconciliation is done within the period of iddah talak raj'i, or whether the woman who he is going to reconcile is really his own ex-wife.

(4) The next step is the husband declares the reconciliation statement and each of the party together with the witnesses sign the Reconciliation Registration Book.

(5) Upon the completeness of the signatures, the Marriage Registrar Official or the Assistant to it gives advices to the newly reconciled husband and wife on their obligation related to the reconciliation.

Article 168.

(1) In the case that the reconciliation is done before the Assistant Marriage Registrar Official the reconciliation quotation is made double to be filled in and signed by each of the party together with the witnesses. One copy goes to the Marriage Registrar Official whose territory covers his area, provided with the pertinent documents in order to book in the Reconciliation Registration Book while the other copy is filed.

(2) The delivery of the first page of the reconciliation quotation by the assistant of Marriage Registrar Official is to be done at least 15 (fifteen) days after the reconciliation happens.

(3) If the first page of the reconciliation quotation is lost, the Assistant will make a copy from the second page enclosed with the report on the cause of the lost.

Article 169.

(1) The Marriage Registrar Official makes a statement on the event of reconciliation and send it to the Islamic Court where the talak of the reconciled couple was once declared, and to each of the husband and wife will be given a Quotation of Reconciliation Registration Book based on the example determined by the Minister of Religious Affairs.

(2) The husband and wife or their mandatory go to the Islamic Court where they once declared the talak, and bringing along the quotation of the Reconciliation Registration Book in order to get their Quotation of Marriage Certificates after notes were written in the provided space in the certificate saying that they have truly reconciled.

(3) The notes mentioned in point (2) consists of the place where the reconciliation happened, the date when the reconciliation statement is declared, the number and the date of the Quotation of the Reconciliation Registration Book and the signature of the Clerk of the Islamic Court.

CHAPTER XIX
MOURNING PERIOD

Article 170.

(1) A wife whose husband died is obliged to undertake the mourning during the period of iddah as a token of condolence besides preventing her from any gossips.

(2) A husband whose wife died is to perform a mourning properly in accordance with the norms.

BOOK TWO
INHERITANCE LAW

CHAPTER I
GENERAL RULES

Article 171.

The Definitions

a. Hukum Kewarisan (The inheritance law) is a law that regulates the transfer of ownership from a heir (tirkah), and decides who are the lineal heirs and the amount of each for them.
b. Pewaris is a person, who at the time he/she died or declared as died according to Islamic Law, inherits some wealth to the lineal heirs.
c. Ahli waris (The heir) is a person who has blood relationship or marriage relationship with the deceased person, moslem, and has no legal problem to become a heir(s).
d. Harta peninggalan (The left property) is wealth that once belonged to the deceased person either in the form of property on his/her possession or on his right.
e. Harta waris (The Inheritance) is a self property added with part of the joint property after being deducted for the expense of the late during his/her illness until died, burial costs (tajhiz) debt repayment and gift to some relatives.
f. Wasiat (The will) is a giving of a good from the 'pewaris' to other person or an institution which is effective from the time the 'pewaris' died.
g. Hibah is a thing given voluntarily and at no cost to other person who is still alive for his/her possession.
h. Anak angkat (adopted child) is a child whose living costs, education costs, etc., is taken over from the real parents to his/her foster parents based on the sentence from the Court.
i. Baitual Maal is a Religious Treasury House.

CHAPTER II
THE HEIR

Article 172.

A heir is considered as a moslem from his/her Identification Card or his/her confession, the deed or the testimony, while for a newly born baby or before adolescence follows the religion of the father or the surrounding relatives.

Article 173.

A person is rejected to be the heir upon receiving the verdict of a court, with a fix legal firmness, that he/she was found guilty of:

a. murder or trying to murder or torturing the 'pewaris'
b. guilty of framing the 'pewaris' on doing a crime which can be sentenced for five years imprisonment or more severe punishment.

Article 174.

(1) Classification on heirs is as follows:
a.   According to blood relationship:
    – the male group; father, sons, brothers, uncles and grandfathers.
    – the female group; mother, daughters, sisters and grandmothers.
b.   According to marriage relationship:
    – widow or widower

(2) Should all the people mentioned in point (1) still alive, the inheritance can only goes to; sons and daughters, father, mother, the widow(s) the widowers.

Article 175.

(1) The obligation of the heirs to the 'pewaris' are:
a.   to take care everything in relation with the funeral until the burial is accomplished.
b.   to pay the debt of the deceased such as the medical treatment, caring during the illness period and also collecting the debt of the deceased person.
c.   to settle the will of the 'pewaris'.
d.   to distribute the inheritance of the 'pewaris' to the lineal heirs.

(2) The responsibility of the heirs for the debt of the 'pewaris' is only limited to the amount or the value of the left property/wealth.

CHAPTER III
THE PORTION OF THE INHERITANCE

Article 176.

A daughter, if she is the only one, will get half of the portion, if two or more altogether they will get two third, and if there is also a son, the portion of the son is twice the size as of the daughter's.

Article 177.

A father will get one third if the 'pewaris' has no offspring, should there be ones, father will get one sixth of the portion.

Article 178.

(1) The mother will get one sixth if there is offspring or two brothers/sisters or more. If there are neither children nor brothers/sisters, she will get the third of the portion.

(2) The mother will get the third portion of the remaining wealth after it was deducted by the widow or widower if she is with the father.

Article 179.

A widower will get half portion, if the 'pewaris' has no offspring, should there be ones the widower will get a quarter portion.

Article 180.

A widow will get a quarter portion, if the 'pewaris' has no offspring, should there be ones the widow will get one eighth portion.

Article 181.

If someone dies leaving neither offspring nor a father, the brothers and sisters of the same mother will get one sixth of the portion. If they are two or more, altogether will get one third.

Article 182.

If someone dies leaving neither children nor a father while he/she has one blood sister or from the same father, she will get half portion. If the mentioned sister has one or more sisters they will altogether get two third of the portion.

If the mentioned sister has one blood brother or more or brother of the same father, the portion of those brothers is double as the sisters.

Article 183.

The heirs may make a certain agreement on the distribution of the inheritance, after each of them knows their real portions.

Article 184.

For the heir who is not yet grown up or not capable of exercising his/her right and responsibility, a 'wali' is to be appointed for him/her by the decision of the Judge based on the proposal of the relatives.

Article 185.

(1) For the heir who dies prior to the 'pewaris', his/her right can be transferred to his/her children except those mentioned in article 173.

(2) The portion of the substitute heir cannot be bigger than that of the substituted.

Article 186.

Children from extra marital relationship will only have inheritance relationship with the mother or family from the mother side.

Article 187.

(1) If a 'pewaris' leaves the property, he/she during his/her life, or the heirs may assign some persons as the board of executor of the distribution with the following tasks:

a. make an inventory list of the wealth both the moveable or the non moveable which then legalized by the heirs, the value of the wealth can also be conversed into the money, should it be considered necessary.

b. calculate the expenditure spent for the need of the pewaris in accordance with the article 175 point (1) sub a, b, and c.

(2) The remaining part of the wealth as mentioned above is a property that must be distributed to the lineal heirs.

Article 188.

The heirs either in group or individually may request one to another to execute the distribution of the wealth. Should there be one of the heirs disagree with the request, he/she may appeal to the Islamic Court to do the distribution.

Article 189.

(1) If the property to be distributed is in the form of a farm which is less than 2 hectares in size, it is suggested not to be sliced into pieces, but cultivated for the benefit of all the heirs.

(2) Should the regulation as in point (1) is not possible due to the needs of a certain member of the heir of money, the portion that belongs to the person concerned may be purchased by the other member in accordance with the size of the portion.

Article 190.

For the pewaris who has more than one wives, each of them will have the share of the 'gono-gini' property (the joint property) with their husband. While the whole portion of the pewaris will be the right of his heirs.

Article 191.

Should the pewaris leaves no heir at all or the existence and the place of the heirs are unknown, the wealth based on the decision of the Islamic Court will be donated to the Baitul Maal for the interests of Islam and public welfare.

CHAPTER IV
'AUL' AND 'RAD'

Article 192.

If, during the distribution of the inheritance, there is among the heirs 'dzawil furud' and shows that the nominator is greater than the denominator, the denominator should be increased in accordance with the nominator, afterward the wealth is to be distributed by means of 'aul' according to the nominator figure.

Article 193.

If, during the distribution of the inheritance, there is among the heirs 'dzawil furud' and shows that the nominator is smaller than the denominator, while the heirs are 'asabah', the distribution is to be done by means of 'rad' namely in accordance with portion of each heir while the remaining inheritance will be distributed evenly among them.

CHAPTER V
THE WILL

Article 194.

(1) A person with a minimum age of 21, mentally healthy and not under pressure may bequeath part of his/her property to other person or institution.

(2) The property which is bequeathed must be his/her legitimate property.

(3) Ownership of the wealth as stated in point (1) can only be transferred after the person who bequeath dies.

Article 195.

(1) The will can be declared orally before two witnesses, or written in the presence of two witnesses, or in the present of a Notary.

(2) The property that can be bequeathed is of maximum one third of the inheritance provided that the whole members of the heirs agree.

(3) The will that addressed to the heir is only valid if the whole member of the heirs agree.

(4) Statement of agreement stated in point (2) and (3) this chapter is to be made orally before two witnesses or written in the presence of two witnesses or a Notary.

Article 196.

In the will either oral or written there must be explicitly stated to whom or which institution the bequeathed property is to be given.

Article 197.

(1) The will becomes invalid if the person nominated for the will based on the sentence of a court that has a fix legal firmness, is imprison due to:

a.   found guilty of murdering or trying to murder or torturing the person who bequeaths.

b.   found guilty of framing the person who bequeaths that he/she has committed a crime which can be threatened with five year imprisonment or more severe sentence.

c.   found guilty of doing violence or threatening the person who bequeaths to make or withdraw or change the will for the interest of the nominee concerned.

d.   found guilty of hiding or destroying or forging the will of the person who bequeaths.

(2) The will is void if the person who is nominated to receive the will:

a.   does not know the existence of the will until the time he/she dies before the person who bequeaths dies.

b.   know that there is a will but he/she refuses to accept.

c.   know that there is a will but never say whether or not he/she accept the will until the time he/she dies.

(3) the will become void if the property bequeathed is gone or damaged.

Article 198.

The will which is a product of a certain thing or the benefit of a certain thing must be stated with the certain duration of time.

Article 199.

(1) The 'pewasiat' (the person who bequeaths) may withdraw the will so long as the acceptor of the will has never stated his/her agreement or has stated his/her agreement but then withdraw the statement.

(2) The withdrawal of a will may be done either orally witnessed by two persons or written in the presence of two witnesses or based on the Notary Act if the will had been announced orally.

(3) If the will is made written, it can only be withdrawn also in written in the presence of two witnesses or based on the Notary Act.

(4) If the will is made based on the Notary Act, it can only be withdrawn based on the Notary Act.

Article 200.

The objects of the will which are in the form of non-moveable property, if due to one or more reasons decreases in the value or damage before the 'pewasiat' (person who bequeaths) dies the nominated acceptor of the will only receives the remaining property.

Article 201.

Should the will exceed the amount of one third of the whole inheritance, while there is an objection from a member of the heirs, the execution of the will can only be done up to the amount of one third of the whole inheritance.

Article 202.

If the will is targeted to various noble activities, while the amount of the wealth stated in the will is not sufficient, the heirs may decide which of the activity is to be given the priority.

Article 203.

(1) If the will is in the closed envelope, it should be properly kept at the Notary who made the will or at other places included the documents related to it.

(2) If the will is withdrawn in accordance with the article 199 the withdrawn will is to be returned to the 'pewasiat'.

Article 204.

(1) If the 'pewasiat' dies, the will which is in the envelope and stored in the Notary Office will be opened by the Notary before the heirs and witnessed by two persons, and the Notary will make an official report on the opening of the will.

(2) If the will which is in the envelope stored at a place other than in Notary Office the one who kept the will must submit it to the local Notary or Regional Office of Religious Affairs then the Notary or the Religious Affairs Office will open it as it is stated in article (1) of this chapter.

(3) When the content of the will is clearly understood The Notary or The Religious Affairs Office will hand over the will to the heirs for the follow up actions.

Article 205.

During the war, members of the troop or those who belong to the member of the troop and happen to be in the arena of a battle or in the place which is surrounded by enemies, are allowed to make a will in front of his commander in the presence of two witnesses.

Article 206.

Those who are in the voyage may make a will in front of the ship captain or other high rank official, and if the officials are not available it can be made in front of the secondary official in the presence of two witnesses.

Article 207.

The will cannot in anyway be projected to the person who does the medical care or a person who give a religious guidance to the 'pewasiat' during the illness period until he/she dies, except if it is clearly stated as a thanksgiving.

Article 208.

The will is void for the Notary and the witnesses who make it.

Article 209.

(1) The left-property of the adopted child is divided based on articles 176 up to 193 above, while for the adopting parent who receives no will may be given the 'wasiat wajibah' (compulsory will) as much as one third of the inheritance of the adopted child.

(2) For the adopted child who receives no will may be given a 'compulsory will' as much as one third of the adopting parents' inheritance.

CHAPTER VI
THE HIBAH
(PRESENT)

Article 210.

(1) A grown up person with a minimum age of 21 years old, mentally healthy, not in under pressure may 'present' as much as one third of his wealth to other person or institution in the presence of two witnesses.

(2) The property which is presented must be his/her own real possession.

Article 211.

The 'hibah' from a parent to his/her offspring may be considered as inheritance.

Article 212.

'Hibah' cannot be withdrawn, except the one from the parent to the children.

Article 213.

'Hibah' which is given at the time the presenter is dying or close to the death must be given the approval of the heirs.

Article 214.

Any Indonesian citizens who are in a foreign country can make a declaration of 'hibah' in front of the Consulate or Indonesian Ambassador in the respective country in which the content do not contradict to the conditions on this articles.

BOOK III
THE LAW OF 'WAKAF'
(PROPERTY DONATED FOR RELIGIOUS OR COMMUNITY USE)

CHAPTER I
GENERAL CONDITION

Article 215.

The Definitions

(1) *'Wakaf'* is a legal action of a person or a group of people or an institution which spare some of their property and institutionalize forever for the purpose of ritual or other community use in accordance with the Islamic teaching.
(2) *'Wakif'* is the person or group of people or institution who donate the property of their possession.
(3) *'Ikrar'* is a declaration of the wakif to donate the property in their possession.
(4) The *'benda wakaf'* (the material of the donation) can be anything either moveable or non-moveable which are durable and not of the single-use and bear a value according to Islamic teaching.
(5) *'Nadzir'* is a group of people or a legal board who are trusted to take care or maintain the management of the donated property.
(6) *'Pejabat Pembuat Akta Ikrar Wakaf'* (PPAIW) is a government official who is appointed based on the valid regulation and is obliged to accept the declaration of the 'Wakif' and then hand it over to the 'Nadzir', also to carry out a supervision to preserve the donated property.
(7) The *'Pejabat Pembuat Akta Ikrar Wakaf'* as stated in point (6) is appointed and resigned by the Minister of Religious Affairs.

CHAPTER II
FUNCTION, ELEMENTS AND CONDITIONS OF WAKAF

Part One
The Function of 'Wakaf'

Article 216.

The function of the 'wakaf' is to eternalized the benefit of the 'wakaf' material in accordance with the purpose of the 'wakaf'.

Part Two
The Elements and the Conditions of 'Wakaf'

Article 217.

(1) Indonesian Legal Boards and person or people who have been grown up, mentally healthy and have no legal constrain to exercise a legal action, with his own willingness may donate a property of their own by observing the existing laws and regulations.

(2) In the case of the Legal Institutions, the person who act for and on behalf of his name is the valid care taker according to the existing law.

(3) The material of the 'wakaf' as stated in article 215 point (4) must be of property which is free from any levy, constrain, condemnation and dispute.

Article 218.

(1) Any party who donate the property for 'wakaf' must declare his will clearly and distinctly to the 'Nadzir' in the presence of the PPAIW as stated in article 215 point (6), who then notes down in the form of 'Ikrar Wakaf' witnessed at least by two persons.

(2) In a particular condition, the diversion of the regulation as stated in point (1) may be done after a consultation with and approved by the Minister of Religious Affairs.

Article 219.

(1) 'Nadzir' as stated in article 215 point (4) consists of individual who meets the following criteria:
a.   Indonesian citizen,
b.   Moslem;
c.   Adult;
d.   Physically and mentally healthy;
e.   Not under the care of somebody;
f.   Domicile in the district/borough where the 'wakaf' material located;
   (2) If it takes the form of Legal Institution the 'Nadzir' must meet the following criteria:
a.   An Indonesian Legal board and operating in Indonesia,
b.   It must have a branch in the district/borough where the 'wakaf' material located.

(3) 'Nadzir' as stated in point (1) and (2) must be registered in The Borough Office of Religious Affairs after having recommendation from the 'Camat' (Head of borough) and the Borough Ulemas Council to have the approval.

(4) Before performing his job the 'Nadzir' must pronounce an oath in front of the Borough Office of Religious Affairs witnessed by two persons in the following oath:

"By the name of Allah I swear that to be a Nadzir directly or indirectly by name or whatever reasons will not give or promise or present anything to anybody"

"I swear that I to do or not to do something in my position will not ever accept directly or indirectly from anybody a promise or any gift"

"I swear that I will always consistently respect highly the job and the responsibility which sticks to my position as a Nadzir in taking care of the 'wakaf property' in accordance with its aim and goal"

(5) The number of 'Nadzir' allowed for one unit wakaf property, as stated in article 215 point (5) is of minimum 3 persons and of maximum 10 persons who are appointed by the Borough Office of Religious Affairs in consultancy with the Borough Council of Ulemas.

Part Three
The Rights and Responsibility of 'Nadzir'

Article 220.

(1) 'Nadzir' is obliged to take care and be responsible for the wakaf property and its benefit or profit, and the organization of the property in accordance with its aim as mentioned in the regulation issued by the Minister of Religious Affairs.

(2) 'Nadzir' is obliged to write periodical reports concerning everything under his responsibility as stated in point (1) to the Head of Borough Office of Religious Affairs with copies sent to the Borough Council of Ulemas and the head of Borough.

(3) The procedure in writing reports stated in point (2) is to be carried out in accordance with the regulations of the Minister of Religious Affairs.

Article 221.

(1) A 'Nadzir' is dismissed by the Head of Borough Office of Religious Affairs for the following reasons:
a.   dies;
b.   his own initiative to resign;
c.   not capable in continuing his job as a 'nadzir';
d.   committed a crime that sends him to prison.

(2) Should there be a vacant 'nadzir' position as stated in point (1), the successor is to be appointed by the head of Borough Office of Religious Affairs based on the recommendation from the Council of Ulemas in that borough.

(3) A dismissed 'nadzir', as stated in point (1) letter a, will not automatically be replaced by any of his heirs.

Article 222.

The 'Nadzir' deserves the right to earn some amount of income and facilities of which the amount and the kinds are determined based on the properness as recommended by the Council of Ulemas and the Borough Office of Religious Affairs.

CHAPTER III
THE PROCEDURE OF 'WAKAF'
AND THE REGISTRATION OF THE WAKAF MATERIALS

Part One
The Procedure of Wakaf

Article 223.

(1) The party/person who intends to donate the *wakaf* may declare the 'ikrar wakaf' before the Pejabat Pembuat Akta Ikrar Wakaf (PPAIW) to pronounce the *wakaf*.

(2) The content and the style of wakaf is regulated by the Minister of Religious Affairs.

(3) The event of Ikrar as well as the construction of Ikrar Wakaf Act, will only be considered valid if witnessed by at least two (2) witnesses.

(4) During the event of Ikrar as stated in point (1) the party/person who donate the wakaf is to hand to the Officials as mentioned in article 215 point (6) the following documents:

a.   certificate of ownership of the property or other relevant document;

b.   if the material donated is the non-moveable thing, a document from the Head of Village, legalized by the Head of Borough to confirm the ownership of the mentioned non-moveable property.

c.   the written documents which accompanying the non-moveable property mentioned.

Part Two
The Registration of the Wakaf Material

Article 224.

After the Ikrar Wakaf Act is done by observing the procedure stated in article 223 point (3) and (4), the Head of Borough Office of Religious Affairs on behalf of the respective 'Nadzir' is obliged to propose the Head of Borough to register the mentioned wakaf material in order to secure the wholeness and the continuance.

CHAPTER IV
THE CHANGES, THE SETTLEMENT
AND THE SUPERVISION OF THE WAKAF MATERIAL

Part One
The Changes of The Wakaf Material

Article 225.

(1) Principally, the property that has been donated as wakaf cannot in anyway be changed or be used for other purposes than the one stated in the ikrar wakaf.

(2) The diversion of the regulation as stated in point (1) can only be done in a certain condition after being agreed with the written agreement from the Head of Borough Office of Religious Affairs based on the recommendation of the Council of Ulemas and the Head of Borough where the donated property located with the following reasons:

a.   no more relevant with the aim and purpose of wakaf as declared by the 'wakif';

b.   public utilities.

Part Two
The Settlement of Disputes of Wakaf Material

Article 226.

The settlement of the disputes concerning the wakaf materials and Nadzir will be sued to the local Islamic Court according to the existing rules and regulations.

Part Three
The Supervision

Article 227.

The supervision of tasks and the responsibility of the Nadzir is to be done collectively by the Head of the Borough Office of Religious Affairs, Council of Ulemas and the Islamic Court whose territory covers the place the wakaf property.

CHAPTER V
TRANSITIONAL RULES

Article 228.

The donation of wakaf property as well as the administration that happened before the issuance of this Law, is to be reported and registered to the Borough Officer of Religious Affairs in order to adopt this rules.

The Closing Rules

Article 229.

The Judge who trials the cases which are proposed to him is obliged to pay a serious attention to existing norm and legal values observed in the community so that the sentence will be just and fair.

EXPLANATION ON
COMPILATION BOOK OF ISLAMIC LAW
GENERAL EXPLANATIONS

1. For the country and the people of Indonesia that based on the philosophy of 'Pancasila' and the Constitution of 1945, a national legal system is a 'conditio sine quanon' (a prime necessity) to guarantee the religious life that based on the belief in one God which at the same time as a realization of the consciousness of the people and the nation of Indonesian about law.
2. Based on the Law number 14 of the year 1970 re Broad Regulations of the Judicial Authorization, 'jo' Law Number 14 of the year 1985 re the Supreme Court, The Religious Court is of the same status as other Courts namely as a State Court.
3. The Material law which is applied so far in the Religious Court is Islamic Laws which basically comprise the areas of Marriage law, Inheritance law, and the 'wakaf' (donation) law. Based on the circulation letter of the Religious Court Bureau dated 18 February 1958, Number B/I/735 the material law that serves to be the guidelines for the above legal areas refer to the 13 books which all are based on the religious school of Syafi'ie.
4. By putting the Law number 1 of the year 1974 on the Marriage into effect, and the Government Regulation number 28 of 1977 on the Donation of the Owned Property, the need of law in the society became more developed, thus the aforementioned books need to be enlarged either by adding books from other schools of Islamic religion, widening the interpretation of the stipulations in the books comparing with the

Jurisprudence of the Islamic Court, thoughts of the Ulemas or comparing with those in other countries.

5. The aforementioned Material Law needs to be compiled and put into a Judicial documentation or a Compilation Book of Islamic Law, thus it could serves to be a guideline for Judges within the Religious Court Institutions as an applied law in settling cases put forward to them.

EXPLANATIONS FROM ARTICLE BY ARTICLE

Article 1 to 6.

Sufficiently clear.

Article 7.

This article comes into effect from the date of the sanction of the Law of Religious Court.

Article 8 to 18.

Sufficiently clear.

Article 19.

One that can be a wali is of the blood related family and authorized wali (Wali Hakim), the wali for an adopted child is to be the real father.

Article 20 to 71.

Sufficiently clear.

Article 72.

What it means by deception here is if the husband claimed himself as a bachelor during the wedding but then found out that he had been married to other woman, so that a polygamy occurred without a permit from the Court. Also deception in the self-identity.

Article 73 to 86.

Sufficiently clear.

Article 87.

Condition in this article comes into effect from the date of sanction of the Law of Religious Court.

Article 88 to 93.

Sufficiently clear.

Article 94.

Condition in this article comes into effect from the date of sanction of the Law of Religious Court.

Article 95 to 97.

Sufficiently clear.

Article 98.

Condition in this article comes into effect from the date of sanction of the Law of Religious Court.

Article 99 to 102.

Sufficiently clear.

Article 103.

Condition in this article comes into effect from the date of sanction of the Law of Religious Court.

Article 104 to 106.

Sufficiently clear.

Article 107.

Condition in this article comes into effect from the date of sanction of the Law of Religious Court.

Article 108 to 118.

Sufficiently clear.

Article 119.

Every 'talak' that sentenced by the Religious Court is 'talak ba'in sughra'.

Article 120 to 128.

Sufficiently clear.

Article 129.

Condition in this article comes into effect from the date of sanction of the Law of Religious Court.

Article 130.

Sufficiently clear.

Article 131.

Condition in this article comes into effect from the date of sanction of the Law of Religious Court.

Article 132.

Condition in this article comes into effect from the date of sanction of the Law of Religious Court.

Article 133 to 147.

Sufficiently clear.

Article 148.

Condition in this article comes into effect from the date of sanction of the Law of Religious Court.

Article 149 to 185.

What it means by a child who was born from outside marriage is a child who was born not from the legal marriage or as a result of extra marital relationship.

Article 187 to 228.

Sufficiently clear.

Article 229.

Condition in this article is valid for Book I, Book II, and Book III.

Appendix IV

GOVERNMENT REGULATION NO. 28 OF THE YEAR 1977 ON WAQF OF LANDS WITH THE RIGHT OF OWNERSHIP

REGULATION OF THE GOVERNMENT OF
THE REPUBLIC OF INDONESIA
NUMBER 28 OF THE YEAR 1977
CONCERNING
WAQF OF LANDS WITH THE
RIGHT OF OWNERSHIP

THE PRESIDENT
OF THE REPUBLIC OF INDONESIA

Considering:

a. that waqf is a religious institution which can be used as one of the means for developing religious life, particularly to people professing Islam, within the framework of the national effort to attain spiritual and material welfare toward a just and prosperous society based on Pancasila;

b. that the current statutory regulation, regulating the waqf of lands with the right of ownership, beside not yet meeting the need for waqf procedures, also give opportunities for undesired matters to arise due to the absence of factual complete data on waqf lands;

c. that in line with the provision in Article 14 paragraph (1) under b and Article 49 paragraph (3) of Act Number 5 of the year 1960, it is deemed necessary to provide for the procedures and registration of waqf of lands with the right of ownership by means of a Government Regulation;

Sources: *Peraturan Perwakafan (Waqf Regulations)*, (1998). Ditjen Bimas Islam dan Urusan Haji Direktorat Urusan Agama Islam. Jakarta: Ministry of Religious Affairs of Indonesia.

With a View to:

1. Article 5 paragraph (2) of the 1945 Constitution;
2. Decree of the People's Consultative Assembly Number IV/MPR/1973 on the Basic Outlines of the State's Policies;
3. Act number 5 of the year 1960 on Basic Regulations on Agrarian Principles (State Gazette of the year 1960 number 104; Supplement to the State Gazette number 2043);
4. Government Regulation number 10 of the year 1961 concerning the Registration of Land (State Gazette of the year 1961 number 28; Supplement to the State Gazette number 2171);

HAS DECIDED :

To lay down : REGULATION OF THE GOVERNMENT OF THE REPUBLIC OF INDONESIA CONCERNING WAQF OF LANDS WITH THE RIGHT OF OWNERSHIP.

CHAPTER I
GENERAL PROVISIONS

Article 1.

In this Government Regulation:
(1) "WAQF" means the permanent dedication by any person or corporate body of part of his/its assets in the form of lands with the right of ownership recognized by Muslem Law as serving the interests of Islam or for other public interests in line with the teachings of Islam;
(2) "WAQIF" means any person or persons or corporate body dedicating his/their on its land with the right of ownership for waqf;
(3) "IQRAR" means the statement of intention by the waqif to dedicate his land with the right of ownership for waqf;
(4) "NADHIR" means any group of persons or any corporate body given the task of managing and administering the waqf property.

CHAPTER II
THE FUNCTION OF WAQF

Part One
Article 2.

The function of waqf is to make the waqf property beneficial for an indefinite period of time, in pursuence of the objectives of waqf.

Part Two
Elements of and Conditions of Waqf

Article 3.

(1) Indonesian corporate bodies and a person or persons who is/are (an) adult(s), and of sound reasoning and also which/who by law is/are not prevented to conduct a legal act, at his/its own free will and under no coercion from whomsoever/whichever party, may

submit its/his/their land with the right of ownership for waqf with due regard to the applicable statutory regulations;

(2) In the case of corporate bodies, the party acting for and on behalf of them, is their lawful governing board.

Article 4.

The land as referred to in Article 3, must be land with the right of ownership or title land exempt from any encumbrance, lien, seizure or suit at law.

Article 5.

(1) The party submitting his/their/its land for waqf must state clearly and expressly to the nadhir infront of the Authority — Empowered with issuing the Deeds of Iqrar Waqf as referred to in Article 9 paragraph (2), who then gives such statement of intention the form of an Iqrar Waqf deed, in the presence of at least 2 (two) witnesses.

(2) In specific situations the stipulation as referred to in paragraph (1) may be deviated from, upon prior approval of the Minister of Religious Affairs.

Article 6.

(1) In the event the nadhir as referred to in paragraph (4) of article 1, is an individual, he/she shall fulfil the following conditions:
a.   a citizen of the Republic of Indonesia;
b.   a follower of Islam;
c.   an adult;
d.   physically and spiritually healthy;
e.   not put under guardianship;
f.   having his residence in the sub-district of the location of the waqf land.

(2) In the case of a corporate body being the nadhir, it shall fulfil the following conditions:
a.   an Indonesian corporate body with registered office in Indonesia;
b.   having a representative office in the sub-district where the waqf land is situated.

(3) The nadhir as referred to in paragraph (1) and (2) shall be registered with the local Sub-District Office for Religious Affairs for recognition.

(4) The number of Nadhir as allowed for a certain area, as referred to in paragraph (3), shall be fixed by the Minister of Religions Affairs, as the need may be.

Part Three
Obligations and Rights of a Nadhir

Article 7.

(1) A Nadhir is under the obligation to administer and to exercise control on waqf properties and also on the gains obtained therefrom, under stipulations to be further determined by the Minister of Religious Affairs, such in accordance with the objectives of waqf.

(2) The Nadhir is under the obligation to prepare a periodical report on everything connected with the waqf properties, as referred to in paragraph (1).

(3) The procedure for making the report as referred to in paragraph (2) will be provided for by the Minister of Religious Affairs.

Article 8.

A Nadhir shall have the right to receive renumerations and facilities, the amount and nature of which shall be further determined by the Minister of Religious Affairs.

CHAPTER III
WAQF PROCEDURES AND THE
REGISTRATION THEREOF

Part One
Waqf Procedures of Lands with
the Right of Ownership

Article 9.

(1) The party intending to dedicate his/their/its land for waqf shall appear before the Authority Empowered with issuing the Deeds of Iqrar Waqf, for effecting such intention.

(2) The Authority Empowered with issuing the Deeds of Iqrar Waqf as referred to in paragraph (1) shall be appointed and dismissed by the Minister of Religious Affairs.

(3) The contents and the form of an Iqrar Waqf are laid down by the Minister of Religious Affairs.

(4) The implementation of an Iqrar, and also the preparation of the Deed of Iqrar Waqf shall be regarded as lawful, if done in the presence of and witnessed by at least 2 (two) witnesses.

(5) In carrying out the iqrar as referred to in paragraph (1), the party dedicating piece of land for waqf shall take along and submit to the authority referred to in paragraph (2), the following documents:

a. Certificate of ownership or any other document confirming ownership on the land;
b. a letter issued by the Village-Head, affirmed by the Sub-District-Head, confirming ownership on the land concerned, and that said land is not involved in any dispute;
c. a certificate of land registration;
d. the permit of the District/Municipality-Head, in this case the Head of the Regional Sub-Directorate of Agrarian Affairs.

Part Two
Registration of Waqf of Lands with
the Right of Ownership

Article 10.

(1) After the Deed of Iqrar Waqf is made in accordance with the provisions in paragraphs (4) and (5) of Article 9, the Authority Empowered with issuing the Deeds of Iqrar Waqf, on behalf of the nadhir concerned shall file an application with the District/Municipality-Head, in this case the Head of the Sub-Directorate of Agrarian Affairs, for enrolment of waqf of lands with the right of ownership concerned, as provided for by Government Regulation Number 10 of the year 1961;

(2) The District/Municipality-Head, in this case the Head of the Sub-Directorate of Agrarian Affairs, after having received such application as referred to in paragraph (1) shall enter the waqf of lands with the right of ownership concerned in the Land-Register and on the Certificate thereof.

(3) If the lands with the right of ownership submitted for waqf for which a certificate has not yet been issued, the recording as referred to in paragraph (2) shall be effected after issuance of such certificate.

(4) The Minister of Home Affairs will determine the waqf recording procedures as referred to in paragraphs (2) and (3).

(5) After the recording of the waqf of lands with the right of ownership in the Land-Register and on its Certificate, as referred to in paragraphs (2) and (3), the nadhir concerned is under the obligation to send a report thereabout to the official authorized by the Minister of Religious Affairs.

CHAPTER IV
CHANGES, SETTLEMENT OF DISPUTES, AND
CONTROL OF WAQF OF LANDS WITH
THE RIGHT OF OWNERSHIP

Part One
Changes in the Waqf of Lands with
the Right of Ownership

Article 11.

(1) In principle any place of land with the right of ownership has been submitted for waqf cannot be changed as to its utilization or destination, other than that as referred to in the iqrar waqf.

(2) A deviation from the stipulation as referred to in paragraph (1) may occur only in specific conditions, after having obtained written prior approval of the Minister of Religious Affairs, namely:

a.   if the objective of the waqf as set out in the iqrar of the waqif is no longer in consistence with the present requirements;

b.   of it is in the interest of the general public.

(3) A change in the status of waqf of lands with the right of ownership and a change in its utilization as a consequence of the provision in paragraph (2) shall be reported by the nadhir to the local District/Municipality-Head, in this case the Head of the Sub-Directorate of Agrarian Affairs, for further settlement of the matter.

Part Two
Settlement of Disputes on
Waqf of Lands with the
Right of Ownership

Article 12.

The settlement of a dispute on waqf of lands with the right of ownership, shall be submitted to the local office of the Religious Court of Justice, such as prescribed by the prevailing statutory regulations.

Part Three
Control on Waqf of Lands with the
Right of Ownership

Article 13.

The control of waqf of lands with the right of ownership and the procedures thereof at the various levels of regions shall be laid down further by the Minister of Religious Affairs.

CHAPTER V
JUDICIAL PROVISIONS

Article 14.

Whosoever commits an act in breach of the stipulations as referred to in Article 5, Article 6 paragraph (3), Article 7 paragraphs (1) and (2), Article 9, Article 10 and Article 11, shall be liable to a penalty of detention for not longer than 3 (three) months or a fine of maximum Rp10,000 (ten thousand rupiahs).

Article 15.

If the act as referred to in Article 14 is committed by or on behalf of a corporate body, the criminal prosecution shall be effected and the penalty and disciplinary measure imposed on both the corporate body and those persons having given the order to commit such act, or on the one having acted as the leader or neglect or on both of them.

CHAPTER VI
TRANSITIONAL PROVISIONS

Article 16.

(1) A waqf of lands with the right of ownership as well as the formalities required therefor, which took place before the issuance of this Government Regulation, shall be registered by the nadhir with the local Sub-District Office of Religious Affairs, to be adjusted to the provisions of this Government Regulation.

(2) The procedures and the implementation of the provision as referred to in paragraph (1) shall be further laid down by the Minister of Religious Affairs.

Article 17.

(1) The regulations and or the stipulations on waqf of lands with the right of ownership, as mentioned in the Supplements to the State Gazette number 6196 of the year 1905, number 12573 of the year 1931, number 13390 of the year 1934 and number 13480 of the year 1935 as well as the provisions in the implementation thereof to the extent that they are contrary to the provisions in this Government Regulation, are declared no longer applicable.

(2) Any matter not yet sufficiently provided for in this Government Regulation shall be further regulated by the Minister of Religious Affairs and the Minister of Home Affairs, such in accordance with their respective competencies.

CHAPTER VII
CONCLUDING PROVISION

Article 18.

This Government Regulation shall come into force as from the date of its promulgation. In order that everybody has knowledge hereof, this Government Regulation shall be inserted in the State Gazette of the Republic Indonesia.

Sanctioned in Jakarta
On 17th May, 1977
THE PRESIDENT OF THE REPUBLIC OF INDONESIA

signed.
SOEHARTO

Promulgated in Jakarta on 17th May, 1977
MINISTER/SECRETARY OF STATE OF THE
REPUBLIC OF INDONESIA

signed.
SUDHARMONO S. H.

STATE GAZETTE OF THE REPUBLIC OF INDONESIA
OF THE YEAR 1977 NUMBER 38

ELUCIDATION
OF
THE REGULATION OF THE GOVERNMENT OF
THE REPUBLIC OF INDONESIA NUMBER 28 OF
THE YEAR 1977 CONCERNING WAQF OF LANDS
WITH THE RIGHT OF OWNERSHIP

I. GENERAL

One of the features in the field of religion related with the implementation of agrarian tasks is the waqf of lands with the right of ownership. This issue of waqf of lands with the right of ownership is of such importance viewed from the angle of Act number 5 of the year 1960 on Basic Regulations on Agrarian Principles, that is has been made desirable to regulate it by means of a Government Regulation.

In the past, the issue of waqf of lands with the right of ownership had not been adequately regulated by a statutory regulation, leading to the easy occurrences of deviations from the true meaning and objectives of waqf, primarily caused by the fact that too many varieties of waqf exist (family waqf, general waqf, and others), and by the absence of any obligation of having waqf registered, so that not much is known of many of the things which had been submitted for waqf. Even to the extent that said waqf have come to be considered the property of the heirs of those who were given the tasks of administering waqf (nadhir).

Such occurrences have caused much uneasiness among the faithful, particularly among Muslems, and have led to feelings of antipathy to exist. On the other hand, many instances of dispute about land-property have arisen due to the unclear status of the lands concerned, so that unless a regulation this respect is immediately provided not only will this reduce religious consciousness among Moslems but it will, even obstruct any effort of the Government to activate and guide the faithful toward fulfilling their religious duties, as implied in the Pancasila-teachings and laid down in the Decree of the People Consultative Assembly number IV/MPR/1973.

Regulated in this Government Regulation, are only matters concerning waqf for public interest of lands with the right of ownership. Other forms of waqf, such as family-waqf, are not dealt with in this Government Regulation. This limitation needs to be made in order to prevent confusions to occur concerning the matter of waqf. Furthermore, the waqf object in this regulation is limited to lands with the right of ownership. This also with the purpose of preventing future confusions.

Under Act of the Basic Regulation on Agrarian Principles it is just the right of ownership which has a comprehensive effect, whereas other forms of right on land, such as the right of exploitation, the right of building, the right of utilization, are valid for a limited period of time only so that the holders of such rights do not have the same rights and authority as those holding a right of ownership. Since all forms of waqf hold good for an unlimited period of time, title lands which the right on are temporary in nature cannot be submitted for waqf.

Furthermore, also regulated by this Government Regulation are the administration to be carried out by the waqf (nadhir), waqf procedures, and procedures for granting rights and procedures for acquiring legal certainty concerning the right on waqf land.

II. ARTICLE BY ARTICLE

Article 1.

Paragraph (1) up to and including (3).
   Sufficently clear.
Paragraph (4)
   Means by a group of persons in this paragraph is a group of persons forming one entity or forming one governing board.

Article 2.

   Sufficently clear.

Article 3.

   This article gives a detailed explanation on the conditions to be met by individuals conducting a waqf act, in order to avoid unlawful practice of waqf which may be caused either by internal factors (insanity) or by external factors such as pressure by an (other) party (parties).
   These stipulations are also applicable to corporate body and Indonesian Foundations which are active in the field of religion, by adjusting them, where necessary to the conditions of the legal subjects concerned in line with the current laws.

Article 4.

   As set forth above, the act of waqf is a sacred one, a noble and praiseworthy act in accordance with the teachings of Islam. Therefore, lands to be submitted for waqf shall be the full and perfect property of the submitting party, free from any incorrectness as seen from the angle of the right of ownership. Apart from that, these requisites are meant to prevent the institution of waqf from being involved in a lawsuit, which may lower the prestige and sacred nature of Islam. In view of the above, any piece of land being burdened with liens, like a mortgage, crediet-verband, being disputed through a lawsuit, etc. cannot be submitted as waqf before the attaching matter is first fully settled.

Article 5.

   Sufficiently clear.

Article 6.

   This article regulates the requirements to be met for becoming a nadhir (waqf administrator), so that the nadhir, whether a group of persons or a corporate body, can perform his/their function properly. The number of nadhir in a region needs to be limited and registered, in order to eliminate any seed of dispute which may exist due to the fact that too many persons are focussing on the same matter and the same object. The registration meant to avoid that a waqf takes place deviating from the provisions as laid down and while also to facilitate the exercise of control.

Article 7.

With a view to facilitating control on waqf of lands the appointed nadhir thereto is under the obligation of submitting periodical reports on the land which has been submitted for waqf and administered by him, and also on the use of any proceeds thereof.

Such reporting is also meant to facilitate the exercise of control.

Article 8.

This article provides a basis for determining the income of and granting facilities to a nadhir. By giving the nadhir a reasonable reward/income for covering his needs, it is expected that deviations in the use of the waqf land will be prevented from occurring.

Article 9.

This article makes it obligatory for waqf to be concluded in writing rather than orally with the purpose of providing an authentic proof to be used whenever a problem may arise such as at the time of registering it with the Sub-District/municipality Office of Sub-Directorate of Agrarian Affairs, or the settling of a dispute which may arise later with respect to said waqf land. Thus a person wanting to submit for waqf a piece of land shall take along all evidences of ownership (land-certificate) and other documents confirming that there none whatsoever can prevent the submission for waqf of lands with the right of ownership concerned.

For the implementation of the aforementioned, officials need to be assigned with the specific task or preparing the necessary Deeds. Furthermore, the form and contents of iqrar waqf, must have uniformity of shape.

Article 10.

One feature which has not been provided properly regulated and implemented sofar is the registration of waqf lands along the stipulations as laid down in Act number 5 of the year 1960 and its implementary regulation.

The registration of waqf lands is of immense importance both viewed from the angle of legal certainty and from the angle of the administration of the control and use of the land concerned, in accordance with the prevailing statutory regulation with respect to agrarian affairs.

By registering and recording waqf on the certificate of lands with the right of ownership, submitted for waqf, that land has obtained instrument of evidence which in undeniable.

Article 11.

In the past it was possible for a nadhir to bring about change in the status of a waqf-land without any reasonable grounds. Such occurrences naturally caused reactions in the community, primarily those who have an immediate interest in the waqf-land.

This Government Regulation provides for strict limitations on such practises while also determining that prior approval of the Minister of Religious Affairs or from any authorized official must first obtained for such changes in order to practices damaging the interests of a waqf will be avoided. For the purpose of land-administration, any change in the status of waqf land must be notified to the competent administrator. Any deviation from the provisions as referred to in Article 11 paragraph (2), besides being subject to the sanction under Article 15, will also be considered as null and void by law.

Article 12.

Any settlement of disputes as referred to in this article which comes under the jurisdiction and competence of the Religious Court of justice concerns whether or not an act of waqf has been made in accordance with the provisions of this Government Regulation, and other issues related to waqf based on the teachings of Islam. Consequently, other issues related to Civil law or Criminal law are obviously to be solved procedure of law in the Court of Justice.

Article 13.

Generally a waqf of land takes place in regions at the sub-district level in order to facilitate control, adequate administration is a necessity at the sub-district, district, province level as well as in the central government.

As to the reciproval manner in which control is to be exercised this will be further determined by the Minister of Religious Affairs.

Article 14.

Sufficiently clear.

Article 15.

Sufficiently clear.

Article 16.

This represents a transitional provision on waqf of land having taken place before issuance of this Government Regulation.

In executing his task of adjusting any existing waqf to this Government Regulation it will not suffice if the nadhir solely registers waqf with the local Sub-District Office of Religious Affairs, the status of the land must first be determined and its right of ownership registered through procedures required for the waqf of lands with the right of under Article 10.

The process of adjusting existing waqfs to the provisions in this Government Regulation will consume time and makes it desirable for specific policies to be taken; Consequently further decisions will be taken by the Minister of Religious Affairs as to the procedures, the period of adjustment and a possible extension thereof.

Article 17.

Sufficiently clear.

Article 18.

Sufficiently clear.

SUPPLEMENT OF THE STATE GAZETTE OF THE
REPUBLIC OF INDONESIA NUMBER 3107.

BIBLIOGRAPHY

Abbas Sirajuddin. *40 Masalah Agama* [40 Questions on Religion]. 4 vols. Jakarta: Pustaka Tarbijah, 1972.

Abdullah, Abdul Gani, ed. *Himpunan Perundang-undangan dan Peraturan Peradilan Agama.* Jakarta: Intermasa, 1991.

Abdullah, Abdul Gani. "Pemasyarakatan Inpres No. 1/1991 tentang Kompilasi Hukum Islam". *Mimbar Hukum: Aktualisasi Hukum Islam* III, no. 5 (1992).

————. *Pengantar Kompilasi Hukum Islam dalam Tata Hukum Indonesia.* Jakarta: Gema Insani Press, 1994.

Abdullah, Taufik. "Zakat Collection and Distribution in Indonesia". In *The Islamic Voluntary Sector in Southeast Asia,* edited by Mohammed Ariff. Singapore: Institute of Southeast Asian Studies, 1991.

————. "Islamic Discourse and Muslim Intellectuals in Indonesia: A Historical Sketch on Contemporary Trends". Paper presented at the First International Conference on Islam and the 21st Century, Leiden, June 1996.

Abdurrahman, H. *Kompilasi Hukum Islam di Indonesia.* Jakarta: Akademika Presindo, 1992.

Abdurrahman. *Kompilasi Hukum Islam di Indonesia.* Jakarta: Akademika Presindo, 1995.

Abrahamian, Ervand. *Khomeinism: Essays on the Islamic Republic.* Berkeley: University of California Press, 1993.

Abubakar, Zainal Abidin. "Kebijaksanaan Pelayanan Hukum di Lingkungan Peradilan Agama". *GEMA* XVIII, no. 80 (June 1996).

Abu Dawud, Sulaiman bin al-Asy'as bin Ishaq bin Basyir bin Syidad bin 'Amr al-Azdi al-Sijistani. *Sunan Abi Dawud.* Beirut: al-Maktabah al-'Ashriyah, 1952.

Adnan, Zifirdaus. "Islamic Religion". In *State and Civil Society in Indonesia,* edited by Arief Budiman. Monash Papers on Southeast Asia, no. 22, 1990, pp. 441–78.

Affandi, Ali. *Hukum Keluarga Menurut Kitab Undang-undang Hukum Perdata* [Family law according to *Burgerlijk Wetboek*]. Yogyakarta: Jajasan Badan Penerbit Gadjah Mada, 1964.

Ahmad, Amrullah et al., eds. *Dimensi Hukum Islam dalam Sistem Hukum Nasional: Mengenang 65 tahun Prof. Dr. H. Bustanul Arifin, SH.* Jakarta: Gema Insani Press, 1996.

'Alam, Shaikh Nizam and 'Ulama' al-Hind al-. *al-Fatawa al-'Alamkiriyah al-Ma'rufah bi al-Fatawa al-Hindiyyah,* edited by Ghulam Nabi Tunsawi, 6 vols. Kuitiyah: Maktabah Majidiyah, 1983.

Ali, A. M. *Beberapa Persoalan Agama Dewasa Ini* [Several current matters of religion]. Jakarta: Rajawali, 1987.

Ali, Fachry and Bahtiar Effendy. *Merambah Jalan Baru Islam* [Pioneering a new Islamic path]. Bandung: Mizan, 1986.

Ali, Muhammad Daud. *Asas-asas Hukum Islam.* Jakarta: Rajawali Press, 1990.

Alisjahbana, S. Takdir. *Indonesia: Social and Cultural Revolution.* Kuala Lumpur: Oxford University Press, 1966.

'Alwani, Taha Jabir al-. *Source Methodology in Islamic Jurisprudence.* USA: The International Institute of Islamic Thought, 1993.

Amak F. Z. *Proses Undang-undang Perkawinan.* Bandung: Al-Ma'arif, 1976.

Amidi, Sayf al-Din al-. *al-Ihkam fi Usul al-Ahkam.* Cairo: Dar al-Kutub al-Khidiwiya, 1914.

Angelino, A. D. A. de Kat. *Colonial Policy,* tr. G. J. Renier, vol. 2. The Hague: M. Nijhoff, 1955.

Antonio, M. Syafi'i. *Bank Syariah: Suatu Pengenalan Umum* [*Shari'a* bank: A general introduction]. Jakarta: Tazkia Institute, 2000.

Anwar, M. Syafi'i. "Negara, Umat dan Ijtihad Politik". *Panji Masyarakat,* No. 693, 11–21 August 1991.

Aqsha, Darul, Dick van der Meij, and Johann Hendrik Meuleman. *Islam in Indonesia: A Survey of Events and Developments from 1988 to March 1993.* Jakarta: Indonesia, Netherlands Islamic Services (INIS), 1995.

Ariff, Mohammed. "Resource Mobilization through the Islamic Voluntary Sector in Southeast Asia". In *The Islamic Voluntary Sector in Southeast Asia,* edited by Mohammed Ariff. Singapore: Institute of Southeast Asian Studies, 1991.

Arifin, Bustanul. "Kompilasi: Fiqh dalam Bahasa Undang-Undang". *Pesantren* II, no. 2 (1985).

──────. "Pemahaman Hukum Islam dalam Konteks Perundang-undangan". *Wahyu* VII, no. 108 (May 1985).

Arnold, Thomas W. *The Preaching of Islam,* reprinted ed. Lahore: Ashraf, 1961.

Asrofie, Yusron. *Kiyai Ahmad Dahlan: Pemikiran dan Kepemimpinannya.* Yogyakarta: Yogyakarta Offset, 1983.

Attamimi, A. Hamid S. "Kedudukan Kompilasi Hukum Islam dalam Sistem Hukum Nasional: Suatu Tinjauan dari Sudut Teori Perundang-undangan Indonesia". In *Dimensi Hukum Islam dalam Sistem Hukum Nasional: Mengenang 65 Tahun*

Prof. Dr. H. Bustanul Arifin, SH., edited by Amrullah Ahmad. Jakarta: Gema Insani Press, 1996.

Attas, Sayyid Muhammad Naguib Al-. *Preliminary Statement on A General Theory of the Islamization of the Malay-Indonesian Archipelago*. Kuala Lumpur: Dewan Bahasa & Pustaka, 1970.

Ayata, Sencer. "Patronage, Party and State: The Politicization of Islam in Turkey". Middle East Journal 50, no. 1 (Winter 1996): 40–56.

Azra, Azyumardi. "The Transmission of Islamic Reformism to Indonesia; Networks of Malay-Indonesian Ulama in the 17th and 18th centuries". Ph.D. dissertation, Columbia University, 1992.

—————. "Islamic Perspective on the Nation-State: Political Islam in Post-Soeharto Indonesia". Paper presented at International Conference on "Islamic Perspectives on the New Millennium", Australian National University, Canberra, 20–21 November 2000.

Ball, John. *Indonesian Legal History 1602–1848*. Sydney: Oughtershaw Press, 1982.

—————. *Indonesian Law Commentary and Teaching Materials*. Sydney: Faculty of Law, University of Sydney, 1985.

—————. *The Struggle for National Law in Indonesia*. Sydney: Faculty of Law, University of Sydney, 1986.

Baloch, N. A. *Advent of Islam in Indonesia*. Islamabad: National Institute of Historical and Cultural Research, 1980.

Barton, Gregg. "Neo-Modernism: A Vital Synthesis of Traditionalist and Modernist Islamic Thought in Indonesia". *Studia Islamika* 2, no. 3 (1995): 1–76.

Basran, Masran. "Kompilasi Hukum Islam". *Mimbar Ulama* X, no. 105 (May 1986).

Basri, Hasan. "Perlunya Kompilasi Hukum Islam". *Mimbar Ulama* X, no. 104 (April 1986).

Basyir, Ahmad Azhar. "Pemasyarakatan Kompilasi Hukum Islam melalui Jalur Pendidikan Non Formal". *Mimbar Hukum: Aktualisasi Hukum Islam* III, no. 5 (1992).

—————. *Refleksi atas Persoalan Keislaman*. Bandung: Mizan, 1994.

Benda, Harry. *The Crescent and the Rising Sun*. The Hague: W. van Hoeve, 1958.

Bisri, Cik Hasan. "Aspek-aspek Sosiologis Hukum Islam di Indonesia" [Sociological aspects of Islamic law in Indonesia]. In *Hukum Islam dalam Tatanan Masyarakat Indonesia* [Islamic law in Indonesian social order], edited by Cik Hasan Bisri, pp. 109–44. Jakarta: Logos, 1998.

Boland, B. J. *The Struggle of Islam in Modern Indonesia*. The Hague: Martinus Nijhoff, 1982.

Bowen, John R. *Muslims Through Discourse: Religion and Ritual in Gayo Society*. Princeton: Princeton University Press, 1993.

Bukhari, Abu 'Abd Allah Muhammad bin Isma'il bin Ibrahim bin al-Mugirah bin Bardizbah al-. *Sahih al-Bukhari*. Beirut: Dar al-Qalam, 1987.

Cammack, Mark, Lawrence A. Young, and Tim Heaton. "Legislating Social Change in an Islamic Society—Indonesian Marriage Law". *American Journal of Comparative Law* 44 (1996): 45–73.

Christelow, Allan. *Muslim Law Courts and the France Colonial State in Algeria*. New Jersey: Princeton University Press, 1985.

Coulson, N. J. *A History of Islamic Law*. Edinburgh: Edinburgh University Press, 1964.

Crone, Patricia and Martin Hinds. *God's Caliph: Religious Authority in the First Century of Islam*. Cambridge: Cambridge University Press, 1986.

Crouch, Harold. "Indonesia: An Uncertain Outlook". In *Southeast Asian Affairs 1994*. Singapore: Institute of Southeast Asian Studies, 1994.

Dachlan, M. "Piagam Djakarta Sumber Hukum Mendjiwai U.U.D. 1945". Speech delivered at the Commemoration of Jakarta Charter Day Celebration, 29 June 1968. *Kiblat* XVI, no. 3-4 (1968).

Damanik, Ali Said. *Fenomena Partai Keadilan: Transformasi 20 Tahun Gerakan Tarbiyah di Indonesia* (Jakarta: Teraju, 2002).

Damian, Eddy and Robert N. Homick. "Indonesia's Formal Legal System; An Introduction". *America Journal of Comparative Law* 20, no. 3 (Summer 1972): 492–530.

Darimi, Abu Muhammad al-. *Sunan al-Darimi*. Dar al-Kitab al-'Arabi, 1987.

Dawalibi, Muhammad Ma'ruf al-. *al-Madkhal ila 'Ilm al-Usul al-Fiqh*. Matba'ah Jami'ah Damsyq, 1959.

De Graaf, H. J. "Southeast Asian Islam to the Eighteenth Century". In *The Cambridge History of Islam*, edited by P. M. Holt et al. London: Cambridge University Press, 1987.

Departemen Agama RI. *Pedoman Pembinaan BAZIS: Hasil Pertemuan Nasional I BAZIS se-Indonesia tanggal 3–4 Maret 1992*. Jakarta, 1992.

Ditbinbapera. *Kompilasi Hukum Islam di Indonesia*. Jakarta: Ditbinbapera, 1991/1992.

Ditjen Bimas Islam dan Urusan Haji Depag RI. *Pedoman Zakat*, Jakarta: Proyek Pembinaan Zakat dan Wakaf, 1992/93.

Djamil, Fathurrahman. "The Muhammadiyah and the Theory of Maqasid al-Shari'ah". *Studia Islamika* 2, no. 1 (1995).

————."Manhaj Istinbath Hukum dalam Muhammadiyah". Paper presented at Raker Majelis Tarjih PWM, DKI Jakarta, 30 November 1997.

————. *Metode Majelis Tarjih Muhammadiyah*. Jakarta: Logos Publishing Houses, 1995.

Djamour, J. *The Muslim Matrimonial Court in Singapore*. London: Athlone Press, 1966.

Djojodidigeono. M. M. *Adat Law in Indonesia*. Jakarta: Djambatan, 1952.

Effendy, Bahtiar. "Islam and the State: The Transformation of Islamic Political Ideas and Practices in Indonesia". Ph.D. dissertation, Ohio State University, 1994.

————. *Islam dan Negara: Transformasi Pemikiran dan Praktik Politik Islam di Indonesia* [Islam and the state: Transformation of Islamic political ideas and practices in Indonesia]. Jakarta: Paramadina, 1998.

Emmerson, Donald K. *Indonesia's Elite: Political Culture and Cultural Politics*. Ithaca and London: Cornell University Press, 1976.

Fadlullah, Cholid. *Mengenal Hukum ZIS dan Pengamalannya di DKI Jakarta*. Jakarta: BAZIS DKI, 1993.

Faruqi, Ismail and Lamiya. *The Cultural Atlas of Islam*. New York: Macmillan, 1986.

Fatchurrahman. *Al-Haditsun Nabawy* [Traditions of the Prophet]. 2 vols. Kudus: Menara, 1966 (1979).

Federspiel, Howard M. *Persatuan Islam: Islamic Reform in the Twentieth Century Indonesia*. Ithaca: Modern Indonesia Project Southeast Asia Program, 1970.

————. *Muslim Intellectuals and National Development in Indonesia*. Commack: Nova Science Press, 1992.

————. *The Usage of Traditions of the Prophet in Contemporary Indonesia*. Tempe: Arizona State University Program for International Studies, 1993.

————. *A Dictionary of Indonesian Islam*. Athens, Ohio: Ohio University, Center for International Studies, 1995.

————. "The Endurance of Muslim Traditionalist Scholarship: An Analysis of the Writings of the Indonesian Scholar Sirajuddin Abbas". In *Toward a New Paradigm in Indonesian Islamic Thought,* edited by Mark Woodward. Tempe: ASU Program for Southeast Asian Studies, 1996.

Gaffar, Afan. "Islam dan Politik dalam Era Orde Baru, Mencari Bentuk Artikulasi Yang Tepat". *Ulumul Qur'an* IV, no. 2 (1993).

————. "Islam dan Partai Politik, Bagian Kedua". *Risalah*, No. 7 (November 1994).

Gautama, Soedarto. "Law Reform in Indonesia". *Rabels Zeitschrift* 26 (1961): 535–53.

Gibb, H. A. R. *Modern Trends in Islam*. Chicago: University of Chicago Press, 1945.

Gouwgioksiong. "The Marriage Laws of Indonesia with Special Reference to Mixed Marriages". *Rabels Zeitschrift* 28 (1964): 711–31.

Haar, B. Ter. *Adat Law in Indonesia,* translated from Dutch and edited with an Introduction by E. Adamson Hoebel and A. Arthur Schiller. New York: Institute of Pacific Relation, 1948.

Habir, Ahmad D. "The Emerging Managerial Elite Professionals and Patriachs". In *Southeast Asian Affairs 1993*, pp. 161–82. Singapore: Institute of Southeast Asian Studies, 1993.

Hakim, Muhammad Taqi al-. *al-Usul al-'Ammah li al-Fiqh al-Muqarin*. 1st ed. Dar al-Andalus, Beirut, 1963.

Halimah A. *Kebhinnekaan dan Sifat-Sifat Khas Masyarakat Hukum Adat Indonesia*. Padang: Laboratorium PMP/IKN FPIPS Institute Keguruan Ilmu Pendidikan Padang, 1987.

Hamka. "Hubungan Timbal Balik antara Adat dan Syara' di dalam Kebudayaan Minangkabau". *Panji Masyarakat* 61/IV (1970).

Hanbal, Ahmad bin. *Musnad al-Imam Ahmad*. al-Maktabah al-Islami, n.d.

Harahap, M. Yahya. "Tujuan Kompilasi Hukum Islam". In *Kajian Islam tentang berbagai Masalah Kontemporer,* edited by IAIN Syarif Hidayatullah. Jakarta: Hikmat Syahid Indah, 1988.

Harahap, M. Yahya. "Informasi Materi Kompilasi Hukum Islam: Mempositifkan Abstraksi Hukum Islam". In *Berbagai Pandangan Terhadap Kompilasi Hukum Islam*, edited by Tim Ditbinbapera. Jakarta: Yayasan Al-Hikmah, 1993.

Hartono, C. F. G. Sunaryati. *Politik Hukum Menuju Satu Sistem Hukum Nasional* [Politic of law toward one system of national law]. Bandung: Penerbit Alumni, 1991.

———. "Pembinaan Hukum Nasional Pada Pembangunan Jangka Panjang Tahap II Dalam Konteks Hukum Islam". *Mimbar Hukum* IV, no. 8 (1993).

Harun, Lukman. *Muhammadiyah dan Asas Pancasila*. Jakarta: Pustaka Panjimas, 1986.

Hassan, Ahmad. *Soal Jawab Agama* [Questions and answers concerning Islam]. 4 vols. Bangil: Persatuan Islam, 1985.

Hassan, Kamal. *Modernisasi Indonesia, Respon Cendekiawan Muslim*. Jakarta: LSI, 1987.

Hazairin. *Pergolakan Penyesuaian Adat kepada Islam* [The struggle of *adat* adoption of Islam]. Jakarta: Bulan Bintang, 1952.

———. *Hoekum Islam dan Masjarakat* [Islamic law and society]. Jakarta: Bulan Bintang, 1957.

———. *Hukum Kekeluargaan Nasional* [National family laws]. Jakarta: Tintamas, 1962.

———. *Hukum Kewarisan*. Jakarta: Tintamas, 1964.

Hefner, Robert. "Islamizing Java? Religion and Politics in Rural East Java". *Journal of Asian Studies* 46, no. 3 (August 1987): 533–54.

———. "Islam, State and Civil Society: ICMI and the Struggle for the Indonesian Middle Class". *Indonesia* 56 (October 1993): 1–35.

———. "Islamizing Capitalism: On the Founding of Indonesia's First Islamic Bank". In *Toward a New Paradigm: Recent Developments in Indonesian Islamic Thought*, edited by Mark Woodward. Arizona: Arizona State University Program of Southeast Asian Studies, 1996.

Hisyam, Muhammad. "The Dynamics of Religion and State Relations in Indonesia: The Case of the Islamic Court". Paper presented at the First International Conference on Islam and the 21st Century, Leiden, June 1996.

Hodgson, Marshal G. S. *The Venture of Islam*. Chicago: The University of Chicago Press, 1977.

Hooglund, Eric. "The Social Origins of the Revolutionary Clergy". In *The Iranian Revolution and the Islamic Republic*, edited by Nikki R. Keddie and E. Hooglund. Syracuse: Syracuse University Press, 1986.

Hooker, M. B. *Adat Law in Modern Indonesia*. Kuala Lumpur: Oxford University Press, 1978.

———. *Islamic Law in South-East Asia*. Kuala Lumpur: Oxford University Press, 1984.

———. "The State and Shariah in Indonesia 1945–1995". Lecture and typescript. 1995.

Hooker, Virginia Matheson. *Culture and Society in New Order Indonesia*. Kuala Lumpur: Oxford University Press, 1993.

Horowitz, D. L. "The Qur'an and the Common Law". *Americal Journal of Comparative Law* 42 (1994): 233, 545.

Ibn Majah, Abu 'Abd Allah Muhammad bin Yazid. *Sunan Ibn Majah*. Dar Ihya al-Turas al-Arabi, 1975.

Ibrahim, Ahmad. "The Shari'ah and Codification: Malaysia Experience". *Shari'ah Law Journal* (January 1987).

Indonesia, Departmen Agama. *Organization of the Department of Religious Affairs*. Jakarta: 1985.

Ismail, Faisal. "Pancasila as the Sole Basis for all Political Parties and for all Mass Organizations: An Account of Muslims' Response". Ph.D. Dissertation, McGill University, Montreal, 1995.

Jafizham, T. "Peranan Pengadilan Agama dalam Pelaksanaan Undang-undang Perkawinan". In *Kenang-kenangan Seabad Peradilan Agama,* edited by H. A. Muhaimin Nur et al. Jakarta: Departemen Agama, 1985.

Jainuri, Achmad. "Muhammadiyah sebagai Gerakan Pembaharuan Islam" [Muhammadiyah as an Islamic renewal movement]. *Gebyar Muktamar Muhammadiyah ke-43* [43rd General Congress of the Muhammadiyah], 1995.

—————. "The Formation of the Muhammadiyah's Ideology, 1912–1942"' Ph.D. thesis, McGill University, 1997.

Jenkins, David. *Suharto and His Generals: Indonesian Military Politics 1975–1983*. Ithaca: Cornell, 1984.

Jennings, Sir Ivor. *The Law and the Constitution,* 5th ed. London: The English Language Book Society, 1979.

Johns, Anthony H. "Indonesia; Islam and Cultural Pluralism". In *Islam in Asia; Religion, Politics and Society,* edited by John L. Esposito. New York: Oxford University Press, 1987.

Ka'bah, Rifyal, "Keputusan Lajnah Tarjih Muhammadiyah dan Lajnah Bahsul Masa'il Nahdlatul Ulama Sebagai Keputusan Ijtihad Jama'i di Indonesia". Ph.D. thesis, Universitas Indonesia, Jakarta, 1998.

Kamali, Muhammad Hashim. *Principles of Islamic Jurisprudence*. Cambridge: Islamic Text Society, 1991.

Kansil, C. S. T. *Pengantar Ilmu Hukum dan Tata Hukum Indonesia*. Jakarta: Balai Pustaka, 1986.

Kansil and Erwin. *Kitab Himpunan Karya MPRS*. Djakarta, 1970.

Karim, Rusli. *Dinamika Islam di Indonesia, Suatu Tinjauan Sosial dan Politik*. Jakarta: Hanindita, 1985.

Katz, June and Ronald Katz. "The New Indonesian Marriage Law: A Mirror of Indonesia's Political, Cultural, and Legal System". *American Journal of Comparative Law* 23 (1975): 653.

Kernkamp, WJA. "Government and Islam in the Netherland Indies", translated by NAC. Slotemaker de Bruine. *The Muslim World*, vol. 35, pp. 6–26. Hartford, 1945.

Ketetapan-ketetapan Majelis Permusyawaratan Rakyat Indonesia Tahun 1993. Jakarta: BP7 Pusat, 1993.

Khatib, Muhammad 'Ajaj al-. *Usul al-Hadis: 'Ulumuh wa Mustalahuh*, Beirut: Dar al-Fikr, 1989.

Khin, Mustafa Sa'id al-. *Asar al-Ikhtilaf fi al-Qawa'd al-Usuliyyah fi Ikhtilaf al-Fuqaha*. Beirut: Mu'assasah al-Risalah, 1982.

Kitani, Muhammad Ja'far al-. *Nizam al-Mutanasir min al-Hadis al-Mutawatir*. Beirut: Maktabah al-'Ilm wa al-Iman, 1990.

Koentjaraningrat. *Javanese Culture*. Singapore: Oxford University Press, 1990.

Koesnodiprodjo. *Himpunan Undang-undang, Peraturan-peraturan, Penetapan-penatapan Pemerintah Republik Indonesia 1946* [Compilation of laws, regulations and decrees of the government of the Republic of Indonesia, 1946]. Jakarta: Seno, 1947.

Koesnoe, Mohammad. "Menetapkan Hukum dari Adat" [Making law from *adat*]. *Hukum Nasional* year 2, no. 3 (January-March 1969): 3–11.

————. "Hukum Adat dan Pembangunan Hukum Nasional" [*Adat* law and the development of national law]. *Hukum dan Keadilan* year 2, no. 3 (March/April 1970): 32–43.

Legowo, Tommi. "Religious Issues in Indonesia". *Indonesian Quarterly* XVII, no. 2 (1989).

Lev. Daniel S. "The Lady and the Banyan Tree: Civil Law Change in Indonesia". *American Journal of Comparative Law* 14 (1965): 282–307.

————. *Islamic Courts in Indonesia*. Berkeley: University of California Press, 1972a.

————. "Judicial Institutions and Legal Culture". In *Culture and Politics in Indonesia*, edited by Claire Holt, pp. 246–318. Ithaca, NY: Cornell University Press, 1972b.

————. "Judicial Unification in Post Colonial Indonesia". *Indonesia* 16 (October 1973): 1–37.

————. "Judicial Authority and the Struggle of an Indonesian *Rechtstaat*". *Law and Society Review* 13/1 (Fall 1978).

————. "Colonial Law and the Genesis of the Indonesian State". *Indonesia* 40 (October 1985): 69–74.

Liddle, R. William. "*Media Dakwah* Scripturalism: One Form of Islamic Political Thought and Action in New Order Indonesia". In *Toward a New Paradigm: Recent Development in Indonesian Islamic Thought*, edited by Mark R. Woodward, pp. 323–56. Arizona: Arizona State University, 1996a.

————. "The Islamic Turn in Indonesia: A Political Explanation". *Journal of Asian Studies* 55, no. 3 (1996b): 613–34.

Lubis, Arbiyah. *Pemikiran Muhammadiyah dan Muhammad Abduh: Suatu Studi Perbandingan*. Jakarta: Bulan Bintang, 1993.

Lubis, Nur Ahmad Fadhil. "Institutionalization and the Unification of Islamic Courts under the New Order". *Studia Islamika* 2, no. 1 (1995): 1–51.

Lubis, Todung Mulya. *In Search of Human Right: Legal Political Dilemmas of Indonesia's New Order, 1966–1990*. Jakarta: Gramedia, 1993.

Madkur, Muhammad Salam. *Manahij al-Ijtihad fi al-Islam*. Jami'ah al-Kuwait: al-Matba'ah al-'Ashriyah al-Kuwait, 1974.

Magnis-Suseno, Franz. "Seputar Rencana UU Peradilan Agama". *Kompas*, 16 June 1989.

Mahfud, Mohd. *Politik Hukum di Indonesia* [Legal politics in Indonesia]. Jakarta: LP3ES, 1998.

Majelis Tarjih Muhammadiyah. *Tuntunan Manasik Haji*. Yogyakarta, 1998.

Majelis Ulama Indonesia. *Kumpulan Fatwa Majelis Ulama Indonesia* [Collection of jurisprudential recommendations of the Indonesian Religious Scholars' Council]. Jakarta: Pustaka Panjimas, 1984.

Malik, Abu 'Abd Allah. *al-Muwatta'*. al-Syirkah al-'Alamiyah, 1993.

Mastura, Datu M. O. "Shari'ah and Codification: Islamic Legislation in Relation to Legal Reforms in the Philippines". *Shari'ah Law Journal* (January 1987).

Mas'udi, Masdar F. *Risalah Zakat (Pajak) dalam Islam*. Jakarta: Pustaka Firdaus, 1991.

————. An oration delivered at a seminar on the Dissemination of the Bill of Zakat Laws at Treva Hotel, Jakarta on 19 August 1999.

Mawardi, Abu al-Hasan 'Ali bin Muhammad bin Habib al-. *al-Nukat wa al-'Uyun Tafsir al-Mawardi*, vol. 1. Beirut: Dar al-Kutub al-'Ilmiyah, n.d.

Mayer, Ann Elizabeth. "The Shari'ah: A Methodology or a Body of Substantive Rules". In *Islamic Law and Jurisprudence: Studies in Honor of Farhat J. Ziadeh*, edited by Nicholas Heer. London: University of Washington Press, 1990.

Meeker, Michael E. "The New Muslim Intellectuals in the Republic of Turkey". In *Islam in Modern Turkey: Religion, Politics and Literature in a Secular State*, edited by Richard Tapper, pp. 189–219. London: I. B. Tauris, 1991.

Mehdi, Rubaya. *The Islamization of the Law in Pakistan*. Richmond, U.K.: Curzon Press, 1994.

Menteri Agama RI, *Himpunan Pidato Menteri Agama RI*. Jakarta: Biro Hukum dan Humas Sekretaris Jenderal Departemen Agama, 1988.

Merryemen, J. T. *The Civil Law Tradition*. Stanford University Press, 1969.

Meuleman, Johan. "The Institut Agama Islam Negeri at the Crossroads". Paper presented at the First International Conference on Islam and the 21st Century, Leiden, June 1996.

Mohd Ibrahim, Ahmad bin. "The Administration of Muslim Law in Indonesia". *Islamic Culture* XLIII, no. 2 (April 1969): 113–24 (Hyderabad, The Islamic Culture Board).

Mudzhar, Atho. *Fatwa-Fatwa Majelis Ulama Indonesia* [Advising opinions of the Council of Islamic Scholars]. Jakarta: INIS, 1993.

Muhaimin, Yahhya. "Muslim Society, Higher Education and Development". In *Muslim Society, Higher Education and Development in Southeast Asia*, edited by Sharom Ahmat and Sharon Siddique, pp. 28–42. Singapore: Institute of Southeast Asian Studies, 1987.

Muhammad, Abdul Chalim. "Peradilan Agama dan Kompilasi Hukum Islam sebagai Pranata Hukum Nasional". *Pesantren* VII, no. 2 (1990).

Muhammadiyah. *Himpunan Putusan Tarjih ke 20 di Garut, 21 di Klaten, 22 di Malang*. Jember: Muhammadiyah, 1993.

Mulkhan, Abdul Munir. *Masalah-masalah Teologi dan Fiqh dalam Tarjih Muhammadiyah*. 2nd ed. Yogyakarta: Sipress, 1997.

Munhanif, Ali. "Mukti Ali: Modernisasi Politik Keagamaan Orde Baru". In *Menteri-Menteri Agama RI: Biografi Sosial Politik*, edited by Azyumardi Azra and Saiful Umam. Jakarta: INIS-PPIM-Balitbang Depag RI, 1998.

Muslim, Abu al-Husain al-Qusyari al-Naisaburi. *Sahih Muslim*. Dar Ihya al-Turas al-'Arabi, 1972.

Nadhlatul Ulama. *Kembali ke Khittah 1926* [Return to the 1926 standard]. Bandung: Risalah, 1985.

Na'im, Muchtar. *Menggali Hukum Tanah dan Hukum Waris Minangkabau*. Padang: Center for Minangkabau Studies, 1986.

Nakamura, Mitsuo. *The Crescent Arises over the Banyan Tree*. Yogyakarta: Gadjah Mada University Press, 1983.

Nasa'i, Abu 'Abd al-Rahman al-. *Sunan al-Nasa'i*. Dar al-Basya'ir al-Islamiyah, 1986.

Nasr, Seyyed Hossein. "Islam". In *Our Religions*, edited by Arvind Sharma. New York: Harper Collins, 1993.

Nasr, Seyyed Vali Reza. "Islamic Opposition to the Islamic State: The Jama'at-i-Islami 1977–88". *International Journal of Middle Eastern Studies* 25 (1993): 261–83.

Nasution, A. H. "Tuntutan Persatuan Umat Islam Perlu Dilembagakan Djadi Madjelis Permusjawaratan Islam yang Permanen". Speech delivered at the Commemoration of Jakarta Charter Day Celebration, 29 June 1968. *Kiblat* XVI, no. 4 (1968).

Nasution, Harun and Ahmad Khatib. "The Positions of *Adat* Law, *Shari'a* and Secular Law in Indonesia". *Studies in Islam* 11, no. 1–2 (1974): 62–67.

Nawawi, Abu Zakariya Yahya Muhyiddin bin Syarf al-. *al-Azkar al-Muntakhabah min Kalam Sayyid al-Abrar*. 5th ed. Damascus: Dar al-Khayr, 1993.

Noeh, Zain Ahmad and Abdul Basit Adnan. *Sejarah Singkat Pengadilan Agama*. Surabaya: PT. Bina Ilmu, 1983.

Noer, Deliar. *The Modernist Muslim Movement in Indonesia 1900–1942*. Oxford University Press, 1973.

──────. *The Administration of Islam in Indonesia*. Monograph Series No. 58. Ithaca, New York: Cornell Modern Indonesia Project, 1978.

Notosutanto. *Organisasi dan Jurisrudensi Peradilan Agama di Indonesia* [Organization and jurisprudence of religious courts in Indonesia]. Yogjakarta: Jajasan Badan Penerbit Gadjah Mada, 1963.

Nur, H. A. Muhaimin et al., eds. *Kenang-kenangan Seabad Peradilan Agama di Indonesia*. Jakarta: Departemen Agama, 1985.

Onar, S. S. "The Majallah". In *Law in the Middle East: Origin and Development of Islamic Law*, edited by Majid Khaddury and Herbert J. Liebesny, pp. 292–306. Washington, D.C.: The Middle East Institute, 1955.

Pangestu, Mari. "The Role of the State and Economic Development in Indonesia". *Indonesian Quarterly* 31, no. 3 (1993): 253–83.

Panitia Penyusunan Biografi. *Prof. K.H. Ibrahim Hosen dan Pembaharuan Hukum Islam di Indonesia*. Jakarta: Putra Harapan, 1990.

Pauker, Guy J. "Policy Implication of Political Institutionalization and Leadership Change in Southeast Asia". *Asian Affairs An American Review* 13/3 (Fall 1986).

Peacock, James. *Muslim Puritans: Reformist Psychology in South East Asian Islam*. Berkeley: University of California, 1978.

——. *Purifying the Faith: The Muhammadiyah Movement in Indonesian Islam*, California: The Benjamin/Cummings Publishing Company, 1978.

Permono, Sjechul Hadi. "Sosialisasi Inpres No. 1/1991 tentang Kompilasi Hukum Islam". *Mimbar Hukum: Aktualisasi Hukum Islam* III, no. 5 (1992).

——. *Negara sebagai Pengelola Zakat*. Jakarta: Pustaka Firdaus, 1993.

Poesponegoro, Marwati Djoened and Nugroho Notosusanto. *Sejarah Nasional Indonesia* [Indonesian national history]. 5 vols. Jakarta: Balai Pustaka, 1984.

PP Muhammadiyah. *Pedoman Bermuhammadiyah*. Yogyakarta, 1992.

——. *Buku Panduan Muktamar Tarjih Muhammadiyah XXII*. Malang, 1989.

——. *Himpunan Putusan Majelis Tarjih*. 3rd ed. PP Muhamamdiyah, n.d.

Pranowo, Bambang M. "Which Islam and which Pancasila". In *State and Civil Society in Indonesia*, edited by Arief Budiman. Monash Papers on Southeast Asia, no. 22, 1990, pp. 479–502.

Price, Daniel E. *Islamic Political Culture, Democracy and Human Rights: A Comparative Study*. Westport, Connecticut: Praeger, 1999.

Prodjodikoro, Wirjono. *Hukum Perkawinan di Indonesia* [Marriage Law in Indonesia]. Bandung: Penerbit Sumur Bandung, 1971.

Rahardjo, Dawam. "Zakat dalam Perspektif Sosial Ekonomi". *Pesantren* III, no. 2 (1986).

——. *Perspektif Deklarasi Makkah: Menuju Ekonomi Islam*. Bandung: Mizan, 1987.

Ramage, Douglas E. *Politics in Indonesia: Islam and the Ideology of Tolerance*. London: Routledge, 1995.

Ranuwiharjo, H. Dahlan. "Peranan Badan Peradilan Agama dalam Mewujudkan Cita-cita negara Hukum". In *Kenang-kenangan Seabad Peradilan Agama,* edited by H. A. Muhaimin Nur et al. Jakarta: Departemen Agama, 1985.

Rasjidi. H. M. *Kasus RUU Perkawinan dalam Hubungan Islam-Kristen* [The case of the proposed Marriage Bill in Islamic–Christian relations]. Jakarta: Bulan Bintang, 1974.

Rasyid, M. Ryass. "Indonesia: Preparing for Post-Soeharto Rule and Its Impact on the Democratization Process". In *Southeast Asian Affairs 1995*, pp. 150–63. Singapore: Institute of Southeast Asian Studies, 1995.

Rasyid, Roihan A. "Kompilasi Hukum Islam (Penelitian Tentang Dasar dan Norma Hukum Serta Aplikasinya di Peradilan Agama)". Yogyakarta: Fakultas Syari'ah IAIN Sunan Kalijaga , Mei 1995.

Reid, Anthony. *Southeast Asia in the Age of Commerce 1450–1680*. Vol. I: *The Lands Below the Winds*. New Haven: Yale University Press, 1988.

Ricklefs, M. *A History of Modern Indonesia*. Bloomington: University of Indiana Press, 1981.

Robison, Richard. *Indonesia. The Rise of Capital*. North Sydney: Allen and Unwin, 1986.

Rosyidi, Sahlan. "Ulama, Tarjih, Pendidikan Ulama, Pendidikan Al-Islam" [Religious scholars, religious scholarship, education of the scholars, and islamic education]. In *Muhammadiyah di Penghujung Abad 20* [Muhammadiyah at the end of the twentieth century], by Tim UMS. Surakarta: Muhammadiyah University Press, 1989.

Sabrie, Zuffran, ed. *Peradilan Agama dalam Wadah Negara Pancasila: Dialog Tentang RUUPA* [Religious courts in the room of Pancasila state: Dialogue on Religious Courts Bill]. Jakarta: Pustaka Antara, 1990.

Sadr, Muhammad Baqir al-. "Thematic Approach to Qur'anic Exegesis (1)". *al-Tawhid* VI, no. 3 (May 1989). <http://www.quran.org.uk/ieb_quran_exegesis1.htm>.

Sakallioglu, Umit Cizre. "Parameters and Strategies of Islam-State Interaction in Turkey". *International Journal of Middle Eastern Studies* 28, no. 2 (1996): 231–51.

Saleh, Ismail, Minister of Justice. "Wawasan Pembangunan Hukum Nasional". *Kompas*, 1 and 2 June 1989.

————. "Eksistensi Hukum Islam dan Sumbangannya terhadap Hukum Nasional". *Kompas*, 3 June 1989.

Salim, Arskal. *Etika Intervensi Negara: Perspektif Politik Ibnu Taimiyah* [The ethics of state intervention: Ibn Taymiyah political perspectives]. Jakarta: Logos, 1998.

San'ani, Muhammad bin Isma'il al-Kahlani al-. *Subul al-Salam*. Bandung: Dahlan, n.d.

Schacht, Joseph. "Foreign Elements in the Ancient Islamic Law". *Journal of Comparative Legislation and International Law* 32 (1950).

————. "Talaq". In *The Encyclopedia of Islam*, vol. I, Part 2, Leiden: E. J. Brill, 1978.

————. *Introduction to Islamic Law*. Oxford: Clarendon Press, 1986.

Schumann, Olaf. "Dilema Islam Kontemporer: Antara Masyarakat Madani dan Negara Islam" [Dilemma of contemporary Islam: Between civil society and the Islamic state]. *Jurnal Pemikiran Islam Paramadina* 1, no. 2 (1999): 48–75.

Schwarz, Adam. *A Nation in Waiting: Indonesia in the 1990s*. Boulder: Westview Press, 1995.

Shaham, Ron. "Custom, Islamic Law, and Statutory Legislation: Marriage Registration and Minimum Age at Marriage in the Egyptian Shari'a Courts". *Islamic Law and Society* 2. no. 3 (October 1995).

Shihab, M. Quraish. *Wawasan Al Quran*. Bandung: Mizan, 1996.

Siddiq, Mazheruddin. Preface to *Muwatta' Imam Malik*, trans. and notes by Muhammad Rahimuddin. New Delhi: Kitab Bhavan, 1989.

Simanjutak, Marsilam. *Unsur Hegelian dalam Pandangan Negara Integralistik*. A thesis submitted to the Law School, University of Indonesia, 1992.

Simatupang, T. B. "Menyempurnakan RUUPA demi Makin Mantapnya Persatuan & Kesatuan Bangsa". *Suara Pembaruan*, 29 June 1989.

Simorangkir, B. "*Adat* Versus Emansipasi". *Sinar Harapan*, 10 August 1968.

Sjadzali, Munawir. "Shari'ah: A Dynamic Legal System". Offprint of the Keynote Address to the International Seminar on Shari'ah Codification, Colombo, Sri Lanka, 1985.

————. "Landasan Pemikiran Politik Hukum Islam dalam Rangka Menentukan Peradilan Agama di Indonesia". In *Hukum Islam di Indonesia: Pemikiran dan Praktek*, edited by Eddi Rudiana Arief et al. Bandung: Rosda Karya, 1991.

————. "Peradilan Agama dan Kompilasi Hukum Islam". In *Peradilan Agama dan Kompilasi Hukum Islam dalam Tata Hukum Indonesia*, edited by Moh. Mahfud et al. Yogyakarta: UII Press, 1993.

Soeharto. *Islam dan Pembangunan* [Islam and development]. Jakarta: Islamic Research Institute, 1976.

Soekanto, Soerjono. *Kedudukan dan Peranan Hukum Adat di Indonesia*. Jakarta: Kurnia Esa, 1987.

Soewondo, Nani. *Kedudukan Wanita dalam Hukum dan Masyarakat* [The position of women in law and society], 2nd ed. Jakarta: Timun Mas, 1968.

Starr, June. *Law as Metaphor: From Islamic Courts to the Palace of Justice*. Albany: State University of New York Press, 1992.

Stuers, Cora Vrede-de. *The Indonesian Woman; Struggles and Achievements*. The Hague: Mouton, 1960.

Subekti. *Law in Indonesia*. Jakarta: Gunung Agung, 1973.

Subekti, R. *Law in Indonesian*. Bandung: Karya Nusantara, 1976.

Subekti, R. *Law in Indonesia*. Jakarta: Yayasan Proklamasi, Center for Strategic and International Studies, 1982.

Suma, Muhammad Amin, "Problematika Ijtihad dalam Persyarikatan Muhammadiyah". In *Tarjih Muhammadiyah dalam Sorotan*, edited by Afifi Fauzi Abbas. Jakarta: IKIP Muhammadiyah Press, 1995.

————, et al. "Respon Hakim, Panitera, Karyawan Pengadilan Agama dan Masyarakat Muslim terhadap UU no. 35 tahun 1999" [The responses of judges, clerk of the Religious Court and Muslim community towards the enactment of the Law no. 35 of 1999]. Research Report. Jakarta: Proyek Pengembangan Penelitian Ditbinbapera Depag RI, 2000.

Suminto, H. Aqib. *Politik Islam Hindia Belanda* [Dutch Indies Islamic politics]. Jakarta: LP3ES, 1985.

Sunny, Ismail. "Hukum Islam dalam Hukum Nasional". *Hukum dan Pembangunan* XVII, no. 4 (August 1987): 351–57.

————. "Kompilasi Hukum Islam ditinjau dari Sudut Pertumbuhan Teori Hukum Indonesia". *Suara Muhammadiyah*, No. 16/76 (August 1991).

————. "Kedudukan Hukum Islam dalam Sistem Ketatanegaraan Indonesia". In *Hukum Islam di Indonesia: Perkembangan dan Pembentukan*, edited by Eddi Rudiana Arief et al. Bandung: Remaja Rosda Karya, 1991.

————. "Tradisi dan Inovasi Keislaman di Indonesia dalam bidang Hukum". *Mimbar Hukum* IV, no. 8 (1993).

Suny, Ismail. *Mekanisme Demokrasi Pancasila*. Jakarta: Aksara Bari, 1978.

Supomo. *Sistem Hukum di Indonesia Sebelum Perang II* [Law systems in Indonesia before World War II]. Jakarta: Noodhoff-Kolff, 1953.

Surbakti, R. "Formal Political Institutions". In *Indonesia: The Challenge of Change*, edited by Richard W. Baker et al. Singapore: Institute of Southeast Asian Studies, 1999.

Suryadinata, Leo. *Military Ascendancy and Political Culture: A Study of Indonesia's Golkar*. Athens, Ohio: Ohio University Center for International Studies, 1989.

Sutarmadi, A. A remark delivered at a seminar on the Dissemination of the Bill of Zakat Laws at Treva Hotel, Jakarta on 19 August 1999.

Suthasasna, Arong. "Shari'ah and Codification: Thailand Experience". *Shari'ah Law Journal* (January 1987).

Suwarno, P. J. "Peradilan Agama di Negara Pancasila". *Suara Pembaruan*, 6 April 1989.

Suyuti, Jalal al-Din al-. *al-Jami' al-Sagir*. Beirut: Dar al-Fikr, n.d.

Syahari, 'Abd Allah al-Hadrami al-. *Idah al-Qawa'id al-Fiqhiyah*. Jeddah: al-Haramain, n.d.

Syarifuddin, Amir. *Pelaksanaan Hukum Kewarisan Islam dalam Lingkungan Adat Minangkabau*. Jakarta: Gunung Agung, 1984.

Syaukani, Muhammad bin 'Ali al-. *Nail al-Awtar*. Idarat al-Tiba'ah al-Muniriyah, n.d

Tafal, B. Bastian. "Pengadilan Agama". *Hukum Nasional* year 2, no. 7 (1976).

Tahhan, Mahmud al-. *Taysir Mustalah al-Hadis*. Cairo: Dar al-Turas al-'Arabi, 1981.

Tamara, M. Nasir. *Indonesia in the Wake of Islam*. Kuala Lumpur: Institute of Strategic and International Studies (ISIS), 1986.

Thaba, A. Aziz. *Islam dan Negara dalam Politik Orde Baru*. Jakarta: Gema Insani Press, 1996.

Thalib, Sajuti, ed. *Pembaharuan Hukum Islam di Indonesia* [The renewal of Islamic law in Indonesia]. Jakarta: University of Indonesia Press, 1976.

Thalib, Sajuti. *Politik Hukum Baru* [The new politic of law]. Bandung: Binacipta, 1987.

Tim Ditbinbapera, ed. "Sejarah Penyusunan Kompilasi Hukum Islam di Indonesia". In *Berbagai Pandangan Terhadap Kompilasi Hukum Islam*. Jakarta: Yayasan Al-Hikmah, 1993.

Tirmizi, Abu 'Isa Muhammad al-. *Sunan al-Tirmizi*. Beirut: Dar al-Fikr, 1980.

Tonang, A. Lolo. "Beberapa Pemikiran tentang Mekanisme Badan Amal Zakat". In *Zakat dan Pajak*, edited by B. Wiwoho. Jakarta: PT Bina Rena Pariwara, 1992.

Trubek, David M. "Max Weber on Law and the Rise of Capitalism". *Wisconsin Law Review* 3 (1972): 720–53.

Ula, Mutammimul. "Peluang dan Tantangan Penerapan Syari'ah Islam" [The opportunity and the challenge of *shari'a*]. *Journal Politik Akses* I, no. 1 (2001): 16–20.

Van Bruinessen, Martin. "*Kitab Kuning* [Yellow books]: Books in Arabic Script Used in the Pesantren Milieu". *Bijdragen tot den Koninglijke Instituut voor Taal-, Land- en Volkenkunde* 46 (1990): 226–69.

Van Bruinessen, Martin. *Kitab Kuning*. Bandung: Penerbit Mizan, 1995.

Vatikiotis, Michael R. J. *Indonesian Politics under Suharto*. London: Routledge, 1993.

Voll, John. *Islam: Continuity and Change in the Modern World*. Boulder: Westview Press, 1982.

————. "The Revivalist Heritage". In *The Contemporary Islamic Revival: A Critical Survey and Bibliography*, edited by Y. Y. Haddad, pp. 23–33. New York: Greenwood Press, 1991.

Wahid, Abdurrahman. "The Nahdlatul Islam and Islam in Present Day Indonesia". In *Islam and Society in Southeast Asia*, edited by T. Abdullah and S. Siddique. Singapore: Institute of Southeast Asian Studies, 1986.

Wahyono, "Hak dan Kewajiban Asasi berdasarkan Cara Pandang Integralistik Indonesia". *Forum Keadilan* 9 (1989).

Waluyo, Bambang. *Implementasi Kekuasaan Kehakiman Republik Indonesia*. Jakarta: Sinar Grafika, 1992.

Waster, H. *Custom and Muslim Law in the Nederlands East Indies*. London: Transaction of the Grotius Society, 25, 1940.

Watson, Alan. *The Making of Civil Laws*. Cambridge: Harvard University Press, 1981.

Weiss, Bernard. *The Search for God's Will: Islamic Jurisprudence in the Writings of Sayf al-Din al-Amidi*. University of Utah Press, 1992.

Wertheim, W. F. "Indonesian Moslems under Sukarno and Suharto: Majority with Minority Mentality". Studies on Indonesian Islam, *Occasional Paper* no. 19. Center for Southeast Asian Studies, University of North Queensland Australia, 1986.

White, Elizabeth H. "Legal Reform as an Indicator of Women's Status in Muslim Nations". In *Women in the Muslim World*, edited by Lois Beck and Nikki Keddie. Cambridge, MA: Harvard University Press, 1980.

Widjanarto, *Hukum dan Ketentuan Perbankan di Indonesia*. Jakarta: Grafiti, 1993.

Widjojo, S. "Kesaktian Pancasila dan Tantangan". *Majalah Hidup* 10 (March 1989).

Widjoyo, S. "Antara Negara Agama dan Negara Pancasila". *Majalah Hidup* 7 (12 February 1989).

Wignjodipoero, R. Soerojo. *Kedudukan Serta Perkembangan Hukum Adat Setelah Kemerdekaan*. Jakarta: Gunung Agung, 1982.

Wignjosubroto, Sutandyo. *Dari Hukum Kolonial ke Hukum Nasional* (From colonial law to national law). Jakarta: Raja Grafindo Persada, 1994.

The World Almanac and Book of Facts 1986. New York: Newspaper Enterprise Association Inc., 1985.

Zubaida, Sami. *Islam: The People and the State*. London: I. B. Tauris, 1989.

Zuhaili, Wahbah al-. *al-Wasit fi Usul al-Fiqh al-Islami*. Matba'ah Dar al-Kitab, 1977.

————. *Usul al-Fiqh al-Islami*. 2 vols. Beirut: Dar al-Fikr, 1986.

Laws and Regulations (in chronological order)

Peraturan Menteri Agama no. 4 tahun 1968 tentang Pembentukan Badan Amil Zakat [MORA Regulations no. 4 of 1968 on the Establishment of Zakat Agency].

Instruksi Menteri Agama no. 16 tahun 1968 tentang Pedoman Pelaksanaan dan Penjelasan Mengenai PMA no. 4 tahun 1968 [An Instruction of MORA no. 16 of 1968 on Guides and Explanations of PMA Zakat no. 4 of 1968].

Instruksi Menteri Agama no. 1 tahun 1969 tentang Penundaan Pelaksanaan Peraturan Menteri Agama no. 4 of 1968 [An Instruction of MORA no. 1 of 1969 on the Deferment of the Implementation of PMA Zakat no. 4 of 1968].

Instruksi Menteri Agama no. 16 tahun 1989 tentang Pembinaan Badan Zakat, Infaq dan Shadaqah [An Instruction of MORA no. 16 of 1989 on the Guidance of Zakat, Infaq and Shadaqah Agency].

Surat Keputusan Bersama (SKB) Menteri Agama dan Menteri Dalam Negeri no. 29 tahun 1991 dan no. 47 tahun 1991 tentang Pembinaan Badan Amil Zakat, Infaq dan Shadaqah [Joint Decree between MORA and Minister of Home Affairs no. 29 of 1991 and no. 47 of 1991 on the Guidance of Zakat, Infaq and Shadaqah Agency].

Instruksi Menteri Agama no. 5 tahun 1991 tentang Petunjuk Pelaksanaan Pembinaan Teknis Badan Amil Zakat, Infaq dan Shadaqah. [An Instruction of MORA no. 5 of 1991 on the Guides of the Technical Implementation of Zakat, Infaq and Shadaqah Agency].

Instruksi Menteri Dalam Negeri no. 7 tahun 1998 tentang Pembinaan Umum Badan Amil Zakat, Infaq dan Shadaqah [An Instruction of Minister of Home Affairs no. 7 of 1998 on the General Guides of Zakat, Infaq and Shadaqah Agency].

Undang-undang no. 10 tahun 1998 tentang Perubahan atas Undang-undang no. 7 tahun 1992 tentang Perbankan [Law no. 10 of 1998 on the Amendment over Law no. 7 of 1992 on Banking].

Peraturan Menteri Agama no. 581 tahun 1999 tentang Pelaksanaan UU no. 38 tahun 1999 tentang Pengelolaan Zakat [Decree of Minister of Religious Affairs no. 581 of 1999 on the Implementation of Law no. 38 of 1999 on the Zakat Management].

Undang-undang no. 17 tahun 1999 tentang Penyelenggaraan Haji [Law no. 17 of 1999 on the Hajj Services].

Undang-undang no. 22 tahun 1999 tentang Pemerintahan Daerah [Law no. 22 of 1999 on Regional Government]

Undang-undang no. 23 tahun 1999 tentang Bank Indonesia [Law no. 23 of 1999 on the Indonesian Bank]

Undang-undang no. 25 tahun 1999 tentang Perimbangan Keuangan antara Pemerintah Pusat dan Daerah [Law no. 25 of 1999 on Balancing Finances between the Central and Regional Governments].

Undang-undang no. 35 tahun 1999 tentang Perubahan atas UU no. 14 tahun 1970 tentang Pokok-pokok Kekuasaan Kehakiman [Law no. 35 of 1999 on the Amendment over Law no. 14 of 1970 on the Fundamental Rules of Judicial Power].

Undang-undang no. 38 tahun 1999 tentang Pengelolaan Zakat [Law no. 38 of 1999 on the Management of Zakat].

Undang-undang no. 44 tahun 1999 tentang Penyelenggaraan Keistimewaan Propinsi Daerah Istimewa Aceh [Law no. 44 of 1999 on the Administration of the Specificity of Aceh as the Special Province].

Undang-undang no. 18 tahun 2001 tentang Otonomi Khusus bagi Propinsi Daerah Istimewa Aceh sebagai Propinsi Nanggroe Aceh Darussalam [Law no. 18 of 2001 on the Exclusive Autonomy for the Special Province of Aceh as Nanggroe Aceh Darussalam Province].

Newspapers and Magazines

Adil, 14 December 2000.

Al-Muslimun [The Muslims]. 1955–1966. Bangil.

Fajar, 2 June 2000.

Indonesian Quarterly. Jakarta, Centre for Strategic and International Studies.

Media Indonesia, 30 November 1999.

Panji Masyarakat [The Banner of Society — Panjimas]. 1982–1990. Jakarta.

Panji Masyarakat, No. 502/XXVII, 1 May 1986.

Republika, 11 August 2000.

Sabili VI, no. 16, (24 February 1999); VII, no. 24 (17 May 2000); VIII, no. 6 (6 September 2000); VIII, no. 11 (15 November 2000).

INDEX